555 Powerful AI Prompts for Coaching, Mentoring and Leadership Mastery in Business

555 Powerful AI Prompts for Coaching, Mentoring and Leadership Mastery in Business

Navigate Your Path to Success Easily & Boldly with AI Prompts Suitable for ChatGPT, Microsoft Copilot, Gemini & Llama

Mindscape Artwork Publishing
Mauricio Vasquez

Toronto, Canada

555 Powerful AI Prompts for Coaching, Mentoring and Leadership Mastery in Business
by Mindscape Artwork Publishing [Aria Capri International Inc.]. All Rights Reserved.

Authors:
Mauricio Vasquez

First Printing: December 2023

ISBN-978-1-990709-91-3 (Paperback)

ISBN-978-1-998402-18-2 (Hardcover)

<u>DEDICATION</u>

To the tenacious professionals and aspiring leaders seeking to elevate their career paths: Let this book function as your blueprint, delivering the approaches and insights required to adeptly navigate professional challenges.

INTRODUCTION

Welcome to an unparalleled book that fuses time-honored principles in coaching, mentoring, and leadership with the avant-garde innovation of Generative Artificial Intelligence (AI). Authored by Mauricio Vasquez, an authority in both professional guidance and the vanguard of AI technologies, this book is the roadmap for those looking to leave an indelible imprint on their respective fields.

As professionals, we operate in a milieu where adaptability, ingenuity, and substantive impact are the gold standards. In these pages, you'll find a merger of conventional wisdom and state-of-the-art AI tools, delivering strategies that are both timeless and timely.

Generative AI is not just an adjunct in this book; it serves as a cornerstone. Through its lens, you'll gain a new understanding of how to individualize coaching, refine mentorship strategies, and cultivate dynamic leadership skills, all underpinned by actionable data and empirical evidence.

Our mission is unequivocal: to fortify your professional aptitude across diverse settings and scenarios. Whether you're a novice starting your career, a mid-career pivoter, or a seasoned veteran in the C-suite, this book synthesizes practice and technology into a cohesive strategy for your career evolution. But we aim to do more than arm you with a versatile toolkit. Get ready for immersive journeys into the world of leadership and the fine-tuning of AI-curated prompts.

As you turn these pages, you are not merely absorbing information; you're participating in a transformative process aimed at elevating your level of influence and leadership. Welcome to a groundbreaking shift in how you perceive, and operate in, the world of professional development.

ABOUT THE AUTHOR

Mauricio Vasquez is a multifaceted professional with over 20 years of experience in risk management and insurance, specializing in sectors like mining, power, and renewable energy. He holds an Industrial Engineering degree, a Master's in Business Administration, and a Master's in Marketing and Commercial Management, along with certifications in Enterprise Risk Management and Artificial Intelligence.

Mauricio is also a certified Adler Trained Coach and a self-published author, focusing on personal growth and professional development. His expertise in Artificial Intelligence and Large Language Models Prompt engineering adds a unique layer to his professional background. Fluent in both English and Spanish, Mauricio has worked across Canada, the U.S., Latin America, and the Caribbean. In addition to his corporate roles, he is a Professional and Life Coach, committed to helping immigrants transition successfully to new lives in Canada. His approach is deeply rooted in building long-term relationships and providing tailored, impactful solutions to clients.

If you want to connect with Mauricio, go to this link
https://www.linkedin.com/in/mauriciovasquez or scan this QR code:

WHAT IS GENERATIVE ARTIFICIAL INTELLIGENCE (AI)?

In the advanced landscape of Artificial Intelligence (AI), Generative AI emerges not merely as an incremental milestone but as a transformative narrative that reconfigures the potential of what AI can achieve. This is not a slight enhancement in the realm of data analytics. Rather, it's artificial intelligence capable of generating text, images, or other media, using generative models.

Traditional AI systems are proficient at analyzing and interpreting existing data sets. In contrast, Generative AI elevates this capability by producing entirely original content that is embedded with value. This spans a range of applications, from the composition of persuasive emails to the formulation of comprehensive strategic initiatives and the improvement of coaching dialogues. In essence, Generative AI enhances human capabilities and fundamentally alters the pathways for innovative solutions.

Built on complex neural network architectures, Generative AI goes beyond mere imitation to acquire and extend intricate patterns of human behavior. The impact of this technology is broad and significant, affecting diverse industries such as marketing, executive leadership, and even individual personal development. It is important to note that this is not a theoretical construct confined to research labs; it is a practical innovation with immediate and expansive real-world applications.

As the industry shifts its focus to upcoming developments in Natural Language Processing (NLP) and Chatbots, it is imperative to acknowledge that Generative AI constitutes the foundational architecture for these advanced conversational interfaces. Specifically, in areas such as coaching, mentoring, and leadership development, Generative AI enriches these platforms by facilitating not just relevant, but also deeply contextual and emotionally nuanced dialogues. The outcome is an enhanced coaching model that is underpinned by both data-driven and human-like insights. Neglecting the capabilities of Generative AI would be to bypass a plethora of opportunities for innovation and increased effectiveness that this technology generously affords.

WHAT ARE NATURAL LANGUAGE PROCESSING CHATBOTS?

An Artificial Intelligence (AI) Chatbot is a program within a website or app that uses machine learning (ML) and natural language processing (NLP) to interpret inputs and understand the intent behind a request or "prompt" (more on this later in the book). Chatbots can be rule-based with simple use cases or more advanced and able to handle multiple conversations.

The rise of language models like GPT has revolutionized the landscape of conversational AI. These Chatbots now boast advanced capabilities that can mimic not just a human conversation style but also a (super) human mind. They can find information online and produce unique content and insights.

The most important thing to know about an AI Chatbot is that it combines ML and NLP to understand what people need and bring the best answers. Some AI Chatbots are better for personal use, like conducting research, and others are best for business use, like featuring a Chatbot on your company's website.

With this in mind, we've compiled a list of the best AI Chatbots at the time of the writing of this book. We strongly suggest that you try and test each of the most popular ones and see what works best for you.

ChatGPT:
- Uses NLP to understand the context of conversations to provide related and original responses in a human-like conversation.

- Multiple use cases for things like answering questions, ideating and getting inspiration, or generating new content [like a marketing email].
- Improves over time as it has more conversations.

Microsoft Copilot/Bing Chat:
- Uses NLP and ML to understand conversation prompts.
- The compose feature can generate original written content and images, and its powerful search engine capabilities can surface answers from the web.
- It's a conversational tool, so you can continue sending messages until you're satisfied.

Google Gemini/Bard:
- Google's Bard is a multi-use AI Chatbot.
- It's powered by Google's LaMDA [instead of GPT].
- Use it for things like brainstorming and ideation, drafting unique and original content, or getting answers to your questions.
- Connected to Google's website index so it can access information from the internet.

Meta LLaMa:
- Meta's Chatbot is an open source large language [LLM].
- The tool is trained using reinforcement learning from human feedback [RLHF], learning from the preferences and ratings of human AI trainers.

Starting from now, we will refer to these platforms as Chatbots. For a guide on how to sign up to each, please refer to Appendix No 1.

If you're seeking a beginner-friendly, step-by-step guide to using ChatGPT, please refer to Appendix No. 3. This appendix includes access to our report, "Elevate Your Productivity Using ChatGPT," which offers a detailed guide on leveraging ChatGPT to boost efficiency and productivity across a range of professional environments.

As of the book's publication date, the information herein is current and accurate. The Chatbot industry, however, is dynamic, with constant updates and new entrants. While specifics may evolve, our prompts, core strategies and principles discussed in this book are designed to withstand the test of time, offering you a robust framework for navigating this fast-paced landscape.

THE BENEFITS OF USING AI CHATBOTS IN YOUR COACHING, MENTORING AND LEADERSHIP JOURNEY

In today's complex professional landscape, effective leadership, coaching, and mentorship require a dynamic skill set that can feel like a job in and of itself. Enter Chatbots and conversational agents like ChatGPT, game-changing technologies that are becoming invaluable allies for professionals in these fields.

These AI-driven tools are becoming invaluable assets in the realm of professional development. They offer real-time coaching, behavioral insights, and actionable strategies, which can be a boon for anyone aiming to climb the corporate ladder or make an impact as a leader.

The advantages of integrating Chatbots and the insights from this book into your leadership journey can be broken down into five key areas:

1. **Efficiency Amplified:** The immediacy with which Chatbots can deliver actionable insights is invaluable. Whether you are crafting a leadership manifesto or preparing for a coaching session, Chatbots help you accelerate the process, thereby enhancing your overall productivity.
2. **Quality, Data-Backed Inputs:** While human intuition and experience are irreplaceable, Chatbots can serve as a reliable first draft for your strategies. Grounded in data analytics and pattern recognition, they can churn out initial recommendations that you can fine-tune according to your unique needs.
3. **Strategic Differentiation:** Customization is pivotal in leadership and coaching. Chatbots, due to their scalability, empower you to personalize your approaches effortlessly. This customized strategy provides a competitive edge that is crucial for achieving success in leadership roles.
4. **Innovation Catalyst:** The capacity of Chatbots to sift through vast datasets enables them to offer innovative yet data-driven suggestions. This infusion of new ideas can revolutionize your existing practices, encouraging a more forward-thinking approach to leadership and coaching.
5. **Enhanced Self-Actualization:** The synergy between this book and Chatbots aims to bolster your self-confidence. Tailored recommendations, predicated on your distinct strengths and weaknesses, will not only affirm your capabilities but also point you toward areas for potential growth.

To sum up, the integration of Chatbots and the insights you will get through this book offer an unparalleled arsenal of tools and strategies. This powerful combination has the potential to transform conventional paradigms in leadership, coaching, and mentorship, arming you with the multifaceted skill set required to excel in these intricate roles

WHAT ARE PROMPTS?

Imagine stepping into a high-stakes negotiation with only half the information—you're likely to miss the mark. Similarly, Chatbots rely on well-crafted prompts to deliver precise and valuable responses.

Prompts serve as the guiding questions, suggestions, or ideas that instruct Chatbots on how and what to respond. But these aren't just any text or phrase; prompts are carefully engineered inputs designed to optimize the Chatbot's output for quality, relevance, and accuracy.

Prompts are suggestions, questions, or ideas for what Chatbots should respond. And for Chatbots to provide a helpful response to their users, they need a thorough prompt with some background information and relevant context. Becoming a solid prompt writer takes time and experience, but there are also some best practices that you can use to see success fairly quickly:

1. **Be precise in your instructions:** when interacting with Chatbots for leadership or coaching tasks, specificity is paramount. Clearly define the tone, scope, and objectives you wish the Chatbot to achieve. For instance, you might say, "Generate a team motivational message that emphasizes the importance of collaboration and aligns with our Q4 targets. Keep the message under 150 words and use a motivational tone."

2. **Integrate contextual information:** the more context you provide, the better Chatbots can tailor their responses. Always include any relevant background information or guidelines. For example, in the case of crafting a message to resolve team conflicts, you may want to append specific issues or arguments that the team is facing.

3. **Segment your interactions:** complex leadership tasks often have multiple components. Break these down into discrete tasks and use individual prompts for each. If you're generating materials for a leadership workshop, you could use separate prompts for the introduction, body, and conclusion segments.

4. **Continuous refinement:** Chatbots provide a valuable starting point but shouldn't replace your own expertise and voice. Use the generated material as a draft that can be further honed and personalized. This ensures that the content aligns with your unique leadership style and the specific needs of your team or mentees.

5. **Employ follow-up prompts:** to get more nuanced advice, use follow-up prompts based on initial outputs. For example, if your first prompt is, "Outline the key principles for effective leadership," a good follow-up could be, "Explain the application of each principle in remote team settings." This sequencing enriches the dialogue and makes the Chatbot's advice more actionable. Check Appendix No 2 for 1100 follow-up prompts you could use, but remember they also need to be tailored to the specific conversation you are having with the Chatbot.

HOW TO USE THIS BOOK?

In the current professional ecosystem, the topics of coaching, mentoring, and leadership are intricate but filled with unprecedented opportunities. This book offers a comprehensive guide for leveraging artificial intelligence, specifically Chatbots, to gain a competitive edge in these sectors. While the content is structured around key frameworks and principles of leadership and coaching, you are encouraged to engage with this book in a non-linear fashion, focusing on areas most relevant to your immediate and long-term objectives.

1. **Optimize your outcomes with our specialized GPT:** We are thrilled to provide exclusive access to "*My Coaching, Mentoring & Leadership Advisor*" GPT, a cutting-edge tool developed using OpenAI's ChatGPT technology. This custom GPT model is specifically designed to offer targeted assistance in leadership, coaching, and mentoring, enhancing your professional journey with AI-driven insights. To maximize its impact, we recommend using this GPT in conjunction with the prompts provided in this book. This synergistic approach will amplify your learning experience, offering a unique blend of expert guidance and personalized AI assistance. To access this GPT, please refer to the following chapter in this book.

2. **Prompt engineering for optimal outcomes:** We advocate for an informed, strategic approach to using the prompts provided in this book. Each prompt is meticulously engineered to serve a specific purpose and is accompanied by its intended goal, a guiding formula, and two illustrative examples. Text highlighted in **bold** and terms enclosed in square brackets [ ] are particularly conducive to customization. We encourage you to not just copy these prompts verbatim but to understand their underlying structure and adapt them to your unique circumstances. The more tailored the prompt, the more relevant and actionable the output will be.

3. **Differentiating complexities for broader utility:** The aim is to offer a broader perspective on how these prompts can be employed and customized. By engaging with a diverse array of prompts, you can develop a nuanced understanding of their underlying mechanisms, thereby gaining the flexibility to tailor them to multiple contexts or objectives.

4. **Integrative strategies for customization:** As you move through this book, you are encouraged to blend different strategies and tools to create customized plans. A well-crafted prompt elicits a higher-quality response; thus, investment in tailoring your inquiries is more than just a recommendation—it's a necessity for meaningful engagement with the book's content.

5. **Ethical considerations and critical thinking:** AI provides valuable insights, but it's crucial to critically evaluate this information. Use Chatbots' advice as a starting point for your strategies, complementing it with further research and ethical considerations. It's essential to remember that while AI can augment decision-making, it can't replace human wisdom.

6. **Communication excellence:** When crafting prompts for Chatbots, aim for clarity and precision. Open-ended questions often lead to more in-depth responses. For a tailored experience, you can also specify the persona or role you want the AI to assume, thereby aligning its feedback with your specific leadership or coaching context.

7. **Target audience, industry, and specificity:** Clearly defining your target audience and industry will enable you to fine-tune the strategies and insights you derive from this book and the accompanying AI resources. Whether you are a leadership consultant, executive coach, or HR professional, audience specificity enhances the utility of the guidance offered.

8. **Getting started with Chatbots:** For those new to the Chatbots platform, we provide a step-by-step guide to get you up and running, empowering you to leverage AI capabilities for your professional development in leadership and coaching.

Here is an overview of the appendices and how they can be integrated into your prompting:

- **Appendix No. 4** - Professions in Mentoring, Coaching, and Leadership: This appendix enumerates key professions that support personal and organizational development through guidance, training, and inspiration. Select the profession most relevant to your current challenge or opportunity to tailor your prompts, ensuring the most pertinent input from the Chatbot.

- **Appendix No. 5** - Specializations in Mentoring, Coaching, and Leadership: This section presents specialized roles within these fields, emphasizing excellence, innovation, and resilience in professional settings. Choose a specialization closely aligned with your specific challenge or opportunity to create effective prompts and receive the most relevant input from the Chatbot.
- **Appendix No. 6** - Tones for Responses from Chatbots: This appendix explores various writing tones you may want Chatbots to use in their responses to your prompts, ensuring alignment with your communication preferences.
- **Appendix No. 7** - Writing Styles for Responses from Chatbots: This section explores a variety of writing styles designed to enhance the clarity and effectiveness of the responses you seek to obtain from Chatbots, ensuring tailored and impactful communication.
- **Appendix No. 8** - Tagging System for Prompt Navigation: This appendix extends beyond the table of contents by offering three tags for each prompt in the book. These tags are carefully selected to assist readers in easily finding the most relevant prompts for their specific challenges or opportunities, ensuring a targeted and efficient use of the book's resources.

By strategically integrating AI tools and best practices, you can enhance not just your personal growth, but also the development of those you coach, mentor, and lead.

MEET *"MY COACHING, MENTORING & LEADERSHIP ADVISOR"* GPT

My Coaching, Mentoring & Leadership Advisor GPT, developed with OpenAI's ChatGPT technology, enhances your interaction with ChatGPT, offering a more tailored and responsive experience.

This custom GPT (Generative Pre-trained Transformer) model is expertly crafted to provide targeted help in leadership, coaching, and mentoring.

As a dynamic Artificial Intelligence companion, it aligns with your unique professional style and needs, providing tailored advice and insights to help navigate your leadership path.

Engaging with this GPT is incredibly intuitive, and simpler than you might expect. Once you access to ChatGPT, you'll be greeted by a user-friendly interface where you can input your questions or prompts.

The GPT responds almost instantly, offering valuable insights and guidance.

Whether you aim to enhance your leadership abilities, improve team dynamics, or foster personal and professional growth, *My Coaching, Mentoring & Leadership Advisor GPT* stands as your gateway to innovative professional development.

Accompanying this section is a screenshot showcasing the user interface you'll encounter when accessing 'My Coaching, Mentoring & Leadership Advisor' GPT. This visual reference provides a clear preview of what to expect, guiding you through your first steps in utilizing this innovative tool.

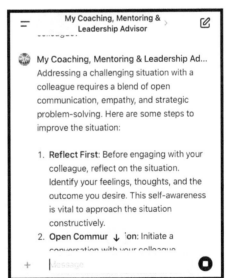

To start your journey towards advanced leadership and coaching skills, and to experience this unique blend of knowledge and technology, please scan this QR code.

Disclaimer: There's a monthly fee for using OpenAI's Plus plan, which you need to access the GPT I created for this book. Wanted to be clear – I don't get any income from OpenAI for suggesting their service. It's all about giving you great tools, and that's why I produced this GPT specifically for the book and for you. As of now, us GPT builders don't get a share of OpenAI's earnings, but if that ever changes – I'll update the disclaimer right away. Mauricio

FREE GOODWILL

Would you consider investing a minute to leave a lasting impression on someone's professional journey? Your experience and insights matter.

Right now, there's a professional, a mentor, or a leader seeking to elevate their capabilities. They're navigating the challenges of leadership, coaching, and perhaps even career transition. Your review could be a pivotal guide for them.

Think of reviews as more than just responses—they're endorsements, collective knowledge, and indicators of reliability. If this book offers you actionable insights or innovative strategies, could you share those experiences through a quick review? By doing so, you contribute to:

- Directing someone to tools and strategies that can heighten their leadership skills.
- Facilitating an individual's capacity to better mentor and coach.
- Enriching someone's perspective, which they might have otherwise overlooked.
- Catalyzing transformation in another's professional path.

By reviewing this book, you contribute to broadening the horizon of effective leadership, mentorship, and coaching for someone else. If you find value in this book, don't hesitate to share it within your network. People remember fondly those who introduced them to beneficial resources.

Enjoyed our book? Scan the QR code to quickly leave a review where you purchased it. Your feedback is invaluable!

Your engagement is much appreciated. Thank you for becoming an advocate for impactful leadership and personal development.

Best regards,

Mauricio

Scan the QR code to access our book collection.

TABLE OF CONTENTS

PROMPT No 1

Accountability - Leadership - Performance

Engage in a transformative process to foster a culture of accountability and ownership within the team, thereby enhancing task completion, work quality, and overall team performance and cohesion.

Given the **present challenges** my team faces with **accountability and task ownership**, as a **leadership coach**, could you provide an in-depth exploration of proven strategies and actionable steps to **nurture a culture of responsibility and engagement**? The ultimate aim is to **enhance task adherence, elevate work quality, and foster team harmony**, while maintaining a **supportive and encouraging atmosphere**.

Given the **[specific challenges]** my team faces with **[issue area]**, as a **[profession]**, could you provide an in-depth exploration of proven strategies and actionable steps to **[desired outcome]**? The ultimate aim is to **[long-term benefits]**, while maintaining a **[desired tone and atmosphere]**.

PROMPT No 2

RemoteWork - Self-Accountability - Commitment

To gain insights on methods for fostering and maintaining self-accountability within a team, enhancing their commitment to goals.

Given the challenge of **remote work**, as a **leadership coach** and in a **supportive and encouraging tone**, could you detail methods **I** can use to maintain the **self-accountability** of my **team** towards their **goals**?

Given the challenge of **[contextual challenge/opportunity]**, as a **[profession]** and in a **[tone of voice]**, could you detail methods **[I/Name/Role]** can use to maintain the **[desired outcome]** of my **[team/group/department]** towards their **[responsibilities/tasks/goals]**?

PROMPT No 3

Engagement - Virtual Environment - Team Presence

To acquire strategies for promoting and ensuring the full presence and engagement of a team member with their colleagues.

In the context of a **virtual working environment**, as a **Professional Coach** and in an **empathetic and understanding tone**, could you explain the steps **I** should take to ensure **the full presence** of a **colleague** with their **colleagues**?

In the context of **[contextual challenge/opportunity]**, as a **[profession]** and in a **[tone of voice]**, could you explain the steps **[I/Name/Role]** should take to ensure the **[desired outcome]** of a **[colleague/employee/team member]** with their **[colleagues/team/client]**

PROMPT No 4

Accountability - Manager Review - Professionalism

To equip professionals with a structured, respectful, and assertive approach for holding their manager accountable during a performance review, thereby enhancing the quality of leadership and fostering a culture of mutual accountability.

As a **Professional Coach** specializing in **career development** within the **insurance industry**, provide an exhaustive and meticulous examination, incorporating innovative insights and inventive strategies, for outlining a nuanced approach that individuals can employ during a performance review to respectfully and assertively hold their manager accountable for various aspects such as **setting clear expectations, providing timely feedback, and ensuring a supportive work environment**. Additionally, offer insights into how to prepare for potential pushbacks and secure mutual understanding and respect.

As a **[profession]** specializing in **[topic/field]** within the **[industry]**, provide an exhaustive and meticulous examination, incorporating innovative insights and inventive strategies, for outlining a nuanced approach that individuals can employ during a [performance review] to respectfully and assertively hold their manager accountable for various aspects such as **[setting clear expectations/providing timely feedback/ensuring a supportive work environment]**. Additionally, offer insights into how to prepare for potential pushbacks and secure mutual understanding and respect.

PROMPT No 5

Responsibility - Supportive Identification - Workplace Culture

To gain specific strategies or methods that colleagues can employ to accurately and comprehensively identify individuals who can effectively support them in upholding their accountability and responsibility towards their work, fostering a culture of accountability and responsibility within the workplace.

As a **Leadership Development Consultant**, adopting a **respectful and solution-oriented tone**, could you provide specific strategies or methods that **colleagues** can employ to accurately and comprehensively identify individuals who can effectively support them in **upholding their accountability and responsibility towards their work**? This is particularly relevant given the goal of **fostering a culture of accountability and responsibility within the workplace**.

As a **[profession]**, adopting a **[tone of voice]**, could you provide specific strategies or methods that **[colleagues/team/group]** can employ to accurately and comprehensively identify individuals who can effectively support them in **[contextual challenge/opportunity]**? This is particularly relevant given the goal of **[desired outcome]**.

PROMPT No 6

Team Accountability -Solution-Oriented - Professional Setting

To provide a robust methodology for establishing and maintaining accountability, thereby enhancing performance, fostering responsibility, and achieving organizational goals

Act as a **Leadership Consultant** with a specialization in **team accountability** in the **aerospace industry**. Could you provide insights on **specific and effective ways that team members can maintain accountability among themselves in a professional setting**? Please include **accountability frameworks, peer-review mechanisms, and communication protocols**. Make sure to cover how **to set clear expectations and how to handle accountability lapses constructively**. Investigate unconventional **accountability practices** and cutting-edge **performance tracking technologies** to **ensure sustained accountability**. Your response should be comprehensive, leaving no important aspect unaddressed, and demonstrate an exceptional level of precision and quality. Let's think about this step by step. Write using a **solution-oriented** tone and a **professional advisory** style.

Act as a **[profession]** with a specialization in **[area of expertise]** in the **[industry]**. Could you provide insights on **[specific challenge/opportunity]**? Please include **[methods/techniques]**. Make sure to cover how **[key areas/topics]**. Investigate unconventional **[area for innovation]** and cutting-edge **[technologies/methods]** to **[desired outcome]**. Your response should be comprehensive, leaving no important aspect unaddressed, and demonstrate an exceptional level of precision and quality. Let's think about this step by step. Write using a **[type]** tone and **[style]** writing style.

PROMPT No 7

Strategic Plan - Team Motivation - Revenue Alignment

To obtain a comprehensive and detailed strategy that can ensure that a team remains focused on their assigned tasks and aligns with the corporate objective of increasing revenue or other objectives, including specific steps, measures, and techniques to keep the team on track and motivated to achieve this goal.

As a **Business Consultant**, adopting a **strategic and motivational tone**, could you provide a **thorough and detailed plan** that can successfully guarantee that my team stays dedicated to their **designated tasks and works** towards the overarching corporate goal of **revenue growth**? In your response, please include **precise** steps, measures, and techniques that can be implemented to maintain the team's **focus, motivation, and alignment** with this objective.

As a **[profession]**, adopting a **[tone of voice]**, could you provide a **[detailed/thorough/comprehensive plan]** that can successfully guarantee **that [my/their] [team/group/department]** stays dedicated to their **[designated/assigned]** tasks and works towards the **[overarching/corporate]** goal of **[contextual challenge/opportunity]**? In your response, please include **[precise/specific]** steps, measures, and techniques that can be implemented to maintain the team's **[focus/motivation/alignment]** with this objective.

PROMPT No 8

Courage Enhancement - Risk-Taking - Innovative Culture

To gain insights on specific ways to provide a team with the necessary tools, resources, and support to enhance their courage and enable them to take more risks and make bolder decisions, fostering a culture of innovation and growth.

Given the goal of **enhancing courage and risk-taking in decision-making**, as a **Leadership Development Facilitator** and in an **empowering and motivational tone**, could you suggest specific ways **I** can provide my **team** with the necessary tools, resources, and support?

Given the goal of **[contextual challenge/opportunity]**, as a **[profession]** and in a **[tone of voice]**, could you suggest specific ways **[I/Name/Role]** can provide **[my/their] [team/group/department]** with the necessary tools, resources, and support?

PROMPT No 9

Effort Acknowledgment - Team Commitment - Appreciative Strategy

To gain insights on specific strategies or actions that can be employed to effectively acknowledge and value the diligent efforts and unwavering commitment exhibited by each member of a team.

As a **Leadership Coach**, adopting an **appreciative and respectful tone**, could you provide specific strategies or actions that **I** can employ to ensure that **I** effectively acknowledge and value the **diligent efforts and unwavering commitment** exhibited by each member of **my team**?

As a **[profession]**, adopting a **[tone of voice]**, could you provide specific strategies or actions that **[I/Name/Role]** can employ to ensure that **[I/Name/Role]** effectively acknowledges and values the **[contextual challenge/opportunity]** exhibited by each member of **[my/their]** **[team/group/department]**?

PROMPT No 10

Accountability - Relationships - Collaboration

To understand how to leverage peer relationships as a tool for enhancing accountability within a team.

In the context of a **collaborative work environment**, as a **Professional Coach** and in a **supportive and encouraging tone**, could you explain how **my team** could utilize their work relationships with their **peers** as a measure of **accountability**?

In the context of **[contextual challenge/opportunity]**, as a **[profession]** and in a **[tone of voice]**, could you explain how **[I/Name/Role]**'s team could utilize their work relationships with their **[peers/colleagues]** as a measure of **[desired outcome]**?

ACTION

PROMPT No 11

Growth Cultivation - Fulfillment Fostering - Team Development

To gain a detailed understanding of the specific steps that can be implemented to effectively cultivate a growth mindset within a team, fostering a sense of fulfillment and enabling them to achieve their dreams.

As a **Leadership Development Consultant**, adopting an **encouraging and supportive tone**, could you provide a detailed explanation of the precise and comprehensive steps that **I** can implement to effectively cultivate a **growth mindset** within **my team**? This is particularly relevant given the goal of **fostering a sense of fulfillment and enabling them to achieve their dreams**.

As a **[profession]**, adopting a **[tone of voice]**, could you provide a detailed explanation of the precise and comprehensive steps that **[I/Name/Role]** can implement to effectively cultivate a **[desired outcome]** within **[my/their]** **[team/group/department]**? This is particularly relevant given the goal of **[desired outcome]**.

PROMPT No 12

Client Acquisition - Business Development - Detailed Strategy

To provide a comprehensive strategy for successfully attracting and acquiring new clients, thereby driving revenue growth and enhancing market position.

Act as a **Business Development Consultant** with a specialization in **client acquisition** in the **automotive industry**. Could you provide a comprehensive and detailed response outlining **the specific steps that my team should take in order to ensure the successful attraction and acquisition of new clients?** Please include **lead generation techniques, client engagement strategies, and sales funnel optimization**. Make sure to cover how **to qualify leads and how to tailor pitches to different client needs**. Investigate unconventional **client acquisition channels** and cutting-edge **CRM technologies** to **maximize success rates**. Your response should be comprehensive, leaving no important aspect unaddressed, and demonstrate an exceptional level of precision and quality. Let's think about this step by step. Write using a **clear and concise** tone and a **tactical guide** style.

Act as a **[profession]** with a specialization in **[area of expertise]** in the **[industry]**. Could you provide a comprehensive and detailed response outlining **[specific challenge/opportunity]**? Please include **[methods/techniques]**. Make sure to cover how **[key areas/topics]**. Investigate unconventional **[area for innovation]** and cutting-edge **[technologies/methods]** to **[desired outcome]**. Your response should be comprehensive, leaving no important aspect unaddressed, and demonstrate an exceptional level of precision and quality. Let's think about this step by step. Write using a **[type]** tone and **[style]** writing style.

PROMPT No 13

Strategic Planning - Competitive Advantage - Team Performance

To gain a comprehensive and detailed strategic plan that can be implemented by the team to successfully achieve their objectives or gain a significant competitive advantage, with the aim of enhancing team performance and competitiveness.

As a **Management Consultant**, adopting a **clear and concise tone**, could you please provide a comprehensive and detailed strategic plan that can be implemented by **my team** to **successfully achieve their objectives or gain a significant competitive advantage**? Your response should include a thorough outline of the steps, strategies, and tactics that need to be taken into consideration. This is particularly relevant given the goal of **enhancing team performance and competitiveness**.

As a **[profession]**, adopting a **[tone of voice]**, could you please provide a comprehensive and detailed strategic plan that can be implemented by **[my/their] [team/group/department]** to **[contextual challenge/opportunity]**? Your response should include a thorough outline of the steps, strategies, and tactics that need to be taken into consideration. This is particularly relevant given the goal of **[desired outcome]**.

PROMPT No 14

Business Planning - Detailed Explanation - Organizational Structure

To meticulously outline and comprehend the multifaceted process of crafting a robust business plan, ensuring a clear trajectory towards business objectives and a concrete foundation for operational, financial, and strategic decision-making.

As a **Business Consultant**, with a focus on **clarity and precision**, could you delineate a step-by-step methodology to **devise a comprehensive and well-structured business plan**? This discussion should meticulously cover **each phase of the process**, the significance of each **step**, and how they collectively contribute to **a sound business blueprint** capable of **guiding organizational decision-making and tracking progress towards defined objectives**.

As a **[Profession]**, with a focus on **[desired tone attributes]**, could you delineate a step-by-step methodology to **[specific task or objective]**? This discussion should meticulously cover **[key areas or steps]**, the significance of each **[step/phase/element]**, and how they collectively contribute to **[desired outcome or final product]** capable of **[further benefits or implications]**.

PROMPT No 15

Team Resilience - Problem-Solving - Supportive Leadership

To gain specific and practical strategies or actions that can be adopted to greatly improve support and assistance to the team when they encounter a problem, with the aim of enhancing team resilience and problem-solving capabilities.

As a **Leadership Coach**, adopting a **supportive and solution-oriented tone**, could you please provide specific and practical strategies or actions that I can adopt to greatly improve my support and assistance to **my team** when they encounter a problem? Your response should include detailed and comprehensive suggestions that **will help me enhance my effectiveness in providing assistance and support during challenging situations**. This is particularly relevant given the goal of **improving team resilience and problem-solving capabilities**.

As a **[profession]**, adopting a **[tone of voice]**, could you please provide specific and practical strategies or actions that I can adopt to greatly improve my support and assistance to **[my/their]** **[team/group/department]** when they encounter a problem? Your response should include detailed and comprehensive suggestions that **[contextual challenge/opportunity]**. This is particularly relevant given the goal of **[desired outcome]**.

PROMPT No 16

Management - Diversity - Strategies

To acquire strategies for effectively managing various types of professionals within a team.

Given the challenge of **managing diverse team members**, could you, as an **organizational development consultant** and in a **solution-oriented tone**, explain strategies **I** could consider to manage them?

Given the challenge of **[contextual challenge/opportunity]**, could you, as a **[profession]** and in a **[tone of voice]**, explain strategies **[I/Name/Role]**'s team could consider to manage their **[suppliers/subordinates/peers]**?

PROMPT No 17

Effective Communication - Team Cooperation - Initiative Implementation

To gain insights on specific actions that can enhance communication with a team member and effectively gain their cooperation for a new initiative.

As a **Team Leader**, adopting a **persuasive and respectful tone**, could you provide specific actions that I can take to enhance communication with a team member and effectively gain their cooperation for **a new initiative**? This is particularly relevant given the goal of **fostering effective communication and cooperation within the team**.

As a **[profession]**, adopting a **[tone of voice]**, could you provide specific actions that [I/Name/Role] can take to enhance communication with a **[team member/colleague]** and effectively gain their cooperation for a **[contextual challenge/opportunity]**? This is particularly relevant given the goal of **[desired outcome]**.

PROMPT No 18

Self-Discovery - Personal Development - Strengths

To gain a comprehensive and detailed step-by-step process that can be followed to effectively engage in self-discovery, enabling the identification and understanding of personal strengths and weaknesses.

As a **Personal Development Coach**, adopting an **encouraging and supportive tone**, could you provide a **precise and comprehensive step-by-step process** that **I** can adopt to

thoroughly and successfully engage in self-discovery? This is particularly relevant given the goal of **identifying and understanding my individual strengths and weaknesses**.

As a **[profession]**, adopting a **[tone of voice]**, could you provide a **[description of process]** that **[I/Name/Role]** can adopt to **[contextual challenge/opportunity]**? This is particularly relevant given the goal of **[desired outcome]**.

PROMPT No 19

Team Dynamics - Goal Accomplishment - Behavioral Mitigation

To gain a comprehensive analysis of methods and strategies that a team can utilize to identify and mitigate activities or behaviors that impede progress or negatively impact team dynamics, and to learn about effective measures for enhancing team dynamics and achieving goals.

As a **Team Development Consultant**, adopting a **solution-oriented and analytical tone**, could you provide a comprehensive analysis outlining the various methods and strategies that **my team** can utilize to accurately identify and mitigate any activities or behaviors that impede their progress in **meeting their quota or have a detrimental effect on team dynamics**? Moreover, could you suggest measures that have proven to be effective in **enhancing team dynamics and bringing the team closer to accomplishing their goals**?

As a **[profession]**, adopting a **[tone of voice]**, could you provide a comprehensive analysis outlining the various methods and strategies that **[my/their]** **[team/group/department]** can utilize to accurately identify and mitigate any activities or behaviors that impede their progress in **[contextual challenge/opportunity]**? Moreover, could you suggest measures that have proven to be effective in **[desired outcome]**?

PROMPT No 20

Task Prioritization - Team Autonomy - Efficiency Enhancement

To gain a comprehensive understanding of the procedures and strategies that can be utilized by the team to autonomously identify and prioritize crucial tasks or projects, with the aim of enhancing team autonomy and efficiency in task prioritization.

As a **Performance Coach**, adopting a **clear and concise tone**, could you please provide a comprehensive explanation of the step-by-step procedures and effective strategies that **my team** can utilize to **autonomously identify and prioritize the utmost crucial tasks or projects that demand their immediate attention**? This is particularly relevant given the goal of **enhancing team autonomy and efficiency in task prioritization**.

As a **[profession]**, adopting a **[tone of voice]**, could you please provide a comprehensive explanation of the step-by-step procedures and effective strategies that **[my/their]** **[team/group/department]** can utilize to **[contextual challenge/opportunity]**? This is particularly relevant given the goal of **[desired outcome]**.

PROMPT No 21

Sustainability - Expenses - Debt Mitigation

To gain a detailed plan of specific initial actions a team can undertake to decrease variable expenses or outstanding debts, fostering financial management and business sustainability.

Given the challenge of **decreasing variable expenses or outstanding debts**, as a **Management Consultant** and in a **clear and concise tone**, could you provide a detailed plan of specific initial actions **my team** can undertake?

Given the challenge of **[contextual challenge/opportunity]**, as a **[profession]** and in a **[tone of voice]**, could you provide a detailed plan of specific initial actions **[my/their]** **[team/group/department]** can undertake?

PROMPT No 22

Relationship Maintenance - Collaborative Strategies - Professional Interaction

To obtain strategies for maintaining healthy and productive relationships with colleagues or suppliers.

Considering the importance of **maintaining healthy relationships in a professional setting**, could you, as a **leadership development consultant** and in a **collaborative tone**, share the strategies **my team** could implement to **foster such relationships** with colleagues?

Considering the importance of **[contextual challenge/opportunity]**, could you, as a **[profession]** and in a **[tone of voice]**, share the strategies **[I/Name/Role]'s** team could implement to **[desired outcome]** with **[colleagues/suppliers/subordinates]**?

PROMPT No 23

Decision-Making - Bold Choices - Informed Analysis

To gain insights on the specific factors that should be thoroughly analyzed and considered when making a bold decision that will affect a team, ensuring informed and effective decision-making.

As a **Decision-Making Expert**, adopting a **clear and concise tone**, could you guide **me** on the specific factors that **I** should thoroughly analyze and consider when making a bold decision that will affect **my team**? This is particularly relevant given the goal of **ensuring informed and effective decision-making**.

As a **[profession]**, adopting a **[tone of voice]**, could you guide **[me/Name/Role]** on the specific factors that **[I/Name/Role]** should thoroughly analyze and consider when making a bold decision that will affect **[my/their]** **[team/group/department]**? This is particularly relevant given the goal of **[desired outcome]**.

PROMPT No 24

Motivational Strategies - Perspective Expansion - Opportunity Pursuit

To gain a clear and detailed explanation of the specific strategies, techniques, and approaches that can be utilized to successfully motivate and encourage team members to expand their perspectives and actively pursue new opportunities for action.

As a **Leadership Development Consultant**, adopting an **inspiring and motivational tone**, could you provide a clear and detailed explanation of the specific strategies, techniques, and approaches that can be utilized to successfully **motivate and encourage my team members to expand their perspectives and actively pursue new opportunities for action**?

As a **[profession]**, adopting a **[tone of voice]**, could you provide a clear and detailed explanation of the specific strategies, techniques, and approaches that can be utilized to successfully **[desired outcome]**?

PROMPT No 25

Goal Achievement - Ambition Cultivation - Success Strategies

To gain a detailed and comprehensive understanding of specific strategies a team can explore and implement to successfully attain the goals and achievements they have envisioned for their future, fostering a culture of ambition and success.

Given the aspiration of **attaining envisioned future goals**, as a **Career Coach** and in an **optimistic and clear tone**, could you provide a detailed and comprehensive response on specific strategies **my team** can explore and implement?

Given the aspiration of **[contextual challenge/opportunity]**, as a **[profession]** and in a **[tone of voice]**, could you provide a detailed and comprehensive response on specific strategies **[I/Name/Role]**'s **[team/group/department]** can explore and implement?

PROMPT No 26

Self-Awareness - Work Ethic - High-Performance Culture

To gain detailed recommendations of effective strategies to enhance self-awareness and its influence on work ethic in a team, fostering a high-performance culture and personal growth.

Given the goal of **enhancing self-awareness and its influence on work ethic**, as a **Leadership Development Facilitator** and in an **encouraging and professional tone**, could you provide detailed recommendations of effective strategies **I** can impart to **my team**?

Given the goal of **[contextual challenge/opportunity]**, as a **[profession]** and in a **[tone of voice]**, could you provide detailed recommendations of effective strategies **[I/Name/Role]** can impart to **[my/their] [team/group/department]**?

PROMPT No 27

False Assumptions - Insightful Leadership - Self-Reflection

To gain a detailed understanding of specific strategies and techniques that can be used to improve team members' self-awareness, particularly in recognizing and addressing potential false assumptions in their work environment.

As a **Leadership Development Consultant**, adopting a **supportive and insightful tone**, could you provide some specific strategies and techniques that can be utilized to successfully improve the self-awareness of **my team members** when it comes to **recognizing and addressing potential false assumptions in their work environment**?

As a **[profession]**, adopting a **[tone of voice]**, could you provide some specific strategies and techniques that can be utilized to **[desired outcome]** of **[my/their] [team/group/department]** when it comes to **[work environment/context]**?

PROMPT No 28

Emotional Intelligence - Fear Addressing - Team Morale

To gain specific strategies or methods to uncover the hidden fears or anxieties that team members may have regarding their work, fostering an understanding of these fears and how to address them to enhance team morale and productivity.

As an **Emotional Intelligence Coach**, adopting a **patient and empathetic tone**, could you suggest specific strategies or methods that **I** can employ to uncover **the hidden fears or anxieties** that **my team members** may have regarding their work? This is particularly relevant given the goal of **understanding and addressing these hidden fears to enhance team morale and productivity**.

As a **[profession]**, adopting a **[tone of voice]**, could you suggest specific strategies or methods that [I/Name/Role] can employ to uncover the **[contextual challenge/opportunity]** that **[my/their] [team/group/department]** may have regarding their work? This is particularly relevant given the goal of **[desired outcome]**.

PROMPT No 29

Professional Growth - Development Evaluation - HR Strategies

To gain insights on the most effective methods and strategies to evaluate the current status of a team's professional growth and development.

As a **Human Resources Consultant**, adopting an **analytical and insightful tone**, could you provide insights on the most effective methods and strategies to evaluate the current status of **my team's professional growth and development**? This is particularly relevant given the goal of **understanding and enhancing the professional development of the team**.

As a **[profession]**, adopting a **[tone of voice]**, could you provide insights on the most effective methods and strategies to evaluate the current status of **[my/their] [team/group/department]'s [contextual challenge/opportunity]**? This is particularly relevant given the goal of **[desired outcome]**.

PROMPT No 30

Resource Optimization - Allocation Efficiency - Task Management

To gain specific details that will enable the identification of areas where a team is either allocating too many resources or not enough in their tasks, enhancing resource optimization and team performance.

In the context of **optimizing resource allocation**, as a **Management Consultant** and in a **clear and concise tone**, could you furnish **me** with specific details that will enable **me** to determine the areas where **my team** is either allocating too many resources or not enough in their tasks?

In the context of **[contextual challenge/opportunity]**, as a **[profession]** and in a **[tone of voice]**, could you furnish **[I/Name/Role]** with specific details that will enable **[me/them]** to determine the areas where **[my/their]** **[team/group/department]** is either allocating too many resources or not enough in their tasks?

PROMPT No 31

Autonomous Assessment - Training Effectiveness - Work Enhancement

To equip team leaders, and professionals with a comprehensive approach for training team members effectively, with a focus on empowering them to autonomously assess their work and identify areas for improvement.

Act as a **Training and Development Specialist** with a specialization in **self-assessment and skill enhancement** in the **manufacturing industry**. Could you provide specific strategies and methods that can be employed **to train my team members effectively**? This is particularly relevant given the goal of **empowering them to autonomously assess their own work and recognize areas that need enhancement**. Please include **competency frameworks, self-assessment tools, and feedback loops**. Make sure to cover how **to set performance benchmarks and how to foster a culture of continuous improvement**. Investigate unconventional **training methodologies** and cutting-edge **e-learning platforms** to **facilitate self-assessment**. Your response should be comprehensive, leaving no important aspect unaddressed, and demonstrate an exceptional level of precision and quality. Let's think about this step by step. Write using a **supportive and instructive** tone and a **skill-building guide** style.

Act as a **[profession]** with a specialization in **[area of expertise]** in the **[industry]**. Could you provide specific strategies and methods that can be employed to **[specific challenge/opportunity]**? This is particularly relevant given the goal of **[specific goal]**. Please include **[methods/techniques]**. Make sure to cover how **[key areas/topics]**. Investigate unconventional **[area for innovation]** and cutting-edge **[technologies/methods]** to **[desired outcome]**. Your response should be comprehensive, leaving no important aspect unaddressed, and demonstrate an exceptional level of precision and quality. Let's think about this step by step. Write using a **[type]** tone and **[style]** writing style.

PROMPT No 32

Goal-Setting - Prioritization Strategies - Task Management

To gain specific strategies or methods to effectively assist a team in identifying and establishing distinct priorities or goals, fostering an enhancement in goal-setting and prioritization within the team.

As a **Performance Coach**, adopting a **clear and concise tone**, could you suggest specific strategies or methods that **I** can employ to effectively assist **my team** in identifying and establishing

distinct priorities or goals? This is particularly relevant given the goal of enhancing goal-setting and prioritization within the team.

As a **[profession]**, adopting a **[tone of voice]**, could you suggest specific strategies or methods that **[I/Name/Role]** can employ to effectively assist **[my/their]** **[team/group/department]** in identifying and establishing **[contextual challenge/opportunity]?** This is particularly relevant given the goal of **[desired outcome].**

PROMPT No 33

Personal Growth - Achievement Strategies - Individual Development

To gain specific strategies or methods that can be employed to effectively explore and enhance the personal growth and development of each individual team member, particularly in relation to their accomplishments or setbacks in achieving their goals. This is aimed at fostering personal development and goal achievement within the team.

As a **Leadership Development Consultant**, adopting an **empathetic and supportive tone**, could you provide specific strategies or methods that can be utilized to successfully explore and enhance the **personal growth and development** of each individual **team member**, specifically in regards to their **achievements or obstacles encountered while striving to reach their objectives**?

As a **[profession]**, adopting a **[tone of voice]**, could you provide specific strategies or methods that can be utilized to successfully explore and enhance the **[desired outcome]** of each individual **[team/group/department member]**, specifically in regards to their **[contextual challenge/opportunity]**?

PROMPT No 34

Self-Awareness - Performance - Management

To gain specific steps to assist a team in gaining a thorough understanding by themselves about the current state of their performance levels, fostering self-awareness and performance management.

Given the challenge of **understanding current performance levels**, as a **Performance Management Specialist** and in a **clear and concise tone**, could you suggest specific steps **I** can take to assist **my team** in **gaining a thorough understanding by themselves**?

Given the challenge of **[contextual challenge/opportunity]**, as a **[profession]** and in a **[tone of voice]**, could you suggest specific steps **[I/Name/Role]** can take to assist **[my/their]** **[team/group/department]** in **[desired outcome]**?

PROMPT No 35

Positive Mindset - Motivation Maintenance - Supportive Leadership

To gain a detailed understanding of specific approaches, techniques, or actions that can be adopted to provide effective support and guidance to a team, with the aim of preventing any decrease in their motivation and attitude, and ensuring they consistently maintain a positive mindset.

As a **Leadership Coach**, adopting a **motivational and supportive tone**, could you provide **me** with specific approaches, techniques, or actions that **I** can adopt to provide effective support and guidance to my **team**? This is particularly relevant given the goal of **preventing any decrease in their motivation and attitude, and ensuring they consistently maintain a positive mindset.**

As a **[profession]**, adopting a **[tone of voice]**, could you provide **[me/Name/Role]** with specific approaches, techniques, or actions that **[I/Name/Role]** can adopt to provide effective support and guidance to **[my/their]** **[team/group/department]**? This is particularly relevant given the goal of **[desired outcome]**.

PROMPT No 36

Mission Influence - Organizational Culture - Team Mindset

To understand the influence of a company's mission or vision on a team's thinking patterns and overall mindset.

Given the significant role a **company's mission or vision plays in shaping its culture**, could you, as an **organizational development consultant** and in an **insightful tone**, discuss how these elements influence **my team's thinking patterns**?

Given the significant role of **[contextual challenge/opportunity]**, could you, as a **[profession]** and in a **[tone of voice]**, discuss how these elements influence **[I/Name/Role]**'s team's **[desired outcome]**?

PROMPT No 37

Project Preparation - Team Equipping - Effective Tackling

To gain a detailed understanding of the specific actions to take to prepare a team for an upcoming project, ensuring the team is adequately equipped and ready to tackle the new project effectively.

Given the challenge of **preparing a team for an upcoming project**, as a **Project Management Consultant** and in a **clear and concise tone**, could you provide a detailed explanation of the specific actions **I** can take to ensure that **my team** is adequately equipped and ready to **tackle the new project effectively**?

Given the challenge of **[contextual challenge/opportunity]**, as a **[profession]** and in a **[tone of voice]**, could you provide a detailed explanation of the specific actions **[I/Name/Role]** can take to ensure that **[my/their]** **[team/group/department]** is adequately equipped and ready to **[desired outcome]**?

PROMPT No 38

Role Visualization - Value Articulation - Sense of Belonging

To provide comprehensive strategy for conducting team exercises that enhance the ability of team members to vividly imagine and articulate the symbols or representations that resonate with their perception of their roles and value within the organization.

Act as a **Team Development Consultant** with a specialization in **role perception and value articulation** in the **pharmaceutical industry**. Could you provide precise strategies or approaches that can be employed to **effectively conduct an exercise with my team**? This exercise should **foster their ability to vividly imagine and express the representation or symbol that resonates with their perception of their role, especially considering their value within the organization**. Please include **creative thinking techniques, visualization exercises, and communication frameworks**. Make sure to cover how **to facilitate open dialogue and how to capture and analyze the outcomes for organizational alignment**. Investigate unconventional **team-building activities** and cutting-edge **virtual collaboration** tools to **enrich the exercise**. Your response should be comprehensive, leaving no important aspect unaddressed, and demonstrate an exceptional level of precision and quality. Let's think about this step by step. Write using an **engaging and supportive** tone and an **experiential learning guide** style.

Act as a **[profession]** with a specialization in **[area of expertise]** in the **[industry]**. Could you provide precise strategies or approaches that can be employed to **[specific challenge/opportunity]**? This exercise should **[specific goal]**. Please include **[methods/techniques]**. Make sure to cover how **[key areas/topics]**. Investigate unconventional **[area for innovation]** and cutting-edge **[technologies/methods]** to **[desired outcome]**. Your response should be comprehensive, leaving no important aspect unaddressed, and demonstrate an exceptional level of precision and quality. Let's think about this step by step. Write using a **[type]** tone and **[style]** writing style.

PROMPT No 39

Identity Recognition - True Self - Personal Growth

To gain specific strategies or actions to effectively assist a team in recognizing and understanding the areas where their true personalities and desired identities coincide, fostering an enhancement in self-awareness and personal growth within the team.

As an **Executive Mentor**, adopting an **empathetic and respectful tone**, could you suggest specific strategies or actions that **I** can take to effectively assist **my team** in recognizing and understanding **the areas where their true personalities and desired identities coincide**? This is particularly relevant given the goal of enhancing self-awareness and personal growth within the team.

As a **[profession]**, adopting a **[tone of voice]**, could you suggest specific strategies or actions that **[I/Name/Role]** can take to effectively assist **[my/their]** **[team/group/department]** in recognizing and understanding **[contextual challenge/opportunity]**? This is particularly relevant given the goal of **[desired outcome]**.

PROMPT No 40

Ideal Self - Self-Awareness - Professional Growth

To gain insights on specific actions to assist a team in recognizing the differences between their ideal and actual selves, fostering self-awareness and personal and professional growth.

Considering the importance of **self-awareness in personal and professional growth**, as an **Executive Coach** and in an **empathetic and respectful tone**, could you suggest specific actions **I** can take to assist **my team** in **recognizing the differences between their ideal and actual selves**?

Considering the importance of **[contextual challenge/opportunity]**, as a **[profession]** and in a **[tone of voice]**, could you suggest specific actions **[I/Name/Role]** can take to assist **[my/their]** **[team/group/department]** in **[desired outcome]**?

PROMPT No 41

Cohesive Culture - Organizational Success - Mission Cultivation

To gain detailed and comprehensive recommendations for the most effective and efficient strategies and techniques companies can implement to cultivate a strong and cohesive culture or mission, fostering organizational success and cohesion.

Considering the importance of **cultivating a strong and cohesive culture or mission within an organization**, as an **Organizational Development (OD) Consultant** and in an **inspirational and professional tone**, could you provide detailed and comprehensive recommendations for the most effective and efficient strategies and techniques **companies** can implement?

Considering the importance of **[contextual challenge/opportunity]**, as a **[profession]** and in a **[tone of voice]**, could you provide detailed and comprehensive recommendations for the most effective and efficient strategies and techniques **[companies/organizations]** can implement?

PROMPT No 42

Effective Communication - Team Understanding - Self-Awareness Enhancement

To gain specific strategies and techniques that can be employed to ensure clear and effective communication with a team, with the ultimate goal of enhancing their self-awareness and fostering a deeper understanding among team members.

As a **Communication Coach**, adopting a **clear and concise tone**, could you provide specific strategies and techniques that can be employed to **ensure clear and effective communication** with **my team**? This is particularly relevant given the goal of **enhancing their self-awareness and fostering a deeper understanding among team members**.

As a **[profession]**, adopting a **[tone of voice]**, could you provide specific strategies and techniques that can be employed to **[contextual challenge/opportunity]** with **[my/their]** **[team/group/department]**? This is particularly relevant given the goal of **[desired outcome]**.

PROMPT No 43

Thought Awareness - Responsibility Management - Interaction Impact

To gain specific strategies or techniques that can be used to consistently and effectively maintain awareness of how one's thoughts impact their responsibilities and interactions with team members.

As a **Leadership Development Consultant**, adopting a **reflective and insightful tone**, could you provide specific strategies or techniques that can be used to consistently and effectively maintain awareness of how one's thoughts impact their responsibilities and interactions with team members? This is particularly relevant given the goal of fostering self-awareness and effective team collaboration.

As a **[profession]**, adopting a **[tone of voice]**, could you provide specific strategies or techniques that can be used to **[contextual challenge/opportunity]** of how **[one's/my/their]** thoughts impact **[their/my/one's]** responsibilities and interactions with **[team members/colleagues/group]**? This is particularly relevant given the goal of **[desired outcome]**.

PROMPT No 44

Empowerment - Strategy - Contribution

To gain insights on how to leverage personal skills, expertise, and resources to make a meaningful and substantial contribution to the success and expansion of a company or team.

As a **Business Coach**, adopting an **empowering and strategic tone**, could you provide specific actions that **I** can take to make a meaningful and substantial contribution to the success and expansion of **my company or team**, leveraging **my skills, expertise, and resources** in a way that adds **significant value and has a lasting impact**?

As a **[profession]**, adopting a **[tone of voice]**, could you provide specific actions that **[I/Name/Role]** can take to make a meaningful and substantial contribution to the success and expansion of **[my/their]** **[company/team/group]**, leveraging **[my/their]** **[contextual challenge/opportunity]** in a way that adds **[desired outcome]**?

PROMPT No 45

Questioning - Insight - Understanding

To acquire effective strategies for developing questioning skills that can lead to a deeper understanding of team members' roles, challenges, and opportunities, thereby increasing influence within the team and contributing to the organization's success.

As a **Leadership Development Consultant**, adopting a **supportive and insightful tone**, could you provide me with strategies to **enhance my questioning skills**? I am particularly interested in **asking more impactful and insightful questions to my team members about the challenges they face and the opportunities they encounter**. My ultimate goal is to **gain a comprehensive understanding of their roles and actively contribute to the overall success of our organization**.

As a **[profession]**, adopting a **[tone of voice]**, could you provide me with strategies to enhance my [desired skill]? I am particularly interested in **[specific area of interest]**. My ultimate goal is to **[desired outcome]**.

PROMPT No 46

Resilience - Virtue - Communication

To gain insights on how to effectively communicate to a team the importance of developing self-control and resilience to overcome negative emotions, while emphasizing the crucial role of virtue in promoting happiness.

As a **Leadership Development Consultant**, adopting a **supportive and encouraging tone**, could you provide specific methods or approaches that **I** can employ to ensure that **I** effectively convey to **my team** the importance of **developing self-control and fortitude to overcome harmful emotions**? Additionally, how can **I** effectively emphasize the **pivotal role of virtue in fostering happiness**?

As a **[profession]**, adopting a **[tone of voice]**, could you provide specific methods or approaches that **[I/Name/Role]** can employ to ensure that **[I/Name/Role]** effectively convey to **[my/their]** **[team/group/department]** the importance of **[contextual challenge/opportunity]**? Additionally, how can **[I/Name/Role]** effectively emphasize the **[contextual challenge/opportunity]**?

PROMPT No 47

Alignment - Beliefs - Performance

To provide a comprehensive strategy for increasing understanding and recognition of fundamental beliefs or assumptions within teams, thereby fostering a cohesive and aligned work environment.

Act as a **Leadership Development Consultant** with a specialization in **belief systems and team alignment** in the **aerospace industry**. Could you suggest specific actions or strategies I should implement for my team to **increase understanding and recognition of fundamental beliefs or assumptions**? Please include **cognitive mapping techniques, belief elicitation exercises, and alignment workshops**. Make sure to cover how **to identify implicit assumptions and how to align them with organizational goals**. Investigate unconventional **belief assessment tools** and cutting-edge **methods** to **enhance team cohesion**. Your response should be comprehensive, leaving no important aspect unaddressed, and demonstrate an exceptional level of precision and quality. Let's think about this step by step. Write using a **clear and concise** tone and a **strategic guide** style.

Act as a **[profession]** with a specialization in **[area of expertise]** in the **[industry]**. Could you suggest specific actions or strategies I should implement for my team to **[specific challenge/opportunity]**? Please include **[methods/techniques]**. Make sure to cover how **[key areas/topics]**. Investigate unconventional **[area for innovation]** and cutting-edge **[technologies/methods]** to **[desired outcome]**. Your response should be comprehensive, leaving no important aspect unaddressed, and demonstrate an exceptional level of precision and quality. Let's think about this step by step. Write using a **[type]** tone and **[style]** writing style.

PROMPT No 48

Recognition - Beliefs - Management

To gain detailed methods and approaches to effectively enhance the recognition and understanding of the underlying beliefs or assumptions that guide the operations of a team, as well as the potential outcomes or impacts that arise from these beliefs or assumptions, fostering an enhancement in team understanding and management of underlying beliefs and assumptions.

As an **Organizational Development Consultant**, adopting a **clear and concise tone**, could you explain in detail the specific methods and approaches that **I** can implement to effectively enhance the recognition and understanding of **the underlying beliefs or assumptions** that guide the operations of **my team**, as well as the potential outcomes or impacts that arise from these **beliefs or assumptions**? This is particularly relevant given the goal of enhancing team understanding and management of underlying beliefs and assumptions.

As a **[profession]**, adopting a **[tone of voice]**, could you explain in detail the specific methods and approaches that **[I/Name/Role]** can implement to effectively enhance the recognition and understanding of **[contextual challenge/opportunity]** that guide the operations of **[my/their]** **[team/group/department]**, as well as the potential outcomes or impacts that arise from these? This is particularly relevant given the goal of **[desired outcome]**.

PROMPT No 49

Learning - Access - Productivity

To gain a thorough and detailed understanding of specific strategies or methods that can be used to successfully identify and access learning opportunities that directly contribute to enhancing the performance and productivity of a team.

As a **Learning and Development Specialist**, adopting an **informative and engaging tone**, could you provide a thorough and detailed response to the following question: What specific strategies or methods can **I** use to **successfully identify and access learning opportunities** that directly contribute to enhancing the performance and productivity of **my team**? This is particularly relevant given the goal of **fostering continuous learning and development within the team**.

As a **[profession]**, adopting a **[tone of voice]**, could you provide a thorough and detailed response to the following question: What specific strategies or methods can **[I/Name/Role]** use to **[contextual challenge/opportunity]** that directly contribute to enhancing the performance and productivity of **[my/their]** **[team/group/department]**? This is particularly relevant given the goal of **[desired outcome]**.

PROMPT No 50

Tags

Mindset - Positive - Conversion

Goal

To gain insights on specific and practical strategies and techniques that can be utilized to successfully identify and convert the negative and unproductive mindset displayed by a team into a positive and productive one.

Prompt

As a **Leadership Development Consultant**, adopting a **supportive and encouraging tone**, could you provide specific and practical strategies and techniques that can be utilized to **successfully identify and convert the negative and unproductive mindset** displayed by my team into a **positive and productive one**?

Formula

As a **[profession]**, adopting a **[tone of voice]**, could you provide specific and practical strategies and techniques that can be utilized to **[contextual challenge/opportunity]** displayed by **[my/their] [team/group/department]** into a **[contextual challenge/opportunity]**?

PROMPT No 51

Tags

Reflection - Growth - Learning

Goal

To gain insights on how to guide a team to see the potential for learning and growth even when they do not achieve their desired outcome or solution. This involves fostering a mindset that values the process and the insights gained from it, not just the end result.

Prompt

As a **Leadership Development Consultant**, adopting a **supportive and encouraging tone**, could you provide effective strategies to encourage **my team** to engage in reflection and consider the potential for gaining new insights and understanding when they do not achieve their **desired outcome or solution**?

Formula

As a **[profession]**, adopting a **[tone of voice]**, could you provide effective strategies to encourage **[my/their] [team/group/department]** to engage in reflection and consider the potential for gaining new insights and understanding when they do not achieve their **[contextual challenge/opportunity]**?

PROMPT No 52

Tags

Leadership - Action - Productivity

Goal

To gain specific actions, methods, or strategies to improve leadership abilities and successfully lead a team in creating and implementing action plans with enhanced productivity and success.

Prompt

As a **Leadership Development Consultant**, adopting a **motivational and inspiring tone**, could you provide **me** with specific actions, methods, or strategies that **I** can utilize to improve **my** leadership abilities and successfully lead **my team** in **creating and implementing action plans with enhanced productivity and success**?

As a **[profession]**, adopting a **[tone of voice]**, could you provide **[me/Name/Role]** with specific actions, methods, or strategies that **[I/Name/Role]** can utilize to improve **[my/their]** leadership abilities and successfully lead **[my/their]** **[team/group/department]** in **[contextual challenge/opportunity]**?

PROMPT No 53

Empathy - Emotion - Interpretation

To gain guidance on how to effectively interpret the cues and signals exhibited by team members in order to gain a deeper understanding of their emotions and feelings, fostering an enhancement in emotional intelligence and empathy within the team.

As an **Emotional Intelligence Coach**, adopting a **patient and empathetic tone**, could you guide **me** on how **I** can effectively interpret the cues and signals exhibited by **my team** members in order to gain a deeper understanding of **their emotions and feelings**? This is particularly relevant given the goal of **enhancing emotional intelligence and empathy within the team**.

As a **[profession]**, adopting a **[tone of voice]**, could you guide **[me/Name/Role]** on how **[I/they]** can effectively interpret the cues and signals exhibited by **[my/their]** **[team/group/department]** members in order to gain a deeper understanding of **[contextual challenge/opportunity]**? This is particularly relevant given the goal of **[desired outcome]**.

PROMPT No 54

Assumptions - Strategies - Dynamics

To gain specific instructions on the strategies and techniques that can be employed to effectively uncover and expose the implicit assumptions that a team may have unknowingly depended on while carrying out their assignments or projects, fostering a deeper understanding of team dynamics and decision-making processes.

As a **Business Analyst**, adopting a **detailed and instructive tone**, could you provide specific instructions on the strategies and techniques **I** can employ to effectively uncover and expose the implicit assumptions that **my team** may have unknowingly depended on while carrying out their **assignments or projects**? This is particularly relevant given the goal of **fostering a deeper understanding of team dynamics and decision-making processes**.

As a **[profession]**, adopting a **[tone of voice]**, could you provide specific instructions on the strategies and techniques **[I/Name/Role]** can employ to **[contextual challenge/opportunity]** that **[my/their]** **[team/group/department]** may have unknowingly depended on while carrying out their **[assignments/tasks/projects]**? This is particularly relevant given the goal of **[desired outcome]**.

PROMPT No 55

Barriers - Detection - Progress

To gain a comprehensive understanding of practical strategies that can be used to identify and address both internal and external barriers that could potentially obstruct the actions and progress of a team.

As a **Leadership Development Consultant**, adopting a **solution-oriented and proactive tone**, could you provide concrete and detailed approaches that can be utilized to accurately **detect and tackle internal as well as external barriers** that could hinder **the actions and advancement of my team** in an efficient manner?

As a **[profession]**, adopting a **[tone of voice]**, could you provide **[specific/detailed/concrete]** approaches that can be utilized to accurately **[desired outcome]** that could hinder **[contextual challenge/opportunity]** in an efficient manner?

BELIEF

PROMPT No 56

Assessment - Workload - Balance

To gain a comprehensive understanding of the specific steps that can be taken to thoroughly assess whether a team is efficiently handling their workload and responsibilities, and if they are maintaining a healthy work-life balance.

As a **Human Resources Consultant**, adopting a **supportive and professional tone**, could you guide **me** on the specific steps I can take to thoroughly assess whether **my team** is efficiently handling their **workload and responsibilities**, and if they are maintaining **a healthy work-life balance**? Please provide a comprehensive explanation with detailed actions to follow.

As a **[profession]**, adopting a **[tone of voice]**, could you guide **[me/Name/Role]** on the specific steps **[I/Name/Role]** can take to thoroughly assess whether **[my/their]** **[team/group/department]** is efficiently handling their **[contextual challenge/opportunity]**, and if they are maintaining **[desired outcome]**? Please provide a comprehensive explanation with detailed actions to follow.

PROMPT No 57

Verification - Evidence - Strategy

Goal

To gain a detailed understanding of the precise and comprehensive methods or techniques that can be employed to thoroughly assess and verify the evidence supporting a team's thoughts and ideas regarding their business plan or strategy.

Prompt

As a **Business Consultant**, adopting a **clear and concise tone**, could you provide me with the **precise and comprehensive methods or techniques** that can be employed to **thoroughly assess and verify the evidence supporting my team's thoughts and ideas** regarding **their business plan or strategy**?

Formula

As a **[profession]**, adopting a **[tone of voice]**, could you provide me with the **[specific methods or techniques]** that can be employed to **[desired outcome]** regarding **[contextual challenge/opportunity]**?

PROMPT No 58

Tags

Counter-evidence - Critical-Thinking -Evaluation

Goal

To obtain comprehensive and high-quality suggestions on specific methods or techniques that can effectively foster critical thinking and encourage the consideration of counter-evidence among team members or oneself when evaluating a business plan or strategy.

Prompt

As a **Business Strategy Consultant**, adopting an **informative and insightful tone**, could you provide detailed suggestions on specific methods or techniques that can effectively foster **critical thinking and encourage the consideration of counter-evidence** among **my team members** when **evaluating a business plan or strategy**?

Formula

As a **[profession]**, adopting a **[tone of voice]**, could you provide detailed suggestions on specific methods or techniques that can effectively foster **[desired outcome]** among **[my/their] [team/group/department]** when **[contextual challenge/opportunity]**?

PROMPT No 59

Tags

Empowerment - Beliefs - Goals

Goal

To gain a detailed understanding of specific strategies that can be implemented to cultivate and proficiently convey positive beliefs, empowering a team to accomplish exceptionally ambitious goals or commitments.

As a **Leadership Development Consultant**, adopting an **inspiring and motivating tone**, could you provide a detailed explanation of specific strategies that **I** can implement to **cultivate and proficiently convey positive beliefs** within my team? This is particularly relevant given the goal of **empowering my team to accomplish exceptionally ambitious goals or commitments**.

As a **[profession]**, adopting a **[tone of voice]**, could you provide a detailed explanation of specific strategies that **[I/Name/Role]** can implement to **[contextual challenge/opportunity]** within **[my/their]** **[team/group/department]**? This is particularly relevant given the goal of **[desired outcome]**.

PROMPT No 60

Hindrance - Development - Mindset

To gain insights on improving the approach to discussing beliefs that hinder the team's progress and to learn strategies to assist the team in developing empowering beliefs, fostering a positive mindset and improved performance.

As a **Leadership Development Consultant**, adopting a **supportive and constructive tone**, could you suggest specific steps I can take to enhance **my** approach when addressing the beliefs that are hindering **my team** from reaching their **goals or fulfilling their commitments**? Furthermore, could you recommend strategies **I** can implement to help them develop their own empowering beliefs? This is particularly relevant given the goal of **fostering a positive mindset and improved performance**.

As a **[profession]**, adopting a **[tone of voice]**, could you suggest specific steps **[I/Name/Role]** can take to enhance **[my/their]** approach when addressing the beliefs that are hindering **[my/their]** **[team/group/department]** from reaching their **[contextual challenge/opportunity]**? Furthermore, could you recommend strategies **[I/Name/Role]** can implement to help them develop their own empowering beliefs? This is particularly relevant given the goal of **[desired outcome]**.

PROMPT No 61

Alignment - Work-Ethic - Productivity

To gain insights on effective strategies and methods that can be utilized to align the beliefs and work ethic of a team with their actions, and vice versa, ensuring a harmonious and productive work environment.

As a **Leadership Development Consultant**, adopting a **supportive and insightful tone**, could you provide an in-depth explanation of the strategies and methods that can be utilized to **effectively align the beliefs and work ethic** of **my team** with their actions? Additionally, could you elaborate on the approaches that can be employed to ensure that their actions remain in sync with their beliefs and work ethic? This is particularly relevant given the goal of creating a harmonious and productive work environment.

As a **[profession]**, adopting a **[tone of voice]**, could you provide an in-depth explanation of the strategies and methods that can be utilized to **[contextual challenge/opportunity]** of **[my/their]** **[team/group/department]** with their actions? Additionally, could you elaborate on the approaches that can be employed to **[contextual challenge/opportunity]**? This is particularly relevant given the goal of **[desired outcome]**.

PROMPT No 62

Self-awareness - Improvement - Challenge

To gain a comprehensive understanding of the specific actions that can be taken to effectively challenge the team's beliefs and assumptions about themselves and their work, with the aim of fostering a culture of self-awareness and continuous improvement.

As an **Executive Coach**, adopting a **respectful and solution-oriented tone**, could you please provide a detailed description of the specific actions that I can take to effectively challenge **my team**'s beliefs and assumptions about themselves and their work in a practical manner? This is particularly relevant given the goal of fostering a culture of self-awareness and continuous improvement.

As a **[profession]**, adopting a **[tone of voice],** could you please provide a detailed description of the specific actions that I can take to effectively challenge **[my/their]** **[team/group/department]**'s beliefs and assumptions about **[contextual challenge/opportunity]** in a practical manner? This is particularly relevant given the goal of **[desired outcome].**

PROMPT No 63

Assumptions - Conflict - Resolution

To gain a comprehensive understanding of the underlying assumptions that the team is making while addressing a specific issue, thereby enabling a more effective and informed approach to problem-solving.

As a **Team Development Consultant**, adopting a **detailed and analytical tone**, could you help **me** identify and provide detailed explanations of the various assumptions **my team** is making when addressing **a conflict with their suppliers**? By doing so, we aim to gain a thorough understanding of the underlying beliefs and premises that underpin their approach to this **conflict**.

As a **[profession]**, adopting a **[tone of voice]**, could you help **[me/Name/Role]** identify and provide detailed explanations of the various assumptions **[my/their]** **[team/group/department]** is making when addressing a **[contextual challenge/opportunity]**? By doing so, we aim to gain a thorough understanding of the underlying beliefs and premises that underpin our approach to this **[contextual challenge/opportunity]**.

PROMPT No 64

Tags
Mindset - Performance - Belief

Goal
To gain insights on how to foster a specific belief or mindset within a team to address a particular problem that is causing a decrease in their performance.

Prompt
As a **Leadership Development Consultant**, adopting a **supportive and solution-oriented tone**, could you provide insights on how I can foster a specific belief or mindset **within my team** to address **the particular problem of lack of self-awareness**, which is leading to a decrease in their **performance**?

Formula
As a **[profession]**, adopting a **[tone of voice]**, could you provide insights on how **[I/Name/Role]** can foster a specific belief or mindset within **[my/their]** **[team/group/department]** to address **[contextual challenge/opportunity]**, which is leading to a decrease in their **[performance/productivity/effectiveness]**?

PROMPT No 65

Tags
Assessment - Engagement - Strategies

Goal
To gain insights on the most effective methods or strategies to assess the extent to which my team's beliefs regarding a particular issue or problem are beneficial for them.

Prompt
As a **Leadership Development Consultant**, adopting a **supportive and analytical tone**, could you provide insights on the most effective methods or strategies to assess the extent to which **my team**'s beliefs regarding **their lack of engagement** are beneficial for them?

Formula
As a **[profession]**, adopting a **[tone of voice]**, could you provide insights on the most effective methods or strategies to assess the extent to which **[my/their]** **[team/group/department]**'s beliefs regarding **[particular issue or problem]** are beneficial for them?

PROMPT No 66

Tags
Improvement - Change - Mindset

Goal

To obtain practical steps for changing a team's fixed mindset and fostering a belief in the potential for improvement and change.

Considering the challenge of **overcoming a fixed mindset in a team**, could you, as a **performance coach** and in an **empowering tone**, provide practical steps **I** could take to change my **team's** belief that their **work** can't **improve or change**?

Considering the challenge of **[contextual challenge/opportunity]**, could you, as a **[profession]** and in a **[tone of voice]**, provide practical steps **[I/Name/Role]** could take to change **[team/group/department]'s** belief that their **[work/performance/results]** can't **[improve/change/evolve]**?

PROMPT No 67

Identification - Covert - Motivations

To gain insights on covertly identifying the beliefs held by team members, which can help in understanding their motivations and behavior, and in turn, guide effective team management.

As a **Leadership Consultant**, adopting a **discreet and observant tone**, could you provide specific strategies or techniques that can be utilized to effectively and accurately discern **the beliefs held by my team**, while ensuring that **they remain unaware of my objective to gather this information**?

As a **[profession]**, adopting a **[tone of voice]**, could you provide specific strategies or techniques that can be utilized to effectively and accurately discern the **[desired outcome]**, while ensuring that **[contextual challenge/opportunity]**?

PROMPT No 68

Contradiction - Values - Resolution

Goal

To gain insights on how to handle a workplace situation that directly contradicts personal beliefs or values, ensuring the response is comprehensive, precise, and of high quality.

Prompt

As a **HR Professional**, adopting a **thoughtful and empathetic tone**, could you explain in great detail the specific steps I should take to navigate and resolve a workplace scenario that **directly contradicts my personal beliefs or values**? This is particularly relevant given the goal of **understanding how to handle situations that conflict with personal values in the workplace**.

Formula

As a **[profession]**, adopting a **[tone of voice]**, could you explain in great detail the specific steps that **[I/Name/Role]** can take to navigate and resolve a workplace scenario that **[contextual challenge/opportunity]**? This is particularly relevant given the goal of **[desired outcome]**.

PROMPT No 69

Outcomes - Emotions - Evaluation

Goal

To gain a detailed understanding of the methods or strategies that a team can use to effectively assess the extent to which they find it beneficial to consider alternative outcomes, especially in terms of their emotional response to a problem.

Prompt

As a **Team Development Consultant**, adopting a **supportive and insightful tone**, could you provide specific techniques or approaches that **my team** can employ to effectively assess the degree to which they perceive value in **exploring alternative solutions**, specifically in relation to their **emotional reaction to a problem**?

Formula

As a **[profession]**, adopting a **[tone of voice]**, could you provide specific techniques or approaches that **[my/their]** **[team/group/department]** can employ to effectively assess the degree to which they perceive value in **[contextual challenge/opportunity]**, specifically in relation to their **[desired outcome]**?

PROMPT No 70

Core-Values - Behavior -Professionalism

Goal

To gain insights on identifying the core values that guide team members in their professional journeys and to understand how these beliefs shape their behaviors and choices within the workplace.

Prompt

As a **Leadership Development Consultant**, adopting a **supportive and respectful tone**, could you help **me** identify the specific core values that **my team members** uphold as **guiding principles in their professional journeys**? Additionally, could you explain how these beliefs **shape and impact their behaviors and choices within the workplace**?

Formula

As a **[profession]**, adopting a **[tone of voice]**, could you help **[me/Name/Role]** identify the specific core values that **[my/their]** **[team/group/department]** uphold as **[contextual challenge/opportunity]**? Additionally, could you explain how these beliefs **[contextual challenge/opportunity]**?

PROMPT No 71

Tags

Communication - Losses - Commitment

Goal

To gain insights on how to improve communication within the team and conduct a comprehensive evaluation of potential losses in the team's current situation.

Prompt

As a **Communication Consultant**, adopting a **solution-oriented and empathetic tone**, could you provide specific tactics or methods that **I** can utilize to improve communication and ensure a comprehensive assessment of potential losses in my team's present situation regarding **their lack of commitment to work**?

Formula

As a **[profession]**, adopting a **[tone of voice]**, could you provide specific tactics or methods that **[I/Name/Role]** can utilize to improve communication and ensure a comprehensive assessment of potential losses in **[my/their]** **[team/group/department]**'s present situation regarding **[contextual challenge/opportunity]**?

PROMPT No 72

Tags

Stakeholders - Interaction - Performance

Goal

To identify concrete steps that can be implemented to ensure effective communication within the team, leading to optimal performance and interaction with internal stakeholders.

Prompt

As a **Human Resources Consultant**, adopting a **solution-oriented and professional tone**, could you provide specific steps that **I** can implement to guarantee that **my HR team** excels in their communication with **internal stakeholders**, leading to **the highest level of performance possible**?

Formula

As a **[profession]**, adopting a **[tone of voice]**, could you provide specific steps that **[I/Name/Role]** can implement to guarantee that **[my/their]** **[team/group/department]** excels in their communication with **[contextual challenge/opportunity]**, leading to **[desired outcome]**?

PROMPT No 73

Satisfaction - Fulfillment - Communication

To identify and communicate specific beliefs or assumptions that will contribute to the overall job satisfaction and personal fulfillment of a team.

As a **Team Leader**, adopting a **supportive and encouraging tone**, could you help **me** identify **specific beliefs or assumptions that I can effectively communicate to my team**? This is particularly relevant given the goal of **enhancing their overall job satisfaction and personal fulfillment**.

As a **[profession]**, adopting a **[tone of voice]**, could you help **[me/Name/Role]** identify **[contextual challenge/opportunity]**? This is particularly relevant given the goal of **[desired outcome]**.

PROMPT No 74

Limitations - Independence - Progress

To provide a detailed guide on how a team can independently identify and address any assumptions or beliefs that might be limiting their progress or potential.

As a **Leadership Development Consultant**, adopting a **supportive and encouraging tone**, could you provide specific actions that **my team** can undertake on their own to thoroughly and effectively identify and uncover any **assumptions or beliefs** that might be hindering their advancement or limiting their potential?

As a **[profession]**, adopting a **[tone of voice]**, could you provide specific actions that **[my/their]** **[team/group/department]** can undertake on their own to thoroughly and effectively identify and uncover any **[contextual challenge/opportunity]** that might be hindering their advancement or limiting their potential?

PROMPT No 75

Awareness - Outcomes - Decision-Making

To gain specific strategies, practices, or tools that can be utilized to improve the team's awareness and to ensure that the team has a thorough understanding of the potential outcomes and impacts of their decisions and actions, fostering a more informed and conscious decision-making process within the team.

As a **Leadership Development Consultant**, adopting an **informative and detailed tone**, could you provide specific strategies, practices, or tools that can be utilized to improve **my team's awareness**? Additionally, how can we ensure that **my team** has a thorough understanding of the **potential outcomes and impacts of our decisions and actions**? Please provide detailed and comprehensive suggestions for each question separately.

As a **[profession]**, adopting a **[tone of voice]**, could you provide specific strategies, practices, or tools that can be utilized to improve **[my/their]** **[team/group/department's]** **[desired outcome]**? Additionally, how can we ensure that **[my/their]** **[team/group/department]** has a thorough understanding of the **[contextual challenge/opportunity]**? Please provide detailed and comprehensive suggestions for each question separately.

PROMPT No 76

Beliefs - Progress - Work

To gain insight into the beliefs about work that might be preventing a team from moving forward, fostering an understanding of limiting beliefs and how they impact team progress.

As a **Career Coach**, adopting a **patient and empathetic tone**, could you describe the **beliefs about work** that might be preventing **my team** from moving forward? This is particularly relevant given the challenge of overcoming limiting beliefs to enhance team progress.

As a **[profession]**, adopting a **[tone of voice]**, could you describe the **[contextual challenge/opportunity]** that might be preventing **[my/their]** **[team/group/department]** from moving forward? This is particularly relevant given the **[contextual challenge/opportunity]**.

PROMPT No 77

Viewpoints - Reevaluation - Diversity

To gain a comprehensive understanding of the specific strategies or techniques that can be employed to successfully present alternative viewpoints to the team, motivating them to reevaluate their conduct or mindset in a thoughtful manner, with the aim of fostering a culture of diverse thinking.

As a **Leadership Development Consultant**, adopting a **respectful and solution-oriented tone**, could you please provide a detailed description of the specific strategies or techniques that I can employ to successfully present alternative viewpoints to **my team, motivating them to reevaluate their conduct or mindset in a thoughtful manner**? This is particularly relevant given the goal of fostering a culture of diverse thinking.

Formula

As a **[profession]**, adopting a **[tone of voice]**, could you please provide a detailed description of the specific strategies or techniques that I can employ to successfully present alternative viewpoints to **[my/their] [team/group/department]**, **[contextual challenge/opportunity]**? This is particularly relevant given the goal of **[desired outcome]**.

PROMPT No 78

Tags

Transformation - Assumptions - Facilitation

Goal

To gain insights on how to effectively facilitate a shift in a team's underlying beliefs or assumptions.

Prompt

Given the challenge of **transforming deeply ingrained beliefs or assumptions**, could you, as an **Executive Coach** and in a **respectful and patient tone**, detail how **I** could facilitate this switch in **my team**'s underlying beliefs or assumptions?

Formula

Given the challenge of **[contextual challenge/opportunity]**, could you, as a **[profession]** and in a **[tone of voice]**, detail how **[I/Name/Role]** could facilitate this switch in **[my/their] [team/group/department]'s** underlying beliefs or assumptions?

PROMPT No 79

Tags

Qualities - Development - Professionalism

Goal

To gain insights on how to guide a team towards understanding the professional qualities and skills they need to develop in order to excel in their roles.

Prompt

As a **Leadership Development Consultant**, adopting a **supportive and encouraging tone**, could you provide specific strategies that **I** can employ to engage **my team** in meaningful discussions about the **professional qualities and skills they should develop in order to excel in their roles**?

Formula

As a **[profession]**, adopting a **[tone of voice]**, could you provide specific strategies that **[I/Name/Role]** can employ to engage **[my/their] [team/group/department]** in meaningful discussions about the **[contextual challenge/opportunity]**?

PROMPT No 80

Motivation - Analysis - Evidence

Goal

To gain a detailed understanding of the most effective and specific strategies or methods that can be employed to motivate and inspire a team to conduct a comprehensive and meticulous analysis of evidence and criteria when evaluating a decision or course of action, fostering informed decision-making and effective problem-solving within the team.

Prompt

As a **Leadership Development Consultant**, adopting a **motivational and informative tone**, could you provide the most effective and specific strategies or methods that can be employed to **motivate and inspire my team to conduct a comprehensive and meticulous analysis of evidence and criteria when evaluating a decision or course of action**? This is particularly relevant given the goal of fostering informed decision-making and effective problem-solving within the team.

Formula

As a **[profession]**, adopting a **[tone of voice]**, could you provide the most effective and specific strategies or methods that can be employed to **[contextual challenge/opportunity] [my/their] [team/group/department] [contextual challenge/opportunity]**? This is particularly relevant given the goal of **[desired outcome]**.

PROMPT No 81

Tags

Evolution - Beliefs - Identification

Goal

To gain insights on how to identify the beliefs that the team used to hold but no longer consider to be true, in order to understand their evolving perspectives and adapt leadership strategies accordingly.

Prompt

As a **Leadership Development Consultant**, adopting a **respectful and empathetic tone**, could you provide me with strategies and methods to effectively identify the **beliefs that my team used to hold but no longer consider to be true at present**?

Formula

As a **[profession]**, adopting a **[tone of voice]**, could you provide **[me/Name/Role]** with strategies and methods to effectively identify the **[contextual challenge/opportunity]**?

PROMPT No 82

Tags

Responsibilities - Clarity - Productivity

Goal

To gain insights on the most effective strategies and approaches that can be applied during team discussions about responsibilities, with the aim of achieving maximum effectiveness, clarity, and productivity.

As a **Team Development Specialist**, adopting a **clear and concise tone**, could you provide insights on the most effective strategies and approaches that should be considered and applied when discussing **team responsibilities**, in order to achieve the highest level of **effectiveness, clarity, and productivity?**

As a **[profession]**, adopting a **[tone of voice]**, could you provide insights on the most effective strategies and approaches that should be considered and applied when discussing **[contextual challenge/opportunity]**, in order to achieve the highest level of [**desired outcome**]?

PROMPT No 83

Belief - Motivation - Action

To gain a detailed explanation of actionable steps that can be taken to instill a strong sense of belief within a team, fostering motivation for positive changes in career or performance by altering the decision-making process.

As an **Executive Coach**, adopting an **inspiring and motivating tone**, could you provide a detailed explanation of actionable steps that can be taken to **instill a strong sense of belief** within **my team**? This is particularly relevant given the goal of **motivating them to make positive changes in their career or performance by altering their decision-making process.**

As a **[profession]**, adopting a **[tone of voice]**, could you provide a detailed explanation of actionable steps that can be taken to **[desired outcome]** within **[my/their] [team/group/department]**? This is particularly relevant given the goal of **[contextual challenge/opportunity].**

CHALLENGE

PROMPT No 84

Independence - Strategies - Motivation

To foster independent thinking within the team, enabling them to generate potential next steps for their tasks or projects on their own.

As a **Leadership Development Consultant**, adopting a **motivational and encouraging tone**, could you provide **strategies or techniques** that **I** can employ to **inspire and encourage my team members to independently generate potential next steps for the tasks or projects they are currently engaged in?**

As a **[profession]**, adopting a **[tone of voice]**, could you provide **[strategies/techniques/methods]** that **[I/Name/Role]** can employ to **[desired outcome]**?

PROMPT No 85

Tags

Innovation - Encouragement - Challenges

Goal

To gain specific tactics or methods to inspire and encourage team members to step out of their comfort zones and take on new challenges, fostering a culture of innovation and growth.

Prompt

Given the goal of **inspiring team members to step out of their comfort zones and take on new challenges**, as a **Leadership Coach** and in an **encouraging and motivational tone**, could you outline specific tactics or methods **I** can employ?

Formula

Given the goal of **[contextual challenge/opportunity]**, as a **[profession]** and in a **[tone of voice]**, could you outline specific tactics or methods **[I/Name/Role]** can employ?

PROMPT No 86

Tags

Solutions - Proactivity - Challenges

Goal

To gain a comprehensive list of specific actions that can be implemented by a team to effectively address and overcome new challenges they are currently facing.

Prompt

As a **Team Development Consultant**, adopting a **solution-oriented and proactive tone**, could you provide a detailed and comprehensive list of specific actions that **my team** can implement in order to effectively address and overcome the **new challenges we are currently encountering**?

Formula

As a **[profession]**, adopting a **[tone of voice]**, could you provide a detailed and comprehensive list of specific actions that **[our/my/their]** **[team/group/department]** can implement in order to effectively address and overcome the **[contextual challenge/opportunity]** we are currently encountering?

PROMPT No 87

Tags

Uncertainty - Capabilities - Support

Goal

To develop strategies or approaches that can effectively assist a team in addressing any uncertainties or doubts they may have about their professional capabilities and potential within the workplace.

Prompt

As a **Leadership Coach**, adopting a **supportive and empathetic tone**, could you provide specific strategies or approaches that **I** can employ to effectively assist **my team** in addressing any **uncertainties or doubts they may have about their professional capabilities and potential** within the workplace?

As a **[profession]**, adopting a **[tone]**, could you provide specific strategies or approaches that **[I/Name/Role]** can employ to effectively assist **[my/their] [team/group/department]** in addressing any **[contextual challenge/opportunity]** within the workplace?

PROMPT No 88

Career - Assistance - Progression

To gain insights on identifying signs of a colleague's career going off-course and to learn actionable steps to assist them in getting back on track, fostering career progression and a supportive work environment.

As a **Career Coach**, adopting a **supportive and respectful tone**, could you help **me** identify signs that might indicate a **colleague's career is veering off-course**? Additionally, could you suggest actions **I** can take to assist them in getting back on the right track, especially considering the challenge of maintaining career progression?

As a **[profession]**, adopting a **[tone of voice]**, could you help **[me/Name/Role]** identify signs that might indicate a **[team member/colleague's] [contextual challenge/opportunity]**? Additionally, could you suggest actions **[I/Name/Role]** can take to assist them in **[desired outcome]**, especially considering **[contextual challenge/opportunity]**?

PROMPT No 89

Competencies - Emotional - Resolution

To understand the specific obstacles or issues that arise when a team lacks core competencies in dealing with a lack of emotional intelligence and to learn how to effectively resolve these challenges.

As a **Leadership Trainer**, adopting a **supportive and solution-oriented tone**, could you provide specific obstacles or issues that arise when a team lacks core competencies in dealing with a lack of emotional intelligence? Additionally, could you provide strategies on how these challenges can be effectively resolved? This is particularly relevant given the goal of enhancing emotional intelligence within the team.

As a **[profession]**, adopting a **[tone]**, could you provide specific obstacles or issues that arise when **[my/their] [team/group/department]** lacks **[contextual challenge/opportunity]**?

Additionally, could you provide strategies on how these challenges can be effectively resolved? This is particularly relevant given the goal of **[desired outcome]**.

PROMPT No 90

Tags

Self-awareness - Decision-Making - Beliefs

Goal

To foster self-awareness and improve decision-making skills among employees.

Prompt

As a **Leadership Development Coach**, with a focus on **fostering self-awareness and improving decision-making skills** among employees, I would like to request a comprehensive and detailed explanation on **how personal beliefs have a significant impact on decision-making processes in the workplace**. It would be greatly appreciated if you could adopt a **reflective and instructive tone** while addressing this topic. Additionally, I would like you to **identify specific ways in which these personal beliefs shape choices and guide actions in professional settings**.

Formula

As a **[profession]**, with a focus on **[desired outcome]**, I would like to request a comprehensive and detailed explanation on **[topic]**. It would be greatly appreciated if you could adopt a **[tone of voice]** while addressing this topic. Additionally, I would like you to **[additional request]**.

PROMPT No 91

Tags

Exploration - Diversity - Analysis

Goal

To gain a comprehensive understanding of specific strategies, techniques, or methods that can be utilized to effectively encourage and facilitate a team's exploration of various perspectives and approaches when analyzing a problem.

Prompt

As a **Problem-Solving Expert**, adopting a **solution-oriented and analytical tone**, could you please provide a detailed explanation of the specific strategies, techniques, or methods that **I** can employ to effectively **encourage and facilitate my team's exploration of diverse perspectives and approaches** when **analyzing a problem**?

Formula

As a **[profession]**, adopting a **[tone of voice]**, could you please provide a detailed explanation of the specific strategies, techniques, or methods that **[I/Name/Role]** can employ to effectively **[desired outcome]** when **[contextual challenge/opportunity]**?

PROMPT No 92

Attitudes - Benefit - Mindset

To gain a detailed analysis of the specific ways in which the negative attitudes or mindset of a team might be benefiting them, fostering a deeper understanding of team dynamics and attitudes.

As an **Emotional Intelligence Coach**, adopting an **open-minded and considerate tone**, could you provide a detailed analysis of the specific ways in which the **negative attitudes or mindset** of **my team** might be benefiting them? This is particularly relevant given the **challenge of managing pessimistic perspectives**.

As a **[profession]**, adopting a **[tone of voice]**, could you provide a detailed analysis of the specific ways in which the **[contextual challenge/opportunity]** of **[my/their]** **[team/group/department]** might be benefiting them? This is particularly relevant given the **[contextual challenge/opportunity]**

PROMPT No 93

Diversity - Problem-Solving - Strategies

To gain insights and strategies for facilitating diverse problem-solving perspectives within a team, enhancing the team's ability to approach and solve problems from various angles.

As a **Leadership Coach**, adopting a **collaborative and open-minded tone**, could you provide **me** with strategies and techniques to explore with **my team** different ways to **look at a problem**? This is particularly relevant given the goal of **fostering a diverse problem-solving culture within the team**.

As a **[profession]**, adopting a **[tone of voice]**, could you provide **[me/Name/Role]** with strategies and techniques to explore with **[my/their]** **[team/group/department]** different ways to **[contextual challenge/opportunity]**? This is particularly relevant given the goal of **[desired outcome]**.

PROMPT No 94

Adaptability - Mindset - Leadership

To gain specific and detailed actions that can be implemented to effectively lead a team in embracing a new perspective or mindset, fostering adaptability and open-mindedness within the team.

As a **Leadership Development Consultant**, adopting a **supportive and encouraging tone**, could you provide me with specific and detailed actions that **I** can implement to effectively lead **my team** in embracing a **new perspective or mindset**? This is particularly relevant given the goal of **fostering adaptability and open-mindedness within the team**.

As a **[profession]**, adopting a **[tone of voice]**, could you provide me with specific and detailed actions that **[I/Name/Role]** can implement to effectively lead **[my/their]** **[team/group/department]** in embracing a **[contextual challenge/opportunity]**? This is particularly relevant given the goal of **[desired outcome]**.

PROMPT No 95

Data - Relevance - Strategies

To gain specific actions and strategies that can be employed to assist a team in identifying the most relevant and reliable data sources that can effectively support or challenge their assumptions.

As a **Data Analyst**, adopting a **clear and concise tone**, could you provide specific actions and strategies that **I** can employ to assist **my team** in **identifying the most relevant and reliable data sources** that can effectively **support or challenge their assumptions**?

As a **[profession]**, adopting a **[tone of voice]**, could you provide specific actions and strategies that **[I/Name/Role]** can employ to assist **[my/their]** **[team/group/department]** in **[desired outcome]** that can effectively **[contextual challenge/opportunity]**?

PROMPT No 96

Development - Growth - Challenges

To gain specific actions and strategies for designing a thorough and effective development plan for a team, enabling them to perceive challenges as opportunities for personal and professional growth and enhancement.

As a **Leadership Development Consultant**, adopting a **solution-oriented and supportive tone**, could you guide me through the specific actions and strategies I should implement in order to design a **thorough and effective development plan** for my team? This plan should enable them to perceive challenges as **chances for personal and professional growth and enhancement**.

As a **[profession]**, adopting a **[tone of voice]**, could you guide me through the specific actions and strategies **[I/Name/Role]** should implement in order to design a **[contextual challenge/opportunity]** for **[my/their]** **[team/group/department]**? This plan should enable them to perceive challenges as **[desired outcome]**.

PROMPT No 97

Motivation - Inspiration - Challenges

Goal

To gain precise and comprehensive strategies and techniques that can be used to successfully motivate and inspire team members to enthusiastically embrace new challenges and actively pursue their next major challenge.

Prompt

As a **Leadership Development Consultant**, adopting an **inspiring and motivational tone**, could you provide me with precise and comprehensive strategies and techniques that I can use to successfully **motivate and inspire my team members** to enthusiastically embrace new challenges and actively pursue their next major challenge?

Formula

As a **[profession]**, adopting a **[tone of voice]**, could you provide me with precise and comprehensive strategies and techniques that I can use to successfully **[desired outcome]** **[my/their]** **[team/group/department]** to **[contextual challenge/opportunity]**?

PROMPT No 98

Tags

Resilience - Problem-Solving - Empowerment

Goal

To gain specific strategies or methods for promoting resilience and problem-solving abilities within a team, empowering them to effectively tackle various challenges.

Prompt

As a **Leadership Development Consultant**, adopting a solution-oriented and supportive tone, could you recommend specific strategies or methods that **I** can implement to **promote resilience and problem-solving abilities** within **my team**? I am seeking comprehensive and precise suggestions that will empower them to effectively tackle the various challenges they may face.

Formula

As a **[profession]**, adopting a **[tone of voice]**, could you recommend specific strategies or methods that **[I/Name/Role]** can implement to **[desired outcome]** within **[my/their]** **[team/group/department]**? I am seeking comprehensive and precise suggestions that will empower them to **[contextual challenge/opportunity]**.

PROMPT No 99

Tags

Systematic - Organization - Guidance

Goal

To gain specific strategies or methods that can be implemented to effectively motivate and guide a team towards adopting a systematic and organized approach when faced with obstacles, with the aim of problem-solving and devising action plans.

Prompt

As a **Leadership Development Consultant**, adopting a **solution-oriented and professional tone**, could you recommend specific strategies or methods that **I** can implement to effectively motivate and guide **my team** towards adopting **a systematic and organized approach** when faced with **obstacles**, with the aim of **problem-solving and devising action plans**?

Formula

As a **[profession]**, adopting a **[tone of voice]**, could you recommend specific strategies or methods that **[I/Name/Role]** can implement to effectively motivate and guide **[my/their]** **[team/group/department]** towards adopting a **[desired outcome]** when faced with **[contextual challenge/opportunity]**, with the aim of **[desired outcome]**?

PROMPT No 100

Tags

Problem-Solving - Cultivation - Empowerment

Goal

To gain specific strategies or activities that can be implemented to cultivate a problem-solving mindset within a team, enabling them to effectively confront and surmount any challenges they encounter.

Prompt

As a **Leadership Development Consultant**, adopting an **empowering and solution-oriented tone**, could you recommend specific strategies or activities that **I** can implement to cultivate a **problem-solving mindset** in **my team**, enabling them to effectively **confront and surmount any challenges they encounter**?

Formula

As a **[profession]**, adopting a **[tone of voice]**, could you recommend specific strategies or activities that **[I/Name/Role]** can implement to cultivate a **[desired outcome]** in **[my/their]** **[team/group/department]**, enabling them to effectively **[contextual challenge/opportunity]**?

PROMPT No 101

Tags

Adaptation - Transition - Techniques

Goal

To gain specific techniques or habits that individuals can develop and adopt when preparing to confront a fresh challenge or assume a new role, with the aim of facilitating a smooth transition and improving adaptability.

Prompt

As a **Career Coach**, adopting a **supportive and encouraging tone**, could you recommend specific techniques or habits that individuals can develop and adopt when **getting ready to confront a fresh challenge or assume a new role**? These suggestions should aim to facilitate a smooth transition and improve one's ability to adapt effectively.

Formula

As a **[profession]**, adopting a **[tone of voice]**, could you recommend specific techniques or habits that individuals can develop and adopt when **[contextual challenge/opportunity]**? These suggestions should aim to **[desired outcome]**.

PROMPT No 102

Thriving - Adaptation - Insights

To gain insights on specific practices, attitudes, or behaviors that individuals can adopt to not only successfully adapt but also thrive in a new role or position.

As a **Career Coach**, adopting a **supportive and encouraging tone**, could you share your insights on specific practices, attitudes, or behaviors that individuals can adopt **to not only successfully adapt but also thrive** in a new role or position?

As a **[profession]**, adopting a **[tone of voice]**, could you share your insights on specific practices, attitudes, or behaviors that individuals can adopt to **[contextual challenge/opportunity]** in a new role or position?

PROMPT No 103

Learning - Mistakes - Growth

To gain insights and strategies on how to develop a mindset that perceives mistakes as valuable opportunities for learning, rather than as failures, fostering a growth mindset and a culture of continuous learning.

As a **Personal Development Coach**, adopting an **encouraging and supportive tone**, could you provide detailed insights and strategies on how **I** can help **my team** develop a mindset that perceives **mistakes** as valuable opportunities for learning, rather than as failures? This is particularly relevant given the goal of **fostering a growth mindset and a culture of continuous learning within the team**.

As a **[profession]**, adopting a **[tone of voice]**, could you provide detailed insights and strategies on how **[I/Name/Role]** can help **[my/their]** **[team/group/department]** develop a mindset that perceives **[contextual challenge/opportunity]** as valuable opportunities for learning, rather than as failures? This is particularly relevant given the goal of **[desired outcome]**.

PROMPT No 104

Empowerment - Self-Discovery - Strategies

To gain specific strategies or methods that can be effectively utilized to accurately recognize and utilize personal strengths in order to triumph over obstacles or achieve success in a project.

As a **Personal Development Coach**, adopting an **empowering and solution-oriented tone**, could you share specific strategies or methods that I can effectively utilize to accurately recognize and utilize **my** personal strengths in order to **triumph over obstacles or achieve success in my projects**?

As a **[profession]**, adopting a **[tone of voice]**, could you share specific strategies or methods that **[I/Name/Role]** can effectively utilize to accurately recognize and utilize **[my/their]** personal strengths in order to **[contextual challenge/opportunity]**?

PROMPT No 105

Team-Motivation - Leadership - Empowerment

To gain specific and practical strategies, methods, and approaches to successfully motivate and empower a team to overcome any internal barriers or doubts, fostering an environment that compels decisive action and the accomplishment of shared objectives.

As a **Leadership Coach**, adopting an **empowering and optimistic tone**, could you provide specific and practical strategies, methods, and approaches that **I** can employ to successfully **motivate and empower my team to overcome any internal barriers or doubts they may possess**? I aim to **foster an environment that compels them to take decisive action and ultimately accomplish our shared objectives**.

As a **[profession]**, adopting a **[tone of voice]**, could you provide specific and practical strategies, methods, and approaches that **[I/Name/Role]** can employ to successfully **[contextual challenge/opportunity]** **[my/their]** **[team/group/department]**? I aim to **[desired outcome]**.

PROMPT No 106

Team-Leadership - Strategies - Professional-Development

To equip Leadership Coaches, team leaders, and organizational decision-makers with a robust strategy for encouraging teams to view situations or challenges from alternative viewpoints, thereby fostering a culture of diverse thinking and enhanced problem-solving.

Act as a **Leadership Coach** with a specialization in **cognitive diversity and problem-solving** in the **renewable energy industry**. Could you suggest specific tactics or methods that I can implement to **encourage my team to view situations or challenges from alternative viewpoints**? This is particularly relevant given the goal of **fostering a culture of diverse**

thinking. Please include **lateral thinking exercises, perspective-shifting workshops, and cognitive diversity assessments**. Make sure to cover how **to facilitate inclusive discussions** and how **to measure the impact of diverse thinking on team performance**. Investigate **unconventional problem-solving techniques and cutting-edge diversity analytics tools** to **enrich team dynamics**. Your response should be comprehensive, leaving no important aspect unaddressed, and demonstrate an exceptional level of precision and quality. Let's think about this step by step. Write using an **open-minded and supportive** tone and a **diversity-enhancing** guide style.

Act as a **[profession]** with a specialization in **[area of expertise]** in the **[industry]**. Could you suggest specific tactics or methods that I can implement to **[specific challenge/opportunity]**? This is particularly relevant given the goal of **[specific goal]**. Please include **[methods/techniques]**. Make sure to cover how **[key areas/topics]**. Investigate **[technologies/methods]** to **[desired outcome]**. Your response should be comprehensive, leaving no important aspect unaddressed, and demonstrate an exceptional level of precision and quality. Let's think about this step by step. Write using a **[type]** tone and **[style]** writing style.

PROMPT No 107

Diverse-Thinking - Problem-Solving - Leadership

To gain specific tactics or methods to encourage a team to view situations or challenges from alternative viewpoints, fostering a culture of diverse thinking and problem-solving.

As a **Leadership Coach**, adopting an **open-minded and supportive tone**, could you suggest specific tactics or methods that **I** can implement to encourage **my team** to **view situations or challenges from alternative viewpoints**? This is particularly relevant given the goal of fostering a culture of diverse thinking.

As a **[profession]**, adopting a **[tone of voice]**, could you suggest specific tactics or methods that **[I/Name/Role]** can implement to encourage **[my/their]** **[team/group/department]** to **[desired outcome]**? This is particularly relevant given the **[contextual challenge/opportunity]**.

PROMPT No 108

Communication - HR - Obstacle-Resolution

To gain specific strategies and techniques to enhance communication within a team and effectively address and overcome obstacles encountered in their work.

As a **Human Resources (HR) Consultant**, utilizing a **clear and concise tone**, could you provide strategies and techniques to **enhance communication** within the **HR team** and **address obstacles** encountered during **recruitment efforts**?

As a **[profession]**, utilizing a **[tone of voice]**, could you provide strategies and techniques to **[desired outcome]** within **[my/their]** **[team/group/department]** and **[desired outcome]** encountered during **[contextual challenge/opportunity]**?

PROMPT No 109

Risk-Taking - Team-Discussion - Positive-Outcome

To gain effective strategies for initiating a discussion with a team, encouraging them to share their experiences of taking risks that ultimately led to positive outcomes.

As a **Leadership Consultant**, adopting an **engaging and supportive tone**, could you suggest effective strategies that I can employ to initiate a discussion with **my team**, encouraging them to share their experiences of **taking risks that ultimately led to positive outcomes**?

As a **[profession]**, adopting a **[tone of voice]**, could you suggest effective strategies that **[I/Name/Role]** can employ to initiate a discussion with **[my/their]** **[team/group/department]**, encouraging them to share their experiences of **[contextual challenge/opportunity]**?

PROMPT No 110

Comfort-Zone - Performance - Team-Dynamics

To gain specific strategies or methods to accurately determine the boundaries of a team's comfort zone, fostering an understanding of team dynamics and enabling the expansion of comfort zones for enhanced performance

As a **Performance Coach**, adopting a **respectful and professional tone**, could you suggest specific strategies or methods that **I** can use to accurately determine the **boundaries of my team's comfort zone**? This is particularly relevant given the goal of **understanding and expanding comfort zones for enhanced performance**.

As a **[profession]**, adopting a **[tone of voice]**, could you suggest specific strategies or methods that **[I/Name/Role]** can use to accurately determine the **[contextual challenge/opportunity]** of **[my/their]** **[team/group/department]**? This is particularly relevant given the goal of **[desired outcome]**.

PROMPT No 111

Productive-Discussion - Impediment - Insight

To gain specific strategies and approaches to enhance the ability to have productive and insightful discussions with a team about the factors that have impeded their progress or work towards achieving their goals.

As a **Leadership Development Consultant**, adopting a **supportive and understanding tone**, could you provide specific strategies and approaches that **I** can employ to enhance **my** ability to have productive and insightful discussions with **my team** about the factors that have impeded their **progress or work towards achieving their goals**?

As a **[profession]**, adopting a **[tone of voice]**, could you provide specific strategies and approaches that **[I/Name/Role]** can employ to enhance **[my/their]** ability to have productive and insightful discussions with **[my/their] [team/group/department]** about the factors that have impeded their **[contextual challenge/opportunity]**?

CHANGE

PROMPT No 112

Mindset-Change - Productivity - Organizational-Development

To gain specific tactics or methods to successfully alter the mindset of a team, fostering a change in mindset for enhanced productivity and overall effectiveness.

As an **Organizational Development (OD) Consultant**, adopting an **encouraging and solution-oriented tone**, could you suggest specific tactics or methods that **I** can employ to **successfully alter the mindset** of my team? This is particularly relevant given the ultimate goal of **enhancing their productivity and overall effectiveness**.

As a **[profession]**, adopting a **[tone of voice]**, could you suggest specific tactics or methods that **[I/Name/Role]** can employ to **[desired outcome]** of **[my/their]** **[team/group/department]**? This is particularly relevant given the ultimate goal of **[desired outcome]**.

PROMPT No 113

Relationship-Building - Collaboration - Work-Environment

To gain a detailed plan of action to enhance the working relationships of a team with their colleagues and clients, fostering a positive and productive work environment.

As a **Business Coach**, adopting a **collaborative and respectful tone**, could you provide a detailed plan of action that **I** can implement to **enhance the working relationships** of **my team** with their colleagues and clients? This is particularly relevant given the goal of **fostering a positive and productive work environment**.

As a **[profession]**, adopting a **[tone of voice]**, could you provide a detailed plan of action that **[I/Name/Role]** can implement to **[desired outcome]** of **[my/their]** **[team/group/department]** with their colleagues and clients? This is particularly relevant given the goal of **[desired outcome]**.

PROMPT No 114

Sales-Communication - Obstacle-Resolution - Client-Service

To gain strategies or approaches for effectively communicating with a team about the specific areas in the sales process or client service process where they are facing the most challenges, and to understand the steps that can be taken to successfully address and overcome these obstacles.

As a **Sales Manager**, adopting a **solution-oriented and empathetic tone**, could you suggest strategies or approaches that **I** can employ to effectively communicate with **my team** about the specific areas in the **sales process or client service process** where we are facing the most challenges? Additionally, what steps can we take to successfully **address and overcome these obstacles**?

As a **[profession]**, adopting a **[tone of voice]**, could you suggest strategies or approaches that **[I/Name/Role]** can employ to effectively communicate with **[my/their]** **[team/group/department]** about the specific areas in the **[contextual challenge/opportunity]** where we are facing the most challenges? Additionally, what steps can we take to successfully **[desired outcome]**?

PROMPT No 115

Change-Management - Innovation - Adaptability

To gain specific methods and strategies that leaders can employ to effectively anticipate and navigate rapid changes and innovations in their industry, while also ensuring their team is well-prepared and adaptable.

As a **Change Management Consultant**, adopting a **proactive and strategic tone**, could you provide specific methods and strategies that **I**, as a leader, can employ to effectively anticipate and navigate **rapid changes and innovations** in **my** industry, while also ensuring **my team** is **well-prepared and adaptable**? This is particularly relevant given the **dynamic nature of our industry**.

As a **[profession]**, adopting a **[tone of voice]**, could you provide specific methods and strategies that **[I/Name/Role]**, as a leader, can employ to effectively anticipate and navigate **[contextual challenge/opportunity]** in **[my/their]** industry, while also ensuring **[my/their]** **[team/group/department]** is **[desired outcome]**? This is particularly relevant given the **[contextual challenge/opportunity]**.

PROMPT No 116

Diplomacy - Communication - Team-Feedback

To gain strategies for effectively and tactfully addressing aspects of a situation or project that did not go well with a team, without making them feel defensive or threatened.

As a **Leadership Development Consultant**, adopting a **diplomatic and understanding tone**, could you suggest strategies that **I** can employ to effectively and tactfully address the aspects of a **situation or project** that did not go well with **my team**, without making them feel defensive or threatened by **my** approach? This is particularly relevant given the goal of **maintaining a positive and open communication environment**.

As a **[profession]**, adopting a **[tone of voice]**, could you suggest strategies that **[I/Name/Role]** can employ to effectively and tactfully address the aspects of a **[contextual challenge/opportunity]** that did not go well with **[my/their]** **[team/group/department]**, without making them feel defensive or threatened by **[my/their]** approach? This is particularly relevant given the goal of **[desired outcome]**.

PROMPT No 117

Celebration - Team-Morale - Appreciation

To gain specific details and suggestions on how to make the celebration of a successful work or project more memorable and meaningful for everyone involved, fostering team morale and appreciation.

As a **Team Building Specialist**, adopting an **enthusiastic and appreciative tone**, could you provide specific details and suggestions on how **I** can improve and make the celebration of a successful **work or project** that **my team** has accomplished more memorable and meaningful for everyone involved? This is particularly relevant given the goal of **fostering team morale and appreciation**.

As a **[profession]**, adopting a **[tone of voice]**, could you provide specific details and suggestions on how **[I/Name/Role]** can improve and make the celebration of a successful **[work/project/task]** that **[my/their]** **[team/group/department]** has accomplished more memorable and meaningful for everyone involved? This is particularly relevant given the goal of **[desired outcome]**.

PROMPT No 118

Tags

Future-Readiness - Leadership - Perspective-Shift

Goal

To acquire specific knowledge or skills at present that will enable the effective recognition and guidance of necessary changes in a team's perspectives in the future.

Prompt

As a **Leadership Development Consultant**, adopting an **educational and forward-thinking tone**, could you suggest what specific knowledge or skills **I** should acquire at present in order to effectively recognize and guide **my team** towards the necessary changes in their perspectives in the future?

Formula

As a **[profession]**, adopting a **[tone of voice]**, could you suggest what specific knowledge or skills **[I/Name/Role]** should acquire at present in order to effectively recognize and guide **[my/their]** **[team/group/department]** towards the necessary changes in their perspectives in the future?

PROMPT No 119

Tags

Self-Motivation - Performance - Change

Goal

To gain strategies or methods that can be employed to motivate a team to independently contemplate the necessary changes they should make in order to enhance their performance.

Prompt

As a **Leadership Development Consultant**, adopting a **motivational and encouraging tone**, could you suggest strategies or methods that **I** can employ to motivate **my team** to independently contemplate the necessary changes they should make in order to enhance their performance?

Formula

As a **[profession]**, adopting a **[tone of voice]**, could you suggest strategies or methods that **[I/Name/Role]** can employ to motivate **[my/their] [team/group/department]** to independently contemplate the necessary changes they should make in order to **[desired outcome]**?

PROMPT No 120

Tags

Forward-Thinking - Impact - Strategy

Goal

To gain specific strategies or tools to effectively engage in a discussion with a team about how their current work will impact and shape future outcomes, fostering a forward-thinking mindset within the team.

Prompt

69

As a **Leadership Development Consultant**, adopting a **forward-thinking and engaging tone**, could you provide specific strategies or tools that **I** can utilize to effectively engage in a discussion with **my team** about how their current work will **impact and shape future outcomes**? This is particularly relevant given the goal of **fostering a forward-thinking mindset within the team**.

As a **[profession]**, adopting a **[tone of voice]**, could you provide specific strategies or tools that **[I/Name/Role]** can utilize to effectively engage in a discussion with **[my/their]** **[team/group/department]** about how their current work will **[contextual challenge/opportunity]**? This is particularly relevant given the goal of **[desired outcome]**.

PROMPT No 121

Skills-Assessment - Implementation - Team-Development

To gain specific strategies for thoroughly assessing the existing abilities and skills of a team, and to understand how to effectively utilize these capacities to successfully implement any required modifications or improvements.

As a **Team Development Specialist**, adopting a **solution-oriented tone**, could you suggest specific strategies to thoroughly assess the existing abilities and skills of **my team**? Additionally, how can we effectively utilize these capacities to successfully implement any required **modifications or improvements**?

As a **[profession]**, adopting a **[tone of voice]**, could you suggest specific strategies to thoroughly assess the existing abilities and skills of **[my/their]** **[team/group/department]**? Additionally, how can we effectively utilize these capacities to successfully implement any required **[contextual challenge/opportunity]**?

PROMPT No 122

Proposal-Development - Positive-Change - Work-Habits

To create a thorough and successful proposal for a team, with the aim of transforming their work routine and overall attitude, fostering a positive change in work habits and mindset.

As a **Leadership Development Consultant**, adopting an **empowering and optimistic tone**, could you guide **me** through the specific steps **I** can take to create a thorough and successful proposal for **my team**? The goal is to successfully **transform their work routine and overall attitude**, fostering **a positive change in work habits and mindset**.

As a **[profession]**, adopting a **[tone of voice]**, could you guide **[me/Name/Role]** through the specific steps **[I/Name/Role]** can take to create a thorough and successful proposal for **[my/their]**

[team/group/department]? The goal is to successfully **[desired outcome]**, fostering **[contextual challenge/opportunity]**.

PROMPT No 123

Evaluation - Consequence - Work-Methods

To gain specific techniques or approaches that can be employed to conduct a comprehensive evaluation of the impacts on a team's work if they decide to continue with their existing work methods and routines, fostering an understanding of the consequences of maintaining current work practices.

As an **Organizational Development Consultant**, adopting an **analytical and strategic tone**, could you suggest specific techniques or approaches that **I** can employ to conduct a comprehensive evaluation of the impacts on **my team's** work if they decide to **continue with their existing work methods and routines**? This is particularly relevant given the goal of understanding the consequences of **maintaining current work practices**.

As a **[profession]**, adopting a **[tone of voice]**, could you suggest specific techniques or approaches that **[I/Name/Role]** can employ to conduct a comprehensive evaluation of the impacts on **[my/their] [team/group/department]**'s work if they decide to **[contextual challenge/opportunity]**? This is particularly relevant given the goal of **[desired outcome]**.

PROMPT No 124

Transformation - Mindset - Improvement

To gain concrete and specific strategies and techniques to successfully shift a team's mindset and overall attitude, resulting in positive transformation and improvement, fostering a positive transformation and improvement within the team.

As a **Performance Coach**, adopting an **encouraging and motivating tone**, could you suggest what concrete and specific strategies and techniques **I** can implement to successfully shift **my team's** mindset and overall attitude, resulting in **positive transformation and improvement**? This is particularly relevant given the goal of **fostering a positive transformation and improvement within the team.**

As a **[profession]**, adopting a **[tone of voice]**, could you suggest what concrete and specific strategies and techniques **[I/Name/Role]** can implement to successfully shift **[my/their] [team/group/department]**'s mindset and overall attitude, resulting in **[contextual challenge/opportunity]**? This is particularly relevant given the goal of **[desired outcome]**.

PROMPT No 125

Prioritization - Decision-Making - Task-Management

To obtain a list of criteria that a team should consider when deciding which tasks or projects to let go of in order to prioritize effectively.

In the context of a **team needing to prioritize and let go of certain tasks or projects**, as a **performance management specialist** and in a **clear and concise tone**, could you list the criteria **my team** needs to consider when **making these decisions**?

In the context of **[contextual challenge/opportunity]**, as a **[profession]** and in a **[tone of voice]**, could you list the criteria **[I/Name/Role]'s [team/group/department]** needs to consider when **[desired outcome]**?

PROMPT No 126

Development - Skills - Adaptability

To gain insights on identifying areas for ongoing development within a team, enhancing their skills and adaptability.

As a **talent development specialist**, in an **encouraging and supportive tone**, could you help **me** in identifying the areas of ongoing development for **my team**, particularly in the context of a **rapidly evolving industry**?

As a **[profession]**, in a **[tone of voice]**, could you help **[I/Name/Role]** in identifying the areas of ongoing development for **[my/their] [team/group/department]**, particularly in the context of **[contextual challenge/opportunity]**?

PROMPT No 127

Assessment - Improvement - Team-Development

To gain a clear understanding of the specific factors or criteria that should be considered when assessing areas that need improvement within a team, fostering effective team development and performance enhancement.

As a **Performance Improvement Consultant**, adopting a **clear and concise tone**, could you elaborate on the specific factors or criteria that **I** should consider when assessing **areas that need improvement** within **my team**? This is particularly relevant given the goal of **fostering effective team development and performance enhancement**.

As a **[profession]**, adopting a **[tone of voice]**, could you elaborate on the specific factors or criteria that **[I/Name/Role]** should consider when assessing **[contextual challenge/opportunity]** within **[my/their]** **[team/group/department]**? This is particularly relevant given the goal of **[desired outcome]**.

COMMITMENT

PROMPT No 128

Motivation - Ownership - Vision

To gain specific and detailed strategies or approaches to successfully motivate and inspire a team to take full ownership of their responsibilities and actively work towards accomplishing a common vision, fostering a sense of ownership and shared vision within the team.

As a **Leadership Development Facilitator**, adopting an **inspirational and motivating tone**, could you provide specific and detailed strategies or approaches that I can implement to successfully motivate and inspire **my team** to take full ownership of their responsibilities and actively work towards accomplishing **our common vision**? This is particularly relevant given the goal of **fostering a sense of ownership and shared vision within the team**.

As a **[profession]**, adopting a **[tone of voice]**, could you provide specific and detailed strategies or approaches that **[I/Name/Role]** can implement to successfully motivate and inspire **[my/their]** **[team/group/department]** to take full ownership of their responsibilities and actively work towards accomplishing **[contextual challenge/opportunity]**? This is particularly relevant given the goal of **[desired outcome]**.

PROMPT No 129

Distribution - Evaluation - Task-Management

To gain strategies or methods for accurately evaluating and determining the distribution of tasks among team members, taking into consideration their individual strengths and weaknesses, while also prioritizing the best interests of the company.

As a **Management Consultant**, adopting a **solution-oriented tone**, could you suggest strategies or methods that **I** can employ to accurately evaluate and determine the distribution of tasks among **my team members**, considering their **individual strengths and weaknesses**, while also prioritizing **the best interests of our company**?

As a **[profession]**, adopting a **[tone of voice]**, could you suggest strategies or methods that **[I/Name/Role]** can employ to accurately evaluate and determine the distribution of tasks among

[my/their] [team/group/department], considering their **[contextual challenge/opportunity]**, while also prioritizing **[contextual challenge/opportunity]**?

PROMPT No 130

Influence - Commitment - Goal-Orientation

To gain strategies on how to effectively influence a team to commit to their goals, enhancing their performance and productivity.

In the context of **fostering a goal-oriented team culture**, as a **leadership coach** and in **an inspiring and motivating tone**, could you advise on how **I** could influence **my team** to commit themselves to achieving their **goals**?

In the context of **[contextual challenge/opportunity]**, as a **[profession]** and in a **[tone of voice]**, could you advise on how **[I/Name/Role]** could influence **[my/their]** **[team/group/department]** to commit themselves to achieving their **[goals/targets/objectives]**?

PROMPT No 131

Engagement - Productivity - Remote-Work

To gain insights on measures to implement in order to support a team's commitment to their work, enhancing their engagement and productivity.

As a **leadership development manager**, in a **clear and concise tone**, could you outline what measures **I** could implement to support **my team's** commitment to their work, particularly in the context of a **remote working environment**?

As a **[profession]**, in a **[tone of voice]**, could you outline what measures **[I/Name/Role]** could implement to support **[my/their]** **[team/group/department]**'s commitment to their **[work/tasks/projects]**, particularly in the context of **[contextual challenge/opportunity]**?

PROMPT No 132

Communication - Promotion - Motivation

To learn effective methods to subtly communicate to a team about the potential for a promotion or salary increase, contingent on performance improvement, fostering motivation and performance enhancement.

As a **Human Resources Consultant**, adopting a **diplomatic and professional tone**, could you suggest specific and effective methods that **I** can use to subtly convey to **my team** that they have the potential for a **promotion or salary increase**, without directly stating it, as long as **they improve their performance**? This is particularly relevant given the goal of fostering motivation and performance enhancement.

As a **[profession]**, adopting a **[tone of voice]**, could you suggest specific and effective methods that **[I/Name/Role]** can use to subtly convey to **[my/their]** **[team/group/department]** that they have the potential for **[contextual challenge/opportunity]**, without directly stating it, as long as they **[contextual challenge/opportunity]**? This is particularly relevant given the goal of **[desired outcome]**

PROMPT No 133

Dedication - Strategy - Goal-Progress

To gain specific strategies to effectively encourage and enhance a team's dedication and motivation in fulfilling their responsibilities and progressing towards their goals.

As a **Leadership Development Consultant**, adopting a **motivational and encouraging tone**, could you provide specific strategies that I can implement to effectively encourage and enhance my **team's dedication and motivation** in fulfilling their responsibilities and progressing towards **our company's goals**?

As a **[profession]**, adopting a **[tone of voice]**, could you provide specific strategies that **[I/Name/Role]** can implement to effectively encourage and enhance **[my/their]** **[team/group/department]'s** **[desired outcome]** in fulfilling their responsibilities and progressing towards **[contextual challenge/opportunity]**?

PROMPT No 134

Accountability - Performance - Reliability

To gain insights on strategies for holding a team accountable to their commitments, enhancing their performance and reliability.

Given the importance of **accountability in team performance**, as an **Executive Coach** and in a **constructive and professional tone**, could you explain a strategy **I** could adopt for holding **my team** accountable to their **commitments**?

Given the importance of **[contextual challenge/opportunity]**, as a **[profession]** and in a **[tone of voice]**, could you explain a strategy **[I/Name/Role]** could adopt for holding **[my/their]** **[team/group/department]** accountable to their **[commitments/tasks/goals]**?

PROMPT No 135

Composure - Support - Well-being

To an actionable framework for assisting team members in managing personal issues while maintaining professional composure, thereby fostering a supportive work environment and enhancing overall team well-being.

As an **Employee Relations Manager** specializing in the **healthcare sector**, could you **delineate specific methods** I can **employ** to **assist** my team in **managing personal issues** while **maintaining composure** at work? Include **evidence-based practices, psychological theories, and real-world case studies**. Let's think about this step by step. Write using an **empathetic** tone and a **respectful** writing style.

As an **[Employee Relations Manager/HR Specialist/Well-being Coordinator]** specializing in the **[healthcare/technology/finance]** sector, could you **[delineate/suggest/elaborate on]** **[specific methods/strategies/approaches]** I can **[employ/use/implement]** to **[assist/support/guide]** my team in **[managing/handling/addressing]** **[personal issues/life challenges/emotional struggles]** while **[maintaining/keeping/sustaining]** **[composure/professionalism/equanimity]** at work? Include **[evidence-based practices/empirical data]**, **[psychological theories/behavioral models]**, and **[real-world case studies/practical examples]**. Let's **[think about this step by step/methodically dissect each component]**. Write using a **[empathetic/respectful/compassionate]** tone and a **[respectful/considerate/tactful]** writing style.

CREATIVITY

PROMPT No 136

Collaboration - Innovation - Originality

To gain specific techniques, approaches, and actions to foster effective collaboration with a team, enabling the generation of innovative and original ideas for projects or tasks, fostering effective collaboration and innovation within the team.

As a **Change Management Consultant**, adopting a **collaborative and solution-oriented tone**, could you provide specific techniques, approaches, and actions that **I** can utilize to foster effective collaboration with **my team**, enabling us to generate **innovative and original ideas for our projects or tasks**? This is particularly relevant given the goal of fostering effective collaboration and innovation within the team.

As a **[profession]**, adopting a **[tone of voice]**, could you provide specific techniques, approaches, and actions that **[I/Name/Role]** can utilize to foster effective collaboration with **[my/their]** **[team/group/department]**, enabling us to generate **[contextual challenge/opportunity]**? This is particularly relevant given the goal of **[desired outcome].**

PROMPT No 137

Satisfaction - Engagement - Productivity

To gain insights on ways to enhance job satisfaction and enjoyment in a team, thereby improving their engagement and productivity.

Considering the importance of **job satisfaction in team productivity**, as an **employee engagement manager** and in an **optimistic and enthusiastic tone**, could you propose ways **my team** can find more enjoyment in accomplishing their **responsibilities**?

Considering the importance of **[contextual challenge/opportunity]**, as a **[profession]** and in a **[tone of voice],** could you propose ways **[I/Name/Role]'s [team/group/department]** can find more enjoyment in accomplishing their **[responsibilities/tasks/goals]?**

PROMPT No 138

Self-Assessment - Evaluation - Improvement

To gain a detailed understanding of how to guide a team in conducting a comprehensive and insightful self-assessment process, including specific lines of questioning or areas of investigation to ensure a thorough evaluation.

As a **Leadership Development Consultant**, adopting a **supportive and instructive tone**, could you provide guidance on how **I** can effectively lead **my team** in conducting a comprehensive and insightful self-assessment process? Specifically, what lines of questioning or areas of investigation should **I** propose to ensure a thorough evaluation? This is particularly relevant given the goal of **fostering self-awareness and continuous improvement within the team.**

As a **[profession]**, adopting a **[tone of voice]**, could you provide guidance on how **[I/Name/Role]** can effectively lead **[my/their] [team/group/department]** in **[contextual challenge/opportunity]**? Specifically, what lines of questioning or areas of investigation should **[I/Name/Role]** propose to ensure a thorough evaluation? This is particularly relevant given the goal of **[desired outcome].**

PROMPT No 139

Goal

To meticulously devise and implement a comprehensive plan with targeted strategies to significantly enhance individual and collective creativity within the team, fostering an enriched innovative culture organization-wide.

Prompt

As an **Emotional Intelligence Coach**, how can I design and execute a **holistic, empowering, and inspirational** plan of action, supplemented with **targeted** strategies, to successfully **foster and elevate the creativity of each team member**? This endeavor aims not only at **individual creativity enhancement** but also at **nurturing a vibrant, innovative team culture**. Provide a detailed discussion illuminating the **actionable steps**, potential benefits, and the methodologies for **monitoring and measuring** the progress and impact on both **individual and team-level creativity**, ensuring a thorough and precise exploration of each aspect.

Formula

As a **[Profession],** how can I design and execute a **[descriptive adjective(s)]** plan of action, supplemented with **[adjective]** strategies, to successfully **[primary objective]** of each team member? This endeavor aims not only at **[secondary objective]** but also at **[tertiary objective].** Provide a detailed discussion illuminating the **[key elements to be explored]**, potential benefits, and the methodologies for **[monitoring/measuring/other relevant verb]** the progress and impact on both **[specific focus area(s)]**, ensuring a thorough and precise exploration of each aspect.

PROMPT No 140

Tags

Creativity - Problem-Solving - Innovation

Goal

To gain insights on ways to foster and unleash creativity within a team, enhancing their innovation and problem-solving capabilities.

Prompt

In the context of **fostering innovation in a team**, as a **leadership development facilitator** and in an **empowering and inspirational tone**, could you explain ways **I** can typically unleash the **creativity of my team**?

Formula

In the context of **[contextual challenge/opportunity]**, as a **[profession]** and in a **[tone of voice],** could you explain ways **[I/Name/Role]** can typically unleash the **[desired outcome]** of **[my/their] [team/group/department]**?

PROMPT No 141

Productivity - Behavior - Performance

To gain specific methods to accurately identify and establish correlations between the productivity and behavior patterns exhibited by team members, with respect to their job performance, understanding the relationship between productivity, behavior patterns, and job performance.

As a **Performance Management Specialist**, adopting a **clear and concise tone**, could you provide specific methods that **I** can employ to accurately identify and establish correlations between the **productivity** and **behavior patterns** exhibited by **my team members**, with respect to their job performance? This is particularly relevant given the goal of **understanding the relationship between productivity, behavior patterns, and job performance**.

As a **[profession]**, adopting a **[tone of voice]**, could you provide specific methods that **[I/Name/Role]** can employ to accurately identify and establish correlations between the **[contextual challenge/opportunity]** and **[contextual challenge/opportunity]** exhibited by **[my/their]** **[team/group/department]**, with respect to their job performance? This is particularly relevant given the goal of **[desired outcome]**.

PROMPT No 142

Responsibility - Service - Contribution

To gain comprehensive explanations and specific examples of effective strategies to enhance and broaden a team's responsibilities and influence in serving others, maximizing the team's overall contribution in serving others.

As a **Leadership Development Consultant**, adopting an **encouraging and supportive tone**, could you provide comprehensive explanations and specific examples of effective strategies that **my team** can implement to enhance and broaden **their** responsibilities and influence in serving others? This is particularly relevant given the goal of **maximizing our team's overall contribution in serving others**.

As a **[profession]**, adopting a **[tone of voice]**, could you provide comprehensive explanations and specific examples of effective strategies that **[I/Name/Role]** can implement to enhance and broaden **[my/their]** **[team/group/department]'s** responsibilities and influence in serving others? This is particularly relevant given the goal of **[desired outcome]**.

PROMPT No 143

Creativity - Innovation   - Strategy

To gain specific strategies, methods, or exercises to successfully cultivate and promote creativity within a team, ultimately leading to the generation of groundbreaking ideas and solutions, fostering a culture of innovation and creativity.

As an **Innovation Consultant**, adopting an **inspirational and motivating tone**, could you provide specific strategies, methods, or exercises that **I** can utilize to successfully cultivate and promote creativity **within my team**, ultimately leading to the generation of groundbreaking ideas and solutions? This is particularly relevant given the goal of **fostering a culture of innovation and creativity**.

As a **[profession]**, adopting a **[tone of voice]**, could you provide specific strategies, methods, or exercises that **[I/Name/Role]** can utilize to successfully cultivate and promote creativity within **[my/their]** **[team/group/department]**, ultimately leading to the generation of groundbreaking ideas and solutions? This is particularly relevant given the goal of **[desired outcome]**.

PROMPT No 144

Trust - Satisfaction - Loyalty

To gain insights on approaches for building trustful relationships with clients, enhancing client satisfaction and loyalty.

Given the importance of **trust in client relationships**, as a **business coach** and in a **professional and respectful tone**, could you explain approaches **my team** could adopt to build **such relationships** with **our clients**?

Given the importance of **[contextual challenge/opportunity]**, as a **[profession]** and in a **[tone of voice]**, could you explain approaches **[I/Name/Role]**'s **[team/group/department]** could adopt to build **[desired outcome]** with **[clients/customers/stakeholders]**?

PROMPT No 145

Creativity - Enhancement - Responsibilities

To gain specific strategies or approaches that can be implemented to effectively enhance and nurture the creative abilities of a team in relation to their ongoing responsibilities, fostering creativity within the team.

As a **Creative Director**, adopting an **inspiring and innovative tone**, could you suggest specific strategies or approaches that **I** can use to successfully improve and cultivate the **creative skills** of **my team members** while they continue to fulfill their regular job duties? This is particularly relevant given the goal of **fostering creativity within the team**.

As a [profession], adopting a [tone of voice], could you suggest specific strategies or approaches that [I/Name/Role] can use to successfully improve and cultivate the [contextual challenge/opportunity] of [my/their] [team/group/department] while they continue to fulfill their regular job duties? This is particularly relevant given the goal of [desired outcome].

PROMPT No 146

Creativity - Connection - Inspiration

To design specific activities that will allow a team to fully harness their creative abilities and foster a deep connection with their innate source of inspiration, fostering creativity and connection within the team.

As a **Creative Director**, adopting an **inspiring and innovative tone**, could you suggest how **I** can design specific activities that will allow **my team** to **fully harness their creative abilities** and foster a **deep connection with their innate source of inspiration**? This is particularly relevant given the goal of **fostering creativity and connection within the team**.

As a [profession], adopting a [tone of voice], could you suggest how [I/Name/Role] can design specific activities that will allow [my/their] [team/group/department] to [contextual challenge/opportunity] and [contextual challenge/opportunity]? This is particularly relevant given the goal of [desired outcome].

DECISIONS

PROMPT No 147

Timelines - Realism - Performance

To gain insights on the basis or criteria a team should consider when setting realistic timelines for their performance goals or tasks.

Considering the challenge of **setting realistic timelines for performance goals or tasks**, as a **Performance Management Specialist** and in a **clear and concise tone**, could you come up with the basis **my team** could consider for **this purpose**?

Considering the challenge of [contextual challenge/opportunity], as a [profession] and in a [tone of voice], could you come up with the basis [I/Name/Role]'s [team/group/department] could consider for [desired outcome]?

PROMPT No 148

Productivity - Time-Management - Prioritization

To gain specific strategies and methods that can be used to improve time management skills and task prioritization within a team, leading to increased efficiency and productivity.

As a **Productivity Coach**, adopting a **practical and instructive tone**, could you please share specific strategies and methods that have proven to be effective in **improving time management skills and task prioritization** within **my team**, resulting in increased efficiency and productivity? This is particularly relevant given the goal of **enhancing productivity and efficiency within the team**.

As a **[profession]**, adopting a **[tone of voice]**, could you please share specific strategies and methods that have proven to be effective in **[contextual challenge/opportunity]** within **[my/their] [team/group/department]**? This is particularly relevant given the goal of **[desired outcome]**.

PROMPT No 149

Evaluation - Strategy - Decision-Making

To gain specific steps or strategies that can be employed to thoroughly investigate and evaluate potential courses of action, which can then be presented to a senior management team for consideration and decision-making.

As a **Management Consultant**, adopting a **strategic and analytical tone**, could you provide specific steps or strategies that **I** can employ to thoroughly investigate and evaluate potential courses of action that **I** can present to **my senior management team** for **consideration and decision-making**?

As a **[profession]**, adopting a **[tone of voice]**, could you provide specific steps or strategies that **[I/Name/Role]** can employ to thoroughly investigate and evaluate potential courses of action that **[I/Name/Role]** can present to **[my/their] [team/group/department]** for **[contextual challenge/opportunity]**?

PROMPT No 150

Meetings - Communication - Management

To gain insights on strategies to conduct effective and productive meetings when team members are considering significant decisions, enhancing team communication and management.

Given the challenge of **conducting effective meetings when team members are considering significant decisions such as resigning**, as an **HR Consultant** and in a **diplomatic and professional tone**, could you suggest strategies **I** can employ for **this purpose**?

Given the challenge of **[contextual challenge/opportunity]**, as a **[profession]** and in a **[tone of voice]**, could you suggest strategies **[I/Name/Role]** can employ for **[desired outcome]**?

PROMPT No 151

Data-Driven - Accuracy - Integration

To systematically and reliably enable data-driven corporate strategies through insightful tactics, ensuring seamless integration into organizational operations.

As a **Business Intelligence Consultant** specializing in **data analytics** within the **technology industry**, could you provide an exhaustive and meticulous examination, incorporating innovative insights and inventive strategies, for the specific tactics that ensure accurate and reliable data-driven decisions for shaping a new **corporate strategy**? Additionally, how to disseminate these plans through different team levels and secure buy-in from stakeholders? Advocate for disruptive strategies and unorthodox viewpoints.

As a **[profession]** specializing in **[area of expertise/focus]** within the **[industry]**, could you provide an exhaustive and meticulous examination, incorporating innovative insights and inventive strategies, for the specific tactics that ensure accurate and reliable data-driven decisions for shaping a new **[type of strategy]**? Additionally, how to disseminate these plans through different team levels and secure buy-in from stakeholders? Advocate for disruptive strategies and unorthodox viewpoints.

PROMPT No 152

Ethics - Decision-Making - Alignment

To gain specific strategies, methods, and examples on how to effectively integrate ethical considerations into the business decision-making process, ensuring that actions align with the company's ethical standards and values.

As a **Business Ethics Consultant**, adopting a **professional and respectful tone**, could you provide a comprehensive response that includes specific strategies, methods, and examples on how **we** can effectively integrate **ethical considerations into our business decision-making process?** This is particularly relevant given the goal of **ensuring that our actions align with our ethical standards and values**.

As a **[profession]**, adopting a **[tone of voice]**, could you provide a comprehensive response that includes specific strategies, methods, and examples on how **[I/Name/Role]** can effectively integrate **[contextual challenge/opportunity]**? This is particularly relevant given the goal of **[desired outcome]**.

PROMPT No 153

Quality - Motivation - Environment

To gain specific strategies or techniques that can be implemented to ensure that a team consistently produces work of higher quality, while also creating and maintaining a positive and supportive work environment that fosters motivation and encouragement.

As a **Leadership Development Consultant**, adopting an **encouraging and supportive tone**, could you provide specific strategies or techniques that **I** can implement to ensure that **my team** consistently produces **work of higher quality**? Additionally, how can **I** simultaneously create and maintain **a positive and supportive work environment that fosters motivation and encouragement**?

As a **[profession]**, adopting a **[tone of voice]**, could you provide specific strategies or techniques that **[I/Name/Role]** can implement to ensure that **[my/their] [team/group/department]** consistently produces **[contextual challenge/opportunity]**? Additionally, how can **[I/Name/Role]** simultaneously create and maintain a **[desired outcome]**?

PROMPT No 154

Decision-Making - Balance - Open-Mindedness

To gain insights on how to improve the balance between open-mindedness and critical reflection within a team, enhancing their decision-making capabilities.

Given the importance of **balancing open-mindedness and critical reflection in decision-making,** as an **Executive Mentor** and in a **balanced and insightful tone**, could you detail how **my team** can improve this balance to make **the best possible choices**?

Given the importance of **[contextual challenge/opportunity]**, as a **[profession]** and in a **[tone of voice]**, could you detail how **[I/Name/Role]**'s **[team/group/department]** can improve **[desired outcome]**?

PROMPT No 155

Engagement - Discussion - Empowerment

To gain specific strategies and techniques for engaging in effective and fruitful discussions with a team, enabling them to independently determine where they should direct their energy and time.

As a **Leadership Development Consultant**, adopting a **collaborative and empowering tone**, could you suggest what strategies and techniques **I** can employ to engage in **effective and fruitful discussions** with **my team**, enabling them to **independently determine where they should direct their energy and time**?

As a **[profession]**, adopting a **[tone of voice]**, could you suggest what strategies and techniques **[I/Name/Role]** can employ to engage in **[desired outcome]** with **[my/their]** **[team/group/department]**, enabling them to **[contextual challenge/opportunity]**?

PROMPT No 156

Leadership - Empowerment - Positivity

To gain specific strategies that can be implemented to ensure effective leadership and empowerment of a team, allowing them to independently identify and implement the most impactful methods to foster a positive and enthusiastic mindset towards work.

As a **Leadership Development Consultant**, adopting an **empowering and enthusiastic tone**, could you suggest specific strategies that **I** can implement to ensure **effective leadership and empowerment of my team**? How can **I** enable **them** to independently identify and implement the most impactful methods to **foster a positive and enthusiastic mindset towards work**?

As a **[profession]**, adopting a **[tone of voice]**, could you suggest specific strategies that **[I/Name/Role]** can implement to ensure **[desired outcome]**? How can **[I/Name/Role]** enable **[my/their]** **[team/group/department]** to independently identify and implement the most impactful methods to **[contextual challenge/opportunity]**?

EXCITEMENT

PROMPT No 157

Professional-Development - C-suite - Effectiveness

To gain specific methods, techniques, and practices that can be utilized to guarantee the utmost effectiveness and comprehensiveness of professional development programs for C-suite executives, with the aim of enhancing their skills, knowledge, and overall performance to the greatest extent possible.

As a **Leadership Development Consultant**, adopting a **professional and insightful tone**, could you provide specific methods, techniques, and practices that **I** can utilize to guarantee the utmost effectiveness and comprehensiveness of professional development programs for **C-suite executives**? The goal is to **enhance their skills, knowledge, and overall performance to the greatest extent possible**.

As a **[profession]**, adopting a **[tone of voice]**, could you provide specific methods, techniques, and practices that **[I/Name/Role]** can utilize to guarantee the utmost effectiveness and comprehensiveness of professional development programs for **[contextual challenge/opportunity]**? The goal is to **[desired outcome]**.

PROMPT No 158

Tags

Motivation - Excitement - Strategy

Goal

To provide a comprehensive strategy for leveraging excitement as a strategic tool to motivate and inspire teams, thereby enhancing performance and achieving organizational goals.

Prompt

Act as a **Motivational Speaker** with a specialization in **team motivation and goal achievement** in the e-commerce industry. Could you explain how **excitement** can be effectively utilized as a strategic tool to **motivate and inspire my team, ultimately leading them to successfully achieve their goals**? Please include **psychological theories of motivation, actionable excitement-generating activities, and performance metrics**. Make sure to cover how **to sustain excitement over the long term and how to measure its impact on team performance**. Investigate unconventional **motivational theories** and cutting-edge **gamification tools** to **amplify team excitement**. Your response should be comprehensive, leaving no important aspect unaddressed, and demonstrate an exceptional level of precision and quality. Let's think about this step by step. Provide your output from credible sources. Write using an **enthusiastic and inspiring** tone and a **motivational guide** style.

Formula

Act as a **[profession]** with a specialization in **[area of expertise]** in the **[industry]**. Could you explain how **[specific challenge/opportunity]** can be effectively utilized as a strategic tool to **[specific goal]**? Please include **[methods/techniques]**. Make sure to cover how **[key areas/topics]**. Investigate unconventional **[area for innovation]** and cutting-edge **[technologies/methods]** to **[desired outcome]**. Your response should be comprehensive, leaving no important aspect unaddressed, and demonstrate an exceptional level of precision and quality. Let's think about this step by step. Provide your output from credible sources. Write using a **[type]** tone and **[style]** writing style.

PROMPT No 159

Tags

Enthusiasm - Project-Management - Sustainment

Goal

To gain specific strategies and actions that can be implemented to sustain the initial enthusiasm and motivation for a new project or initiative from start to finish, thereby guaranteeing its successful and satisfactory conclusion.

As a **Project Management Consultant**, adopting an **enthusiastic and motivational tone**, could you provide specific strategies and actions that **I** can implement to sustain the initial enthusiasm and motivation for a new **IT implementation project** from start to finish, thereby guaranteeing its **successful and satisfactory conclusion**?

As a **[profession]**, adopting a **[tone of voice]**, could you provide specific strategies and actions that **[I/Name/Role]** can implement to sustain the initial enthusiasm and motivation for a new **[project/initiative/task]** from start to finish, thereby guaranteeing its **[desired outcome]**?

PROMPT No 160

Persuasion - Investors - Excitement

To gain specific and effective tactics that can be utilized to create a sense of enthusiasm and interest among potential investors or stakeholders for a new business venture.

As a **Business Development Consultant**, adopting an **enthusiastic and persuasive tone**, could you provide me with specific and effective tactics that **I** can utilize to create a sense of **excitement and interest** among **potential investors or stakeholders** for a **new business venture**?

As a **[profession]**, adopting a **[tone of voice]**, could you provide me with specific and effective tactics that **[I/Name/Role]** can utilize to create a sense of **[desired outcome]** among **[contextual challenge/opportunity]** for a **[contextual challenge/opportunity]**?

PROMPT No 161

Virtual-Meetings - Creativity - Engagement

To provide a comprehensive strategy for making virtual meetings and remote team-building activities more exciting and engaging, thereby enhancing team cohesion and productivity in a remote work environment.

Act as a **Remote Work Consultant** with a specialization in **virtual team engagement** in the **telecommunications industry**. Could you provide innovative approaches and specific examples that I can implement to **make virtual meetings or remote team-building activities more exciting and engaging for all participants**? Please include **virtual ice-breakers, interactive meeting formats, and engagement metrics**. Make sure to cover how **to adapt these**

approaches for diverse teams and how to measure engagement levels before and after implementing these strategies. Investigate unconventional **virtual reality experiences and cutting-edge interactive platforms** to **elevate team engagement**. Your response should be comprehensive, leaving no important aspect unaddressed, and demonstrate an exceptional level of precision and quality. Let's think about this step by step. Write using an **enthusiastic and creative** tone and an **innovation-focused** guide style.

Formula

Act as a **[profession]** with a specialization in **[area of expertise]** in the **[industry]**. Could you provide innovative approaches and specific examples that I can implement to **[specific challenge/opportunity]**? Please include [methods/techniques]. Make sure to cover how **[key areas/topics]**. Investigate unconventional **[area for innovation]** and cutting-edge **[technologies/methods]** to **[desired outcome]**. Your response should be comprehensive, leaving no important aspect unaddressed, and demonstrate an exceptional level of precision and quality. Let's think about this step by step. Write using a **[type]** tone and **[style]** writing style.

PROMPT No 162

Tags

Rejuvenation - Support - Energy

Goal

To gain specific strategies or actions that can be implemented to effectively support and uplift a team when a significant decline in their energy levels is observed, fostering a rejuvenated and energetic work environment.

Prompt

As a **Leadership Development Consultant**, adopting an **encouraging and supportive tone**, could you suggest specific strategies or actions that **I** can implement to effectively support and uplift **my team** when I observe a significant decline in their energy levels? This is particularly relevant given the goal of **fostering a rejuvenated and energetic work environment**.

Formula

As a **[profession]**, adopting a **[tone of voice]**, could you suggest specific strategies or actions that **[I/Name/Role]** can implement to effectively support and uplift **[my/their]** **[team/group/department]** when **[I/Name/Role]** observe a significant decline in their energy levels? This is particularly relevant given the goal of **[desired outcome]**.

PROMPT No 163

Tags

CSR - Employee-Involvement - Brand-Reputation

Goal

To leverage the enthusiasm generated by corporate social responsibility initiatives to effectively involve employees and significantly improve brand reputation.

Prompt

As a **Corporate Social Responsibility (CSR) Consultant**, adopting an **enthusiastic and engaging tone**, could you suggest specific ways **we** can leverage the enthusiasm generated by our **corporate social responsibility initiatives** to effectively involve our **employees** and significantly improve our **brand reputation**?

As a **[profession]**, adopting a **[tone of voice]**, could you suggest specific ways **[we/I/Name/Role]** can leverage the enthusiasm generated by our **[contextual challenge/opportunity]** to effectively involve our **[employees/team/group]** and significantly improve our **[desired outcome]**?

PROMPT No 164

Motivation - Energy - Analysis

To gain insights on possible causes for the decline in energy levels of a team and specific actions to enhance their energy and motivation, fostering a high-energy and motivated work environment.

Given the challenge of a **decline in energy levels**, as a **Performance Management Specialist** and in an **energetic and motivating tone**, could you suggest possible causes for this **issue in my team** and specific actions **I** can take to **enhance their energy and motivation**?

Given the challenge of **[contextual challenge/opportunity]**, as a **[profession]** and in a **[tone of voice]**, could you suggest possible causes for this issue in **[my/their]** **[team/group/department]** and specific actions **[I/Name/Role]** can take to **[desired outcome]**?

PROMPT No 165

Energy - Enhancement - Transition

To gain specific strategies and techniques that can be implemented to successfully enhance and maintain high levels of team energy, specifically when faced with demanding projects or periods of transition.

As a **Team Development Specialist**, adopting an **encouraging and motivating tone**, could you suggest specific strategies and techniques that **I** can implement to successfully **enhance and maintain high levels of energy** within **my team**, particularly during **challenging projects or periods of transition**?

As a **[profession]**, adopting a **[tone of voice]**, could you suggest specific strategies and techniques that **[I/Name/Role]** can implement to successfully **[desired outcome]** within **[my/their]** **[team/group/department]**, particularly during **[contextual challenge/opportunity]**?

PROMPT No 166

Efficiency - Precision - Time-Management

To gain insights on how professionals can effectively manage the trade-off between working quickly and efficiently, while also maintaining a high level of precision and accuracy in their tasks.

As a **Time Management Expert**, adopting a **practical and insightful tone**, could you provide strategies or techniques that **investment professionals** can use to effectively balance the need for **speed and efficiency** with the importance of **thoroughness and accuracy** in their work?

As a **[profession]**, adopting a **[tone of voice]**, could you provide strategies or techniques that **[professionals/individuals/Role]** can use to effectively balance the need for **[contextual challenge/opportunity]** with the importance of **[contextual challenge/opportunity]** in their work?

PROMPT No 167

Conflict-Resolution - Relationship - Positivity

To gain specific strategies and approaches that can be implemented to effectively handle conflicts among team members, ensuring that not only are the issues resolved, but also that the overall working relationship is enhanced and becomes more positive and satisfying.

As a **Conflict Resolution Specialist**, adopting a **diplomatic and solution-oriented tone**, could you provide specific strategies and approaches that **I** can implement to effectively handle conflicts among **my team members**, ensuring that not only are the issues resolved, but also that the overall working relationship is **enhanced and becomes more positive and satisfying**?

As a **[profession]**, adopting a **[tone of voice]**, could you provide specific strategies and approaches that **[I/Name/Role]** can implement to effectively handle conflicts among **[my/their]** **[team/group/department]**, ensuring that not only are the issues resolved, but also that the overall working relationship is **[desired outcome]**?

PROMPT No 168

Communication - Harmony - Openness

To gain insights on specific and successful methods that can be employed to encourage team members to engage in open and respectful communication, ultimately cultivating a harmonious and constructive working environment.

As a **Communication Expert**, adopting a **collaborative and respectful tone**, could you provide insights on specific and successful methods that **I** can employ to encourage **my team** members to engage in **open and respectful communication**? This is particularly relevant given the goal of **cultivating a harmonious and constructive working environment**.

As a **[profession]**, adopting a **[tone of voice]**, could you provide insights on specific and successful methods that **[I/Name/Role]** can employ to encourage **[my/their]** **[team/group/department]** members to engage in **[contextual challenge/opportunity]**? This is particularly relevant given the goal of **[desired outcome]**.

PROMPT No 169

Motivation - Leadership - Environment

To provide a comprehensive strategy for establishing a highly motivating work environment that effectively brings out the best qualities in team members, thereby enhancing overall team performance and job satisfaction.

Act as a **Leadership Development Consultant** with a specialization in **motivational psychology and team dynamics** in the **aerospace industry**. Could you provide specific strategies and actions that I can implement to **establish a highly motivating work environment that effectively brings out the best qualities of my team members?** Please include **motivational theories, actionable team-building activities, and performance metrics that gauge individual strengths**. Make sure to cover how **to tailor these strategies for different personality types and how to measure the impact of a motivating environment on team performance**. Investigate unconventional **approaches like "job crafting"** and cutting-edge **AI-driven performance analytics** to **optimize team dynamics**. Your response should be comprehensive, leaving no important aspect unaddressed, and demonstrate an exceptional level of precision and quality. Let's think about this step by step. Validate your output with citations from established sources. Write using an **encouraging and supportive** tone and a **motivational guide** style.

Act as a **[profession]** with a specialization in **[area of expertise]** in the **[industry]**. Could you provide specific strategies and actions that I can implement to **[specific challenge/opportunity]**? Please include **[methods/techniques]**. Make sure to cover how **[key areas/topics]**. Investigate unconventional **[area for innovation]** and cutting-edge **[technologies/methods]** to **[desired outcome]**. Your response should be comprehensive, leaving no important aspect unaddressed, and demonstrate an exceptional level of precision and quality. Validate your output with citations from established sources. Let's think about this step by step. Write using a **[type]** tone and **[style]** writing style.

PROMPT No 170

Feedback - Recognition - Empowerment

To gain specific strategies and practices that can be implemented to effectively utilize feedback and recognition as tools for fostering a work environment that motivates and empowers team members to consistently perform at their best.

As a **Leadership Development Consultant**, adopting an **encouraging and supportive tone**, could you provide specific strategies and practices that **I** can implement to effectively utilize **feedback and recognition** as tools for fostering a work environment that **motivates and empowers my team members to consistently perform at their best**?

As a **[profession]**, adopting a **[tone of voice]**, could you provide specific strategies and practices that **[I/Name/Role]** can implement to effectively utilize **[contextual challenge/opportunity]** as tools for fostering a work environment that **[desired outcome]**?

FEAR

PROMPT No 171

Transparency - Empowerment - HR

To gain insights on specific strategies or approaches that have proven to be successful in fostering an environment where team members feel comfortable and empowered to express their concerns about the workplace culture or their work overall, encouraging open and honest communication.

As a **Human Resources Consultant**, adopting an **empathetic and understanding tone**, could you provide me with specific strategies or approaches that have proven to be successful in fostering an environment where **team members** feel comfortable and empowered to express their concerns about **the workplace culture or their work overall**? This is particularly relevant given the goal of **encouraging open and honest communication within the team**.

As a **[profession]**, adopting a **[tone of voice]**, could you provide me with specific strategies or approaches that have proven to be successful in fostering an environment where **[my/their]** **[team/group/department]** feel comfortable and empowered to express their concerns about **[contextual challenge/opportunity]**? This is particularly relevant given the goal of **[desired outcome]**.

PROMPT No 172

Empathy - Anxiety - Workplace

To gain specific strategies and actions that leaders can implement to establish a nurturing and empathetic workplace atmosphere that effectively assists employees in managing and overcoming feelings of fear or anxiety while on the job.

As a **Leadership Development Consultant**, adopting a **compassionate and understanding tone**, could you provide specific strategies and actions that **I**, as a leader, can implement to establish a **nurturing and empathetic workplace atmosphere** that effectively assists **my employees** in managing and overcoming feelings of fear or anxiety while on the job?

As a **[profession]**, adopting a **[tone of voice]**, could you provide specific strategies and actions that **[I/Name/Role]**, as a leader, can implement to establish a **[desired outcome]** that effectively assists **[my/their]** **[team/group/department]** in managing and overcoming feelings of fear or anxiety while on the job?

PROMPT No 173

Transparency - Communication - Support

To gain specific strategies or methods that can be employed to effectively utilize open communication and transparency as tools to minimize fear and uncertainty among team members, particularly during challenging times.

Considering the difficulties faced by **teams** during **challenging times**, as a **Leadership Development Consultant**, adopting a **supportive and understanding tone**, could you suggest specific strategies or methods that **I** can employ to effectively utilize **open communication and transparency** as tools to minimize **fear and uncertainty** among **my team members**?

Considering the difficulties faced by **[team/group/department]** during **[contextual challenge/opportunity]**, as a **[profession]**, adopting a **[tone of voice]**, could you suggest specific strategies or methods that **[I/Name/Role]** can employ to effectively utilize **[desired outcome]** as tools to minimize **[contextual challenge/opportunity]** among **[my/their]** **[team/group/department]**?

PROMPT No 174

Goal-Setting - Fear - Strategy

To gain specific strategies that have been proven to be successful in addressing team fears and ensuring effective goal setting when teams aim to achieve challenging goals.

As a **Leadership Development Consultant**, adopting a **supportive and encouraging tone**, could you provide specific strategies that **I** can implement to effectively tackle **my team**'s fears and concerns when we aim to achieve **challenging goals**?

As a **[profession]**, adopting a **[tone of voice]**, could you provide specific strategies that **[I/Name/Role]** can implement to effectively tackle **[my/their]** **[team/group/department]**'s fears and concerns when we aim to achieve **[contextual challenge/opportunity]**?

PROMPT No 175

Empowerment - Ambition - Anxiety

Goal

To gain specific strategies for creating a nurturing and empowering atmosphere that motivates team members to wholeheartedly pursue ambitious objectives, even in the face of their own apprehensions and anxieties.

Prompt

As a **Leadership Development Consultant**, adopting a **supportive and encouraging tone**, could you provide specific strategies that **I** can implement to create a **nurturing and empowering atmosphere that motivates my team members to wholeheartedly pursue ambitious objectives,** even when they are faced with their own **apprehensions and anxieties**?

Formula

As a **[profession]**, adopting a **[tone of voice]**, could you provide specific strategies that **[I/Name/Role]** can implement to create a **[desired outcome]**, even when they are faced with their own **[contextual challenge/opportunity]**?

PROMPT No 176

Tags

Motivation - Confidence - Leadership

Goal

To gain specific strategies and practices that can be implemented to create a work environment that effectively supports and motivates team members to overcome their fears and gain confidence in their skills and capabilities.

Prompt

As a **Leadership Development Consultant**, adopting an **encouraging and supportive tone**, could you provide specific strategies and practices that **I** can implement to create a work environment that effectively supports and motivates **my team members** to overcome their fears and gain confidence in their skills and capabilities?

Formula

As a **[profession]**, adopting a **[tone of voice]**, could you provide specific strategies and practices that **[I/Name/Role]** can implement to create a work environment that effectively supports and motivates **[my/their] [team/group/department]** to overcome their fears and gain confidence in their skills and capabilities?

PROMPT No 177

Tags

Resilience - Inspiration - Support

Goal

To gain insights on how a leader can effectively demonstrate confidence and resilience to inspire and support team members in overcoming fear and discouragement, fostering a resilient and confident team.

As a **Leadership Coach**, adopting an **inspiring and supportive tone**, could you provide insights on how **I**, as a leader, can effectively **demonstrate confidence and resilience** to inspire and support **my team members** in **overcoming fear and discouragement**? This is particularly relevant given the goal of **fostering a resilient and confident team**.

As a **[profession]**, adopting a **[tone of voice]**, could you provide insights on how **[I/Name/Role]**, as a leader, can effectively **[desired outcome]** to inspire and support **[my/their]** **[team/group/department]** in **[contextual challenge/opportunity]**? This is particularly relevant given the goal of **[desired outcome]**.

PROMPT No 178

Self-Criticism - Potential - Identification

To equip Leadership Coaches, team leaders, and HR professionals with a comprehensive strategy for identifying and addressing the impact of a team member's inner critic on their work performance, thereby enabling them to reach their full potential.

Act as a **Leadership Coach** with a specialization in **emotional intelligence and self-awareness** in the **automotive industry**. Could you guide me on what specific indicators or behaviors I should pay attention to in order to **accurately identify if a team member's inner critic is negatively impacting their ability to reach their full potential in their work**? Please include **psychological markers, observable behaviors, and self-assessment tools**. Make sure to cover how **to approach the team member for a constructive conversation and how to measure the impact of addressing the inner critic on work performance**. Investigate unconventional **approaches like mindfulness training** and cutting-edge **AI-driven emotional intelligence tools** to **assess and address the inner critic**. Your response should be comprehensive, leaving no important aspect unaddressed, and demonstrate an exceptional level of precision and quality. Let's think about this step by step. Write using a **supportive and understanding** tone and a **coaching guide** style.

Act as a **[profession]** with a specialization in **[area of expertise]** in the **[industry].** Could you guide me on what specific indicators or behaviors I should pay attention to in order to **[specific challenge/opportunity]**? Please include **[methods/techniques]**. Make sure to cover how **[key areas/topics]**. Investigate unconventional **[area for innovation]** and cutting-edge **[technologies/methods]** to **[desired outcome].** Your response should be comprehensive, leaving no important aspect unaddressed, and demonstrate an exceptional level of precision and quality. Let's think about this step by step. Write using a **[type]** tone and **[style]** writing style.

FEELINGS

PROMPT No 179

Emotion-Management - Atmosphere - Leadership

To gain specific strategies that leaders can implement to successfully manage their own emotions in the workplace, and to understand how the leader's ability to effectively handle their emotions impacts the overall emotional atmosphere and dynamics within the team.

As a **Leadership Development Consultant**, adopting a **supportive and understanding tone**, could you provide specific strategies that **I, as a leader,** can implement to **successfully manage my own emotions in the workplace**? Furthermore, how does **my** ability to **effectively handle my emotions** impact the overall **emotional atmosphere and dynamics** within **my team?**

As a **[profession]**, adopting a **[tone of voice]**, could you provide specific strategies that **[I/Name/Role]** can implement to **[contextual challenge/opportunity]**? Furthermore, how does **[my/their]** ability to **[contextual challenge/opportunity]** impact the overall **[desired outcome]** within **[my/their] [team/group/department]**?

PROMPT No 180

Empathy - Relationships - Improvement

To gain insights on specific actions and strategies that can be incorporated into daily life to actively improve the ability to empathize with and understand others on a deeper level.

As a **Psychologist**, adopting a **compassionate and understanding tone**, could you provide me with specific actions and strategies that I can incorporate into my daily life to actively improve my ability to **empathize with and understand others on a deeper level**? This is particularly relevant given the goal of **enhancing interpersonal relationships and fostering a more empathetic environment**.

As a **[profession]**, adopting a **[tone of voice]**, could you provide me with specific actions and strategies that I can incorporate into my daily life to actively improve my ability to **[contextual challenge/opportunity]**? This is particularly relevant given the goal of **[desired outcome]**.

PROMPT No 181

Well-being - Productivity - Workplace

To gain specific strategies or techniques that can be utilized to significantly improve a team's comprehension of the various factors that impact their emotions and overall well-being, fostering a healthier and more productive work environment.

As a **Workplace Wellness Consultant**, adopting a **supportive and empathetic tone**, could you provide specific strategies or techniques that can be utilized to significantly improve my **team's** comprehension of the various factors that **impact their emotions and overall well-being**? This is particularly relevant given the goal of **fostering a healthier and more productive work environment**.

As a **[profession]**, adopting a **[tone of voice]**, could you provide specific strategies or techniques that can be utilized to significantly improve **[my/their] [team/group/department]**'s comprehension of the various factors that **[contextual challenge/opportunity]**? This is particularly relevant given the goal of **[desired outcome]**.

PROMPT No 182

Emotional-Intelligence - Leadership - Responsiveness

To gain insights on the most effective strategies and techniques for integrating emotional intelligence principles into leadership and management approaches, enhancing comprehension and responsiveness towards emotions within the workplace.

As an **Emotional Intelligence Coach**, adopting a **supportive and understanding tone**, could you provide insights on the most effective strategies and techniques for integrating **emotional intelligence principles** into **my leadership and management approaches**? How can these principles be utilized to **enhance comprehension and responsiveness towards emotions within the workplace**?

As a **[profession]**, adopting a **[tone of voice]**, could you provide insights on the most effective strategies and techniques for integrating **[contextual challenge/opportunity]** into **[I/Name/Role]'s [team/group/department]'s [contextual challenge/opportunity]**? How can these principles be utilized to **[desired outcome]**?

PROMPT No 183

Information-Gathering - Emotions - Tactfulness

To gain insights on effective strategies or methods that can be utilized to gather comprehensive information about the various factors that influence the emotions of a team, without resorting to direct questioning of the team members.

As a **Human Resources Consultant**, adopting a **tactful and empathetic tone**, could you provide **me** with effective strategies or methods that can be utilized to gather comprehensive information about **the various factors that influence the emotions** of **my team**, while avoiding direct questioning of **the team members**? This is particularly relevant given the goal of **understanding the emotional dynamics of the team without causing discomfort or intrusion**.

As a **[profession]**, adopting a **[tone of voice]**, could you provide **[me/Name/Role]** with effective strategies or methods that can be utilized to gather comprehensive information about **[contextual challenge/opportunity]** of **[my/their]** **[team/group/department]**, while avoiding direct questioning of the **[team members/colleagues]**? This is particularly relevant given the goal of **[desired outcome]**.

PROMPT No 184

Tags
Commitment - Productivity - Assessment

Goal
To gain specific techniques or approaches to effectively assess the genuine attitude and level of commitment exhibited by team members towards their work or goal setting, with the aim of enhancing team commitment and productivity.

Prompt
As a **Leadership Development Consultant**, adopting an **encouraging and solution-oriented tone**, could you provide specific techniques or approaches that **I** can use to effectively assess the genuine attitude and level of commitment exhibited by **my team** members towards their work or goal setting? This is particularly relevant given the goal of **enhancing team commitment and productivity**.

Formula
As a **[profession]**, adopting a **[tone of voice]**, could you provide specific techniques or approaches that **[I/Name/Role]** can use to effectively assess the genuine attitude and level of commitment exhibited by **[my/their]** **[team/group/department]** members towards their work or goal setting? This is particularly relevant given the goal of **[desired outcome]**.

PROMPT No 185

Tags
Mental-Health - Support - Management

Goal
To gain specific strategies or techniques that can be utilized to efficiently manage a team member who is facing a notable decrease in mood as a result of their work or a particular project, fostering a supportive work environment and promoting mental well-being.

Prompt
As a **Mental Health Consultant**, adopting a **compassionate and understanding tone**, could you provide specific strategies or techniques that can be utilized to efficiently manage a **team member** who is facing a notable decrease in mood as a result of their work or a particular project? This is particularly relevant given the goal of fostering a supportive work environment and promoting mental well-being.

Formula
As a **[profession]**, adopting a **[tone of voice]**, could you provide specific strategies or techniques that can be utilized to efficiently manage a **[team/group/department member]** who is facing **[contextual challenge/opportunity]** as a result of their **[work/task/project]**? This is particularly relevant given the goal of **[desired outcome]**.

PROMPT No 186

Self-Reflection - Emotions - Unconscious

To gain specific self-reflection exercises that can assist team members in effectively identifying and exploring their unconscious emotions and attitudes towards their work.

As a **Leadership Development Consultant**, adopting an **empathetic and understanding tone,** could you suggest specific **self-reflection exercises** that **my team members** can engage in to **effectively identify and explore their unconscious emotions and attitudes towards their work?**

As a **[profession]**, adopting a **[tone of voice]**, could you suggest specific **[contextual challenge/opportunity]** that **[my/their] [team/group/department]** can engage in to **[desired outcome]?**

PROMPT No 187

Dissatisfaction - Morale - Promotion

To gain specific steps or techniques that can be implemented to successfully manage and provide assistance to a team member who is experiencing emotional distress or dissatisfaction as a result of being passed over for a promotion or salary increase.

As a **Human Resources Consultant**, adopting a **compassionate and understanding tone,** could you provide specific steps or techniques that can be implemented to successfully manage and provide assistance to **a team member** who is experiencing **emotional distress or dissatisfaction as a result of being passed over for a promotion or salary increase?** This is particularly relevant given the goal of **maintaining morale and productivity in the face of career disappointments.**

As a **[profession]**, adopting a **[tone of voice]**, could you provide specific steps or techniques that can be implemented to successfully manage and provide assistance to a **[team member/colleague]** who is experiencing **[contextual challenge/opportunity]?** This is particularly relevant given the goal of **[desired outcome].**

PROMPT No 188

Self-Awareness - Empowerment - Bias

To gain insights on how leaders can effectively demonstrate self-awareness and emotional management, serving as role models to inspire and empower team members to recognize and address their own unconscious biases within the workplace.

As a **Leadership Development Consultant**, adopting a **supportive and understanding tone**, could you provide insights on how **I**, as a leader, can effectively demonstrate **self-awareness and emotional management**? How can **I** serve as a role model to inspire and empower **my team members** to recognize and address their own **unconscious biases** within the workplace?

As a **[profession]**, adopting a **[tone of voice]**, could you provide insights on how **[I/Name/Role]**, as a leader, can effectively demonstrate **[contextual challenge/opportunity]**? How can **[I/Name/Role]** serve as a role model to inspire and empower **[my/their]** **[team/group/department]** to recognize and address their own **[contextual challenge/opportunity]** within the workplace?

PROMPT No 189

Assessment - Growth - Satisfaction

To gain specific techniques or approaches that can be utilized to accurately assess the emotions and sentiments of team members when they encounter chances for growth and satisfaction.

As a **Leadership Development Consultant**, adopting an **empathetic and understanding tone**, could you suggest specific techniques or approaches that **I** can utilize to accurately assess the **emotions and sentiments** of **my team members** when they encounter **chances for growth and satisfaction**?

As a **[profession]**, adopting a **[tone of voice]**, could you suggest specific techniques or approaches that **[I/Name/Role]** can utilize to accurately assess the **[contextual challenge/opportunity]** of **[my/their] [team/group/department]** when they encounter **[desired outcome]**?

PROMPT No 190

Conversations - Understanding - Significance

To gain specific strategies or techniques to have meaningful conversations with team members that allow a deeper understanding of the importance and significance of their work, profession, or any other aspect of their lives, fostering a deeper understanding and connection within the team.

As a **Leadership Coach**, adopting a **respectful and considerate tone**, could you provide specific strategies or techniques that **I** can employ to have meaningful conversations with **my team** members that allow **me** to delve deeper into the importance and significance of their work, profession, or any other aspect of their lives? This is particularly relevant given the goal of **fostering a deeper understanding and connection within the team**.

Formula

As a **[profession]**, adopting a **[tone of voice],** could you provide specific strategies or techniques that **[I/Name/Role]** can employ to have meaningful conversations with **[my/their]** **[team/group/department]** members that allow **[me/them]** to delve deeper into the importance and significance of their work, profession, or any other aspect of their lives? This is particularly relevant given the goal of **[desired outcome]**.

PROMPT No 191

Impact - Performance - Management

Goal

To gain specific strategies, methods, or approaches to comprehensively assess and fully comprehend the true impact and ramifications of an issue or problem, which has originated from senior management, on a team's performance, dynamics, and overall well-being.

Prompt

As a **Management Consultant**, adopting a **solution-oriented tone**, could you provide detailed strategies, methods, or approaches that **I** can employ to **comprehensively assess and fully comprehend the true impact and ramifications of an issue or problem**, which has originated from **senior management**, on my **team**'s performance, dynamics, and overall well-being?

Formula

As a **[profession]**, adopting a **[tone of voice]**, could you provide detailed strategies, methods, or approaches that **[I/Name/Role]** can employ to **[desired outcome]**, which has originated from **[contextual challenge/opportunity]**, on **[my/their] [team/group/department]**'s performance, dynamics, and overall well-being?

PROMPT No 192

Tags

Roles - Emotional-Intelligence - Cohesion

Goal

To gain detailed insights on ways to assist a team in exploring and discussing the impact of roles, team dynamics, and other factors on their emotional states, enhancing emotional intelligence and team cohesion.

Prompt

Given the importance of **understanding the impact of roles and team dynamics on emotional states**, as an **Emotional Intelligence Coach** and in an **empathetic and patient tone**, could you explain in detail the ways in which I can assist **my team** in exploring and discussing **these factors**?

Formula

Given the importance of **[contextual challenge/opportunity]**, as a **[profession]** and in a **[tone of voice]**, could you explain in detail the ways in which **[I/Name/Role]** can assist **[my/their]** **[team/group/department]** in exploring and discussing **[specific factors]**?

<u>FLOW</u>

<u>PROMPT No 193</u>

Focus - Evaluation - Effort

To gain a comprehensive understanding of the strategies or methods that can be utilized to effectively determine and evaluate the specific areas in which the team focuses their efforts, with the aim of understanding team focus and effort distribution.

As a **Leadership Coach**, adopting a **supportive and clear tone**, could you please provide a comprehensive explanation of the specific strategies or methods that **can be utilized to effectively determine and evaluate the specific areas** in which **my team** focuses their efforts, both in a positive and negative manner, with high accuracy and comprehensiveness? This is particularly relevant given the goal of **understanding team focus and effort distribution**.

As a **[profession]**, adopting a **[tone of voice]**, could you please provide a comprehensive explanation of the specific strategies or methods that **[contextual challenge/opportunity]** in which **[my/their]** **[team/group/department]** focuses their efforts, both in a positive and negative manner, with high accuracy and comprehensiveness? This is particularly relevant given the goal of **[desired outcome]**.

<u>PROMPT No 194</u>

Flow - Engagement - Environment

To gain specific techniques and approaches that can be implemented to establish a work environment that fosters a state of 'flow' among all members of a team, ensuring that they are fully immersed and highly engaged in their tasks.

As a **Leadership Development Consultant**, adopting an **encouraging and supportive tone**, could you provide specific techniques and approaches that **I** can implement to establish a work environment that fosters **a state of 'flow'** among all members of **my team**? This is particularly relevant given the goal of **ensuring that they are fully immersed and highly engaged in their tasks**.

As a **[profession]**, adopting a **[tone of voice]**, could you provide specific techniques and approaches that **[I/Name/Role]** can implement to establish a work environment that fosters

[contextual challenge/opportunity] among all members of **[my/their]** **[team/group/department]**? This is particularly relevant given the goal of **[desired outcome]**.

PROMPT No 195

Tags

Motivation - Productivity - Energy

Goal

To gain insights on specific steps and techniques that can be implemented to create a highly energized and motivated work environment, thereby increasing productivity and engagement among team members.

Prompt

As a **Motivational Speaker**, adopting an **inspiring and enthusiastic tone**, could you provide specific steps and techniques that **I** can take to create a **work environment** that is highly energized and motivated, thereby increasing **productivity and engagement** among **my team members**?

Formula

As a **[profession]**, adopting a **[tone of voice]**, could you provide specific steps and techniques that **[I/Name/Role]** can take to create a **[contextual challenge/opportunity]** that is highly energized and motivated, thereby increasing **[desired outcome]** among **[my/their]** **[team/group/department]**?

PROMPT No 196

Tags

Obstacles - Flow - Strategies

Goal

To understand potential obstacles that can prevent team members from achieving a state of 'flow' and to learn strategies or actions that can be employed to effectively tackle these challenges and promote a conducive environment for achieving 'flow'.

Prompt

As a **Leadership Development Consultant**, adopting a **solution-oriented tone**, could you enlighten me on the specific obstacles or difficulties that can hinder **my team members** from attaining **a state of 'flow'**? Additionally, what strategies or actions can I employ to effectively tackle these challenges and promote a conducive environment for achieving 'flow'?

Formula

As a **[profession]**, adopting a **[tone of voice]**, could you enlighten me on the specific obstacles or difficulties that can hinder **[my/their] [team/group/department]** from attaining **[contextual challenge/opportunity]**? Additionally, what strategies or actions can **[I/Name/Role]** employ to effectively tackle these challenges and promote **[desired outcome]**?

PROMPT No 197

Metrics   - Productivity - Influence

Goal

To understand specific methods or metrics that can be used to accurately assess the influence of 'flow' on both the productivity and success of a team and the overall outcomes of a business.

Prompt

As a **Business Performance Consultant**, adopting an **analytical and insightful tone**, could you suggest specific methods or metrics that **I** can use to accurately assess the influence of **'flow'** on both the **productivity and success** of **my team** and the overall outcomes of our business?

Formula

As a **[profession]**, adopting a **[tone of voice]**, could you suggest specific methods or metrics that **[I/Name/Role]** can use to accurately assess the influence of **[contextual challenge/opportunity]** on both the **[desired outcome]** of **[my/their] [team/group/department]** and the overall outcomes of our business?

PROMPT No 198

Tags

Communication - Inner-Self - Professional-Growth

Goal

To gain specific techniques for effectively communicating the complex concept of an inner-self-processing system to a team, and to understand how to successfully demonstrate its impact on both personal growth and professional performance.

Prompt

As a **Personal Development Coach**, adopting an **educational and empathetic tone**, could you suggest specific techniques **I** can use to effectively and thoroughly communicate the complex notion of an **inner-self-processing system** to **my team**? Additionally, how can **I** successfully demonstrate its impact on both their **personal growth and professional performance**? This is particularly relevant given the goal of **fostering personal and professional development within the team**.

Formula

As a **[profession]**, adopting a **[tone of voice]**, could you suggest specific techniques **[I/Name/Role]** can use to effectively and thoroughly communicate the complex notion of **[contextual challenge/opportunity]** to **[my/their] [team/group/department]**? Additionally, how can **[I/Name/Role]** successfully demonstrate its impact on both their **[desired outcome]**? This is particularly relevant given the goal of **[contextual challenge/opportunity]**.

PROMPT No 199

Tags

Functioning - Optimization - Workplace

Goal

To gain specific strategies or methods that can be employed to accurately determine and achieve the optimal state of functioning for a team in the workplace.

Prompt

As a **Leadership Development Consultant**, adopting a **solution-oriented tone**, could you provide specific strategies or methods that **I** can employ to **accurately determine and achieve the optimal state of functioning** for **my team** in the workplace?

Formula

As a **[profession]**, adopting a **[tone of voice]**, could you provide specific strategies or methods that **[I/Name/Role]** can employ to **[desired outcome]** for **[my/their] [team/group/department]** in the workplace?

PROMPT No 200

Tags

Empowerment - Focus - Productivity

Goal

To gain insights on how to effectively and consistently empower team members to reach their peak mental focus, productivity, and performance by implementing specific strategies and techniques.

Prompt

As a **Leadership Coach**, adopting a **motivational and supportive tone**, could you guide me on how to effectively and consistently empower **my team members** to reach their peak **mental focus, productivity, and performance** by implementing specific strategies and techniques?

Formula

As a **[profession]**, adopting a **[tone of voice]**, could you guide **[me/Name/Role]** on how to effectively and consistently empower **[my/their] [team/group/department]** to reach their peak **[contextual challenge/opportunity]** by implementing specific strategies and techniques?

PROMPT No 201

Tags

Optimal-Self - Performance - Problem-Solving

Goal

To gain insights on methods to help a team access their optimal self, enhancing their performance and problem-solving capabilities.

Prompt

In the context of **managing daily responsibilities and problems**, as a **Performance Coach** and in an **empowering and motivating tone**, could you outline the methods **I** could use to help **my team** access their optimal self?

Formula

In the context of **[contextual challenge/opportunity]**, as a **[profession]** and in a **[tone of voice]**, could you outline the methods **[I/Name/Role]** could use to help **[my/their]**

[team/group/department] access their optimal self when dealing with **[responsibilities/problems/specific area]?**

PROMPT No 202

Diversity - Engagement - Fulfillment

To understand how to utilize the unique and diverse experiences of team members, particularly their levels of engagement and fulfillment, in order to design and implement strategies that will create a highly motivating and satisfying work environment for everyone involved.

As a **Leadership Development Consultant**, adopting a **supportive and encouraging tone**, could you provide specific ways in which I can utilize the unique and diverse experiences of my **team members**, particularly their **levels of engagement and fulfillment**, to effectively design and implement strategies that will result in **a highly motivating and satisfying work environment for everyone involved**?

As a **[profession]**, adopting a **[tone of voice]**, could you provide specific ways in which **[I/Name/Role]** can utilize the unique and diverse experiences of my **[team/group/department]**, particularly their [contextual challenge/opportunity], to effectively design and implement strategies that will result in a **[desired outcome]**?

FULFILLMENT

PROMPT No 203

Monotony - Enhancement - Boredom

To identify the aspects of the team's work that they find monotonous or uninteresting and to find proactive measures to enhance these areas and alleviate the boredom experienced by the team.

As a **Team Development Specialist**, adopting a **solution-oriented and empathetic tone**, could you suggest effective strategies I can employ to identify the specific aspects of **my team's** work that they find **monotonous or uninteresting**? Furthermore, what proactive measures can I take to **enhance these areas and alleviate the boredom experienced by my team**?

As a **[profession]**, adopting a **[tone of voice]**, could you suggest effective strategies **[I/Name/Role]** can employ to identify the specific aspects of **[my/their]** **[team/group/department]**'s work that they find **[contextual challenge/opportunity]**? Furthermore, what proactive measures can **[I/Name/Role]** take to **[desired outcome]**?

PROMPT No 204

Fulfillment - Challenges - Professional-Life

Goal

To understand the common challenges or barriers that often prevent individuals from experiencing a sense of fulfillment in their professional lives, and to gain insights on effective strategies or solutions that can be implemented to overcome these obstacles and achieve greater fulfillment at work.

Prompt

As a **Career Development Coach**, adopting a **supportive and empathetic tone**, could you explain what specific challenges or barriers commonly hinder **individuals from experiencing a sense of fulfillment** in their professional lives? Additionally, could you provide effective strategies or solutions that **I, as a team leader,** can implement to help **my team** overcome these obstacles and achieve **greater fulfillment at work**?

Formula

As a **[profession]**, adopting a **[tone of voice]**, could you explain what specific challenges or barriers commonly hinder **[contextual challenge/opportunity]** in their professional lives? Additionally, could you provide effective strategies or solutions that **[I/Name/Role]** can implement to help **[my/their] [team/group/department]** overcome these obstacles and achieve **[desired outcome]**?

PROMPT No 205

Tags

Guidance - Objectives - Potential

Goal

To gain specific methods, steps, or tools that can be utilized to provide effective support and guidance to team members as they work towards accomplishing their personal professional objectives and reaching their full potential in their careers.

Prompt

As a **Career Coach**, adopting a **supportive and encouraging tone**, could you provide specific methods, steps, or tools that **I** can utilize to provide effective support and guidance to **my team members** as they work towards accomplishing their **personal professional objectives** and reaching their full potential in their careers?

Formula

As a **[profession]**, adopting a **[tone of voice]**, could you provide specific methods, steps, or tools that **[I/Name/Role]** can utilize to provide effective support and guidance to **[my/their] [team/group/department]** as they work towards accomplishing their **[contextual challenge/opportunity]** and reaching their full potential in their **[contextual challenge/opportunity]**?

PROMPT No 206

Cohesion - Development - Realization

To gain insights on the steps and items to consider when identifying factors that hinder a team from becoming more fully realized, enhancing their development and cohesion.

Given the goal of **developing a more fully realized team**, as an **Organizational Development Consultant** and in a **solution-oriented tone**, could you confirm the steps and items to consider when trying to identify the factors that hinder **my team** from **achieving this**?

Given the goal of **[contextual challenge/opportunity]**, as a **[profession]** and in a **[tone of voice]**, could you confirm the steps and items to consider when trying to identify the factors that hinder **[I/Name/Role]'s [team/group/department]** from **[desired outcome]**?

PROMPT No 207

Attributes - Leadership - Empathy

To gain insights on the specific personal attributes, abilities, or shifts in mindset that one should prioritize cultivating within themselves to become an exceptionally effective leader, especially considering a current deficiency in abilities.

As a **Leadership Development Consultant**, adopting a **supportive and constructive tone**, could you guide **me** on the precise personal attributes, abilities, or shifts in mindset **I** should prioritize cultivating within **myself** to become an exceptionally effective **leader**? This is particularly relevant given my current deficiency in empathy towards my team members.

As a **[profession]**, adopting a **[tone of voice]**, could you guide **[me/Name/Role]** on the precise personal attributes, abilities, or shifts in mindset **[I/Name/Role]** should prioritize cultivating within **[myself/themselves]** to become an exceptionally effective **[leader/role]**? This is particularly relevant given **[contextual challenge/opportunity]**.

PROMPT No 208

Exemplary - Boss - Effectiveness

To gain insights on the steps to undertake to become an exemplary boss, leader, or other specific role, enhancing leadership skills and effectiveness.

Considering the aspiration to be **an exemplary leader**, as a **Leadership Coach** and in an **inspiring and motivational tone**, could you outline the steps **I** need to undertake to achieve this in **my role**?

Formula

Considering the aspiration to be **[contextual challenge/opportunity]**, as a **[profession]** and in a **[tone of voice]**, could you outline the steps **[I/Name/Role]** need to undertake to achieve this in **[my/their] [role/position/job]**?

PROMPT No 209

Tags

Alignment - Passions - Fulfillment

Goal

To understand specific strategies or approaches that can be implemented to effectively align the unique passions and strengths of each team member with their respective job roles, thereby optimizing job satisfaction, productivity, and overall fulfillment at work.

Prompt

As a **Leadership Development Consultant**, adopting a **supportive and encouraging tone**, could you provide a thorough and detailed response that encompasses practical steps, potential challenges, and potential benefits of implementing strategies or approaches to **effectively align the unique passions and strengths of each team member with their respective job roles**? This is particularly relevant given the goal of **optimizing job satisfaction, productivity, and overall fulfillment at work**.

Formula

As a **[profession]**, adopting a **[tone of voice]**, could you provide a thorough and detailed response that encompasses practical steps, potential challenges, and potential benefits of implementing strategies or approaches to **[contextual challenge/opportunity]**? This is particularly relevant given the goal of **[desired outcome]**.

GOALS

PROMPT No 210

Tags

Purpose - Professional - Personal

Goal

To gain insights on specific strategies and actions that can be implemented to effectively guide and support a team in discovering a sense of purpose both in their professional roles and personal lives.

Prompt

As a **Life Coach**, adopting an **empathetic and supportive tone**, could you suggest specific strategies and actions **I** can implement to effectively guide and support **my team** in **discovering a sense of purpose both in their professional roles and personal lives**?

Formula

As a **[profession]**, adopting a **[tone of voice]**, could you suggest specific strategies and actions **[I/Name/Role]** can implement to effectively guide and support **[my/their]** **[team/group/department]** in **[desired outcome]**?

PROMPT No 211

Tags

Values - Integration - Aspirations

Goal

To gain insights on how leaders can effectively align their personal values, goals, and aspirations with their professional duties and obligations, ensuring that their personal purpose is integrated into their professional roles and responsibilities.

Prompt

As a **Leadership Development Consultant**, adopting an **insightful and strategic tone**, could you provide a comprehensive and detailed explanation of the strategies that **leaders** can employ to effectively align **their personal values, goals, and aspirations** with **their professional duties and obligations**? This is particularly relevant given the goal of **integrating personal purpose into professional roles and responsibilities**.

Formula

As a **[profession]**, adopting a **[tone of voice]**, could you provide a comprehensive and detailed explanation of the strategies that **[I/Name/Role]** can employ to effectively align **[contextual challenge/opportunity]** with **[contextual challenge/opportunity]**? This is particularly relevant given the goal of **[desired outcome]**.

PROMPT No 212

Tags

Evaluation - Growth - KPIs

Goal

To gain insights on how to effectively measure and evaluate the professional growth of a team in a specific skill, including the implementation of specific key performance indicators (KPIs) and the use of methods or tools for monitoring and assessing the progress of the development process.

Prompt

As a **Human Resources Consultant**, adopting a **clear and concise tone**, could you provide insights on how **I** can effectively measure and evaluate the professional growth of **my team** in in their **problem solving skills**? Please provide specific key performance indicators (KPIs) that can be implemented for this purpose. Furthermore, what methods or tools can be utilized to accurately monitor and assess the progress of this development process?

Formula

As a **[profession]**, adopting a **[tone of voice]**, could you provide insights on how **[I/Name/Role]** can effectively measure and evaluate the professional growth of **[my/their]** **[team/group/department]** in **[contextual challenge/opportunity]**? Please provide specific key performance indicators (KPIs) that can be implemented for this purpose. Furthermore, what methods or tools can be utilized to accurately monitor and assess the progress of this development process?

PROMPT No 213

Synchronization - Learning - Objectives

To gain insights on specific methods and approaches that can be utilized to effectively synchronize individual learning goals with the overall objectives of a team or organization, ensuring precision, comprehensiveness, and high-quality insights.

As a **Leadership Development Consultant**, adopting a **strategic and detailed tone**, could you provide me with specific methods and approaches that **I** can utilize to effectively synchronize **individual learning goals** with **the overall objectives of my team or organization**?

As a **[profession]**, adopting a **[tone of voice]**, could you provide me with specific methods and approaches that **[I/Name/Role]** can utilize to effectively synchronize **[contextual challenge/opportunity]** with **[desired outcome]**?

PROMPT No 214

Empowerment   - Recognition - Problem-Solving

To gain specific strategies or methods that can be employed to empower a team to independently recognize and address the factors that divert their attention and hinder their progress towards achieving their objectives, fostering a culture of self-awareness and proactive problem-solving.

As a **Leadership Development Consultant**, adopting a **supportive and empowering tone**, could you provide specific strategies or methods that **I** can employ to empower **my team** to independently recognize and address **the factors that divert their attention** and **hinder their progress towards achieving their objectives**?

As a **[profession]**, adopting a **[tone of voice]**, could you provide specific strategies or methods that **[I/Name/Role]** can employ to empower **[my/their]** **[team/group/department]** to independently recognize and address **[contextual challenge/opportunity]** and **[contextual challenge/opportunity]**?

PROMPT No 215

Synergy - Goal - Frameworks

To explore methods and frameworks to identify a pivotal goal that, when accomplished, would simplify or enable the achievement of other related objectives, providing a synergistic effect within an organization.

Act as a **Leadership Development Consultant** specializing in the **renewable energy industry**. Could you elucidate **the strategies, frameworks, or methods that can be employed to determine the goal that, once achieved, would simplify or enable other objectives within a team or organization?** This is central to **aligning efforts and maximizing efficiency in strategic planning**. Include uncommon advice and underrated resources in an all-encompassing and comprehensive manner, considering different organizational structures, cultures, and industries. Let's consider each facet of this topic. Write using an insightful tone and analytical writing style.

Act as a **[profession]** specializing in the **[industry of specialty]**. Could you elucidate **[contextual challenge/opportunity]**? This is central to **[desired outcome]**. Include uncommon advice and underrated resources in an all-encompassing and comprehensive manner, considering different organizational structures, cultures, and industries. Let's consider each facet of this topic. Write using a **[type]** tone and **[style]** writing style.

PROMPT No 216

Empowerment - Leadership - Strategies

To gain detailed insights on actions and strategies a team leader can implement to support and empower team members in leveraging their strengths towards achieving collective goals, enhancing team performance and success.

As a **Leadership Coach**, in an **empowering and supportive tone**, could you explain in detail the actions and strategies that I, **as a team leader**, can implement to effectively support and empower **my team members** to leverage their individual strengths and abilities towards achieving our **collective goals**?

As a **[profession]**, in a **[tone of voice]**, could you explain in detail the actions and strategies that **[I/Name/Role]**, as a **[specific role]**, can implement to effectively support and empower **[my/their]** **[team/group/department]** members to leverage their individual strengths and abilities towards achieving our **[specific goal/outcome]**?

PROMPT No 217

Collaboration - Frameworks - Cohesiveness

To explore various frameworks, methodologies, or strategies that can be employed by a team to align their efforts, increase collaboration, and effectively work towards achieving their collective goals.

Act as a **Team Development Specialist** specializing in the **corporate training industry**. Could you provide an **exhaustive overview of the different frameworks, methodologies, or strategies that my team and I could consider implementing to work cohesively and effectively toward our goals**? This includes **strategies that are both well-established and**

those that might be unconventional but effective. Provide unique insights and overlooked opportunities, considering various team dynamics, organizational structures, and industries. Let's analyze this piece by piece. Write using an informative tone and analytical writing style.

Act as a **[profession]** specializing in the **[industry]**. Could you provide **[contextual challenge/opportunity]**? This includes **[desired outcome]**. Provide unique insights and overlooked opportunities, considering various team dynamics, organizational structures, and industries. Let's analyze this piece by piece. Write using a **[type]** tone and **[style]** writing style.

PROMPT No 218

Prioritization - Goals - Alignment

To help you in identifying various methods or techniques for prioritizing your many goals. This will help in selecting the most critical and significant goals to focus on, ensuring alignment with long-term objectives and efficient use of resources.

Act as a **Leadership Development Consultant** specializing in the **event planning industry**. What are the various **methods** available to me for **sifting through and prioritizing** all the **goals** I have, enabling me to **single out** the **key and most impactful** goals I should set for **myself**? How can these **techniques** be **applied** in **different contexts**, and what are the **potential benefits** of each? Respond to each question separately. Let's **dissect** this **step by step**. Write using a **confident** tone and **analytical** writing style.

Act as a **[profession]** specializing in the **[industry]**, what are the various **[methods/techniques/strategies]** available to me for **[sifting through/prioritizing/organizing]** all the **[goals/objectives/targets]** I have, enabling me to **[select/identify/choose]** the **[key/most important/most impactful]** goals I should set for **[myself/my team/my organization]**? How can these **[techniques/methods]** be **[applied/implemented/used]** in **[different contexts/various scenarios/multiple situations]**, and what are the **[potential risks/benefits/challenges]** of each? Respond to each question separately. Let's **[analyze/dissect/consider]** this **[step by step/piece by piece]**. Write using a **[type]** tone and **[style]** writing style.

PROMPT No 219

Feasibility - Evaluation - Decision-making

To guide you in evaluating the feasibility and alignment of specific goals for your team. It involves providing techniques and considerations for determining whether a particular goal is worth pursuing, taking into account various factors such as relevance, impact, resources, alignment with organizational strategy, and potential challenges.

Act as a **Team Development Specialist** specializing in the **strategy consulting industry**. What various **techniques** should I consider to **assess** if my **team** should **genuinely** pursue a **specific goal** or not? How can these **techniques** be **tailored** to fit **different** types of **goals** and **organizational contexts**? What are the **common pitfalls** that must be **avoided**, and how can the **decision-making process** be **effectively communicated** with the **team**? Let's **dissect** this **step by step**. Write using a **professional** tone and **analytical** writing style.

Act as a **[profession]** specializing **[industry]**, what are the **[methods/techniques/criteria]** I should consider to **[evaluate/assess/determine]** if my **[team/department/organization]** should **[genuinely/really/seriously]** pursue a **[specific/particular/certain]** goal or not? How can these **[methods/techniques]** be **[tailored/adapted/customized]** to fit **[different/various/multiple]** types of **[goals/objectives/targets]** and **[organizational contexts/business environments/corporate settings]**? What are the **[common pitfalls/challenges/mistakes]** that must be **[avoided/considered/addressed]**, and how can the **[decision-making process/evaluation procedure]** be **[effectively/efficiently/clearly]** **[communicated/presented/shared]** with the **[team/department/group]**? Let's **[analyze/dissect/consider]** this **[step by step/piece by piece]**. Write using a **[type]** tone and **[style]** writing style.

PROMPT No 220

Monitoring - Intervention - Accountability

To provide guidance on monitoring your team's progress toward annual goals and intervening appropriately when necessary. The focus is on understanding the ways to track progress, identify barriers, and provide constructive and polite intervention to ensure that the goals are met.

Act as a **Performance Coach** specializing in the **food industry**. What are the **tools** I can employ to **continually** monitor my **team's** progress toward their **annual objectives**? How can I **identify potential obstacles**, and what are the **best practices** for **providing timely, constructive, and respectful interventions** to **ensure** they **stay on track** to **meet** their **goals**? What **strategies** can be **employed** to **create** a **supportive and accountable environment** without **micromanaging**? Let's **think this step by step**. Write using a **supportive** tone and **engaging** writing style.

Act as a **[profession]** specializing in the **[industry]**, what are the **[methods/tools/techniques]** I can employ to **[continually/consistently/regularly]** monitor my **[team's/department's/group's]** progress toward their **[annual/quarterly/monthly]** **[objectives/goals/targets]**? How can I **[identify/detect/recognize]** **[potential/possible/likely]** **[challenges/obstacles/barriers]**, and what are the **[best practices/guidelines/approaches]** for **[providing/offering]** **[timely/constructive/respectful]** **[interventions/support/assistance]** to **[ensure/guarantee/confirm]** they **[stay on track/remain aligned/keep focused]** to **[meet/achieve/accomplish]** their **[goals/targets/objectives]**? What **[strategies/tactics/methods]** can be **[employed/used/applied]** to **[create/build/develop]** a **[supportive/accountable/responsible]** **[environment/culture/atmosphere]** without *[micromanaging/overseeing excessively/over-controlling]*? Let's **[analyze/think**

about/consider] this **[step by step/systematically]**. Write using a **[type]** tone and **[style]** writing style.

PROMPT No 221

Resources - Development - Support

To gain insights on the specific resources, tools, and support colleagues require at each stage of their professional development, enhancing their ability to achieve their desired objectives.

Considering the importance of providing adequate resources and support for professional development, as a **Talent Development Specialist** and in a **solution-oriented and respectful tone**, could you identify what specific resources, tools, and support **my colleagues** require at each stage of their professional development in order to successfully achieve their desired objectives?

Considering the importance of **[contextual challenge/opportunity]**, as a **[profession]** and in a **[tone of voice]**, could you identify what specific resources, tools, and support **[I/Name/Role]'s [colleagues/team/group/department]** require at each stage of their **[specific area]** in order to successfully achieve their **[desired outcome]?**

PROMPT No 222

Assessment - Performance - Accountability

to assist you in evaluating the current progress of your team members towards achieving set goals. It aims to provide a comprehensive framework for tracking, measuring, and assessing performance, identifying gaps or areas of improvement, and implementing strategies to ensure alignment with the desired outcomes.

Act as a **Performance Management Expert** specializing in the **insurance brokerage industry**. Every successful team relies on clearly defined goals and a systematic evaluation of progress towards achieving those goals. How can a **leader** effectively **assess** where their team is **currently** positioned in terms of **reaching** their **targets** compared to the **set expectations**? Provide a **detailed** guide that includes **understanding** the **goals, setting clear KPIs, utilizing tools and techniques** for **tracking and monitoring, conducting regular reviews** and **feedback sessions, identifying areas of concern or improvement, realigning strategies or approaches** if necessary, and **fostering a culture of transparency, accountability, and collaboration**. Include practical examples, best practices, methodologies, and resources suitable for the **nsurance brokerage industry.** Respond separately to each question. Explore unconventional solutions and alternative perspectives. Let's take this one step at a time. Write using a friendly tone and approachable writing style.

Act as a **[profession]** specializing in the **[industry]**. Every successful team relies on clearly defined goals and a systematic evaluation of progress towards achieving those goals. How can a

[leader/manager/supervisor] effectively **[assess/evaluate/measure]** where their team is **[currently/now/presently]** positioned in terms of **[reaching/achieving/meeting]** their **[targets/objectives/aims]** compared to the **[set/established/planned]** **[expectations/benchmarks/standards]**? Provide a **[detailed/comprehensive/in-depth]** guide that includes **[understanding/knowing/getting clear on] [the goals/objectives/targets/vision/mission]**, **[setting/creating/establishing]** **[clear/definite/specific] [benchmarks/KPIs/standards/indicators]**, **[utilizing/using/applying] [tools and techniques/methods and approaches/systems and technology]** for **[tracking/monitoring/observing]** and **[monitoring/measuring/evaluating]**, **[conducting/organizing/holding]** **[regular/frequent/consistent] [reviews/feedback sessions/evaluation meetings]**, **[identifying/recognizing/pinpointing] [areas of concern or improvement/opportunities for growth/challenges or roadblocks]**, **[realigning/adjusting/tweaking] [strategies or approaches/methods or tactics/plans or directions]** if **[necessary/required/needed]**, and **[fostering/encouraging/promoting]** a **[culture/environment/atmosphere]** of **[transparency/accountability/responsibility]** and **[collaboration/cooperation/teamwork]**. Include **[practical/real-life/actual] [examples/scenarios/case studies]**, **[best practices/guidelines/recommendations]**, **[methodologies/techniques/processes]**, and **[resources/tools/materials]** suitable for the **[industry]**. Respond separately to each question. Explore unconventional solutions and alternative perspectives. Let's take this one step at a time. Write using a **[type]** tone and **[style]** writing style.

PROMPT No 223

Tags

Learning - Engagement - Objectives

Goal

To empower business leaders, managers, and executives with an effective method for discovering the specific learning goals that align with their team's performance objectives. The intention is to facilitate the creation of tailored development plans that can accelerate progress, boost employee engagement, and contribute to the overall success of the organization.

Prompt

Act as a **Talent Development Strategist** specializing in **performance coaching** for the **retail industry**. Could you guide me through **an in-depth process to identify the learning goals that would propel my team toward achieving their performance objectives**? I would like to ensure these goals meet the SMART (Specific, Measurable, Achievable, Relevant, Time-bound) criteria. Please provide **a systematic framework, including assessment tools, questioning techniques, and data analysis strategies** to uncover these learning objectives. Also, offer advice on how to integrate these learning goals into **individual and team development plans**. The performance objectives of my team are to **increase customer satisfaction and increase sales**. Let's examine this systematically. Write using a **focused** tone and a **strategic** writing style.

Formula

Act as a **[profession]** specializing in **[topic]** for the **[industry]**. Could you guide me through **[contextual challenge/opportunity]**? I would like to ensure these goals meet **[specific criteria such as SMART]**. Please provide **[tools/techniques/strategies]** to uncover these learning objectives. Also, offer advice on how to integrate these learning goals into **[specific individual or team development plans]**. The performance objectives of my team are **[performance objectives]**. Let's examine this systematically. Write using a **[Tone]** tone and a **[Style]** writing style.

PROMPT No 224

Fulfillment - Conversations - Emotional

To equip team leaders, managers, and executives with a holistic methodology for discussing work fulfillment with their team members. This aims to foster self-awareness, improve team morale, and lead to better alignment between personal satisfaction and organizational objectives.

Act as a **Workplace Fulfillment Coach** specializing in **emotional intelligence** for the **finance industry**. Could you guide me through **an all-inclusive approach to preparing myself for discussions with my team on what they might experience emotionally when reaching their point of work fulfillment**? The goal is to **facilitate conversations that will help both the leadership and the team to understand the emotional landscape associated with achieving work fulfillment**. Please provide a **step-by-step guide, conversation frameworks, reflective exercises, and probing questions** that can be utilized in **one-on-ones meetings**. Also, offer ways to handle potential emotional sensitivities that may arise during such conversations. Suggest actionable strategies and practical solutions. Let's dissect this carefully. Write using an **empathetic** tone and a **thoughtful** writing style.

Act as a **[profession]** specializing in **[topic/specialization]** for the **[industry]**. Could you guide me through **[contextual challenge/opportunity]?** The goal is to **[desired goal].** Please provide **[methodology components, e.g., a step-by-step guide, conversation frameworks, reflective exercises, probing questions]** that can be used in **[one-on-ones/team meetings].** Also, offer ways to handle potential emotional sensitivities that may arise during such conversations. Suggest actionable strategies and practical solutions. Let's dissect this carefully. Write using a **[type]** tone and **[style]** writing style.

PROMPT No 225

Professionalism - Improvement - Objectives

To facilitate the exploration and formulation of new professional objectives within a team, encouraging individual growth, alignment with organizational goals, and fostering a culture of continuous improvement and ambition. The ultimate aim is to empower team members to set challenging yet achievable targets that contribute to both personal development and overall team success.

Act as a **Professional Development Coach** specializing in the **banking industry**. Could you guide me on how to **explore and articulate new professional objectives with my team that they could set for themselves**? This exploration is key to **stimulating growth, fostering alignment with company goals, and driving ambition within the team**. Please provide a comprehensive framework that includes individual **assessment techniques, goal-setting methodologies, collaboration strategies, and monitoring processes to ensure ongoing progress**. Let's approach this methodically. Write using an inspiring tone and instructive writing style.

Act as a **[profession]** specializing in the **[industry]**. Could you guide me on how to **[contextual challenge/opportunity]**? This exploration is key to **[desired outcome]**. Please provide a comprehensive framework that includes **[specific components or methods]**. Let's approach this methodically. Write using a **[type]** tone and **[style]** writing style.

PROMPT No 226

Self-Improvement - Career - Conflict

To gain insights on specific steps or actions to plan for advancing personal growth and development, enhancing self-improvement and goal achievement.

As a **Career Coach**, in an **encouraging and supportive tone**, could you describe in detail what specific steps or actions **someone** should plan to take in order to advance their personal growth and development about **learning to deal with conflict**? This advice is sought particularly considering the importance of continuous learning in today's fast-paced professional environment.

As a **[profession]**, in a **[tone of voice]**, could you describe in detail what specific steps or actions **[someone/I/Name/Role]** should plan to take in order to advance their **[desired outcome]** about **[Topic]?** This advice is sought particularly considering the importance of **[contextual challenge/opportunity]**.

PROMPT No 227

Team-Reflection - Motivation - Goal-Setting

To guide the team in thoughtful reflection and candid discussion about their individual and collective aspirations. This exercise aims to clarify what team members genuinely want to achieve, both for themselves and as a part of the team, thereby setting the stage for focused, purposeful work and strategy planning.

Act as a **Motivational Coach** specializing in **goal-setting and vision alignment** for the **real estate industry**. Could you provide an **exhaustive guide** on how to **effectively conduct a team session aimed at reflecting on what each member truly desires to accomplish?** I am particularly interested in **engaging exercises and questioning techniques that can unlock deeper levels of personal and professional desire**. The guide should be organized into into preparation, discussion facilitation, and conclusion and follow-up. Include uncommon advice and underrated resources. Let's sequentially address each element. Write using an **inspiring** tone and a **holistic** writing style.

Act as a **[profession]** with expertise in **[specialization/topic]** for the **[industry]**. Could you provide a **[type of resource/tool]** on how to **[targeted goal/challenge]?** I am particularly interested in **[particular methods/aspects]**. The guide should be organized into

[sections/themes]. Include uncommon advice and underrated resources. Let's sequentially address each element. Write using a **[type]** tone and **[style]** writing style.

PROMPT No 228

Tags

Leadership - Conversations - Alignment

Goal

To create guidelines or approaches for leaders to enhance their conversations with team members regarding their future goals and desired accomplishments. It focuses on building clarity, understanding, and alignment with the team's personal and professional aspirations within the business context.

Prompt

Act as an **Executive Leadership Consultant** specializing in the **technology industry**. How can I improve **the way I conduct conversations with my team about the type of accomplishments they want to achieve in the future?** The aim is to **align individual goals with the team's mission and company vision, creating a supportive environment for personal growth and success.** Let's take this one step at a time. Write using an empathetic tone and engaging writing style.

Formula

Act as a **[profession]** specializing in the **[industry]**. How can I improve **[contextual challenge/opportunity]**? The aim is to **[goal]**. Let's take this one step at a time. Write using a **[type]** tone and **[style]** writing style.

HABITS

PROMPT No 229

Tags

Behavior - Analysis - Team-Dynamics

Goal

To help leaders and managers accurately identify the recurring actions or thought patterns that their teams engage in, irrespective of the situational context. This information is crucial for understanding team dynamics, work habits, and cultural fit.

Prompt

Act as a **Behavioral Analyst** specializing in **team dynamics** for the **retail industry**. Could you outline **a systematic approach to identify actions or thoughts that my team consistently engages in, regardless of the context?** The approach should include **methodologies for observation, data collection, and analysis, as well as strategies for effectively communicating these insights back to the team.** The ultimate goal is to **achieve team improvement, personal development, and better organizational alignment.** Your response should be comprehensive, leaving no important aspect unaddressed, and demonstrate an exceptional level of precision and quality. Let's break down each step in detail to gain a full understanding. Write using a **clear, instructive** tone and a **logical, step-by-step** writing style.

Formula

Act as a **[profession]** specializing in **[topic/specialization]** for the **[industry]**. Could you outline **[contextual challenge/opportunity]?** The approach should include **[tools/strategies/considerations]**. The ultimate goal is to**[desired objective]**. Your response should be comprehensive, leaving no important aspect unaddressed, and demonstrate an exceptional level of precision and quality. Let's break down each step in detail to gain a full understanding. Write using **[type]** tone and **[style]** writing style.

PROMPT No 230

Tags
Competency - Assessment - Talent-Assessment

Goal
To equip team leaders, managers, and HR professionals with a comprehensive toolkit for effectively assessing the fit between team members' skills and the organization's needs. This includes the implementation of competency models, talent assessments, and a deep dive into both soft and hard skills.

Prompt
Act as a **Talent Management Specialist** specializing in **organizational alignment** for the **manufacturing industry**. Could you provide **a step-by-step guide to assess and determine the best fit between my team's skills and the organizational needs**? The ultimate goal is to **achieve higher team performance, job satisfaction, and long-term retention rates**. Your input should include **methods for evaluating both hard and soft skills**, a framework for matching these skills to company goals, and strategies for actionable follow-through. Explore unconventional solutions and alternative perspectives. Let's thoroughly explore each component for the most comprehensive understanding. Write using a **solution-oriented** tone and a **systematic** writing style.

Formula
Act as a **[profession]** specializing in **[topic/specialization]** for the **[industry]**. Could you provide **[contextual challenge/opportunity]?** The ultimate goal is to **[desired outcomes]**. Your input should include **[tools/techniques/considerations]**, a framework for matching these skills to company goals, and strategies for actionable follow-through. Explore unconventional solutions and alternative perspectives. Let's thoroughly explore each component for the most comprehensive understanding. Write using a **[type]** tone and **[style]** writing style.

PROMPT No 231

Tags
Quality - Efficiency - Error-Reduction

Goal
To identify and implement strategies to reduce errors or miscalculations within a team's workflow, thereby enhancing accuracy, efficiency, and overall performance. The ultimate aim is to cultivate a culture of excellence, attention to detail, and continuous improvement that ensures the delivery of high-quality work.

Prompt
Act as a **Quality Assurance Specialist** specializing in the **manufacturing industry**. Could you delineate strategies that my team could consider implementing to **significantly reduce errors or miscalculations in their daily operations**? This reduction is crucial for **maintaining product**

quality, improving efficiency, safeguarding compliance, and building customer trust. Please present a comprehensive plan, encompassing **training initiatives, process refinement, technology solutions, monitoring mechanisms, and feedback loops**. Let's examine this **step by step**. Write using an **authoritative** tone and **clear** writing style.

Act as a **[profession]** specializing in the **[industry]**. Could you delineate strategies that my team could consider implementing to **[contextual challenge/opportunity]**? This reduction is crucial for **[desired outcome]**. Please present a comprehensive plan, encompassing **[specific components or methods]**. Let's examine this **[methodically/step by step/one piece at a time]**. Write using a **[type]** tone and **[style]** writing style.

PROMPT No 232

Obstacles - Methodologies - Strategy

To explore and outline methodologies or strategies that can be employed to identify potential external obstacles that might obstruct the achievement of targeted deliverables. This guidance aims to help professionals anticipate challenges, adapt, and strategize accordingly to ensure that they meet their business targets.

Act as a **Change Management Consultant** specializing in the **manufacturing industry**. What are some **crucial methodologies or strategies I should consider to identify potential external obstacles that might hinder achieving my targeted deliverables**? The intent is **to understand the external factors and to develop proactive strategies to mitigate or overcome these challenges**. Let's dissect this carefully. Write using an **analytical** tone and **technical** writing style.

Act as a **[profession]** specializing in the **[industry]**. What are some **[contextual challenge/opportunity]**? The intent is to **[desired outcome]**. Let's dissect this carefully. Write using a **[type]** tone and **[style]** writing style.

PROMPT No 233

Self-Sabotage - Transportation - Leadership

To scrutinize personal behaviors, habits, or thought patterns that may unintentionally impede one's progression in professional growth or leadership development. This understanding aims to foster self-awareness, enabling one to take proactive measures for personal and career fulfillment.

Act as a **Leadership Development Consultant** specializing in the **transportation industry**. Could you provide **an exhaustive analysis of the various ways in which I might unintentionally hinder my own progression toward becoming a more fulfilled professional or leader**? Please include **both common and obscure behaviors, mental frameworks, or patterns that might lead to self-sabotage or stagnation**. Share distinctive guidance and unexplored options that could assist in recognizing and overcoming these barriers. Let's dissect this carefully. Write using an empathetic tone and analytical writing style.

Act as a **[profession]** specializing in the **[industry]**. Could you provide **[contextual challenge/opportunity]**? Please include **[specific details or considerations]**. Share distinctive guidance and unexplored options that could assist in recognizing and overcoming these barriers. Let's dissect this carefully. Write using a **[type]** tone and **[style]** writing style.

PROMPT No 234

Creativity - Perspective - Innovation

To identify and explore diverse methods or techniques that you can use to expand current perspectives or thinking patterns. This is aimed at fostering growth, creativity, and adaptability in one's professional life, enabling a more comprehensive approach to problem-solving and decision-making.

Act as a **Personal Development Coach** specializing in the **technology industry**. What are some methods for **expanding my current perspective or thinking patterns**? The goal is to **infuse creativity and broaden my understanding to foster innovation and agility in my professional pursuits**. Impart comprehensive and profound methods. Let's dissect this carefully. Write using an **inspiring** tone and **creative** writing style.

Act as a **[profession]** specializing in the **[industry]**. What are some methods for **[contextual challenge/opportunity]**? The goal is to **[desired outcome]**. Impart comprehensive and profound methods. Let's dissect this carefully. Write using an inspiring tone and creative writing style.

PROMPT No 235

Patterns - Management - Team-Development

To uncover and explore methodologies or strategies that can be utilized to identify recurring patterns or behaviors within a team throughout their career. Recognizing these patterns could lead to understanding underlying issues or habits and enable effective management, development, and growth.

Act as a **Team Development Specialist** specializing in the **e-commerce industry**. What are some ways in which **I can find out patterns that have been recurring for my team throughout their career**? Recognizing these patterns may assist in **identifying both opportunities and challenges that might impact their performance and personal development**. Present a detailed and broad-ranging response. Let's dissect this carefully. Write using an **analytical** tone and **informative** writing style.

Act as a **[profession]** in the **[industry]**. What are some ways in which **[contextual challenge/opportunity]**? Recognizing these patterns may assist in **[desired outcome]**. Present a detailed and broad-ranging response. Let's dissect this carefully. Write using an analytical tone and informative writing style.

PROMPT No 236

Productivity - SocialMedia - Distractions

To gain insights on specific measures to overcome the unhealthy tendency of being distracted by social media during work hours, enhancing work productivity.

Given the challenge of **social media distractions during work hours**, as a **Performance Coach** and in a **clear and concise tone**, could you suggest specific measures that can be taken to overcome this **unhealthy tendency** with the aim of **enhancing work productivity**?

Given the challenge of **[contextual challenge/opportunity]**, as a **[profession]** and in a **[tone of voice]**, could you suggest specific measures that can be taken to overcome **[issue]** with the aim of **[desired outcome]**?

PROMPT No 237

Communication - ActiveListening - Self-awareness

To identify the signs, triggers, or behaviors that might indicate a lapse in active listening to team members, and to reflect on those situations or circumstances where this tends to occur. The understanding of these elements aims to promote self-awareness and improve communication within the team.

Act as a **Communication Specialist** specializing in the **power generation industry**. Could you provide a **profound and detailed analysis of how I can recognize when I am not actively listening to my team**? Furthermore, what **methods or reflective practices can I employ to understand the specific situations where I tend to disengage from listening**? Respond separately to each question. Include both readily observable indicators and subtle signs of inattention, along with actionable strategies for self-reflection and improvement. Let's consider each facet of this topic. Write using an **instructive** tone and **engaging** writing style.

Act as a **[profession]** specializing in the **[industry]**. Could you provide **[contextual challenge/opportunity]**? Furthermore, what **[contextual challenge/opportunity]**? Respond separately to each question. Include both readily observable indicators and subtle signs of inattention, along with actionable strategies for self-reflection and improvement. Let's consider each facet of this topic. Write using a **[type]** tone and **[style]** writing style.

PROMPT No 238

Engagement - Meetings - Incentivize

To explore methods or strategies to motivate and engage a team fully in meetings. This engagement leads to enhanced participation, increased collaboration, and more productive outcomes in team meetings.

Act as a **Leadership Development Consultant** specializing in the **risk management industry**. How can I incentivize my team to **be fully present and actively participate in our team meetings**? Engaging the team in this manner is pivotal for **collaboration, problem-solving, and driving the success of projects**. Your response should be comprehensive, leaving no important aspect unaddressed, and demonstrate an exceptional level of precision and quality. Let's think about this step by step. Write using an **inspiring** tone and **constructive** writing style.

Act as a **[profession]** specializing in the **[industry]**. How can I incentivize my team to **[contextual challenge/opportunity]**? Engaging the team in this manner is pivotal for **[desired outcome]**. Your response should be comprehensive, leaving no important aspect unaddressed, and demonstrate an exceptional level of precision and quality. Let's think about this step by step. Write using a **[type]** tone and **[style]** writing style.

PROMPT No 239

Networking - Efficacy - Optimism

To gain detailed and optimistic suggestions on specific strategies or modifications to improve work efficacy, particularly in light of a challenge with inadequate professional connections in the workplace.

As a **Networking Coach**, what specific strategies or modifications would you recommend to improve the efficacy of **my work** as **manager of the IT team**, given the challenge of **inadequate professional connections in the workplace**? Please provide detailed and **optimistic** suggestions.

As a **[profession]**, what specific strategies or modifications would you recommend to improve the efficacy of **[I/Name/Role]'s** work as **[profession/role]**, given the challenge of **[contextual challenge/opportunity]**? Please provide detailed and **[tone of voice]** suggestions.

LEARNING

PROMPT No 240

Goal

To explore diverse techniques and methodologies that a team can implement to learn and comprehend new topics or subjects efficiently. It emphasizes not just the acquisition of new knowledge but the understanding and application of that knowledge within a team setting.

Prompt

Act as a **Professional Mentor** specializing in the **education sector**. What are some techniques **my team and I should consider to learn and understand any new topic**? This is crucial for **continuous growth, adapting to change, and enhancing our expertise in various domains**. Offer unconventional strategies and underused techniques. Let's dissect this carefully. Write using an **instructive** tone and **engaging** writing style.

Formula

Act as a **[profession]** specializing in the **[sector]**. What are some techniques **[contextual challenge/opportunity]**? This is crucial for **[desired outcome]**. Offer unconventional strategies and underused techniques. Let's dissect this carefully. Write using a **[type]** tone and **[style]** writing style.

PROMPT No 241

Tags

Reflection - Growth - Improvement

Goal

To provide guidance and insights on reflecting and learning from recent experiences. It aims to empower teams to identify key takeaways, learn from them, and integrate these learnings into future actions and decisions.

Prompt

Act as a **Leadership Development Consultant** specializing in the **event planning industry**. What are some **tips I could share with my team to reflect on and learn from the key takeaways from a recent experience**? This reflection is crucial for **personal and professional growth, fostering a culture of continuous improvement and resilience**. Ensuring that your response is thorough, precise, and of the highest quality possible. Let's analyze this piece by piece. Write using a **motivational** tone and **conversational** writing style.

Formula

Act as a **[profession]** specializing in the **[industry]**. What are some **[contextual challenge/opportunity]**? This reflection is crucial for **[desired outcome]**. Ensuring that your response is thorough, precise, and of the highest quality possible. Let's analyze this piece by piece. Write using a **[type]** tone and **[style]** writing style.

PROMPT No 242

Tags

Energy - Motivation - Leadership

Goal

To recognize early signs of declining energy or motivation within a team and to explore strategic interventions to rejuvenate and increase energy and enthusiasm. The focus is on proactive leadership that fosters a vibrant and engaged team culture.

Act as a Leadership Development Consultant specializing in the e-commerce industry. What are the symptoms or signs that the energy of my team is decreasing?, and what actionable strategies can I employ to correct this trend and increase their vitality and motivation? Respond to each question separately. Identifying and addressing these factors is vital for maintaining team productivity and morale. Provide exhaustive and all-encompassing responses. Let's analyze this piece by piece. Write using an enthusiastic tone and engaging writing style.

Act as a **[profession]** specializing in the **[industry].** What are the symptoms or signs that **[contextual challenge/opportunity]?** And what actionable strategies can **I [contextual challenge/opportunity]?** Respond to each question separately. Identifying and addressing these factors is vital for **[desired outcome]**. Provide exhaustive and all-encompassing responses. Let's analyze this piece by piece. Write using a **[type]** tone and **[style]** writing style.

PROMPT No 243

Assessment - Opportunities - Methodologies

To help identify challenges or deficiencies in one's work or professional activities and explore ways to uncover and leverage missed opportunities. This requires a thorough examination of the current state of affairs, clear insights into potential obstacles, and the formulation of strategies to overcome them.

Act as an **Organizational Development Consultant** specializing in the **manufacturing industry**. How can I **critically assess what is not working in my current projects or workflow**? And what methodologies or practices can I **employ to uncover missed opportunities that might be linked to these shortcomings**? This understanding is crucial for **growth and innovation within my role**. Respond to each question separately. Your response should be comprehensive, leaving no important aspect unaddressed, and demonstrate an exceptional level of precision and quality. Let's dissect this carefully. Write using a **methodical** tone and **analytical** writing style.

Act as a **[profession]** specializing in the **[industry]**. How can I **[contextual challenge/opportunity]?** And what methodologies or practices can I **[contextual challenge/opportunity]?** This understanding is crucial for **[desired outcome]**. Respond to each question separately. Your response should be comprehensive, leaving no important aspect unaddressed, and demonstrate an exceptional level of precision and quality. Let's dissect this carefully. Write using a **[type]** tone and **[style]** writing style.

PROMPT No 244

Self-Critique - EmotionalIntelligence - Plan

To gain a detailed and comprehensive plan of action to assist a team in further exploring and connecting their thoughts so as to counteract their inner critic, fostering personal growth and team performance.

Considering the importance of **counteracting the inner critic for personal growth**, as an **Emotional Intelligence Coach** and in an **empathetic and supportive tone**, could you provide a detailed and comprehensive plan of action **I** can implement to assist **my team** in **further exploring and connecting their thoughts**?

Considering the importance of **[contextual challenge/opportunity]**, as a **[profession]** and in a **[tone of voice]**, could you provide a detailed and comprehensive plan of action **[I/Name/Role]** can implement to assist **[my/their] [team/group/department]** in **[desired outcome]**?

PROMPT No 245

Experiences - Beliefs - Self-Awareness

To help leaders effectively communicate to their teams the concept that individual experiences shape beliefs and assumptions. By achieving clarity on this topic, the team can better understand their behavior, make more informed decisions, and foster a culture of self-awareness and continuous improvement.

Act as a **Leadership Communication Expert** specializing in the **finance industry**. Could you provide **a comprehensive guide for explaining to my team how their personal experiences shape their beliefs and assumptions**? Include specific **strategies for presentation, the psychological underpinnings to consider, and a set of key talking points**. This is vital for **enhancing self-awareness and making better team decisions**. Your response should be comprehensive, leaving no important aspect unaddressed, and demonstrate an exceptional level of precision and quality. Let's dissect each element in a detailed manner. Write using an **empathetic** tone and an **instructive** writing style.

Act as a **[profession]** specializing in **[industry]**. Could you provide **[contextual challenge/opportunity]**? Include **[tools/strategies]**. This is vital for **[desired objective]**. Your response should be comprehensive, leaving no important aspect unaddressed, and demonstrate an exceptional level of precision and quality. Let's dissect each element in a detailed manner. Write using a **[type]** tone and **[style]** writing style.

PROMPT No 246

Improvement - Recognition - Learning

To gain specific actions or methods that can be employed to successfully improve a team's understanding and recognition of the areas that were not successful or did not achieve the desired outcomes, fostering a culture of continuous learning and improvement.

As a **Performance Coach**, adopting a **constructive and supportive tone**, could you provide specific actions or methods that **I** can employ to successfully improve **my team's** understanding and recognition of the areas that were not successful or did not achieve the desired outcomes? This is particularly relevant given the goal of **fostering a culture of continuous learning and improvement**.

Formula

As a **[profession]**, adopting a **[tone of voice]**, could you provide specific actions or methods that **[I/Name/Role]** can employ to successfully improve **[my/their]** **[team/group/department]'s** understanding and recognition of **[contextual challenge/opportunity]**? This is particularly relevant given the goal of **[desired outcome]**.

PROMPT No 247

Tags

Opportunities - Vigilance - Identification

Goal

To equip business leaders with a robust methodology for proactively identifying and seizing business opportunities that align with the company's strategic objectives. The focus is on creating an organizational environment that encourages vigilance, collaboration, and quick decision-making.

Prompt

Act as a **Business Opportunity Analyst** specializing in **competitive intelligence** for the **energy industry**. Could you provide a **comprehensive guide on how I can ensure my team doesn't miss a great opportunity for our business in the future**? This is crucial for **maintaining a competitive edge and achieving long-term success**. Your guide should be inclusive of techniques for opportunity identification, risk assessment, and decision-making processes. Explore unconventional solutions and alternative perspectives. Let's tackle this in a phased manner. Write using an **authoritative** tone and a **detailed, systematic** writing style.

Formula

Act as a **[profession]** specializing in **[focus area]** for the **[industry]**. Could you provide a **[specific challenge or opportunity]**? This is crucial for **[desired outcome]**. Your guidance should include **[tactics/considerations/strategies]**. Explore unconventional solutions and alternative perspectives. Let's tackle this in a phased manner. Write using a **[type]** tone and **[style]** writing style.

PROMPT No 248

Tags

Introspection - Conversations - Improvement

Goal

To empower leaders with the right approach and tools to facilitate introspective conversations within their teams. These conversations aim to identify actionable lessons from past experiences, encouraging a culture of continuous improvement.

Prompt

Act as a **Team Development Coach** specializing in the **reflective practice** for the **professional services industry**. Could you provide a **comprehensive guide** on how to **discuss with my** team if they have ideas on how they could improve upon past situations, given another chance? Your output is crucial for **fostering an environment of continuous learning and adaptability**. Your guide should be all-encompassing, covering **preparation, facilitation techniques, and follow-up actions to ensure the team translates insights into future behavior**. Investigate unexpected avenues and creative pathways. Let's deconstruct this subject stepwise. Write using a **coaching** tone and a **detailed, practical** writing style.

Act as a **[profession]** specializing in **[focus area]** for the **[industry]**. Could you provide a **[comprehensive guide/detailed framework]** on how to **[specific challenge or opportunity]**? Your output is crucial for **[desired outcome]**. Your guide should be all-encompassing, covering **[methods/considerations]**. Investigate unexpected avenues and creative pathways. Let's sequentially unravel this issue. Write using a **[type]** tone and **[style]** writing style.

PROMPT No 249

Communication - Engagement - Curiosity

To gain specific strategies or techniques that can be utilized to promote effective communication and facilitate productive discussions within a team, particularly when it comes to addressing and nurturing their work-related interests and curiosities.

As a **Communication Coach**, adopting a **collaborative and engaging tone**, could you provide precise strategies or techniques that can be utilized to **promote effective communication and facilitate productive discussions** within **my software development team**, particularly when it comes to **addressing and nurturing their work-related interests and curiosities**?

As a **[profession]**, adopting a **[tone of voice]**, could you provide precise strategies or techniques that can be utilized to **[contextual challenge/opportunity]** within **[my/their]** **[team/group/department]**, particularly when it comes to **[desired outcome]**?

PROMPT No 250

Blindspots - Leadership - Biases

help leaders in business settings identify and understand their blind spots. Blind spots are areas where a leader might have limitations or biases they are unaware of, which could affect their leadership effectiveness. Recognizing and addressing these blind spots can enhance a leader's ability to guide their team and make unbiased decisions.

Act as a **Leadership Development Consultant** specializing in the **FinTech industry**. How can I **identify** my **blind spots** as a **leader**? What are the **tools** that can **help** me **uncover areas** where I might have **biases** that I'm **not aware of**? How can I **work** with my **team** to **gain insights** into these **hidden** areas, and what **steps** should I **take** to **address** them? What are some **examples** of

common leadership blind spots, and how have **other** leaders successfully **overcome** them? Respond separately to each question. Suggest fresh approaches and inventive ideas. Let's take this one step at a time. Write using an **introspective** tone and **analytical** writing style.

Act as a **[profession]** specializing in the **[industry]**. How can I **[discover/identify/detect]** my **[blind spots/hidden biases/unknown limitations]** as a **[leader/guide/manager]**? What are the **[tools/techniques/strategies]** that can **[help/assist/guide]** me **[uncover/reveal/find]** **[areas/zones/aspects]** where I might have **[biases/limitations/restrictions]** that I'm **[not aware of/unconscious of/ignorant of]**? How can I **[work/collaborate/coordinate]** with my **[team/mentors/coaches]** to **[gain/obtain/acquire]** **[insights/knowledge/understanding]** into these **[hidden/obscured/unseen]** areas, and what **[steps/measures/actions]** should I **[take/implement/follow]** to **[address/resolve/rectify]** them? What are some **[examples/instances/cases]** of **[common/widespread/typical]** **[leadership/management/guidance]** blind spots, and how have **[other/successful/experienced]** leaders **[successfully/efficiently/effectively]** **[overcome/addressed/solved]** them? Respond separately to each question. Suggest fresh approaches and inventive ideas. Let's take this one step at a time. Write using a **[type]** tone and **[style]** writing style.

PROMPT No 251

Growth - Criteria - Evaluation

To guide an individual in identifying and evaluating the various criteria that will influence their selection of areas for personal or professional growth. This includes understanding one's current strengths and weaknesses, values, career or life objectives, opportunities available, and other relevant factors

Act as a **Personal Development Coach** specializing in the **environmental assessment industry**. What are the distinct criteria or factors I **should weigh and assess to pinpoint the domains where I could focus on growing either professionally or personally**? How do these aspects interplay with **my long-term objectives, values, and current capabilities**? Respond to each question separately. Explore unconventional solutions and alternative perspectives. Let's dissect this carefully. Write using an **insightful** tone and **informative** writing style.

Act as a **[profession]** specializing in the **[industry]**. What are the distinct criteria or factors I **[contextual challenge/opportunity]**? How do these aspects interplay with **[contextual challenge/opportunity]**? Respond to each question separately. Explore unconventional solutions and alternative perspectives. Let's dissect this carefully. Write using a **[type]** tone and **[style]** writing style.

PROMPT No 252

Motivation - Reflection - Positivity

To guide leaders in developing effective strategies for motivating their team to engage in reflective practices, focusing on what went well in a recent project or task. By doing so, the team can identify best practices, enhance their skills, and maintain a positive work environment.

Act as a **Business Performance Coach** specializing in **intrinsic motivation and positive reinforcement** for the **logistics industry**. Could you provide a **comprehensive guide** on how to **incentivize my team to reflect on what worked well in a recent project**? I'd like to understand **techniques for encouraging self-reflection and group discussions that focus on the positives, thereby fostering an environment of continuous improvement and team morale**. Please include both individual and group activities, along with appropriate metrics to gauge success. Give a complete and in-depth interpretation. Let's consider each facet of this topic. Write using a **formal** tone and **concise** writing style.

Act as a **[profession]** specializing in **[focus area]** for the **[industry]**. Could you provide a **[comprehensive guide/detailed framework]** on how to **[specific challenge or opportunity]**? I'd like to understand **[sub-goals/specific techniques]**. Please include **[specific elements/additional requirements]**. Give a complete and in-depth interpretation. Let's consider each facet of this topic. Write using a formal tone and concise writing style.

PROMPT No 253

Problem-solving - Communication - Safety

To equip leaders with effective methodologies and conversational strategies for identifying the underlying issues in team performance without alienating or threatening team members. This ensures that root causes are accurately identified and that the team is engaged in the process.

Act as a **Conflict Resolution Specialist** specializing in **non-threatening communication** for the **insurance industry**. Could you provide a **step-by-step guide on how to identify the root-cause of a problem in recent situations or projects, without making my team feel threatened or defensive**? This is essential for **achieving long-term solutions and fostering a psychologically safe workspace**. Your guide should be comprehensive, covering **specific techniques for identifying root causes, and how to navigate potential defensive reactions**. Provide an unbounded and meticulous examination. Let's take this one step at a time. Write using a reassuring tone and a diplomatic writing style.

Act as a **[profession]** specializing in **[focus area]** for the **[industry]**. Could you provide a **[specific challenge or opportunity]**? This is essential for **[desired outcome]**. Your guide should be comprehensive, covering **[techniques/tactics]**. Provide an unbounded and meticulous examination. Let's take this one step at a time. Write using a **[type]** tone and **[style]** writing style.

PROMPT No 254

Development - Environment - Learning

To gain specific strategies and actions that can be implemented by an organization to effectively establish and maintain an environment that consistently fosters and facilitates ongoing learning and professional development for its individuals.

Prompt

As a **Learning and Development Consultant**, adopting an **encouraging and supportive tone**, how can an organization effectively establish and maintain an environment that consistently fosters and facilitates **ongoing learning and professional development** for its individuals? Please provide specific strategies and actions that can be implemented to achieve this goal.

Formula

As a **[profession]**, adopting a **[tone of voice]**, how can an organization effectively establish and maintain an environment that consistently fosters and facilitates **[desired outcome]** for its individuals? Please provide specific strategies and actions that can be implemented to achieve this goal.

PROMPT No 255

Tags

Identification - Application - Performance

Goal

To gain specific strategies or methods that can be utilized to efficiently and accurately identify and access learning opportunities that are directly applicable to enhancing the performance and work of a team.

Prompt

As a **Learning and Development Specialist**, adopting an **informative and supportive tone**, could you provide specific strategies or methods that **I** can utilize to efficiently and accurately identify and access learning opportunities that are directly applicable to enhancing the performance and work of **my sales team**?

Formula

As a **[profession]**, adopting a **[tone of voice]**, could you provide specific strategies or methods that **[I/Name/Role]** can utilize to efficiently and accurately identify and access learning opportunities that are directly applicable to **[desired outcome]** of [my/their] **[team/group/department]**?

PROMPT No 256

Tags

Leadership - Wellbeing - Collaboration

Goal

To identify critical variables that can help a leader ensure the wellbeing and happiness of their team in a business environment. These variables might include factors related to work-life balance, job satisfaction, mental and physical health, collaboration, and motivation. Understanding and monitoring these variables can enable the team leader to create a supportive and fulfilling workplace.

Prompt

Act as a **Leadership Development Consultant** specializing in the **banking industry**. What are the **essential** variables that I should **observe** when **working** with my **team** to **ensure** their

well-being? How can I **recognize** signs of **stress**, and what **tools** can I implement to promote a **healthy** work **environment**? What are some **real-world examples** that have been **effective** in **maintaining team** well-being? Respond separately to each question. Explore unconventional solutions and alternative perspectives. Let's take this one step at a time. Write using an **empathetic** tone and **constructive** writing style.

Act as a **[profession]** specializing in the **[industry]**. What are the **[essential/critical/key]** variables that I should **[observe/monitor/consider]** when **[working/engaging/collaborating]** with my **[team/staff/employees]** to **[ensure/maintain/guarantee]** their **[wellbeing/happiness/satisfaction]**? How can I **[recognize/identify/detect]** **[signs/symptoms/indicators]** of **[stress/burnout/dissatisfaction]**, and what **[tools/strategies/methods]** can I **[implement/employ/use]** to **[promote/support/create]** a **[healthy/motivating/positive]** work **[environment/atmosphere/culture]**? What are some **[real-world/practical/actual]** **[examples/cases/instances]** **[best practices/guidelines/standards]** that have been **[effective/successful/proven]** in **[maintaining/supporting/upholding]** **[team/group/staff]** wellbeing? Respond separately to each question. Explore unconventional solutions and alternative perspectives. Let's take this one step at a time. Write using a **[type]** tone and **[style]** writing style.

PROMPT No 257

Reflection - ProjectManagement - Self-awareness

To enable leaders to harness the momentum and positive energy generated by a successful project to foster self-awareness and continuous growth within their teams. By approaching this conversation effectively, leaders can help team members identify strengths, lessons learned, and areas for future development.

Act as a **Professional Development Coach** specializing in **team dynamics** for the **project management industry**. Could you provide a **structured outline on how I should conduct a reflective conversation with my team about what they could learn from a recently successful project**? This is essential for **encouraging self-awareness, reinforcing strengths, and identifying areas for further growth**. Your outline should include **key talking points, appropriate timing for such discussions, and tips for encouraging an open and honest dialogue**. Offer a meticulous and expansive response. Let's tackle this in a phased manner. Write using an **encouraging** tone and an **action-oriented** writing style.

Act as a **[profession]** specializing in **[topic/specialization]** for the **[industry]**. Could you provide a **[contextual challenge/opportunity]**? This is essential for **[desired outcome]**. Your outline should include **[method/strategy/approach]**. Offer a meticulous and expansive response. Let's tackle this in a phased manner. Write using a **[type]** tone and **[style]** writing style.

PROMPT No 258

LearningCulture - Innovation - Insurance

To empower organizational leaders in establishing and nurturing a culture of continuous learning within their teams and broader company. This aims to enhance individual skill sets, foster innovation, and ultimately contribute to the long-term success of the organization.

Act as an **Organizational Development Expert** specializing in **corporate culture transformation** for the **insurance industry**. Could you provide a **comprehensive strategy for creating a culture of continuous learning within my team and the larger company**? This is crucial for **not only keeping up with industry trends but also for fostering innovation and enhancing employee satisfaction**. Your advice should include **goal-setting, skills assessment, knowledge sharing, and formal training programs**. Excavate untapped resources and unconventional tactics. Let's arrange the elements in a logical order. Write using an **insightful** tone and a **future-focused** writing style.

Act as a **[profession]** specializing in **[topic/specialization]** for the **[industry]**. Could you provide a **[contextual challenge/opportunity]**? This is crucial for **[desired outcome]**. Your advice should include **[tactics/methods/approaches]**. Excavate untapped resources and unconventional tactics. Let's arrange the elements in a logical order. Write using a **[type]** tone and **[style]** writing style.

PROMPT No 259

Diplomacy - Self-Awareness - Improvement

To guide leaders in effectively approaching sensitive conversations with their teams about missed opportunities in performance that team members may not be aware of. This will enable the identification of blind spots and pave the way for constructive feedback and improvement. The ultimate goal is to elevate team performance while preserving a positive and trusting team dynamic.

Act as an **Expert in Conflict Resolution and Team Dynamics** specializing in **the field of professional development** for the **renewable energy industry**. Could you provide me with a **comprehensive outline for how to initiate and guide a conversation with my team about missed opportunities in their performance, which they may not be aware of**? This is essential for **fostering self-awareness, opening avenues for improvement, and ensuring long-term success**. Your outline should include **crucial talking points, recommendations on timing and setting, and strategies**. Highlight imaginative thoughts and avant-garde solutions. Let's think about this step by step. Write using a **diplomatic** tone and a **detail-oriented** writing style.

Act as a **[profession]** specializing in **[topic/specialization]** in the **[industry]**. Could you provide me with a **[contextual challenge/opportunity]**? This is essential for **[desired outcome]**. Your outline should include **[parameters/methods/strategies]**. Highlight imaginative thoughts and avant-garde solutions. Let's think about this step by step. Write using a **[type]** tone and **[style]** writing style.

PROMPT No 260

PositiveCulture -Productivity - KnowledgeTransfer

To provide organizational leaders with a well-rounded approach for transferring positive working experiences from a successful team to the broader company. This strategy aims to multiply the benefits of effective practices, thus improving the work culture, increasing productivity, and boosting overall job satisfaction.

Act as a **Corporate Culture Transformation Specialist** specializing in **positive work environments** for the **banking industry**. Could you provide a **detailed framework for how I can successfully transfer the positive working experiences within my team to the rest of the company**? This is key for **fostering a healthy organizational culture and replicating successful work habits on a larger scale**. Your guidance should include key aspects like knowledge dissemination, inter-departmental collaboration, and feedback loops. Examine overlooked possibilities and imaginative routes. Let's articulate each point for thorough understanding. Write using an **enthusiastic** tone and a **practical, actionable** writing style.

Act as a **[profession]** specializing in **[specialization/topic]** for the **[industry]**. Could you provide a **[specific challenge or opportunity]?** This is key for **[desired outcome]**. Your guidance should include **[tactics/methods/strategies]**. Examine overlooked possibilities and imaginative routes. Let's articulate each point for thorough understanding. Write using a **[type]** tone and **[style]** writing style.

PROMPT No 261

CriticalReview - Solutions - ActionableInsights

To create an open and psychologically safe environment for the team to critically examine and discuss the least beneficial aspects of their work. The objective is to collectively identify these aspects, explore their root causes, and brainstorm actionable solutions, all while avoiding blame or discouragement.

Act as an **Organizational Behavior Expert** specializing in **critical review and feedback systems** for the **health care industry**. Could you provide **a well-rounded guide** on how **to initiate and facilitate a team discussion about the least beneficial aspects of their work?** I am particularly interested in **strategies that promote openness and critical thinking, as well as techniques for turning identified issues into actionable insights**. The guide should be divided into **stages: preparation, execution, and follow-up**. Deliver an all-inclusive and extensive output. Let's systematically explore each facet.
Write using a **constructive** tone and a **solutions-focused** writing style.

Act as a **[profession]** specializing in **[expertise/specialization]** for the **[industry]**. Could you provide a **[comprehensive type of resource/tool]** on how to **[specific objective]?** I am particularly interested in **[specific methods/techniques/goals]**. The guide should be divided into **[specific stages/sections]**. Deliver an all-inclusive and extensive output. Let's systematically explore each facet. Propose a comprehensive and elaborate response. Let's carefully evaluate each aspect. Write using a **[type]** tone and **[style]** writing style.

PROMPT No 262

TalentDevelopment - Alignment - Interests

To understand how to identify and assess the areas or topics that team members are eager to learn about, ensuring that they are congruent with the organization's mission, values, and strategic objectives.

Act as a **Talent Development Specialist** specializing in the **banking industry**. Could you provide **a comprehensive and elaborate depiction of how I can ascertain the subjects or fields my team is keen to explore and learn abou**t? Furthermore, how can I **align these interests with the company's priorities, values, and strategic direction**? Include methodologies for surveying interests, evaluating relevance, and creating a symbiotic learning plan that benefits both the team members and the organization. Let's analyze this piece by piece. Write using an **inspirational** tone and **creative** writing style.

Act as a **[profession]** specializing in the **[industry]**. Could you provide **[contextual challenge/opportunity]?** Furthermore, how can **I [contextual challenge/opportunity]**? Include methodologies for surveying interests, evaluating relevance, and creating a symbiotic learning plan that benefits both the team members and the organization. Let's analyze this piece by piece. Write using a **[type]** tone and **[style]** writing style.

PROMPT No 263

Facilitation - Reflection - Assessment

Goal

To receive a comprehensive and detailed plan of action to effectively facilitate a team reflection process, ensuring that the process is thorough and productive, and assessing the impact of both failures and successes on the individual responsibilities of team members, as well as their overall work.

Prompt

As a **Leadership Development Facilitator**, I would like to receive a comprehensive and detailed plan of action to effectively facilitate a team reflection process. The aim is to ensure that the process is thorough and productive. It is crucial to assess the impact of both failures and successes on the individual responsibilities of team members, as well as their overall work. Please provide a specific plan that can be implemented in a constructive and professional manner.

Formula

As a **[profession]**, I would like to receive a comprehensive and detailed plan of action to effectively facilitate a **[contextual challenge/opportunity]**. The aim is to ensure that the process is thorough and productive. It is crucial to **[desired outcome]** of **[team/group/department]**, as well as their overall work. Please provide a specific plan that can be implemented in a **[tone of voice]** manner.

PROMPT No 264

PersonalGrowth - Effectiveness - Construction

Goal

To gain insights into identifying unexplored or unacknowledged areas in one's professional life that may require enhancement or development, leading to overall effectiveness and personal growth.

Prompt

Act as a **Personal Development Coach** specializing in the **construction sector**. Could you propose a comprehensive and elaborate depiction of the **techniques and frameworks I can employ to identify new areas in my professional life where I seek to enhance my effectiveness**? Share **distinctive guidance and unexplored options** that would help me **recognize hidden potential and unutilized strengths**. Let's dissect this carefully. Write using an inspirational tone and analytical writing style.

Formula

Act as a **[profession]** specializing in the **[industry]**. Could you propose a comprehensive and elaborate depiction of the **[contextual challenge/opportunity]**? Share **[specific insights or resources]** that would help **[desired outcome or transformation]**. Let's dissect this carefully. Write using a **[type]** tone and **[style]** writing style.

PROMPT No 265

ContinuousLearning - Self-awareness - LessonLearned

To foster a culture of continuous learning by creating an environment where team members can openly discuss and extract the most significant lessons from both recent successes and failures. The goal is to help the team understand the factors that contributed to the outcome, reinforce positive behaviors, and identify areas for improvement.

Act as a **Business Learning and Development Expert** specializing in **reflective practices** for the **investment banking industry**. Could you offer a **comprehensive guide** on how **to effectively lead a team discussion centered around the most significant lesson learned from a recent success or failure**? I am interested in **methods that encourage self-awareness, critical thinking, and collective wisdom**. Please include **segments on setting the agenda, question prompts, and follow-up activities to ensure ongoing learning**. Impart unconventional wisdom and under-the-radar tools. Let's go through this systematically. Write using an encouraging tone and a future-focused writing style.

Act as a **[profession]** specializing in **[specialization/expertise]** for the **[industry]**. Could you offer a **[type of resource/tool]** on how to **[specific task]**? I am interested in **[particular methods/techniques]**. Please include **[distinct elements of the discussion/stages/activities]**. Impart unconventional wisdom and under-the-radar tools. Let's go through this systematically. Write using a **[type]** tone and **[style]** writing style.

PROMPT No 266

Preparation - Conversation - Learning

To gain insights on practical strategies or steps to prepare for an effective conversation with the team about valuable lessons they've learned from challenging professional experiences, fostering a culture of shared learning and growth.

As an **Executive Coach**, adopting an **empathetic and encouraging tone**, could you outline the specific strategies or steps that I can take to ensure that I am fully prepared to engage in a meaningful and effective conversation with my team regarding the valuable lessons they have gained from a challenging experience in their professional lives? This is particularly pertinent in fostering a culture of shared learning and growth.

As a **[profession]**, adopting a **[tone of voice]**, could you outline the specific strategies or steps that **[team/group/department]** can take to ensure that I am fully prepared **[contextual challenge/opportunity]**? This is particularly pertinent in fostering **[desired outcome]**.

PROMPT No 267

Investigation - Failure - Improvement

To gain a detailed and specific plan of action to thoroughly investigate and analyze a recent failure with a team, with the goal of identifying and learning from any mistakes made, fostering a learning culture and continuous improvement.

Prompt

Given the challenge of **learning from a recent failure**, as a **Leadership Development Facilitator** and in a **constructive and professional tone**, could you provide a detailed and specific plan of action **I** can use to thoroughly investigate and analyze **this experience** with **my team**, with the goal of **identifying and learning from any mistakes made**?

Formula

Given the challenge of **[contextual challenge/opportunity]**, as a **[profession]** and in a **[tone of voice]**, could you provide a detailed and specific plan of action **[I/Name/Role]** can use to thoroughly investigate and analyze **[specific situation]** with **[my/their]** **[team/group/department]**, with the goal of [**desired outcome**]?

PROMPT No 268

Tags

Reflection - Sacrifices - Outcomes

Goal

To facilitate deep reflection and discussion within the team about instances where sacrifices led to better outcomes. The aim is to extract meaningful lessons and insights from these experiences that can help in future decision-making, foster a culture of understanding, and encourage a sense of unity and purpose within the team.

Prompt

Act as an **Executive Coach** specializing in **leadership psychology and team dynamics**. Could you create a **comprehensive guide** that helps my team **thoughtfully reflect on instances where they've made sacrifices that resulted in better outcomes**? I am particularly interested in **interactive activities, key questions for discussion, and psychological techniques that can foster a safe space for sharing and growth**. Explore unconventional recommendations and alternative perspectives. Please divide the guide into distinct sections and ensure that each recommendation is actionable. Let's sequentially address each section. Write using a **motivational** tone and a **solutions-oriented** writing style.

Formula

Act as a **[profession]** specializing in **[sub-discipline]**. Could you create a **[specific guide/task]** that helps my team **[specific challenge/opportunity]**? I am particularly interested in **[elements/methods/tactics]**. Explore unconventional recommendations and alternative perspectives. Please divide the guide into distinct sections and ensure that each recommendation is actionable. Let's sequentially address each section. Write using a **[tone]** and **[style]** writing style.

PROMPT No 269

Tags

Challenge - Motivation - Goals

Goal

To guide you to properly challenge your team members. This involves setting more ambitious and diverse goals without overwhelming them. It requires insight into motivation, individual and team capabilities, clear communication, and supportive leadership.

Act as a **Leadership Development Consultant** specializing in the **financial services industry**. How can I **appropriately challenge** my team to **achieve more, explore new areas, and strive for various goals**? What are the **techniques** I should **employ** to **ensure** that these challenges **are motivating and not demoralizing**? How can I **align** them with **individual strengths**? What are some **pitfalls** to **avoid**? Respond to each question separately. Explore unconventional solutions and alternative perspectives. Write using a constructive tone and engaging writing style.

Act as a **[profession]** specializing in the **[industry]**, how can I **[properly/adequately/appropriately]** **[challenge/encourage/motivate]** my team to **[achieve/accomplish/attain]** **[more/different/ambitious]** **[goals/targets/objectives]**? What are the **[techniques/methodologies/strategies]** I should **[employ/use/apply]** to **[ensure/make certain]** that these challenges are **[motivating/inspiring/encouraging]** and not **[demoralizing/discouraging/detrimental]**? How can I **[align/synchronize/coordinate]** them with **[individual strengths/organizational objectives/team dynamics]**? What are some **[pitfalls/mistakes/errors]** to **[avoid/steer clear of/dodge]**? Respond to each question separately. Explore unconventional solutions and alternative perspectives. Write using a **[type]** tone and **[style]** writing style.

PROMPT No 270

Authenticity - Communication   - Introspection

To foster authentic communication and self-awareness by guiding you in discussing what you've learned from a recent challenge. The objective is to ensure that your reflections are not only insightful but also sincere, which can help to cultivate trust and openness within your team while promoting personal growth.

Act as a **Communication Coach** with expertise in **leadership transparency**. Could you provide a **detailed guide** on how to **genuinely discuss what I have learned from facing a recent challenge**? I'm specifically looking for a **structured approach that includes a set of key questions I should consider, conversational techniques to maintain authenticity, and psychological tips to encourage introspection**. Segment this guide into clear steps and ensure all advice is actionable. Let's think about this step by step. Write using an **honest** tone and a **straightforward** writing style.

Act as a **[profession]** with expertise in **[specialized area]**. Could you provide a **[type of guide/resource]** on how to **[specific challenge/opportunity]**? I'm specifically looking for **[particular elements/techniques]**. Segment this guide into clear steps and ensure all advice is actionable. Let's think about this step by step. Write using a **[specified tone]** and **[writing style]**.

PROMPT No 271

Reflection - Improvement - Strategy

Goal

To gain insights on specific strategies or methods to encourage a team to reflect on a past situation where their actions could have been improved, fostering reflective learning and continuous improvement.

Prompt

Considering the importance of **reflective learning for continuous improvement**, as a **Leadership Coach** and in an **empathetic and respectful tone**, could you suggest specific strategies or methods **I** can implement with **my team** to **encourage them to reflect on a past situation where their actions could have been improved**?

Formula

Considering the importance of **[contextual challenge/opportunity]**, as a **[profession]** and in a **[tone of voice]**, could you suggest specific strategies or methods **[I/Name/Role]** can implement with **[my/their]** **[team/group/department]** to **[desired outcome]**?

PROMPT No 272

Tags

Learning - Reflection - Actionability

Goal

To create a constructive learning environment where team members can openly reflect on situations they wish they had handled differently, fostering personal and professional growth. The objective is to provide a framework that not only facilitates honest discussion but also leads to actionable insights for future improvement.

Prompt

Act as an **Organizational Learning Expert** specializing in **reflective practices**. Could you provide a **comprehensive guide** on how to **lead my team in learning from situations where they wish they had acted differently**? I'm particularly interested in **methods to encourage open dialogue, psychological techniques to reduce defensive behavior, and activities to promote reflection and learning**. Break down the guide into pre-session planning, during the session, and follow-up activities for sustained learning. Investigate unexpected avenues and creative pathways. Let's unpack this topic. Write using a **supportive** tone and an **insightful** writing style.

Formula

Act as a **[profession]** specializing in **[specialized area]**. Could you provide a **[guide/resources]** on how to **[specific challenge/opportunity]**? I'm particularly interested in **[particular elements/techniques]**. Break down the guide into pre-session planning, during the session, and follow-up activities for sustained learning. Investigate unexpected avenues and creative pathways. Let's unpack this topic. Write using a **[specified tone]** and **[writing style]**.

PROMPT No 273

Tags

Understanding - Motivation - Alignment

To gain insights on specific methods or strategies to acquire a deep understanding of the individual motivations and overall goals of team members, fostering alignment with company values and enhancing team performance.

Given the goal of **understanding individual motivations and overall goals**, as a **Talent Management Specialist** and in an **empathetic and respectful tone**, could you suggest specific methods or strategies **I** can use to acquire a deep understanding of **my team members**?

Given the goal of **[contextual challenge/opportunity]**, as a **[profession]** and in a **[tone of voice]**, could you suggest specific methods or strategies **[I/Name/Role]** can use to acquire a deep understanding of **[my/their] [team/group/department]**?

PROMPT No 274

Learning - Engagement - Team-building

To provide information on how to engage a team in discussions about impactful learning experiences at work. The aim is to foster a culture of shared learning and self-improvement, with an emphasis on adopting an encouraging and supportive tone.

As a **Personal Development Coach**, adopting an **encouraging and supportive tone**, could you outline the specific strategies or steps that I can employ to explore with **my team** the specific learning experiences **at work that have had a highly positive impact on their personal growth and development**? This is particularly relevant given the goal of **promoting a culture of shared learning and self-improvement**.

As a **[profession]**, adopting a **[tone of voice]**, could you outline the specific strategies or steps that I can employ to explore with **[my/their] [team/group/department]** the specific learning experiences **[contextual challenge/opportunity]**? This is particularly relevant given the goal of **[desired outcome]**.

PROMPT No 275

Leadership - Risk-Management - Reflection

To help leaders facilitate discussions or reflections where team members can identify and articulate instances where they successfully navigated challenges or took calculated risks that led to positive outcomes. This serves multiple purposes: validating the team's skills and decision-making, boosting morale, and distilling insights that can be applied in future challenges.

Act as a **Leadership and Risk Management Expert** for the **publishing industry**. Could you provide a **comprehensive guide** on how to **guide my team in articulating a situation where** they successfully managed a challenge, took a risk, and it paid off? I'd like to explore **a range of strategies that facilitate this conversation, including question prompts, possible activities, and ways to record and disseminate these success stories for future learning within the team and organization**. Develop a comprehensive and penetrating insight. Let's think about this step by step. Write using an **informative** tone and **factual** writing style.

Act as a **[profession]** specializing in the **[industry]**. Could you provide a **[comprehensive guide/detailed framework]** on how to **[specific challenge or objective]**? I would like to explore **[sub-goals/specific techniques]**. Develop a comprehensive and penetrating insight. Let's think about this step by step. Write using an informative tone and factual writing style.

LISTENING

PROMPT No 276

Project-Management - Strategy - Progress

To gain insights on specific strategies or methods to facilitate the progress of a project being undertaken by a team, enhancing project management and team performance.

In the context of **facilitating the progress of a project**, as a **Project Management Consultant** and in a **clear and concise tone**, could you suggest specific strategies or methods **I** can implement with **my team**?

In the context of **[contextual challenge/opportunity]**, as a **[profession]** and in a **[tone of voice]**, could you suggest specific strategies or methods **[I/Name/Role]** can implement with **[my/their] [team/group/department]**?

PROMPT No 277

Performance-Enhancement - Conversation - Improvement

To facilitate a constructive conversation among team members about missed opportunities stemming from subpar performance. The objective is to help the team identify what led to these missed opportunities and develop strategies for improvement, thereby contributing to both personal and team growth

Act as a **Performance Enhancement Expert** specializing in **learning from setbacks**. Could you provide **a detailed guide** on how to **initiate and lead conversations with my team about the opportunities they've missed due to not performing at their best**? I am particularly interested in **establishing a safe space for these discussions, using evidence-based methods to guide the conversation, and formulating actionable steps for avoiding similar issues in the future**. Divide the guide into sections addressing the preparation, execution, and follow-up of these conversations. Offer extraordinary advice and non-mainstream opinions. Let's unpack this topic. Write using a **respectful** tone and a **solution-oriented** writing style.

Formula

Act as a **[profession]** specializing in **[specialized area].** Could you provide a **[type of guide/resource]** on how to **[specific challenge/opportunity]?** I am particularly interested in **[particular elements/techniques].** Divide the guide into sections addressing the preparation, execution, and follow-up of these conversations. Offer extraordinary advice and non-mainstream opinions. Let's unpack this topic. Write using a **[specified tone]** and **[specified writing style].**

PROMPT No 278

Tags

Resilience - Discussion - Failure

Goal

To foster a culture of psychological safety and resilience by encouraging open conversations about failures and setbacks within the team. This allows team members to analyze, learn, and grow from these experiences without fear of judgment, while also building a sense of camaraderie and collective wisdom.

Prompt

Act as a **Leadership and Resilience Expert** for the **real estate industry**. Could you provide an **all-encompassing guide on how to effectively lead a discussion with my team about the failures we've all encountered on our journey to success**? I'm looking for a **well-rounded set of strategies that includes question prompts, activities, and psychological techniques to make the team comfortable in sharing their setbacks and learning from them**. Explore unconventional solutions and alternative perspectives. Let's partition the problem into smaller challenges. Write using a **respectful** tone and **considerate** writing style.

Formula

Act as a **[prof**ession] for the **[industry].** Could you provide an **[specific challenge or opportunity]?** I am interested in **[sub-goals or specific techniques].** I'm looking for a **[sub-goals/specific techniques]** to make the team comfortable in sharing their setbacks and learning from them. Explore unconventional solutions and alternative perspectives. Let's partition the problem into smaller challenges. Write using a **[type]** tone and **[style]** writing style.

PROMPT No 279

Tags

Communication - Obstacle-Identification - Team-Dynamics

Goal

To identify and overcome obstacles that may prevent you and your team from actively listening to or assisting others. This includes recognizing individual biases, systemic issues, or any other psychological and logistical hurdles that can impair effective communication and support within the team.

Prompt

Act as a **Communication and Team Dynamics Expert** specializing in **conflict resolution**. Could you provide a comprehensive guide on **identifying the obstacles that might prevent me and my team from listening to or helping others effectively**? I am particularly interested in

understanding both individual and collective hindrances. Provide a multi-dimensional strategy that encompasses **psychological aspects, workflow challenges, and potential external influences**. Let's categorize these obstacles into types and explore potential solutions for each. Write using a **constructive** tone and **solution-focused** writing style.

Act as a **[profession]** specializing in **[sub-discipline]**. Could you provide a comprehensive guide on **[specific challenge or opportunity]**? I'm particularly interested in **[sub-goals/areas of focus]**. Provide a multi-dimensional strategy that encompasses **[considerations/tactics]**. Let's categorize these obstacles into types and explore potential solutions for each. Write using a **[tone]** and **[style]** writing style.

PROMPT No 280

Problem-Solving - Bottleneck-Identification - Innovation

To enhance the understanding and skill set of identifying bottlenecks, challenges, or areas where a team might be stuck within a project or problem, and exploring strategies, methods, or tools to effectively overcome these challenges.

Act as a **Problem-Solving Specialist** specializing in the **technology industry**. Could you provide **an in-depth analysis of the techniques, strategies, and tools that I can employ to identify where my team is most stuck in a project or problem**? This is critical for **timely intervention and to facilitate the progress of ongoing projects**. Include both conventional wisdom and innovative approaches, considering various team dynamics, project complexity, and industries. Let's **dissect this carefully**. Write using an **instructive** tone and **analytical** writing style.

Act as a **[profession]** specializing in the **[industry]**. Could you provide **[contextual challenge/opportunity]**? This is critical for **[desired outcome]**. Include both conventional wisdom and innovative approaches, considering various team dynamics, project complexity, and industries. Let's **[approach]**. Write using a **[type]** tone and **[style]** writing style.

PROMPT No 281

Public-Speaking - Professional-Development - Confidence

To help you in enhancing your public speaking skills. It covers all aspects of public speaking, from understanding the audience to crafting the message, using effective body language, managing anxiety, utilizing visual aids, and continuous improvement through feedback and practice.

Act as a **Professional Development and Communication Coach** specializing in the **technology industry**. **Public speaking** is an **essential** skill for **leaders**. How can **I develop my** public speaking skills to **convey ideas** with **confidence**? Provide a **comprehensive** guide that includes **understanding** the **audience's needs, crafting compelling content, utilizing** storytelling, **body language**, **vocal variety**, **visual aids**, **handling questions**, **managing anxiety**, and **creating opportunities** for **feedback** and continuous practice. Include **actionable steps, tools, resources**, and **examples** of how these **strategies** can be **applied** in **various professional contexts**. Respond separately to each question. Provide exhaustive and all-encompassing responses. Let's break this down into manageable parts. Write using a **confident** tone and **assertive** writing style.

Act as a **[profession]** specializing in the **[industry]**. **[public speaking/presentation/communication]** is a **[crucial/essential/vital]** skill for **[professionals/leaders/managers/employees]**. How can **[individual/professional/speaker]** **[develop/refine/enhance]** **[my/their]** public speaking skills to **[convey/communicate/present]** **[ideas/messages/information]** with **[confidence/clarity/impact]**? Provide a **[comprehensive/thorough/complete]** guide that includes **[understanding/analyzing/assessing]** the **[audience's needs/preferences]**, **[crafting/composing/creating]** **[compelling/engaging/effective]** **[content/message/speech]**, **[utilizing/employing/leveraging]** **[storytelling/metaphors/anecdotes]**, **[body language/gestures/facial expressions]**, **[vocal variety/tone/pacing]**, **[visual aids/slides/props]**, **[handling/responding to/questions]**, **[managing/overcoming/reducing]** **[anxiety/nervousness/fear]**, and **[creating/seeking/finding]** **[opportunities/venues/channels]** for **[feedback/evaluation/practice]**. Include **[actionable steps/tips/strategies]**, **[tools/resources/guides]**, and **[examples/scenarios/case studies]** of how these **[strategies/techniques/methods]** can be **[applied/implemented/used]** in **[various/different/multiple]** **[professional contexts/settings/environments]**. Respond separately to each question. Provide exhaustive and all-encompassing responses. Let's break this down into manageable parts. Write using a **[type]** tone and **[style]** writing style.

PROMPT No 282

Resilience - Mindfulness - Strategy

To provide targeted strategies to a team so that they can prevent minor issues from affecting their performance and morale in the future. This inquiry focuses on resilience, proactive problem-solving, and mindfulness within a specific industry setting.

Act as a **Team Development Specialist** specializing in the **manufacturing industry**. What are some **comprehensive and effective strategies I can share with my team to enable them to avert the influence of minor issues on their future performance and morale**? These strategies should foster resilience, mindfulness, and proactive problem-solving. The goal is to **improve overall team robustness and emotional intelligence**. Let's dissect this carefully. Write using an **encouraging** tone and **engaging** writing style.

Act as a **[profession]** specializing in the **[industry]**. What are some **[contextual challenge/opportunity]?** These strategies should foster resilience, mindfulness, and proactive problem-solving. The goal is to **[goal]**. Let's dissect this carefully. Write using a **[type]** tone and **[style]** writing style.

PROMPT No 283

Self-Reflection - Growth - FinTech

To enable a culture of self-improvement and resilience by providing a structured approach for reflecting on one's own successes and failures. The objective is to leverage both positive and negative experiences for personal and professional growth, thereby fostering skills like self-awareness, emotional intelligence, and adaptability.

Act as a **Career Development Professinal** specializing in **self-reflection** for the **FinTech industry**. Could you provide a **comprehensive guide** on how to **effectively engage in a self-reflective practice that covers both successes and failures for the purpose of professional and personal growth**? I am particularly interested in **cognitive frameworks, journaling techniques, and actionable steps**. Please break down the **guide** into **stages** and provide **examples** for each stage. Suggest rare insights and underappreciated resources. Let's take this one step at a time. Write using an **informative** tone and **factual** writing style.

Act as a **[profession]** specializing in **[area of expertise]** for the **[industry]**. Could you provide a **[type of resource/action plan]** on how to **[specific task]**? I am particularly interested in **[particular methods/techniques]**. Please break down the **[process/guide]** into **[stages/sections]** and provide **[specific examples/scenarios]** for each. Suggest rare insights and underappreciated resources. Let's take this one step at a time. Write using a **[type]** tone and **[style]** writing style.

PROMPT No 284

Emotional-Intelligence - Relationship - Assessment

To enable leaders to effectively evaluate the influence of emotional states within their teams on the quality of relationships between supervisors and subordinates. This assessment aims to foster emotional intelligence, enhance communication, and improve organizational relationships, thereby contributing to a more productive and harmonious work environment.

Act as a **Business Psychologist** specializing in **Emotional Intelligence and Workplace Relationships** for the **Automotive Manufacturing industry**. Could you offer an **in-depth guide** on how to **assess the emotional states of my team and their impact on relationships with supervisors or subordinates**? I am particularly interested in **psychological assessments, qualitative interviews, and practical exercises that I can implement**. Please divide the **guide** into **logical segments for easy execution, and include real-world examples to illustrate key points**. Explore unconventional solutions and alternative perspectives. Let's sequentially address each element. Write using a **friendly** tone and **approachable** writing style.

Act as a **[profession]** specializing in **[area of expertise]** for the **[industry]**. Could you offer an **[all-encompassing guide/manual/resource]** on **[contextual challenge/opportunity]**? I am particularly interested in **[types of methods/approaches/tools]**. Please divide the **[guide/resource]** into **[stages/sections/steps]**. Explore unconventional solutions and alternative perspectives. Let's sequentially address each element. Write using a **[specified tone]** and **[specified style]**.

PROMPT No 285

Work-Environment - Empowerment - Assessment

To equip team leaders with comprehensive strategies for assessing the impact of the current work environment on their team's performance and well-being. This evaluation aims to identify factors that either empower or limit the team, enabling leaders to make data-driven adjustments to the work environment.

Act as an **Organizational Psychologist** specializing in **Workplace Environment and Team Dynamics** for **biotechnology industry**.

Could you provide an **exhaustive guide** on **how to assess whether the current work environment is either limiting or empowering my team**? I'm particularly interested in questionnaires, observational techniques, and real-time analytics that can give me a holistic view. Please divide the guide into manageable sections and include illustrative examples and case studies to clarify key points. Investigate unexpected avenues and creative pathways. Let's scrutinize this topic incrementally. Write using an analytical tone and systematic writing style.

Act as a **[profession]** specializing in **[expertise/topic]** for the **[industry]**. Could you provide an **[all-encompassing guide/manual/resource]** on **[contextual challenge/opportunity]**? I am particularly interested in **[types of methods/approaches/tools]**. Please divide the **[guide/resource]** into **[stages/sections/steps]**. Investigate unexpected avenues and creative pathways. Let's scrutinize this topic incrementally. Write using a **[type]** tone and **[style]** writing style.

PROMPT No 286

Operational - Efficiency - Barriers

To provide team leaders with a thorough framework for assessing the barriers or obstacles that prevent their team from acting on their priorities or ideas. This framework aims to uncover both internal and external factors hindering progress, allowing for tailored interventions to remove or mitigate these barriers and to help the team achieve their objectives effectively.

Act as a **Business Strategy Consultant** specializing in **operational efficiency** for the **healthcare services industry**. Could you provide an **all-encompassing guide** on the **assessment of what is hindering my team from taking action on their current priorities** or ideas? I'm interested in **specific diagnostic tools such as questionnaires, SWOT analyses, and real-time feedback mechanisms**. Please segment the **guide** into **clear sections covering identification, analysis, and solution implementation**. Reveal lesser-known practices and innovative techniques. Let's systematically explore each facet. Write using a **visionary** tone and **innovative** writing style.

Formula

Act as a **[profession]** specializing in **[topic/expertise]** for the **[industry]**. Could you provide an **[all-encompassing guide/manual/resource]** on **[contextual challenge/opportunity]?** I'm interested in **[types of methods/approaches/tools]**. Please segment the **[guide/resource]** into **[stages/sections/steps]**. Reveal lesser-known practices and innovative techniques. Let's systematically explore each facet. Write using a **[type]** tone and **[style]** writing style.

PROMPT No 287

Tags

Leadership - Transparency - Accountability

Goal

To enhance preparedness in having candid conversations with team members regarding their individual successes or failures and the implications of these outcomes on their roles, contributions to the team, and alignment with company goals. The ultimate objective is to foster transparency, encourage personal accountability, facilitate growth, and cultivate a shared understanding of performance standards and expectations.

Prompt

Act as a **Leadership Development Coach** specializing in the **food & beverage manufacturing**. Could you guide me through the process of **effectively preparing to have sincere conversations with my team about what their success or failure means, in terms of work and contribution to the team and company**? This involves **understanding individual perceptions, recognizing performance metrics, communicating expectations, and facilitating reflective dialogue**. Please provide a thorough framework, including **preparation strategies, communication techniques, emotional intelligence insights, and follow-up actions**. Produce a sweeping and meticulous response. Let's analyze this from multiple angles. Write using an **encouraging** tone and **insightful** writing style.

Formula

Act as a **[profession]** specializing in the **[industry]**. Could you guide me through the process of **[contextual challenge/opportunity]**? This involves **[desired outcome]**. Please provide a thorough framework, including **[specific components or methods]**. Produce a sweeping and meticulous response. Let's analyze this from multiple angles. Write using a **[type]** tone and **[style]** writing style.

PROMPT No 288

Tags

Mindset - Professionalism - Self-Reflection

Goal

To provide guidance to professionals and leaders seeking to evaluate their belief systems or mindsets and their effects on their professional careers. It aims to outline methods for analyzing whether these beliefs are helping or hindering progress, fostering or limiting growth, and aligning or conflicting with professional objectives and values. This process is integral for personal development, career progression, and leadership effectiveness.

Act as an **expert in Professional Development and Mindset Coaching** specializing in the Healthcare Services industry. In the dynamic world of business, an **individual's beliefs and mindsets** play a **crucial** role in **shaping behavior**. How can I critically **evaluate** if my **mindset** is **serving me well in my career**? Provide a **comprehensive** guide that includes **understanding one's values, assessing alignment with professional objectives, identifying limiting beliefs, leveraging feedback** from **peers, practicing self-reflection, utilizing assessments,** and **creating actionable plans** for **continuous growth**. Include **practical steps, examples,** and **resources** relevant to the **Healthcare Services industry.** Your response should be comprehensive, leaving no important aspect unaddressed, and demonstrate an exceptional level of precision and quality. Let's approach this methodically. Write using a **confident** tone and **assertive** writing style.

Act as a **[profession]** specializing in the **[industry].** In the dynamic world of business, **[beliefs/mindsets/attitudes]** play a **[crucial/important/vital] role** in **[shaping/determining/influencing] [behavior/decisions/performance].** How can a[n] **[individual/professional/leader]** critically **[evaluate/assess/analyze]** if **[my/their] [belief system/mindset/philosophy]** is **[serving/supporting/enabling] [me/them] [well/positively/effectively]** in **[my/their] [career/professional life/job]**? Provide a **[comprehensive/thorough/detailed]** guide that includes **[understanding/recognizing/identifying]** one's **[values/principles/goals],** [assessing/evaluating/examining] [alignment/congruence/fit] with **[professional objectives/career goals/organizational values], [identifying/spotting/uncovering] [limiting/restrictive/negative]** beliefs, **[leveraging/utilizing/seeking] [feedback/insights/opinions]** from **[peers/mentors/coaches], [practicing/engaging in/embracing] [self-reflection/mindfulness/self-awareness], [utilizing/employing/using] [assessments/tools/methods],** and **[creating/developing/formulating] [actionable plans/strategies/steps]** for **[continuous growth/ongoing alignment/personal development].** Include [practical steps/tips/advice], [examples/scenarios/experiences], [resources/guides/tools], and **[case studies/anecdotes/real-life situations]** relevant to the **[industry].** Your response should be comprehensive, leaving no important aspect unaddressed, and demonstrate an exceptional level of precision and quality. Let's approach this methodically. Write using a **[type]** tone and **[style]** writing style.

PROMPT No 289

Cognitive - Decision-Making - Fintech

To equip professionals with an exhaustive guide for evaluating the factors that influence their conscious or unconscious choice of mindset at work. This guide aims to promote a deeper understanding of how mindset affects performance, decision-making, and relationships, enabling individuals to deliberately cultivate a more productive and positive mental approach.

Act as a **Business Psychologist** specializing in **cognitive behavior** for the **FinTech industry.** Could you provide a **holistic guide** on **the key considerations for selecting consciously or**

unconsciously the mindset I assume at work? I am particularly interested in **cognitive frameworks, emotional triggers, and external environmental factors that could play a role**. Please divide the **guide** into **introspective exercises, empirical methodologies, and actionable takeaways**. Furnish exceptional counsel and offbeat perspectives. Let's think about this step by step. Write using an **informative** tone and **factual** writing style.

Act as a **[profession]** specializing in **[expertise/topic]** for the **[industry]**. Could you provide a **[comprehensive guide/manual/resource]** on **[contextual challenge/opportunity]**? I am particularly interested in **[types of methods/approaches/tools]**. Please divide the **[guide/resource]** into **[sections/stages/steps]**. Furnish exceptional counsel and offbeat perspectives. Let's think about this step by step. Write using a **[type]** tone and **[style]** writing style.

PROMPT No 290

Team-Dynamics - Awareness - Questioning

To create a well-rounded resource that equips leaders and managers with pointed questions aimed at facilitating team members' awareness of their operating mindsets. The objective is to encourage self-reflection, spark open discussions, and inspire shifts towards more constructive mindsets that enhance productivity and team dynamics.

Act as a **Business Psychologist** specializing in **Cognitive Dynamics in a Team Setting** for the Energy industry. Could you provide an **exhaustive list of questions** designed to **prompt my team members to become more aware of their operating mindsets**? I am especially interested in **questions that elicit insights into default thinking patterns, emotional triggers, and interpersonal dynamics**. Also, include guidance on when and how to ask these questions for maximal impact. Please divide the material into **three parts: initial assessment, ongoing development, and intervention scenarios**. Identify latent opportunities and avant-garde approaches. Let's consider each facet of this topic. Write using a supportive and insightful tone.

Act as a **[profession]** specializing in **[topic/expertise]** for the **[industry]**. Could you provide a **[comprehensive guide/list/resource]** designed to **[contextual challenge/opportunity]**? I am especially interested in **[areas of focus/types of methods]**. Please divide the **[guide/list/resource]** into **[sections/stages/steps]**. Identify latent opportunities and avant-garde approaches. Let's consider each facet of this topic. Write using a **[type]** tone and **[style]** writing style.

PROMPT No 291

Comfort - Productivity - Workplace

To understand the unique comfort preferences of each team member in order to create an inclusive and productive work environment. The focus will be on identifying the various factors, such as physical settings, work styles, communication preferences, and interpersonal dynamics, that contribute to each team member's comfort and productivity.

Act as a **workplace culture consultant** with a specialization in **employee well-being** for the **IT sector**. Could you guide me through **the process of setting up work conditions where each of my team members feels most comfortable**? Please include **the steps for identifying individual comfort preferences and integrating them into a cohesive workplace strategy**. Make sure to cover how **these conditions will be communicated, measured, and periodically reviewed**. Probe into nonconformist solutions and divergent viewpoints to continually adapt and refine our approach. Let's dissect this in a structured manner. Write using a personable tone and an instructive writing style.

Act as a **[profession]** with a specialization in **[area of expertise]** for the **[industry]**. Could you guide me through **[specific challenge/opportunity]**? Please include **[methods/techniques]**. Make sure to cover how **[key areas/topics]**. Probe into nonconformist solutions and divergent viewpoints to continually adapt and refine our approach. Let's dissect this in a structured manner. Write using a **[type]** tone and **[style]** writing style.

PROMPT No 292

Vulnerability - Well-being - Psychological-Safety

To equip team leaders, managers, and executives with the tools and strategies to identify conditions where their team feels most vulnerable at work. Understanding these aspects is crucial for optimizing team performance, mental health, and long-term job satisfaction.

Act as an **Organizational Well-being Specialist** specializing in **psychological safety and employee wellness** for the **retail industry**. Could you guide me through **the methods to discover what conditions make my team feel most vulnerable at work**? I'm also interested in creating a framework to improve overall well-being within my team. Please provide a **step-by-step guide** to improve the psychological landscape of my team. Suggest actionable strategies to address discovered vulnerabilities and improve the team's sense of safety and well-being. Explore unconventional solutions and alternative perspectives. Let's tackle this request comprehensively. Write using a **nurturing** tone and an **empathetic** writing style.

Act as a **[profession]** specializing in **[topic/specialization]** for the **[industry]**. Could you guide me through **[contextual challenge/opportunity]**? I'm also interested in creating a framework to improve overall well-being within my team. Please provide a **[step-by-step guide/questionnaires/tools/strategy]** to improve the psychological landscape of my team. Explore unconventional solutions and alternative perspectives. Let's tackle this request comprehensively. Write using a **[type]** tone and **[style]** writing style.

PROMPT No 293

Growth-Mindset - Resilience - Learning

To provide team leaders, managers, and executives with a multi-faceted toolkit for instigating a shift from a fixed to a growth mindset within their teams. This transformation is pivotal for fostering resilience, encouraging continuous learning, and ultimately driving high performance.

Prompt

Act as a **Mindset Transformation Consultant** specializing in **neuro-linguistic programming (NLP)** for the **e-commerce industry**. Could you delineate a comprehensive strategy to help me facilitate a shift from a fixed to a growth mindset within my team? I'd like insights into **the psychological principles that can be leveraged, effective messaging strategies, and daily practices that can induce this mindset shift**. Please provide **actionable steps** to induce this mindset shift. Additionally, outline potential pitfalls and how to avoid them. Let's dissect this systematically. Write using a **strategic** tone and an **analytical** writing style.

Formula

Act as a **[profession]** specializing in topic/specialization] for the **[industry]**. Could you delineate a comprehensive strategy to help me facilitate a shift from a fixed to a growth mindset within my team? I'd like insights into **[psychological principles, messaging strategies, daily practices]**. Please provide **[actionable steps/workshop ideas/team activities/KPIs]** to induce this mindset shift. Additionally, outline potential pitfalls and how to avoid them. Let's dissect this systematically. Write using a **[type]** tone and **[style]** writing style.

PROMPT No 294

Tags

Curiosity - Innovation - Exploration

Goal

To cultivate and sustain curiosity within a team, fostering a culture of continuous learning, innovative thinking, exploration, and creative problem-solving. The ultimate objective is to identify and implement strategies that encourage questioning, experimentation, and active engagement in order to enhance the team's adaptability, collaboration, and overall performance.

Prompt

Act as an **Organizational Culture Consultant** specializing in **creativity and innovation** for the **financial services industry**. Could you share **an extensive range of strategies to nurture curiosity within my team, encouraging members to seek new information, question existing processes, explore various perspectives, and engage in innovative thinking**? Please provide actionable methods that consider **diverse learning styles, organizational culture, team dynamics, and industry-specific needs**. Explore unconventional solutions and alternative perspectives. Let's explore this methodically and creatively. Write using an **inspiring** tone and **constructive** writing style.

Formula

Act as a **[profession]** specializing in the **[topic]** for the **[industry]**. Could you share **[contextual challenge/opportunity]**? Please provide actionable methods that consider **[desired outcome]**. Explore unconventional solutions and alternative perspectives. Let's explore this methodically and creatively. Write using a **[type]** tone and **[style]** writing style.

PROMPT No 295

Possibilities - Reflection - Engagement

To equip team leaders, managers, and executives with an exhaustive framework for fostering a culture of reflection and possibility within their teams. This framework aims to help team members explore the full range of opportunities and potentials in their current roles, thereby boosting engagement, satisfaction, and productivity.

Act as an **Organizational Development Consultant** specializing in **employee engagement** for the **SaaS industry**. Could you guide me through **a comprehensive method to help my team reflect on what's possible in their current roles**? Please offer specific methods and **conversation guides** to foster progress. Additionally, identify any **overlooked opportunities** that might be encountered. Explore unconventional solutions and alternative perspectives. Let's tackle this step by step. Write using an **in-depth** tone and a **structured** writing style.

Act as a **[profession]** specializing in **[topic/specialization]** for the **[industry]**. Could you guide me through **[contextual challenge/opportunity]**? Please offer specific methods and **[specific tools/exercises/conversation guides/tracking metrics]** to foster progress. Additionally, identify any **[overlooked opportunities/potential obstacles]**. Explore unconventional solutions and alternative perspectives. Let's tackle this step by step. Write using a **[type]** tone and **[style]** writing style.

PROMPT No 296

Communication - Leadership - Retention

To provide leaders with a comprehensive framework for initiating and managing sensitive conversations with their team members about potential dissatisfaction with their current roles or positions. The aim is to open channels of communication, collect honest feedback, and identify actionable solutions while maintaining a psychologically safe environment.

Act as an **Executive Coach** specializing in **Employee Engagement and Retention** for the **food & beverage manufacturing industry**. Could you provide a **detailed guide** on how to **skillfully initiate and handle a delicate conversation with my team regarding where they'd rather be if they had a choice, compared to their current positions**? I am interested in **techniques that encourage openness, reduce defensiveness, and elicit actionable insights**. Include **questions, prompts, potential answers to expect, and guidance on interpreting and acting on the feedback** and organize the guide into **sections such as setting the stage, initiating the conversation, and following through with actionable steps**. Explore unconventional solutions and alternative perspectives. Let's sequentially address each element. Write using a **professional** tone and **clear** writing style.

Act as a **[profession]** specializing in **[topic/expertise]** for the **[industry]**. Could you provide a **[comprehensive guide/list/resource]** on how to **[specific challenge/opportunity]**? I am interested in **[focus areas/techniques]**. Include **[question/prompts/examples]** and organize the guide into **[sections/stages]**. Explore unconventional solutions and alternative perspectives. Let's sequentially address each element. Write using a **[type]** tone and **[style]** writing style.

PROMPT No 297

Talent - Identification - Delegation

To guide team leaders in identifying the unique qualities, strengths, and talents of each team member. Doing so allows for more tailored coaching, better delegation, and a more cohesive, effective team environment.

Act as a **Talent Identification Specialist** specializing in the **technology sector**. Could you lay out **a comprehensive methodology for discovering what is unique about each of my software engineers**? This should include **assessment techniques, observation strategies, and conversation prompts** that can help me to pinpoint each team member's unique qualities. This is crucial for **effective team management and individual development**. Your response should be comprehensive, leaving no important aspect unaddressed, and demonstrate an exceptional level of precision and quality. Let's think about this step by step. Write using an **analytical** tone and an **instructive** writing style.

Act as a **[profession]** specializing in **[industry]**. Could you lay out **[contextual challenge/opportunity]?** This should include **[tools/techniques]**. This is crucial for **[desired objectives]**. Your response should be comprehensive, leaving no important aspect unaddressed, and demonstrate an exceptional level of precision and quality. Let's think about this step by step. Write using a **[type]** tone and **[style]** writing style.

PROMPT No 298

Self-Awareness - Performance - Optimization

To equip leaders with a holistic approach for facilitating conversations that help team members articulate their professional identities at their best. This involves not only defining what 'best' means but also recognizing the conditions that enable each individual to thrive. The goal is to boost self-awareness within the team, promote psychological safety, and identify ways to optimize work conditions for peak performance.

Act as a **Leadership Development Consultant** specializing in **Self-Awareness and Peak Performance** for the **automotive transportation industry**. Could you provide a **thorough guide** on how **to initiate and navigate conversations with my team members about who they are professionally when they're performing at their best**? I am particularly interested in **creating an environment that encourages self-exploration and open dialogue**. Include **specific question prompts, potential follow-up questions, and recommendations for facilitating a non-judgmental and constructive discussion** and organize the guide into **key sections such as preparation, engagement, and action steps**. Investigate unexpected avenues and creative pathways. Let's piece-by-piece analyze this matter. Write using a **constructive** tone and **solution-focused** writing style.

Act as a **[profession]** specializing in **[expertise/topic]** for the **[industry]**. Could you provide a **[comprehensive guide/list/resource]** on how to **[specific challenge/opportunity]**? I am particularly interested in **[focus areas/techniques]**. Include **[questions/prompts/examples]** and organize the guide into **[sections/stages]**. Investigate unexpected avenues and creative pathways. Let's piece-by-piece analyze this matter. Write using a **[type]** tone and **[style]** writing style.

PROMPT No 299

Empowerment - Responsibility - Decision-Making

To guide you to inspire your team to understand that choices and decisions they make regularly can significantly impact their results. The intention is to help them instill a sense of responsibility and empowerment within the team, enabling them to take charge of their own progress and outcomes.

Act as a **Performance Coach** specializing in the **telecommunications industry**. How can I **lead** my team to **recognize** that their **choices**, both big and small, **have direct effects** on the **results** they **obtain**? What **strategies** can I **employ** to **emphasize** the **importance** of **wise decision-making**? How can I **inspire** a **mindset** of **continual self-improvement**, **encouraging** them to **change choices** when **necessary** to **improve outcomes**? What are some common **misconceptions** that I may need to **address**? Respond to each question separately. Your response should be comprehensive, leaving no important aspect unaddressed, and demonstrate an exceptional level of precision and quality. Let's dissect this carefully. Write using a motivational tone and engaging writing style.

Act as a **[profession]** specializing in the **[industry]**. How can I **[guide/lead/teach]** my team to **[recognize/understand/realize]** that their **[choices/decisions/actions]** **[have direct effects/are consequential/influence]** on the **[results/outcomes/achievements]** they **[obtain/reach/secure]**? What **[strategies/techniques/methods]** can I **[employ/use/apply]** to **[emphasize/highlight/stress]** the **[importance/significance/value]** of **[wise/prudent/sound]** **[decision-making/choice-making/action-taking]**? How can I **[inspire/encourage/motivate]** a **[mindset/attitude/thinking]** of **[continual/constant/ongoing]** **[self-improvement/growth/development]**, **[encouraging/motivating/urging]** them to **[change/alter/modify]** **[choices/decisions/actions]** when **[necessary/needed/required]** to **[improve/enhance/boost]** **[outcomes/results/performance]**? What are some **[common/widespread/typical]** **[misconceptions/misunderstandings/barriers]** that I may need to **[address/resolve/tackle]**? Respond to each question separately. Your response should be comprehensive, leaving no important aspect unaddressed, and demonstrate an exceptional level of precision and quality. Let's dissect this carefully. Write using a **[type]** tone and **[style]** writing style.

Empathy - Career - Feedback

To obtain a comprehensive, methodical approach for leadership development in the technology sector, focusing on understanding team members' career aspirations. It seeks actionable strategies in conversation techniques, feedback mechanisms, assessment tools, and ongoing support, all delivered in an empathetic and engaging tone.

Act as a **Leadership Development Specialist** specializing in the **technology industry**. Could you guide me on how I can **effectively discover what my team members are actively pursuing in their professional careers**? Understanding **their professional goals, interests, and aspirations** is vital for **my team synergy, motivation, and alignment with our company's mission and vision**. Please provide a detailed and methodical approach, including **conversation techniques, feedback strategies, assessment tools, and a plan for ongoing support**. Let's dissect this carefully. Write using an **empathetic** tone and **engaging** writing style.

Act as a **[profession]** specializing in the **[industry]**. Could you guide me on how I can **[contextual challenge/opportunity]**? Understanding **[desired outcome]** is vital for **[specific team or organizational goals]**. Please provide a detailed and methodical approach, including **[specific techniques or tools]**. Let's dissect this carefully. Write using a **[type]** tone and **[style]** writing style.

Alignment - Goal-Setting - Entertainment

To equip leaders with a comprehensive toolkit for engaging their teams in thoughtful discussions about what they seek to gain from specific experiences or challenges. The aim is to enhance clarity, alignment, and purpose, thereby enabling both individual and collective growth. This will involve creating a space for self-reflection, articulation of personal and team goals, and identifying pathways to achieve those goals.

Act as an **Executive Coach** specializing in **Team Alignment and Goal-Setting** for the **entertainment industry**. Could you provide a **detailed guide** on how to **approach a conversation with my team regarding what they most want to gain from a specific experience or challenge**? I am interested in **methodologies that facilitate self-discovery and teamwork, including frameworks for goal-setting**. Include **question prompts, interactive exercises, and even digital tools that could assist in this process**. Organize the guide into **key components such as setting the stage, opening the discussion, diving deeper, and wrapping up with action plans**. Offer extraordinary advice and non-mainstream opinions. Let's think about this step by step. Write using a **dynamic** tone and **energetic** writing style.

Act as a **[profession]** specializing in **[topic/expertise]** for the **[industry]**. Could you provide a **[comprehensive guide/list/resource]** on how to **[specific challenge/opportunity]**? I am interested in **[focus areas/techniques]**. Include **[questions/prompts/examples]**. Organize the guide into **[sections/stages]**. Offer extraordinary advice and non-mainstream opinions. Let's think about this step by step. Write using a **[type]** tone and **[style]** writing style.

PROMPT No 302

Transparency - Role-Clarity - Objectives

To equip leaders with a comprehensive guide for conducting conversations with team members about their current objectives and roles within the team. The aim is to foster a culture of transparency, alignment, and engagement, encouraging team members to take ownership of their responsibilities and align their individual goals with the team's broader objectives.

Act as an **Executive Coach** specializing in **Role Clarity and Team Alignment** for the **real estate development industry**. Could you provide an **exhaustive guide** on how to **lead a conversation with my team to discuss their current objectives and their roles within the team**? I am particularly interested in **techniques that will make team members comfortable in opening up about their personal and professional goals**. Include a **variety of question prompts, interactive exercises, and perhaps even digital tools that can facilitate this discussion**. Divide the guide into **key phases such as preparation, the actual conversation, and post-discussion actions**. Present novel interpretations and visionary possibilities. Let's analyze this piece by piece. Write using a **reflective** tone and **thoughtful** writing style.

Act as a **[profession]** specializing in **[expertise/topic]** for the **[industry]**. Could you provide a **[comprehensive guide/methodology]** on how to **[contextual challenge/opportunity]**? I am particularly interested in **[specific techniques/areas of focus]**. Include **[question prompts/interactive exercises/digital tools]**. Divide the guide into **[specific phases/sections]**. Present novel interpretations and visionary possibilities. Let's analyze this piece by piece. Write using a **[type]** tone and **[style]** writing style.

PROMPT No 303

Purpose - Engagement - Mission

To provide leaders with a comprehensive strategy for facilitating discussions with team members about the underlying purpose served when striving to achieve company goals. These conversations aim to deepen team members' connection to their work by aligning individual values and motivations with the organizational mission, thereby enhancing engagement and performance.

Act as a **Transformational Leadership Coach** specializing in **Purpose-Driven Organizations** for the **investment banking industry**. Could you offer a **comprehensive guide** on how to **initiate and manage a conversation with my team concerning the deeper purpose they are serving when working towards company objectives? I'm particularly interested in **methods that help team members align their personal values with the corporate mission**. Include **varied question prompts, storytelling techniques, and, if applicable, software tools designed to map values to objectives**. Divide the guide into **segments such as the preparatory phase, conversation initiation, in-depth discussions, and post-conversation follow-up.** Examine overlooked possibilities and imaginative routes. Let's think about this step by step. Write using an engaging tone and interactive writing style.

Act as a **[profession]** specializing in **[specific area of focus]** for the **[industry]**. Could you offer a **[comprehensive guide/method]** on how to **[specific challenge/opportunity]**? I'm particularly interested in **[specific techniques/focus areas]**. Include **[interactive activities/questions/tools]**. Divide the guide into **[sections/phases/dialogue initiation/deep discussions]**. Examine overlooked possibilities and imaginative routes. Let's think about this step by step. Write using a **[type]** tone and **[style]** writing style.

PROMPT No 304

Leadership - Self-Management - Emotional-Intelligence

To equip leaders with the tools and strategies needed to foster an environment of self-observation among team members. This involves teaching methods that encourage employees to reflect on their performance, decisions, and interactions independently. The ultimate goal is to enhance self-awareness, leading to personal and professional development, as well as improved team dynamics and overall organizational performance.

Act as a **Leadership Coach** with a specialization in **Self-Management and Emotional Intelligence** for the **tech industry**, could you guide me through **cultivating self-observation skills within my team**? Please include **specific exercises or methodologies to promote self-reflection, questions that inspire critical self-examination, and tips for establishing a culture where self-observation is valued and implemented**. Make sure to cover how **these skills can be linked back to tangible outcomes like increased productivity or improved collaboration**. Unfold alternative perspectives and pioneering approaches to sustain this practice. Let's dissect this in a structured manner. Write using a **professional** tone and **clear** writing style.

Act as a **[profession]** with a specialization in **[area of expertise]** for the **[industry]**, could you guide me through **[specific challenge/opportunity]**? Please include **[methods/techniques]**. Make sure to cover how **[key areas/topics]**. Unfold alternative perspectives and pioneering approaches to sustain this practice. Let's dissect this in a structured manner. Write using a **[type]** tone and **[style]** writing style.

PROMPT No 305

Readiness - Team-Dynamics - Project-Management

To equip business leaders with insights and strategies to accurately gauge their team's readiness to take specific actions for progressing on projects. Understanding team readiness is crucial for optimizing resource allocation, setting realistic timelines, and ensuring the quality of project outcomes.

Act as a **Project Management Consultant** with a specialization in **team dynamics** for the **tech industry**, could you guide me through **assessing what actions my team is ready to take to move their projects forward**? Please include **frameworks for readiness assessment and techniques to elicit honest and constructive feedback**. Make sure to cover how **to evaluate both individual and collective readiness levels**. Unfold alternative perspectives and pioneering approaches to sustain this practice. Let's dissect this in a structured manner. Write using an **informative** tone and a **factual** writing style.

Act as a [**profession**] with a specialization in [**area of expertise**] for the [**industry**], could you guide me through [**specific challenge/opportunity**]? Please include [**methods/techniques**]. Make sure to cover how [**key areas/topics**]. Unfold alternative perspectives and pioneering approaches to sustain this practice. Let's dissect this in a structured manner. Write using a [**type**] tone and [**style**] writing style.

PROMPT No 306

Resilience - Coping - Oil-and-Gas

To provide strategies and techniques for individuals and teams to endure and overcome challenging periods at work. These difficult times may include heightened stress, project failures, interpersonal conflicts, organizational changes, or other work-related challenges. The focus is on resilience, coping mechanisms, support systems, positive thinking, and actionable steps to navigate through these difficulties.

Act as a **Resilience Coach** specializing in the Oil & Gas industry. During **challenging** periods at work, such as **meeting tight deadlines**, what are the **effective** strategies that **professionals** can **adopt**? How can **emotional intelligence** play a role in enduring these times? What **methodologies** can be **implemented** within a **team** to foster **resilience and adaptability**? Share **real-life examples** that **demonstrate** the **successful** application of these methodologies. Respond separately to each question. Explore unconventional solutions and alternative perspectives. Let's approach this methodically. Write using an **empathetic** tone and **constructive** writing style.

Act as a [**profession**] specializing in the [**industry**]. During [**challenging/difficult/stressful**] periods at work, such as [**list specific situations**], what are the [**effective/practical/proven**] strategies that [**professionals/individuals/teams**] can [**adopt/implement/employ**]? How can [**list qualities or approaches like mindfulness, teamwork**], play a role in [**enduring/overcoming/navigating**] these times? What [**tools/methodologies/systems**] can be [**implemented/utilized/applied**] within a [**team/group/organization**] to foster [**resilience/adaptability/positivity**]? Share [**real-life/actual/practical**] [**examples/case studies/scenarios**] that [**demonstrate/illustrate/showcase**] the [**successful/effective/proven**] application of these strategies. Respond separately to each question. Explore unconventional solutions and alternative perspectives. Let's approach this methodically. Write using a **[type]** tone and **[style]** writing style.

OPTIONS

<u>PROMPT No 307</u>

Proactive - Collaboration - Bankruptcy

To catalyze a proactive, collaborative, and innovative mindset among the team, enabling them to devise robust strategies and choices to navigate potential bankruptcy or economic crises, ensuring business continuity and resilience.

Act as a **Crisis Management Strategist** specializing in **Financial Resilience** within the **retail industry**. Could you guide me through **a structured approach to ignite my team's proactive thinking and collaborative effort in devising choices for navigating a potential bankruptcy or economic crisis**? Please include **brainstorming techniques, scenario planning, and financial analysis tools**. Make sure to cover how **to foster a conducive environment for open discussion and innovative thinking**. Delve into unconventional solutions and emerging best practices that could provide a fresh perspective on crisis management. Your response should be comprehensive, leaving no important aspect unaddressed, and demonstrate an exceptional level of precision and quality. Let's think about this step by step. Write using an **empowering** tone and a **detailed, instructional** writing style.

Act as a **[profession]** specializing in **[area of expertise]** within the **[industry]**. Could you guide me through **[specific challenge/opportunity]**? Please include **[methods/techniques]**. Make sure to cover how **[key areas/topics]**. Delve into unconventional solutions and emerging best practices that could provide a fresh perspective on crisis management. Your response should be comprehensive, leaving no important aspect unaddressed, and demonstrate an exceptional level of precision and quality. Let's think about this step by step. Write using a **[type]** tone and a **[style]** writing style.

<u>PROMPT No 308</u>

Decision-Making - Analysis - Strategy

To assist teams in critically evaluating and weighing the options available to them at work. This process will guide them in making informed decisions that align with their objectives and the overall mission of the company.

Act as a **Decision-Making Strategist** specializing in the **higher education industry**. Could you describe **an array of techniques that my team could consider to carefully analyze the pros and cons of the different options they currently have at their work**? This is essential in **facilitating better decisions that align with our strategic goals**.

Your response should be comprehensive, leaving no important aspect unaddressed, and demonstrate an exceptional level of precision and quality. Let's consider each facet of this topic. Write using an **informative** tone and **analytical** writing style.

Act as a **[profession]** specializing in **[industry]**. Could you describe **[contextual challenge/opportunity]?** This is essential in **[desired outcome]**. Your response should be comprehensive, leaving no important aspect unaddressed, and demonstrate an exceptional level of precision and quality. Let's consider each facet of this topic. Write using a **[type]** tone and **[style]** writing style.

PROMPT No 309

Resilience - Challenge-Management - Personal-Growth

To guide you in enhancing your ability to face challenges, whether in a business environment, leadership role, or personal growth journey. The focus is on providing strategies, methodologies, and psychological insights to understand, face, and overcome challenges, and to foster resilience, adaptability, and problem-solving capabilities.

Act as an expert **Business Resilience and Challenge Management Coach** specializing in the **higher education industry. Challenges** are **inevitable** in **any professional journey.** How can **I enhance my** ability to **face** and **overcome** challenges **effectively**? Provide a **comprehensive** guide that includes **identifying** the **nature** of challenges, understanding **professional strengths and weaknesses, setting realistic** goals, **adopting** a **positive** mindset, **using problem-solving techniques, seeking** support from **mentors, practicing resilience and adaptability, learning from** failures, and **creating a personalized challenge management plan.** Include **practical steps, exercises, real-life examples**, and **resources** relevant to **various professional settings.** Respond separately to each question. Ensure your responses are thorough, precise, and of the highest quality possible. Let's analyze this piece by piece. Write using a **strategic** tone and **forward-thinking** writing style.

Act as a **[profession]** specializing in the **[industry]**. **[challenges/difficulties/obstacles]** are **[inevitable/common/unavoidable]** in **[any/every] [professional journey/career/business]**. How can a[n] **[individual/professional/leader] [enhance/improve/develop] [my/their]** ability to **[face/confront/tackle]** and **[overcome/solve/navigate]** challenges **[effectively/efficiently/successfully]?** Provide a **[comprehensive/thorough/complete]** guide that includes **[identifying/recognizing/understanding]** the **[nature/type/essence]** of challenges, **[understanding/knowing/assessing] [professional/personal strengths and weaknesses/individual capabilities/one's abilities], [setting/establishing/creating] [realistic/achievable/practical]** goals, **[adopting/embracing/fostering]** a **[positive/proactive/constructive]** mindset, **[using/applying/employing] [problem-solving techniques/methods/strategies], [seeking/leveraging/gaining]** support from **[mentors/peers/colleagues], [practicing/cultivating/developing] [resilience/adaptability/flexibility], [learning from/analyzing/reflecting on]** failures, and **[creating/developing/making]** a **[personalized/customized/tailored] [challenge management plan/strategy for overcoming difficulties/approach to problem-solving].** Include **[practical steps/tips/hacks], [exercises/drills/practices], [real-life** examples/scenarios/stories], and [resources/tools/guides] relevant to [various/different/multiple] [professional settings/industries/roles]. Respond separately to each question. Ensure your responses are thorough, precise, and of the highest quality possible. Let's analyze this piece by piece. Write using a [type] tone and [style] writing style.

PROMPT No 310

Opportunities - Development - Learning

To equip leaders with a robust framework for identifying opportunities within problems that can serve as catalysts for their team's professional development, thereby fostering a culture of continuous learning and adaptability.

Act as a **Professional Development Coach** specializing in the **SaaS industry**. Could you **elucidate** the **strategies** for **identifying opportunities** within **problems** that **my** team could **leverage** for **further professional development**? Include **analytical tools, problem-solving methodologies, and team workshops that can be utilized**.

Let's systematically explore each facet. Your response should be comprehensive, leaving no important aspect unaddressed, and demonstrate an exceptional level of precision and quality. Write using an analytical tone and a prescriptive writing style.

Act as a [profession] specializing in the [industry]. Could you [elucidate/explain/guide] the [strategies/methodologies/approaches] for [identifying/spotting/uncovering] [opportunities/chances/potentials] within [problems/challenges/issues] that [my/our/the] team could [leverage/utilize/exploit] for [further/additional/ongoing] [professional/career] development? Include [analytical tools/problem-solving methodologies/team workshops]. Let's systematically explore each facet. Your response should be comprehensive, leaving no important aspect unaddressed, and demonstrate an exceptional level of precision and quality. Write using a [type] tone and [style] writing style.

PROMPT No 311

Decision-Making - Development - Strategy

To empower team leaders, managers, and executives with a holistic strategy for fostering a growth mindset within their teams. By re-framing challenges as learning opportunities, you can boost team morale, enhance problem-solving skills, and contribute to ongoing professional development.

Act as a **Leadership Coach** specializing in **growth mindset training** for the **manufacturing industry**. Could you guide me through a structured method to teach my team to approach problems as opportunities for learning? I want to understand how to **instill a growth mindset, encourage creative problem-solving, and promote collaborative learning**. Please provide a **best practices** that can be incorporated into our daily interactions and team meetings. Also, identify any potential obstacles and how we can mitigate them. Deliver a rigorous and thoroughgoing examination. Let's dissect this carefully. Write using an **enlightening** tone and an **analytical** writing style.

Act as a **[profession]** specializing in **[topic/specialization]** for the **[industry].** Could you guide me through **[contextual challenge/opportunity]**? I want to understand **[desired objective].** Please provide **[specific tools/best practices/actionable tips]** that can be integrated into our daily interactions and team meetings. Also, identify any potential obstacles and how we can mitigate them. Deliver a rigorous and thoroughgoing examination. Let's dissect this carefully. Write using a **[type]** tone and **[style]** writing style.

PROMPT No 312

Resilience - Challenge-Management - Personal-Growth

To identify and explore common blind spots and biases that leaders may possess and to present strategies for recognizing and overcoming them. This information will serve to enhance self-awareness, promote inclusive leadership, and foster a more effective decision-making process.

Act as a **Leadership Development Expert** specializing in **identifying and addressing biases within leadership roles** for the **consulting industry**. Could you explore **some common blind spots that are often persistent with leaders and present strategies to recognize and deal with those biases**? This includes **reflecting on personal tendencies and systematic biases in decision-making**. Provide both established insights and innovative perspectives to **aid in personal and professional growth**. Let's analyze this step by step. Write using an **insightful** tone and **reflective** writing style.

Act as a **[profession]** specializing in **[specific focus]** for the **[industry]**. Could you explore **[contextual challenge/opportunity]**? This includes **[additional specifications].** Provide both established insights and innovative perspectives to **[desired outcome]**. Let's analyze this **[approach]**. Write using a **[type]** tone and **[style]** writing style.

PROMPT No 313

Appreciation - Feedback - Listening

To provide leaders with a structured approach for effectively discussing the positive aspects of a work experience or project with their team. This aims to foster a culture of appreciation, constructive feedback, and continuous improvement.

Act as a **Leadership Communication Specialist** specializing in the **automotive industry**. Could you **outline** the **best practices** for discussing what **went right** in a **recent work experience or project** with **my** team? Include **frameworks for positive feedback, techniques for active listening, and methods for encouraging team dialogue**. Let's sequentially address each element. Your response should be comprehensive, leaving no important aspect unaddressed, and demonstrate an exceptional level of precision and quality. Write using a **constructive** tone and a **facilitative** writing style.

Act as a **[profession]** specializing in the **[industry].** Could you **[outline/describe/explain]** the **[best practices/guidelines/methodologies]** for discussing what **[went right/succeeded/excelled]** in a **[recent/past/current] [work experience/project/assignment]** with **[my/our/the]** team? Include **[frameworks/techniques/methods]** for **[positive feedback/active listening/team dialogue].** Let's sequentially address each element. Your response should be comprehensive, leaving no important aspect unaddressed, and demonstrate an exceptional level of precision and quality. Write using a **[type]** tone and **[style]** writing style.

PROMPT No 314

Innovation - Problem-Solving - Resilience

To equip team leaders with strategies, insights, and tools that will enable their teams to identify and explore new possibilities and creative solutions to address and improve challenging situations at work. The underlying objective is to foster a culture of adaptability, problem-solving, collaboration, and resilience within the team, facilitating growth and innovation.

Act as a **Solution-Oriented Coach** specializing in **team problem-solving and innovation** for the **Healthcare industry.** Could you guide me through the process of **helping my team to uncover new possibilities for addressing and enhancing difficult situations at work?** Include methodologies, techniques, and tools that **can be implemented in various scenarios, considering the team's dynamics, industry challenges, and organizational constraints.** Offer extraordinary advice and non-mainstream opinions. Let's dissect this methodically and creatively. Write using an **instructive** tone and **constructive** writing style.

Act as a **[profession]** specializing in **[topic]** for the **[industry].** Could you guide me through the process of **[contextual challenge/opportunity]?** Include methodologies, techniques, and tools that **[desired outcome].** Offer extraordinary advice and non-mainstream opinions. Let's **[approach].** Write using a **[type]** tone and **[style]** writing style.

PROMPT No 315

Stability - Individual-Preferences - Human-Resources

To gain insights on strategies to effectively initiate a discussion with team members regarding their individual preferences for either stability or challenge in their work environment, fostering a work environment that meets individual needs and enhances team satisfaction and performance.

Given the goal of **understanding individual preferences for stability or challenge in the work environment**, as a **Human Resources Consultant** and in a **diplomatic and**

professional tone, could you suggest strategies **I** can employ to effectively initiate a discussion with **my team members**?

Given the goal of **[contextual challenge/opportunity]**, as a **[profession]** and in a **[tone of voice]**, could you suggest strategies **[I/Name/Role]** can employ to effectively initiate a discussion with **[my/their] [team/group/department]**?

PROMPT No 316

Risk-Mitigation - Opportunity-Leverage - Analysis

To equip your team with the ability to discern the critical factors, both internal and external, that could significantly influence their projects or daily work. This includes understanding methodologies, tools, and strategic thinking to analyze the environment, stakeholders, risks, and opportunities, leading to informed decisions and successful outcomes.

Act as a **Project Management Expert** specializing in the **software development industry**. Could you guide me on how my team can **systematically identify the factors that may have the most substantial impact on their projects or work**? We are looking to **both mitigate risks and leverage opportunities, considering various aspects like market trends, stakeholder expectations, technological advancements, regulations, and internal dynamics**. Please provide a comprehensive response, including applicable frameworks, analytical tools, and best practices. Let's analyze this piece by piece. Write using an **informative** tone and **analytical** writing style.

Act as a **[profession]** specializing in the **[industry]**. Could you guide me on how my team can **[contextual challenge/opportunity]?** We are looking to **[desired outcome]**, considering various aspects like **[specific factors or conditions]**. Please provide a comprehensive response, including applicable frameworks, analytical tools, and best practices. Let's analyze this piece by piece. Write using a **[type]** tone and **[style]** writing style.

PROMPT No 317

Decision-making - Frameworks - Participation

To equip leaders with a comprehensive toolkit for effectively discussing various options with their team regarding specific decisions that need to be made at work. The aim is to facilitate informed decision-making, encourage team participation, and build consensus.

Act as a **Decision-Making Facilitator** specializing in the **retail industry**. Could you **provide** a **structured** approach for discussing **various** options that **appeal to my team** concerning a **specific** decision they need to **make** at work? Include **frameworks** for **decision analysis, techniques for eliciting team input, and methods for achieving consensus**. Let's systematically explore each facet. Explore unconventional solutions and alternative perspectives.

Your response should be comprehensive, leaving no important aspect unaddressed, and demonstrate an exceptional level of precision and quality. Write using a consultative tone and an advisory writing style.

Formula

Act as a **[profession]** specializing in the **[industry]**. Could you **[provide/outline/delineate]** a **[structured/applicable/effective]** approach for discussing **[various/multiple/different]** options that **[appeal to/resonate with]** **[my/our/the]** team concerning a **[specific/particular/targeted]** decision they need to **[make/arrive at/decide]** at work? Include **[frameworks/techniques/methods]** for **[decision analysis/team input/achieving consensus]**.

Let's systematically explore each facet. Explore unconventional solutions and alternative perspectives. Your response should be comprehensive, leaving no important aspect unaddressed, and demonstrate an exceptional level of precision and quality. Write using a **[type]** tone and **[style]** writing style.

PROMPT No 318

Tags

Organizational-Behavior - Empathy - Motivation

Goal

To enable team leaders and managers to understand the underlying factors and motivations that influence their team members' choices at work. This understanding will lead to more effective management, improved communication, and the ability to align team choices with organizational goals and values.

Prompt

Act as an **Organizational Behavior Specialist** specializing in the **retail industry**. Could you guide me through the process of identifying and understanding **the factors that have influenced my team members' choices at work**? This includes considering **individual motivations, environmental influences, organizational culture, and other underlying elements**. Gaining this understanding is crucial for **more targeted coaching, better decision-making, and fostering a culture of empathy and alignment**. Please provide a comprehensive and insightful approach, considering various **psychological theories, assessment tools, and practical strategies**. Let's analyze this piece by piece. Write using an **instructive** tone and **analytical** writing style.

Formula

Act as a **[profession]** specializing in the **[industry]**. Could you guide me through the process of identifying and understanding **[contextual challenge/opportunity]**? This includes considering **[specific factors or elements]**. Gaining this understanding is crucial for **[desired outcome]**. Please provide a comprehensive and insightful approach, considering various **[methods, theories, or tools]**. Let's analyze this piece by piece. Write using a **[type]** tone and **[style]** writing style.

PROMPT No 319

Tags

Reflecting - Effectiveness - Decision-making

Goal

To provide leaders with a robust methodology for reflecting on the effectiveness of their team's decision-making processes. The objective is to identify what has been working well, thereby enabling the team to replicate successful strategies and improve overall performance.

Act as a **Decision Analysis Expert** specializing in the **risk management industry**. Could you **elucidate** the o**ptimal** approach for reflecting on what has been **effective** for **my** team when making **choices**? Include **analytical frameworks, key performance indicators, and best practices for team retrospectives**. Let's systematically explore each facet. Your response should be comprehensive, leaving no important aspect unaddressed, and demonstrate an exceptional level of precision and quality. Write using a consultative tone and an advisory writing style.

Act as a **[profession]** specializing in the **[industry]**. Could you **[elucidate/explain/outline]** the **[optimal/best/most effective]** approach for reflecting on what has been **[effective/successful/working well]** for **[my/our/the]** team when making **[choices/decisions]**? Include **[analytical frameworks/key performance indicators/best practices]** for **[team retrospectives/decision analysis/feedback loops].** Let's systematically explore each facet. Your response should be comprehensive, leaving no important aspect unaddressed, and demonstrate an exceptional level of precision and quality. Write using a **[type]** tone and **[style]** writing style.

PROMPT No 320

Decision-Making - Transparency - Leadership

To develop a set of strategies, techniques, and frameworks for improving decision-making skills within a team. This involves understanding the dynamics of decision-making, factors influencing decisions, potential biases, the role of data, and collaborative decision-making processes. The focus is on practical solutions, case examples, training, and mentoring practices to build a cohesive and efficient decision-making process within the team.

Act as a **Decision-making Coach** specializing in the **Cybersecurity industry**. Decision-making is a **crucial** aspect of **professional** life that **influences** the **outcomes** of **projects** and the overall success of an organization. What are some **proven strategies** that can be used to **enhance** the decision-making skills of a **team**? How can **understanding cognitive biases** improve the **quality** of decisions? Additionally, how can **leadership** cultivate a culture of **transparent** decision-making? Share **examples** demonstrating the **successful** implementation of these strategies within the **Cybersecurity industry**. Respond separately to each question. Deliver all-inclusive and extensive responses. Let's take this one step at a time. Write using a formal tone and concise writing style.

Act as a **[profession]** specializing in the **[industry].** Decision-making is a **[critical/essential/vital]** aspect of **[professional/organizational/team]** life that **[influences/impacts/affects]** the **[outcomes/results/success]** of **[projects/endeavors/initiatives].** What are some **[proven/effective/practical]** **[strategies/techniques/models]** that can be used to **[enhance/improve/build]** the decision-making skills of a **[team/group/organization]**? How can **[list factors such as understanding cognitive biases, using collaborative tools]** improve the

[quality/efficiency/effectiveness] of decisions? Additionally, how can **[leadership/management/team members]** cultivate a culture of **[transparent/inclusive/responsible]** decision-making? Share **[examples/case studies/scenarios]** demonstrating the **[successful/efficient/proven]** implementation of these strategies within the **[industry]**. Respond separately to each question. Deliver all-inclusive and extensive responses. Let's take this one step at a time. Write using a **[type]** tone and **[style]** writing style.

PROMPT No 321

Leadership   Improvement Finance

To equip team leaders, managers, and executives with a robust methodology for effectively conversing with their team members about areas they wish to improve. By doing this, leadership can cultivate an environment of continuous growth and skill development, thereby boosting job satisfaction and performance.

Act as a **Professional Development Strategist** specializing in **individual growth and performance** for the **finance industry**. Could you guide me through **a detailed framework to effectively discuss areas of improvement with my team?** The goal is to **establish a culture of continuous growth and professional development**. Your approach should offer a step-by-step conversation guide, key questions, and follow-up mechanisms, all designed to inspire honesty and actionable insights. Let's dissect this topic methodically. Write using an **encouraging** tone and an **analytical** writing style.

Act as a **[profession]** specializing in **[topic/specialization]** for the **[industry]**. Could you guide me through **[contextual challenge/opportunity]?** The objective is to **[desired outcome]**. Your response should be comprehensive, covering all relevant aspects and displaying an exceptional level of precision and quality. Let's dissect this topic methodically. Write using a **[type]** tone and **[style]** writing style.

PERFORMANCE

PROMPT No 322

Adaptability - Growth - Accounting

To equip leaders with strategies and insights to encourage team members to step out of their comfort zones, highlighting the unforeseen benefits that can be achieved through this process. This will foster personal and professional growth, increase adaptability, and enhance creativity within the team.

Act as a **Leadership Development Specialist** specializing in **fostering growth and adaptability** for the **accounting industry**. Could you guide me through the process of **bringing to my team's attention the unforeseen benefits they could experience by stepping**

outside of their comfort zones? What are the **initial steps they can take to start this journey**? Respond separately to each question. Include both **conventional wisdom and innovative strategies in your responses**. Provide specific examples and actionable insights to motivate and inspire action. Let's examine this **methodically**. Write using an **encouraging** tone and a **motivational** writing style.

Act as a [profession] specializing in [specific focus] for the [industry]. Could you guide me through the process of [contextual challenge/opportunity]? What are the [specific requirements]? Respond separately to each question. Include both [additional specifications]. Provide [desired outcome]. Let's examine this [approach]. Write using a [type] tone and [style] writing style.

PROMPT No 323

Recognition - Team-Dynamics - Tech

To equip leaders with a comprehensive guide on how to initiate and facilitate impactful discussions around the professional advancements team members have gained through their involvement in team projects or group tasks. The ultimate aim is to foster an environment of recognition, self-awareness, and enthusiasm for continuous improvement.

As a **Career Development Specialist** with a focus on **team dynamics** for the **tech industry**, could you guide me through **the process of holding a discussion with my team to reflect on how their participation in team projects has contributed to their professional growth?** Please include **techniques for starting the conversation, types of questions to ask for in-depth reflection, and strategies to encourage an open exchange of ideas**. Ensure the guide covers **how to recognize individual and collective accomplishments and how to channel this recognition into future team and personal development goals**. Introduce innovative perspectives and emerging trends. Let's go through this methodically. Write using an informative tone and factual writing style.

As a [profession] with a focus on [topic] for the [industry], could you guide me through [contextual challenge/opportunity]? Please include [methods/techniques]. Ensure the guide covers [aspects/topics to be addressed]. Introduce innovative perspectives and emerging trends. Let's go through this methodically. Write using a [type] tone and [style] writing style.

PROMPT No 324

Underperformance - Methodologies - Advertising

To enable leaders to accurately identify the underlying factors contributing to their team's lack of performance in achieving annual goals, and equip them with actionable strategies for the initial steps to address these challenges. The ultimate aim is to foster enhanced understanding, collaboration, and performance within the team.

Act as an **Organizational Performance Consultant** specializing in **team dynamics and goal alignment** for the **advertising industry**. Could you elucidate the **methodologies to pinpoint the root cause of my team's underperformance in achieving their annual objectives**? What are the **first few crucial steps I should consider to initiate the improvement process**? Respond separately to each question. Include both **data-driven analysis techniques and human-centric approaches, considering various team dynamics, organizational cultures, and industries**. Provide **actionable insights and pragmatic guidance**. Let's dissect this **step by step**. Write using an **analytical** tone and a **solution-oriented** writing style.

Act as a **[profession]** specializing in **[specific focus]** for the **[industry]**. Could you elucidate the **[contextual challenge/opportunity]?** What are the **[specific requirements]?** Respond separately to each question. Include both **[additional specifications]**. Provide **[desired outcome]**. Let's dissect this **[approach].** Write using a **[type]** tone and **[style]** writing style.

PROMPT No 325

Self-Awareness - Performance - Coaching

To gain insights on effective techniques to increase a team's self-awareness regarding their optimal performance, fostering a high-performing and self-aware work environment.

In the context of **enhancing self-awareness for optimal performance**, as a **Performance Coach** and in an **encouraging and supportive tone**, could you outline some effective techniques I can adopt with **my team**?

In the context of **[contextual challenge/opportunity]**, as a **[profession]** and in a **[tone of voice]**, could you outline some effective techniques **[I/Name/Role]** can adopt with **[my/their] [team/group/department]**?

PROMPT No 326

Outcomes - Alignment - Clarity

To provide leaders with a step-by-step guide on how to initiate and carry out a meaningful discussion with their teams about defining the ideal outcomes of their work. The conversation is designed to encourage clarity, mutual understanding, and alignment with broader company objectives, thereby leading to enhanced job satisfaction and productivity.

As an **Executive Coach** with a specialization in **outcome-based team management** for the **healthcare sector**, could you guide me through **the process of conducting a conversation with my team to articulate what they consider the ideal outcome of their work to be?** Please include **tactics for initiating the conversation, specific questions that encourage vision setting, and strategies for harmonizing individual visions with organizational goals**. Ensure the guide covers **how to elicit both tangible and intangible outcomes, as well**

as ways to track and measure these outcomes for future assessment. Introduce novel approaches and emerging paradigms. Let's examine this in a structured manner. Write using an **authoritative** tone and **factual** writing style.

As a **[profession]** with specialization in **[focus area]** for the **[industry]**, could you guide me through **[contextual challenge/opportunity]**? Please include **[methods/techniques]**. Ensure the guide covers **[aspects/topics to be addressed]**. Introduce novel approaches and emerging paradigms. Let's examine this in a structured manner. Write using a **[type]** tone and **[style]** writing style.

PROMPT No 327

Mindset - Transformation - Support

To explore various strategies, techniques, and approaches that you can utilize to facilitate personal change and growth, leading to better results or performance in professional and personal aspects of life. This includes understanding your strengths and weaknesses, setting clear and achievable goals, embracing change, and utilizing support systems.

Act as a **Personal Growth Coach** specializing in the **biotechnology industry**. The path to **achieving desired** results **often** requires **personal change**. What are some **fundamental** mindset shifts that professionals must **consider** to **facilitate** personal change leading to **improved performance**? How can **embracing change** contribute to **lasting** transformation? Provide **step-by-step guidelines** showcasing how **I** can **implement** these mindset shifts. Offer unconventional tips and lesser-known insights. Let's take this one step at a time. Write using a motivational tone and inspiring writing style.

Act as a **[profession]** specializing in the **[industry]**. The path to **[achieving/accomplishing/attaining]** **[desired/better/optimal]** results **[often/usually/frequently]** requires **[personal change/adaptation/transformation]**. What are some **[fundamental/key/essential]** **[strategies/tools/mindset shifts]** that **[professionals/individuals/employees]** must **[consider/adopt/implement]** to **[facilitate/nurture/encourage]** personal change leading to **[improved/enhanced/increased]** **[results/performance/outcomes]**? How can **[list of factors such as understanding oneself, setting clear goals]**, contribute to **[lasting/enduring/sustainable]** transformation? Provide **[practical examples/guidelines/scenarios]** showcasing how **[individuals at various career stages/different backgrounds/unique situations]** can **[implement/apply/use]** these strategies. Offer unconventional tips and lesser-known insights. Let's take this one step at a time. Write with a **[supportive/encouraging/inspiring]** tone and an **[analytical/thoughtful/comprehensive]** writing style.

PROMPT No 328

Obstacles - Self-Improvement - Introspection

To assist individuals, particularly leaders and professionals, in identifying personal barriers that might be hindering their growth or ability to reach their full potential, and guide them through the initial steps they can take to overcome these obstacles. The ultimate aim is to promote self-awareness, personal development, and effective strategies for self-improvement.

Act as a **Personal Development Coach** specializing in **self-awareness and growth strategies** for the **professional services industry**. Could you elucidate the **techniques to recognize what might be obstructing me from realizing my fullest potential**? What are the **initial critical steps I can undertake to cope with these impediments**? Respond separately to each question. Include both **introspective methodologies and practical exercises, considering various personal dynamics, professional contexts, and life stages**. Provide **tailored insights and actionable advice**. Let's unravel this progressively. Write using a **compassionate** tone and an **inspiring** writing style.

Act as a **[profession]** specializing in **[specific focus]** for the **[industry]**. Could you elucidate the **[contextual challenge/opportunity]**? What are the **[specific requirements]**? Respond separately to each question. Include both **[additional specifications]**. Provide **[desired outcome]**. Let's unravel this progressively. Write using a **[type]** tone and **[style]** writing style.

PROMPT No 329

Evaluation - Performance-Management - Productivity

To provide leaders with a comprehensive framework for initiating nuanced conversations that allow them to assess team performance in a non-intrusive manner. The aim is to identify areas for improvement, be it in terms of efficiency or quality, without affecting team morale. The conversation should ideally lead to concrete action plans for improvement that align with organizational goals.

As an **Organizational Psychologist** with a specialization in **performance management** for the **manufacturing industry**, could you guide me through **the art of subtly evaluating my team's performance to uncover areas for improvement**? Please include **techniques for indirect observation, the types of questions that foster self-improvement without being confrontational, and ways to inspire the team to create actionable plans for bettering performance**. Make sure the guide covers **information on balancing the qualitative and quantitative aspects of performance**. Introduces innovative approaches to motivation and productivity. Let's consider each facet carefully. Write using a **diplomatic** tone and a **nuanced** writing style.

As a **[profession]** with a specialization in **[area/topic]** for the **[industry],** could you guide me through **[contextual challenge/opportunity]**? Please include **[methods/techniques]**. Make sure the guide covers **[aspects/topics to be addressed]**. Introduces innovative approaches to motivation and productivity. Let's consider each facet carefully. Write using a **[type]** tone and **[style]** writing style.

PROMPT No 330

Goal

To outline and explore various strategies, behaviors, practices, and attitudes that a leader or manager can adopt to foster and improve their relationship with their team. This includes the importance of effective communication, empathy, trust-building, providing constructive feedback, recognizing achievements, and promoting an inclusive culture. It aims to provide insights, guidelines, and actionable advice for leaders striving for a more harmonious and productive team environment.

Prompt

Act as a **Team Relationship Expert** specializing in the **consumer goods manufacturing industry**. Building and maintaining a **positive** relationship with your team is **foundational** to **achieving success and fostering a healthy work environment**. What are some **key behaviors** that **leaders** must **adopt** to **enhance** their relationships with **team members**? How does **effective communication** contribute to a **stronger** team **connection**? Share **practical steps** illustrating how these **steps** can be implemented within the **consumer goods manufacturing industry.** Respond separately to each question. Deliver an all-inclusive and extensive commentary. Write using a **friendly** tone and **approachable** writing style.

Formula

Act as a [profession] specializing in the [industry]. Building and maintaining a [positive/healthy/strong] relationship with your team is [foundational/critical/essential] to [achieving/attaining/reaching] [success/growth/harmony]. What are some [key/essential/important] [strategies/behaviors/techniques] that [leaders/managers/supervisors] must [adopt/implement/employ] to [enhance/improve/strengthen] their relationships with [team members/staff/colleagues]? How does [select a factor such as effective communication, empathy, regular feedback] contribute to a [stronger/more cohesive/better] team [connection/bond/relationship]? Share [practical steps/examples/scenarios] illustrating how these [principles/guidelines/concepts] can be [implemented/applied/put into practice] within the [industry]. Respond separately to each question. Deliver an all-inclusive and extensive commentary. Write using a [type] tone and [style] writing style.

PROMPT No 331

Tags

Goals - Prioritization - Repercussions

Goal

To assist leaders in identifying critical company goals that, if overlooked or not pursued, could have significant negative repercussions for the business. This includes evaluating the long-term vision, operational necessities, and the economic, social, and environmental impact of not pursuing certain goals.

Prompt

Act as a **business strategist** with a specialization i **enterprise risk management** for the **healthcare industry**. Could you guide me through **the methodology for identifying the goal that, if not pursued, would have the most substantial negative impact on my organization?** Please include a **SWOT analysis, prioritization matrix, and stakeholder input**. Make sure to cover how **this identified critical goal aligns with or deviates from the overall company strategy**. Navigate through unexplored realms and revolutionary paradigms to determine the business risk. Let's dissect this in a structured manner. Write using a **pragmatic** tone and a **scholarly** writing style.

Act as a **[profession]** with a specialization in **[area of expertise]** for the **[industry]**. Could you guide me through **[specific challenge/opportunity]**? Please include **[methods/techniques]**. Make sure to cover how **[key areas/topics]**. [Navigate through unexplored realms and revolutionary paradigms to determine the business risk. Let's dissect this in a structured manner. Write using a **[type]** tone and **[style]** writing style.

PROMPT No 332

Goal-Attainment - Modification - Performance

To gain insights on specific steps to accurately identify areas requiring improvement or modification, enhancing a team's ability to successfully attain their performance objectives.

In the context of **achieving performance objectives**, as a **Performance Coach** and in a **clear and concise tone**, could you outline the specific steps that can be taken to accurately identify the areas that require improvement or modification in order for **my team** to successfully attain their **goals**?

In the context of **[contextual challenge/opportunity]**, as a **[profession]** and in a **[tone of voice]**, could you outline the specific steps that can be taken to accurately identify the areas that require improvement or modification in order for **[I/Name/Role]'s [team/group/department]** to successfully attain their **[desired outcome]**?

PROMPT No 333

Benefits - Organizational-Psychology - Tech

To help team leaders, managers, and executives accurately identify the primary benefits their team members have derived from working at their company. This understanding will enable them to refine their leadership approach, improve team morale, and optimize talent retention strategies.

As an **professional coach** with a focus on **organizational psychology and team dynamics** for **the tech industry**. Could you guide me through a comprehensive method to **find out what my team members consider to be the most beneficial aspects of working in our organization**? This method should include **designing an evaluation framework, choosing the most appropriate tools for data collection (e.g., surveys, interviews, etc.), and analyzing the gathered information to derive actionable insights**. Make sure to address potential biases and ethical considerations, providing examples and templates for each stage of the process. Explore unconventional solutions and alternative perspectives. Let's take this one step at a time. Write using a **formal** tone and **concise** writing style.

Act as a **[profession]** with a focus on **[specific area of expertise]** for the **[industry]**. Could you guide me through a comprehensive method to **[specific task or objective]**? This method should include **[list of detailed components]**. Make sure to address potential biases and ethical considerations, providing examples and templates for each stage of the process. Explore unconventional solutions and alternative perspectives. Let's take this one step at a time. Write using a **[type]** tone and **[style]** writing style.

PROMPT No 334

Leadership - Strategies - Step-by-Step

To help individuals in leadership positions understand and implement a step-by-step process that will enhance their leadership capabilities, leading them to become outstanding leaders in their respective fields. The response will enable the individual to take actionable steps toward growth, encompassing self-awareness, tailored strategies, and alignment with industry-specific needs.

Act as a **Leadership Development Specialist** specializing in the **retail industry**. Could you outline **a comprehensive, step-by-step process for me to follow that will improve my performance as a leader, tailored to my unique challenges and industry requirements**? This is particularly vital in **becoming an outstanding leader in my field**. Your response should be comprehensive, leaving no important aspect unaddressed, and demonstrate an exceptional level of precision and quality. Let's **explore this systematically**. Write using an **encouraging** tone and **instructive** writing style.

Act as a **[profession]** specializing in **[industry]**. Could you outline **[contextual challenge/opportunity]?** This is particularly vital in **[desired outcome]**. Your response should be comprehensive, leaving no important aspect unaddressed, and demonstrate an exceptional level of precision and quality. Let's [approach]. Write using a **[type]** tone and **[style]** writing style.

PROMPT No 335

Achievement - Self-Reflection - Marketing

To guide you in initiating conversations with your team members regarding their proudest achievements, and how this self-reflection can lead to understanding their driving forces, aligning with organizational values, and guiding future behavior and professional growth.

Act as a **Career Development Specialist** specializing in the **marketing industry**. Could you help me understand **how to have meaningful conversations with my team members about what they are most proud of in their careers**? I would like to understand **how this self-reflection can influence their motivation, align them with our company's values, and guide their future decisions and behaviors**. Please provide step-by-step guidance, conversation frameworks, insightful questions, and methods for integrating these insights into our daily workflow and long-term development plans. Suggest fresh approaches and inventive strategies. Let's analyze this piece by piece. Write using an **encouraging** tone and **interactive** writing style.

Act as a **[profession]** specializing in the **[industry]**. Could you help me understand **[contextual challenge/opportunity]?** I would like to understand **[desired outcome]**. Please provide step-by-step guidance, conversation frameworks, insightful questions, and methods for integrating these insights into our daily workflow and long-term development plans. Suggest fresh approaches and inventive strategies. Let's analyze this piece by piece. Write using a **[type]** tone and **[style]** writing style.

PROMPT No 336

Tags

Leadership - Collaboration - OrganizationalCulture

Goal

To assist team leaders, managers, or individuals within a corporate context to identify and instill values that can guide a team toward realizing their potential, fostering collaboration, enhancing performance, and aligning with organizational goals. The ultimate aim is to provide actionable insights that can be customized to various team dynamics and organizational structures.

Prompt

Act as an **Organizational Culture Consultant** specializing in **value-driven team development** for the **broadcasting industry**. Could you delineate the **core values that could direct my team toward realizing their fullest potential**? This includes insights into **how these values can be embedded into daily practices, and how they can align with various organizational goals and industry norms**. Provide applicable examples, strategies, and overlooked opportunities, considering different team dynamics, organizational structures, and the **broadcasting industry**. Let's dissect this systematically. Write using an **analytical** tone and a **strategic** writing style.

Formula

Act as a **[profession]** specializing in **[specific focus]** for the **[industry]**. Could you delineate the **[contextual challenge/opportunity]?** This includes insights into **[specific requirements]**. Provide applicable examples, strategies, and overlooked opportunities, considering different team dynamics, organizational structures, and the **[industry].** Let's dissect this systematically. Write using a **[type]** tone and **[style]** writing style.

PREFERENCES

PROMPT No 337

Tags

Rapport - Creativity - Engagement

Goal

To equip leaders and managers with the understanding and tools necessary to discern what their team members are focusing on outside their primary responsibilities. This awareness can enhance communication, foster empathy, and leverage these interests to create a more engaging and innovative work environment.

Prompt

Act as a **Work-Life Balance Expert** specializing in the **software development industry**. Could you guide me through **the techniques and approaches to discover what my team members** are paying attention to besides their regular work? This includes **hobbies, side projects, passions, or other interests**. Recognizing these aspects is essential for **building rapport, encouraging creativity, and connecting these interests to organizational goals where possible**. Please provide a comprehensive and nuanced guide, including various strategies like **one-on-one conversations, interest surveys, team-building activities, and observation techniques**. Let's explore this systematically. Write using an **empathetic** tone and **engaging** writing style.

Act as a **[profession]** specializing in the **[industry]**. Could you guide me through **[contextual challenge/opportunity]**? This includes **[specific factors or elements]**. Recognizing these aspects is essential for **[desired outcome]**. Please provide a comprehensive and nuanced guide, including various strategies like **[methods or tools]**. Let's explore this **[approach]**. Write using a **[type]** tone and **[style]** writing style.

PROMPT No 338

CognitivePsychology - Behavioral - DecisionMaking

To help team leaders, managers, and executives understand the cognitive and emotional factors that influence what their team members choose to focus on in the workplace. By doing so, leaders can better allocate resources, tailor communication strategies, and improve productivity.

As an **organizational psychology coach** expert in **cognitive psychology and team dynamics** for the **publishing industry**. Could you provide me with a structured approach to **understand what influences my team's decision on what to pay attention to during work**? This should include **how to formulate targeted questions or observations, select appropriate tools for data collection such as behavioral analysis or surveys, and a method to synthesize and apply these insights in a meaningful way**. Also, please outline potential biases and ethical considerations to be aware of in this process. Explore unconventional solutions and alternative perspectives. Let's think about this step by step. Write using a **formal** tone and **concise** writing style.

Act as **[profession]** expert in **[specific area of expertise]** for the **[industry]**. Could you provide me with a structured approach to **[specific task or objective]**? This should include **[list of detailed components]**. Also, please outline **[potential challenges and limitations]** to be aware of in this process. Explore unconventional solutions and alternative perspectives. Let's think about this step by step. Write using a **[type]** tone and **[style]** writing style.

PROMPT No 339

Success - Resilience - Discussion

To equip you with effective communication strategies, frameworks, and insights to engage in meaningful discussions with your team about the concepts of success and failure, thereby fostering a growth mindset, resilience, collaboration, and alignment with organizational values and goals.

Act as a **Leadership Communication Expert** specializing in the **tech industry**. Could you guide me through **the process of discussing the meaning of success or failure with my team**? The aim here is to **build a shared understanding of these concepts, encourage a culture of learning from both successes and failures, and align these insights with our organizational values and goals**. Please provide various strategies, frameworks, scenarios, and potential outcomes, taking into account different personalities, team dynamics, and cultural aspects. Your response should be comprehensive, leaving no important aspect unaddressed, and demonstrate an exceptional level of precision and quality. Let's analyze this piece by piece. Write using an **engaging** tone and **analytical** writing style.

Act as a **[profession]** specializing in the **[industry]**. Could you guide me through **[contextual challenge/opportunity]**? The aim here is to **[explicit desired outcome]**. Please provide various strategies, frameworks, scenarios, and potential outcomes, taking into account different personalities, team dynamics, and cultural aspects. Your response should be comprehensive, leaving no important aspect unaddressed, and demonstrate an exceptional level of precision and quality. Let's analyze this piece by piece. Write using a **[type]** tone and **[style]** writing style.

PROMPT No 340

Trust-building - Mentorship - OpenDialogue

To equip business leaders and managers with the strategies, tools, and psychological insights needed to create a safe space for open, honest dialogue with their team members about the aspects they find both inspiring and uninspiring about the company.

Act as a **Communication and Trust-building Expert** specializing in **coaching and mentoring** for the **tech industry**. Could you guide me through **techniques for discussing with my team what they find the most inspiring and uninspiring about the company**? I aim to do this in a way that encourages openness without inducing feelings of threat or judgment. Provide a systematic approach, including how to set the environment, types of questions to ask, and strategies for ensuring confidentiality and psychological safety. Let's unpack this carefully. Share tailored guidance and personalized insights. Write using a **compassionate** tone and a **detailed** writing style.

Act as a **[profession]** specializing in **[topic]** for the **[industry]**. Could you guide me through **[contextual challenge/opportunity]**? I aim to facilitate this dialogue in a manner that encourages openness without causing fear or apprehension. Provide a systematic approach, including setting the environment, formulating questions, and ensuring confidentiality and psychological safety. Share tailored guidance and personalized insights. Let's unpack this carefully. Write using a **[Tone]** tone and a **[Style]** writing style.

PROMPT No 341

Prioritization - Facilitation - Reflection

To equip team leaders with the necessary skills and approaches to guide their teams through a thoughtful reflection process. The focus is on what actions or decisions they would prioritize if they knew they had limited time. This exercise aims to clarify priorities, streamline focus, and inspire meaningful action.

Act as a **Life Prioritization Coach** specializing in the **financial services industry**. Could you outline **a structured approach to help me prepare my team to reflect on what actions or decisions they would prioritize if they knew they had limited time left**? This should encompass **guided reflective exercises, pointed questions, and tips for facilitating an open and safe discussion**. This is crucial for **enhancing team focus, commitment, and overall productivity**. Uncover scarce wisdom and trailblazing ideas. Let's dissect each facet of this approach. Write using a **motivational** tone and a **detailed, step-by-step** writing style.

Act as a **[profession]** specializing in **[industry]**. Could you outline **[contextual challenge/opportunity]**? This should encompass **[approaches/techniques/tools]**. This is crucial fo**r [desired outcomes]**. Uncover scarce wisdom and trailblazing ideas. Let's dissect each facet of this approach. Write using a **[type]** tone and **[style]** writing style.

PRIORITIES

PROMPT No 342

Productivity - Diagnostics - Behavior Analysis

To obtain a holistic, actionable guide on methods for identifying actions or behaviors that need to be discontinued in order to enhance team productivity, with the aim of fostering a more efficient and effective work environment.

As an **Organizational Psychologist** in the **technology sector**, could you provide an exhaustive guide outlining the methods **my team** and **I** can employ to identify actions or behaviors we need to stop doing **to increase our productivity**? Please include **both diagnostic assessments and observational techniques**. Segment the guide into **distinct categories**, and substantiate each with **empirical data and scholarly references**. Explore unconventional approaches and diverse viewpoints. Let's scrutinize this topic incrementally. Write using an **analytical** tone and a **structured** writing style.

As a **[profession]** in the **[industry],** could you provide an exhaustive guide outlining the methods **[I/Name/Role]** and **[my/our/their]** **[team/group/department]** can employ to identify actions or behaviors we need to stop doing to **[desired outcome]**? Please include both **[diagnostic assessments/observational techniques]**. Segment the guide into **[distinct categories]**, and substantiate each with **[empirical data/scholarly references]**. Explore unconventional approaches and diverse viewpoints. Let's scrutinize this topic incrementally. Write using a **[type]** tone and **[style]** writing style.

PROMPT No 343

TimeManagement - Strategies - Priorities

To furnish business leaders, managers, and team members with a broad spectrum of strategies to manage multiple key priorities simultaneously. This includes traditional and innovative approaches, practical tools, and customized insights that can be implemented across various industries, organizational structures, and team dynamics.

Act as a **Time Management Specialist** specializing in **corporate productivity** for the **natural resources industry**. Could you provide **a comprehensive examination of various strategies, tools, and methodologies for managing multiple key priorities all at once**? This includes **a mix of time-tested techniques, novel approaches, potential pitfalls, and ways to integrate these strategies into daily workflow**. Provide **unique insights and overlooked opportunities**, considering various **industry norms, organizational hierarchies, and team sizes**. Let's dissect this progressively. Write using an **instructive** tone and **analytical** writing style.

Act as a **[profession]** specializing in **[specific focus]** for the **[industry]**. Could you provide **[contextual challenge/opportunity]?** This includes **[specific requirements]**. Provide **[desired outcome]**, considering various **[additional specifications]**. Let's dissect this progressively. Write using a **[type]** tone and **[style]** writing style.

PROMPT No 344

Self-Management - Autonomy - Independence

To provide team leaders, managers, and executives with an in-depth understanding of how team members can autonomously set priorities that align with both personal career objectives and organizational goals. This insight will empower leadership to facilitate environments where team members can take ownership of their roles, thereby fostering a culture of proactive responsibility and long-term success.

Act as a **Prioritization Expert** specializing in **self-management** for the **logistics industry**. Could you elucidate **the factors that my team members should consider when setting their priorities independently?** The aim is to **foster a culture where employees can proactively align their tasks and goals with the broader objectives of the organization**. Your guidance should include a set of criteria for prioritization, potential pitfalls to avoid, and methods for ongoing reassessment of priorities. Let's analyze this comprehensively. Write using an **instructive** tone and a **systematic** writing style.

Act as a **[profession]** specializing in **[industry]**. Could you elucidate **[contextual challenge/opportunity]?** The aim is to **[desired outcome]**. Your response should be comprehensive, covering every angle and demonstrating a high level of attention to detail. Let's analyze this comprehensively. Write using a **[type]** tone and **[style]** writing style.

PROMPT No 345

Goal-setting - Finance - Strategic Planning

To guide business leaders in strategically prioritizing their goals in a manner that aligns with the overall objectives of the organization, individual career aspirations, and team development needs. Prioritizing goals effectively is essential for maintaining focus, maximizing resources, and achieving sustainable results.

Act as a **Business Strategy Consultant** with a specialization in **goal-setting** for the **finance industry**, could you guide me through **the process of prioritizing my goals in relation to the others I have been working on**? Please include **frameworks like the Eisenhower Matrix, or Objectives and Key Results (OKRs) for setting priorities, and techniques for regular reassessment**. Make sure to cover how **to balance short-term objectives against long-term strategic aims**. Unfold alternative perspectives and pioneering approaches to sustain this practice. Let's dissect this in a structured manner. Write using an **insightful** tone and an **analytical** writing style.

Act as a **[profession]** with a specialization in **[area of expertise]** for the **[industry]**, could you guide me through **[specific challenge/opportunity]**? Please include **[methods/techniques]**. Make sure to cover how **[key areas/topics]**. Unfold alternative perspectives and pioneering approaches to sustain this practice. Let's dissect this in a structured manner. Write using a **[type]** tone and **[style]** writing style.

PROMPT No 346

PositiveCulture - Communication - Team-building

To equip leaders, managers, and executives with an in-depth framework to cultivate and sustain a positive work culture within their organizations. Implementing this framework will lead to higher employee morale, better team collaboration, and ultimately, enhanced organizational performance.

Act as an **Organizational Culture Specialist** specializing in the **cultivation of positive work environments** for the **automotive industry**. Could you provide a **multi-faceted plan to instill a culture of positivity within my organization**? Your plan should address **leadership behaviors, team-building activities, communication strategies, and metrics for evaluating the success of these initiatives**. Impart an all-encompassing and rigorous plan. Let's break down each component for better understanding. Write using a **strategic** tone and a **solution-oriented** writing style.

Act as a **[profession]** specializing in **[topic/specialization]** for the **[industry].** Could you provide **[contextual challenge/opportunity]?** The plan should address **[desired outcomes and considerations]**. Impart an all-encompassing and rigorous plan. Let's break down each component for better understanding. Write using a **[type]** tone and **[style]** writing style.

PROMPT No 347

Strategy - Decision-Making - Prioritization

To provide leaders, managers, and professionals with a robust set of strategies to identify and select key priorities to focus on. This encompasses the integration of various methodologies, decision-making frameworks, personal and organizational considerations, and balance between short-term and long-term goals.

Act as a **Strategic Planning Expert** specializing in **corporate decision-making** for the **asset management industry**. Could you provide **a multifaceted overview of the strategies, tools, and thought processes one should consider when selecting the key priorities to focus on?** This includes **an analysis of organizational goals, personal strengths, market trends, opportunity costs, and alignment with overall strategy**. Provide nuanced insights and actionable recommendations. Let's dissect this methodically. Write using an **analytical** tone and a **structured** writing style.

Act as a **[profession]** specializing in **[specific focus]**. Could you provide **[contextual challenge/opportunity]?** This includes **[specific requirements].** Provide nuanced insights and actionable recommendations. Let's dissect this methodically. Write using a **[type]** tone and **[style]** writing style.

PROMPT No 348

To gain insights on specific strategies or techniques to effectively determine the genuine wants and desires of team members, enhancing team management and satisfaction.

Team-Management - Empathy - Satisfaction

Given the importance of **understanding the genuine wants and desires of team members**, as an **Executive Coach** and in an **empathetic and open-minded tone**, could you suggest specific strategies or techniques I can utilize for **this purpose**?

Given the importance of **[contextual challenge/opportunity]**, as a **[profession]** and in a **[tone of voice]**, could you suggest specific strategies or techniques **[I/Name/Role]** can utilize for **[desired outcome]**?

PROMPT No 349

Tags

Communication - Success - Motivation

Goal

To establish techniques, strategies, and communication methods to engage team members in a meaningful conversation about what winning or progress means to them on a personal level. This includes understanding diverse perspectives on success, aligning individual goals with team objectives, and fostering a culture of shared values and motivation.

Prompt

Act as a **Leadership and Team Development Specialist** in the **renewable energy industry**. **Success** can be **subjective** and may vary among **individuals within a team**. How can a **leader** effectively **engage** with **team members** to understand what **winning** means to them **personally**? What are some **communication styles** that can be used to foster an **environment** where team members feel **comfortable** sharing their **personal definitions** of **success** and how they **align** with the **team's overall objectives**? Respond separately to each question. Explore unconventional solutions and alternative perspectives. Let's consider each aspect in detail. Write using a formal tone and concise writing style.

Formula

Act as a **[profession]** specializing in the **[industry]**. **[success/progress/winning]** can be **[subjective/unique/different]** and may vary among **[individuals/team members/employees]**. How can a **[leader/manager/supervisor]** effectively **[engage/communicate/connect]** with **[team members/colleagues/staff]** to understand what **[winning/making progress/achieving success]** means to them **[personally/individually/on a personal level]?** What are some **[strategies/communication styles/question techniques]** that can be used to foster an **[environment/culture/atmosphere]** where team members feel **[comfortable/safe/confident]** sharing their **[personal definitions/views/perceptions]** of **[success/progress/winning]** and how they **[align/integrate/fit]** with the **[team's overall objectives/company's mission/organizational goals]?** Respond separately to each question. Explore unconventional solutions and alternative perspectives. Let's consider each aspect in detail. Write using a **[type]** tone and **[style]** writing style.

PROMPT No 350

Tags

Well-being - Mental-Health - Productivity

Goal

To develop a deep, actionable understanding of how each team member's strengths manifest in their work and responsibilities, thereby enabling the leader to foster a workplace that amplifies these strengths for enhanced productivity and employee engagement.

Prompt

As a **team leader** specializing in **Human Resources** within the **finance industry**, provide an exhaustive and meticulous examination, incorporating innovative insights and inventive strategies, for consciously identifying observable indicators or patterns that signify how each team member's strengths manifest in **tasks such as data analysis, customer interactions, and project management**. Further, share detailed guidance on how to disseminate these insights to secure buy-in from stakeholders.

As a [profession] specializing in [area of expertise/focus] within the [industry], provide an exhaustive and meticulous examination, incorporating innovative insights and inventive strategies, for consciously identifying observable indicators or patterns that signify how each team member's strengths manifest in [specific tasks or responsibilities]. Further, share detailed guidance on how to disseminate these insights to secure buy-in from stakeholders.

PROMPT No 351

Learning - Development - Professionalism

To equip team leaders and managers with the insight and understanding to identify key indicators, milestones, or signposts within the learning process of their team members. This knowledge will help in recognizing progress, diagnosing challenges, and facilitating personalized support, thereby leading to more efficient learning and professional development within the team.

Act as a **Learning and Development Specialist** specializing in the **e-commerce industry**. Could you elucidate the **essential signposts or milestones that my team can recognize in their learning process**? This includes **identifying when they are grasping new concepts, struggling with particular subjects, reaching a plateau, or excelling in certain areas**. Recognizing these signposts is critical for **adapting our training programs, providing timely assistance, and celebrating achievements**. Please deliver an exhaustive guide that details various methods, best practices, and tools to **observe these indicators, both individually and collectively**. Let's explore this systematically. Write using an **informative** tone and **engaging** writing style.

Act as a **[profession]** specializing in the **[industry]**. Could you elucidate the **[contextual challenge/opportunity]**? This includes **[specific factors or elements]**. Recognizing these signposts is critical for **[desired outcome]**. Please deliver an exhaustive guide that details various methods, best practices, and tools to **[action or approach]**. Let's explore this systematically. Write using a **[type]** tone and **[style]** writing style.

PROMPT No 352

Recognition - Morale - Engagement

To provide business leaders with a detailed strategy for initiating and conducting conversations that meaningfully celebrate team successes. The objective is to enhance the team's motivation and morale, reinforce the importance of high-quality work, and improve overall team cohesion and performance.

Act as a **Leadership Coach** with a specialization in **Employee Engagement** for the **tech industry**, could you guide me through **how I can celebrate my team's successes in a meaningful manner that reinforces the importance of high-quality work?** Please include **methods for recognizing achievements, types of rewards that resonate, and communication strategies to make the team feel genuinely appreciated**. Make sure to cover how **the celebration can be leveraged to encourage further high-quality work**. Navigate through unexplored realms and revolutionary paradigms. Let's dissect this in a structured manner. Write using an **inspiring** tone and **engaging** writing style.

Act as a **[profession]** with a specialization in **[area of expertise]** for the **[industry]**, could you guide me through **[specific challenge/opportunity]**? Please include **[methods/techniques]**. Make sure to cover how **[key areas/topics]**. Navigate through unexplored realms and revolutionary paradigms. Let's dissect this in a structured manner. Write using a **[type]** tone and **[style]** writing style.

PROMPT No 353

Inspiration - Alignment - Potential

To guide you in facilitating conversations with your team about the possibilities and potential outcomes when members are performing at their best, thereby fostering motivation, alignment with goals, and collective achievement.

Act as a **Leadership Communication Specialist** specializing in the **financial services industry**. Could you provide me with **insights, strategies, and techniques on how I can be better prepared to have conversations with my team about the possibilities when they are performing at their best?** The ultimate goal is to **inspire them to reach their full potential, align with organizational values, and contribute positively to the team's success**. Share distinctive methods, role-playing scenarios, and communication tips, considering different team dynamics, performance levels, and individual aspirations. Let's dissect this carefully. Write using an **inspirational** tone and **engaging** writing style.

Act as a **[profession]** specializing in the **[industry]**. Could you provide me with **[contextual challenge/opportunity]**? The ultimate goal is to **[explicit desired outcome]**. Share distinctive methods, role-playing scenarios, and communication tips, considering different team dynamics, performance levels, and individual aspirations. Let's dissect this carefully. Write using a **[type]** tone and **[style]** writing style.

PROMPT No 354

Self-Assessment - Transformation - Leadership

To provide leaders with robust self-assessment methods that will allow them to gauge their growth and transformation in leadership roles since they began their current employment. This is not only for self-awareness but also for continuous improvement, aligned with both personal and organizational objectives.

Act as a **Leadership Transformation Analyst** specializing in the **information technology industry**. Could you provide an exhaustive methodology to help me assess how I have evolved as a leader since I started my current job? This should include multi-dimensional self-assessment techniques, tips for seeking external feedback, and a blueprint for capturing this information over time. This is imperative for understanding my leadership journey and for aligning it with the company's broader vision. Examine each part of this comprehensive approach. Write using a reflective tone and a systematic writing style.

Act as a **[profession]** specializing in **[industry]**. Could you provide **[contextual challenge/opportunity]**? This should include **[desired outcomes and considerations]**. This is imperative for **[broader organizational or personal goal].** Examine each part of this comprehensive approach. Write using a **[type]** tone and **[style]** writing style.

PROMPT No 355

Planning - Project-Management - Collaboration

To guide leaders, managers, or team leads in understanding, developing, and implementing an effective and actionable plan for their team's success in projects.

Act as an expert **Project Manager** with a focus on **team dynamics and success planning** for the **technology industry**. Could you outline a detailed roadmap for **setting up a team for success in their projects**? Include the **identification of goals, alignment with organizational objectives, collaboration strategies, roles and responsibilities, monitoring progress, and continuous improvement mechanisms**. Provide insights tailored to my role as **project leader**. Let's break down the process in a **systematic and sequential manner**. Write with **clarity**, providing **practical examples, and addressing potential pitfalls**.

Act as an expert **[profession]** with a focus on **[specific area of expertise]** for the **[industry]. Could you outline a detailed roadmap for [specific task or challenge]?** Include the **[list of detailed considerations]**. Provide insights tailored to my role as **[position/role]**. Let's break down the process in a **[structured manner]**. Write with **[specific writing tone and style]**, providing **[additional content details]**.

PROMPT No 356

Performance - Measurement - Team

To understand various comprehensive measures and systems that can be implemented to track the progress or performance of a team, with an emphasis on all-encompassing solutions that fit various organizational contexts.

Prompt

Act as a **Performance Coach** specializing in the **recruitment industry**. Could you delineate **the various measures or systems that I can implement to meticulously track the progress or performance of my team?** This is pivotal for **ensuring alignment with goals, identifying areas for improvement, and fostering a culture of continuous growth within the team**. Please provide an all-encompassing and comprehensive explanation with detailed actions to follow, covering different methodologies, tools, software, and best practices. Let's take this one step at a time. Write using a **confident** tone and **analytical** writing style.

Formula

Act as a **[profession]** specializing in the **[industry]**. Could you delineate **[contextual challenge/opportunity]?** This is pivotal for **[desired outcome]**. Please provide an all-encompassing and comprehensive explanation with detailed actions to follow, covering different methodologies, tools, software, and best practices. Let's take this one step at a time. Write using a **[type]** tone and **[style]** writing style.

PROMPT No 357

Tags

Reflection - Self-awareness - Goals

Goal

To help individuals or teams in reflecting on and assessing their feelings about their progress towards specific goals or targets, enhancing self-awareness and leading to informed future actions.

Prompt

As a **Performance Coach** specializing in the **risk management industry**. Could you guide me through the process of assessing **how I feel about my progress toward my goals or targets?** This is especially vital in **understanding my alignment with my objectives and identifying the areas where I need to focus or make adjustments**. Provide unique insights and overlooked opportunities in your response, ensuring it is comprehensive and demonstrates an exceptional level of precision and quality. Let's analyze this piece by piece. Write using an **instructive** tone and **engaging** writing style.

Formula

As a **[profession]** specializing in the **[industry]**. Could you guide me through the process of assessing **[contextual challenge/opportunity]?** This is especially vital in **[desired outcome]**. Provide unique insights and overlooked opportunities in your response, ensuring it is comprehensive and demonstrates an exceptional level of precision and quality. Let's analyze this piece by piece. Write using a **[type]** tone and **[style]** writing style.

PROMPT No 358

Tags

Satisfaction - Evaluation - Motivation

Goal

To understand and evaluate the level of satisfaction within a team regarding the pace of their progress in a specific industry, with the aim of identifying areas of alignment or discontent to enhance motivation, satisfaction, and performance.

Act as a **Team Development Specialist** specializing in the **e-commerce industry**. Could you guide me through **a detailed process to evaluate the level of satisfaction of my team regarding the pace of their progress**? This is particularly vital in recognizing areas of contentment or concern and devising strategies tailored to our industry. Please provide a meticulous and wide-ranging response, including methods, tools, or strategies unique to our sector. Let's think about this step by step. Write using an **analytical** tone and **constructive** writing style.

Act as a **[profession]** specializing in the **[industry]**. Could you guide me through **[contextual challenge/opportunity]**? This is particularly vital in **[desired outcome]**. Please provide a meticulous and wide-ranging response, including methods, tools, or strategies unique to our sector. Let's think about this step by step. Write using a **[type]** tone and **[style]** writing style.

PROMPT No 359

Development - Strategies - Engagement

To equip leaders with a holistic understanding of strategies that can keep both them and their team members engaged in continuous personal development. This will encompass practical steps, mental frameworks, and actionable plans tailored to fit a variety of roles and responsibilities within the team.

Act as a **Personal Development Specialist** specializing in the **renewable energy industry**. Could you **elucidate a detailed set of strategies for my team and me to maintain our trajectory toward personal development**? This is crucial for **our professional growth and for achieving the broader objectives of the organization**. Your outline should cover **both individual-level and team-level strategies, including best practices, tools, and timelines for development**. Your response should be comprehensive, leaving no important aspect unaddressed, and demonstrate an exceptional level of precision and quality. Let's think about this step by step. Write using an **engaging** tone and an **analytical** writing style.

Act as a **[profession]** specializing in **[industry]**. Could you **[contextual challenge/opportunity]**? This is crucial for **[desired outcome]**. Your outline should cover **[methods/strategies/best practices]**. Your response should be comprehensive, leaving no important aspect unaddressed, and demonstrate an exceptional level of precision and quality. Let's think about this step by step. Write using a **[type]** tone and **[style]** writing style.

PROMPT No 360

Motivation - OrganizationalBehavior - Stagnation

To empower leaders with actionable strategies, psychological insights, and communication methods for effectively motivating their teams, especially when facing a standstill or a decline in performance. These guidelines should assist in reinvigorating team morale, refocusing efforts, and generating a newfound sense of progress.

Prompt

Act as a **Motivational Strategist** specializing in **organizational behavior** for the **natural resources industry**. Could you provide a comprehensive guide on **how I can better motivate my team when we are encountering stagnation or lack of progress in our work?** This is vital for **re-energizing the team, improving productivity, and aligning with our overall company goals**. Your guidance should touch on **communication strategies, psychological tactics, and actionable steps**, while also highlighting what to avoid. Explore unconventional solutions and alternative perspectives. Let's take this one step at a time. Write using an encouraging tone and a pragmatic writing style.

Formula

Act as a **[profession]** specializing in **[topic/specialization]** for the **[industry]**. Could you offer a detailed guide on **[contextual challenge/opportunity]?** This is vital for **[desired outcome]**. Your guidance should touch on **[detailed parameters, including x, y, z]**, while also noting what to avoid. Explore unconventional solutions and alternative perspectives. Let's take this one step at a time. Write using a **[type]** tone and **[style]** writing style.

PURPOSE

PROMPT No 361

Tags

Self-awareness - Career Trajectory - Introspection

Goal

To aid in identifying recurring themes, patterns, or common threads in one's professional career, enabling deeper self-awareness and alignment with personal values and goals.

Prompt

Act as a **Career Development Coach** specializing in the **information technology industry**. Could you guide me through the process of identifying **the recurring theme or common thread that has been present throughout my professional career?** The ultimate goal is to **gain a profound understanding of my career trajectory, recognizing underlying patterns that can guide my future career decisions**. Share distinctive guidance, tools for introspection, and methods to connect my past and present roles, considering various career stages and transitions. Let's analyze this step by step. Write using an **insightful** tone and **reflective** writing style.

Formula

Act as a **[profession]** specializing in the **[industry]**. Could you guide me through the process of identifying **[contextual challenge/opportunity]?** The ultimate goal is to **[explicit desired outcome]**. Share distinctive guidance, tools for introspection, and methods to connect my past and present roles, considering various career stages and transitions. Let's analyze this step by step. Write using a **[type]** tone and **[style]** writing style.

PROMPT No 362

Tags

Goal

To enable business leaders to facilitate open conversations with their team members about their self-perception within the organizational context. This dialogue should aim to clarify how individuals see their roles and contributions and how these align with the overall mission and vision of the company.

Prompt

Act as a **Leadership Coach** with a specialization in **Self-Perception and Team Dynamics** for the **financial services industry**, could you guide me through **the process of exploring the vision that my team members have about themselves within the company and how to articulate it**? Please include **discussion frameworks, communication techniques, and sample questions to use**. Make sure to cover how **this self-awareness can be leveraged to enhance team cohesion and performance**. Discover rare insights and pioneering ideas. Let's dissect this in a structured manner. Write using a **conversational** tone and an **accessible** writing style.

Formula

Act as a **[profession]** with a specialization in **[area of expertise]** for the **[industry]**, could you guide me through **[specific challenge/opportunity]**? Please include **[methods/techniques]**. Make sure to cover how **[key areas/topics]**. Discover rare insights and pioneering ideas. Let's dissect this in a structured manner. Write using a **[type]** tone and **[style]** writing style.

PROMPT No 363

Tags

Consciousness - Alignment - Leadership

Goal

To gain specific steps and techniques that can be adopted to successfully improve a team's understanding and consciousness of their goals and objectives.

Prompt

As a **Leadership Development Consultant**, adopting an **encouraging and supportive tone**, could you provide specific steps and techniques that **I** can adopt to successfully improve **my team**'s understanding and consciousness of their **goals and objectives**? This is particularly relevant given the goal of **enhancing their alignment with the organization's mission and vision**.

Formula

As a **[profession]**, adopting a **[tone of voice]**, could you provide specific steps and techniques that **[I/Name/Role]** can adopt to successfully improve **[my/their]** **[team/group/department]**'s understanding and consciousness of their **[contextual challenge/opportunity]**? This is particularly relevant given the goal of **[desired outcome]**.

PROMPT No 364

Tags

Purpose - Conversation - Hospitality

Goal

To acquire a comprehensive, actionable guide on methods for approaching a conversation with colleagues to clarify what is essential to them about living in alignment with their purpose, with the aim of fostering individual well-being, team cohesion, and organizational alignment.

As a **Life Purpose Coach** in the **hospitality industry**, could you provide an exhaustive guide outlining the methods **I** can employ to approach a conversation with **colleagues** to clarify what is essential to them about living in alignment with their **purpose**? Please include **active listening techniques**. Structure your guidance into individual components, each backed by **statistical analysis**. Explore unconventional approaches and diverse viewpoints. Let's dissect this carefully. Write using an **analytical** tone and a **structured** writing style.

As a **[profession]** in the **[industry],** could you provide an exhaustive guide outlining the methods **[I/Name/Role]** can employ to approach a conversation with **[colleagues/team members]** to clarify what is essential to them about living in alignment with their **[purpose/values]**? Please include both **[conversation starters/active listening techniques]**. Structure your guidance into individual components, each backed by **[statistical analysis/peer-reviewed studies]**. Explore unconventional approaches and diverse viewpoints. Let's dissect this carefully. Write using a **[type]** tone and **[style]** writing style.

PROMPT No 365

Emotional - Articulation - Morale

To acquire a comprehensive, actionable guide on methods for exploring the emotional connection a team has with their purpose and assisting them in articulating it, with the aim of enhancing team morale, individual well-being, and organizational alignment.

As an **Emotional Intelligence Coach** in the **automotive industry**, could you provide an exhaustive guide outlining the methods **I** can employ to explore the emotional connection **my team** has with their **purpose** and assist them in describing it? Please include both **reflective exercises and group discussion techniques**. Break down your advice into specific sections, reinforcing each with **quantifiable metrics and scholarly literature**. Explore unconventional approaches and diverse viewpoints. Let's dissect this carefully. Write using a **balanced** tone and a **nuanced** writing style.

As a **[profession]** in the **[industry],** could you provide an exhaustive guide outlining the methods **[I/Name/Role]** can employ to explore the emotional connection **[my/our/their]** **[team/group/department]** has with their **[purpose/goals/values]** and assist them in describing it? Please include both **[reflective exercises/group discussion techniques]**. Break down your advice into specific sections, reinforcing each with **[quantifiable metrics/scholarly literature]**. Explore unconventional approaches and diverse viewpoints. Let's dissect this carefully. Write using a **[type]** tone and **[style]** writing style.

PROMPT No 366

To obtain a comprehensive, actionable framework that outlines methods for defining and articulating in simple but engaging terms what one aims to achieve in collaboration with their team. The objective is to enhance team alignment, improve communication, and foster a collaborative work environment.

As a **Communication Expert** in the **retail industry**, could you provide a **detailed toolkit** outlining **methods** to define in simple but engaging terms what **I** aim to achieve in collaboration with **my** team? Additionally, offer **actionable steps** for **immediate** implementation. Break down your insights into distinct modules, each supported by **evidence from reputable industry reports**. Investigate unexpected avenues and creative pathways. Let's **examine each dimension meticulously**. Write using a **captivating** tone and a **relatable** writing style.

As a **[profession]** in the **[industry]**, could you provide a **[comprehensive strategy/thorough toolkit/detailed blueprint]** detailing **[methods/techniques/approaches]** to define in simple but engaging terms what **[I/we/they]** aim to achieve in collaboration with **[my/our/their]** team? Additionally, offer **[actionable steps/initial measures/immediate tactics]** for **[immediate/short-term/long-term]** implementation. Break down your insights into distinct modules, each supported by **[evidence from/references from/data from]** **[reputable journals/credible research/authoritative publications/industry reports]**. Investigate unexpected avenues and creative pathways. Let's **[examine each dimension meticulously/dissect this carefully]**. Write using a **[captivating/inspiring/motivating]** tone and a **[relatable/engaging/innovative]** writing style.

PROMPT No 367

Goal-setting - Articulation - Clarity

To equip leaders with a structured methodology for articulating goals or objectives in a manner that is clear, actionable, and aligned with organizational priorities. The aim is to enhance clarity, foster team alignment, and facilitate the effective execution of strategies.

Act as a **Strategic Planning Expert** specializing in the **manufacturing industry**. Could you **delineate** the **best** approach for **clearly** stating the goal I **aim** to **accomplish**? Include **frameworks** for **goal-setting**, **linguistic techniques** for **clarity**, and strategies for **ensuring** alignment with **broader organizational** objectives. Let's sequentially address each element. Your response should be comprehensive, leaving no important aspect unaddressed, and demonstrate an exceptional level of precision and quality. Write using a prescriptive tone and an instructional writing style.

Act as a **[profession]** specializing in the **[industry]**. Could you **[delineate/elucidate/outline]** the **[best/optimal/most effective]** approach for **[clearly/precisely/unambiguously]** stating the **[goal/objective/target]** I **[aim/seek/intend]** to **[accomplish/achieve/realize]?** Include **[frameworks/techniques/methodologies]** for **[goal-setting/clarity/alignment]**, [linguistic techniques/communication strategies for **[ensuring/maintaining]** alignment with **[broader/wider/organizational]** objectives] for **[clarity/precision]**, and strategies. Let's sequentially address each element. Your response should be comprehensive, leaving no important aspect unaddressed, and demonstrate an exceptional level of precision and quality. Write using a **[type]** tone and **[style]** writing style.

PROMPT No 368

Tags

Metrics - Criteria - Quantitative

Goal

To provide leaders with a robust framework for identifying and measuring the criteria or indicators that signify the successful achievement of their intentions or objectives. The focus is on creating actionable, quantifiable metrics that align with both individual and organizational goals.

Prompt

Act as a **Performance Metrics Analyst** specializing in the **finance industry**. Could you **delineate** the **criteria** that will **signify** the **achievement** of my **intention in a strategic project**? Include **both qualitative and quantitative metrics, and discuss how these align with broader organizational KPIs**. Let's sequentially address each element. Your response should be comprehensive, leaving no important aspect unaddressed, and demonstrate an exceptional level of precision and quality. Write using an **analytical** tone and a **data-driven** writing style.

Formula

Act as a **[profession]** specializing in the **[industry]**. Could you **[delineate/elucidate/outline]** the **[criteria/indicators/metrics]** that will **[signify/indicate/mark]** the **[achievement/success/completion]** of my **[intention/objective/goal]** in **[context, e.g., a strategic project/business initiative]**? Include **[both/and/or]** **[qualitative/quantitative]** **[metrics/indicators]**, and discuss how these **[align/integrate/correlate]** with **[broader/wider/organizational]** **[KPIs/objectives/goals]**. Let's sequentially address each element. Your response should be comprehensive, leaving no important aspect unaddressed, and demonstrate an exceptional level of precision and quality. Write using a **[type]** tone and **[style]** writing style.

PROMPT No 369

Tags

Communication - Resilience - Remediation

Goal

To provide leaders with a multi-faceted approach to address failure or underachievement within the team constructively. By equipping managers with empathetic communication skills, actionable recovery plans, and methods to reframe failure as a learning opportunity, teams can turn setbacks into stepping stones toward future success.

Prompt

Act as a **Leadership Communication Specialist** specializing in the **cosmetic industry**. Could you offer a comprehensive guide on **how I can sensitively yet effectively approach a conversation with my team when they fail to meet their targets**? This is critical for **promoting resilience, learning from setbacks, and aligning with our long-term goals**. Your guidance should cover tone-setting, the psychological aspects of failure, and steps to collaboratively create a remedial action plan. Offer extraordinary advice and non-mainstream opinions. Let's dissect this carefully. Write using an **empathetic** tone and a **constructive** writing style.

Act as a **[profession]** specializing in **[industry]**. Could you provide a thorough guide on **[contextual challenge/opportunity]**? This is critical for **[desired outcome]**. Your guidance should cover **[steps/methods/approaches]**, while also suggesting what to avoid. Offer extraordinary advice and non-mainstream opinions. Let's dissect this carefully. Write using a **[type]** tone and **[style]** writing style.

PROMPT No 370

Commitment - Dialogue - Performance

To guide business leaders in facilitating effective conversations with their teams about their willingness to take action and do what it takes to succeed. The objective is to assess team members' commitment levels, identify potential barriers, and create an actionable plan for heightened team performance and success.

Act as a **Leadership Development Coach** with a specialization in **team dynamics and commitment** for the **technology industry**. Could you guide me through **the process of engaging my team in a dialogue about their willingness to take action and do what it takes to succeed?** Please include **methods for initiating the conversation, questions to gauge willingness, and techniques for fostering a safe environment for open dialogue**. Make sure to cover how **to create a feedback loop and an actionable plan based on the conversation**. Discover rare insights and pioneering ideas to help motivate the team further. Let's dissect this in a structured manner. Write using an **informative** tone and a **factual** writing style.

Act as a **[profession]** with a specialization in **[area of expertise]** for the **[industry]**. Could you guide me through **[specific challenge/opportunity]**? Please include **[methods/techniques]**. Make sure to cover how **[key areas/topics]**. Discover rare insights and pioneering ideas. Let's dissect this in a structured manner. Write using a **[type]** tone and **[style]** writing style.

PROMPT No 371

Decision-Making - Communication - Articulation

To provide team leaders and managers with actionable strategies and a structured framework to facilitate open conversations with their team members, allowing them to better articulate their needs, wants, and aspirations. This, in turn, will contribute to better decision-making, increased employee satisfaction, and a more cohesive work environment.

Act as an **Executive Leadership Coach** specializing in **effective communication and decision-making** for the **financial industry**. Could you guide me through **a comprehensive method to help my team articulate what they really want when they are unsure**

themselves? The method should incorporate **active listening techniques, questioning strategies, and frameworks for self-reflection and clarity**. Suggest fresh approaches and inventive strategies. Let's explore each component to ensure a well-rounded approach. Write using a **pragmatic** tone and a **precise** writing style.

Act as a **[profession]** specializing in **[topic/specialization]** for the **[industry]**. Could you guide me through **[contextual challenge/opportunity]**? The method should incorporate **[desired outcomes/considerations]**. Suggest fresh approaches and inventive strategies. Let's explore each component to ensure a well-rounded approach. Write using a **[type]** tone and **[style]** writing style.

PROMPT No 372

Career Development - Software - Aspirations

To empower leaders and mentors in creating an inclusive and constructive environment that fosters meaningful discussions around professional aspirations. This will help team members clearly articulate their career goals and how these aspirations align with the team's objectives and the company's broader mission.

Act as a **career development coach** with a specialization in **team-building and self-assessment** in the **software development industry**. Can you provide me with **a structured framework to facilitate a discussion with my team about the professionals they aspire to become?** Please include **self-assessment tools, key talking points, and actionable next steps**. Make sure to cover how **their individual aspirations can be aligned with our project goals and overall company vision**. Explore unconventional solutions and alternative perspectives to assist in career planning. Use a **motivational** tone and a **clear, step-by-step** writing style.

Act as a **[profession]** with a specialization in **[area of expertise]** for the **[industry]**. Can you provide me with **[methodology or framework]** to address **[specific challenge/opportunity]**? Please include **[methods/techniques/tools]**. Make sure to cover how **[key areas/topics]**. Explore unconventional solutions and alternative perspectives to assist in career planning. Write using a **[type]** tone and **[style]** writing style.

PROMPT No 373

Interpersonal - Inquiry - Non-Verbal

To empower business leaders, mentors, and coaches to engage in deeper one-on-one conversations with their colleagues. This aims to subtly identify their unexpressed desires or aspirations, which may be crucial for enhancing job satisfaction, team dynamics, and overall productivity.

Act as a **corporate communications expert** with a focus on **interpersonal skills** in the **healthcare industry**. Can you provide me with **nuanced strategies** for understanding **my** colleague desires or aspires to achieve without directly asking them during a **one-on-one discussion**? Please incorporate **non-verbal cues, open-ended questions, and indirect methods of inquiry**. Make sure to cover how to **interpret the information gained and how to utilize it effectively**. Navigate through unexplored realms and revolutionary paradigms. Let's sequentially address each element. Write using a **friendly** tone and **approachable** writing style.

Formula

Act as a **[profession]** with a specialization in **[area of expertise]** in the **[specific industry]**. Could you provide me with **[strategy/framework/method]** for understanding **[challenge or topic]?** Please incorporate **[tools/techniques/areas to focus on]**. Make sure to cover how to **[actions or objectives to meet]**. Navigate through unexplored realms and revolutionary paradigms. Let's sequentially address each element. Write using a **[type]** tone and **[style]** writing style.

PROMPT No 374

Tags

Contribution - Synergy - Alignment

Goal

To equip team leaders, managers, and executives with an in-depth understanding of the unique types of contributions each team member could make within the company. By doing so, they can better align these contributions with individual strengths, roles, and aspirations, leading to increased team synergy, performance, and overall job satisfaction.

Prompt

Act as an **Organizational Development Specialist** specializing in **team role alignment** for the **retail industry**. Could you help me **understand the diverse types of contributions my team members could make to our company**? I want to explore how to better match these contributions with each team member's unique skills. Please provide a **categorization framework and actionable strategies** for realigning roles. Additionally, outline any potential barriers like skill gaps or resistance to change, and suggest ways to overcome them. Let's navigate my request meticulously. Write using an **instructive** tone and a **thorough** writing style.

Formula

Act as a **[profession]** specializing in **[topic/specialization]** for the **[industry]**. Could you help me **[contextual challenge/opportunity]?** I want to explore how to better match these contributions with each team member's unique **[characteristics/roles/skills]**. Please provide **[categorization framework/assessment tools/strategies]** for realigning roles. Additionally, outline any potential barriers like skill gaps or resistance to change, and suggest ways to overcome them. Let's navigate my request meticulously. Write using a **[type]** tone and **[style]** writing style.

PROMPT No 375

Tags

Engagement - Purpose - Satisfaction

Goal

To gain specific steps or techniques that can be implemented as a leader to improve the capacity to have meaningful conversations with team members about their work's purpose and satisfaction, thereby fostering deeper engagement.

As a **Leadership Coach**, adopting a **supportive and engaging tone**, could you provide specific steps or techniques that **I** can implement as a leader to improve my capacity to have meaningful conversations with **my team members** about their **work's purpose and satisfaction**? This is particularly relevant given the goal of **fostering deeper engagement within the team**.

As a **[profession]**, adopting a **[tone of voice]**, could you provide specific steps or techniques that **[I/Name/Role]** can implement as a leader to improve my capacity to have meaningful conversations with **[my/their]** **[team/group/department]** about their **[contextual challenge/opportunity]**? This is particularly relevant given the goal of **[desired outcome]**.

PROMPT No 376

Self-Awareness - Media - Purpose

To acquire a comprehensive, actionable guide on methods for assessing where one currently stands in living in alignment with their purpose, with the aim of fostering self-awareness, personal growth, and professional alignment.

As a **Purpose-Alignment Coach** in the **media industry**, could you provide an exhaustive guide outlining the methods **I** can employ to assess where **I** currently am in living in alignment with **my purpose**? Please include **self-assessment tools**. Break down your advice into specific sections, reinforcing each with **quantifiable metrics and scholarly literature**. Explore unconventional approaches and diverse viewpoints. Let's dissect this carefully. Write using an **empathetic** tone and a **narrative** writing style.

As a **[profession]** in the **[industry]**, could you provide an exhaustive guide outlining the methods **[I/Name/Role]** can employ to assess where **[I/they]** currently am/are in living in alignment with **[my/their]** **[purpose/goals/values]**? Please include both **[self-assessment tools/reflective exercises]**. Break down your advice into specific sections, reinforcing each with **[quantifiable metrics/scholarly literature]**. Explore unconventional approaches and diverse viewpoints. Let's dissect this carefully. Write using a **[type]** tone and **[style]** writing style.

PROMPT No 377

Leadership - Encouragement - Purpose

To gain effective strategies for identifying the factors that contribute to a team's sense of purpose in their work, and to learn specific methods or actions that can be taken to foster and promote this sense of purpose among all team members.

As a **Leadership Development Consultant**, adopting a **supportive and encouraging tone**, could you share effective strategies that can be employed to identify the key factors that contribute to my team's sense of purpose in their work? Furthermore, could you suggest specific methods or actions that I can take to foster and promote this sense of purpose among all members of my team?

As a [profession], adopting a [tone of voice], could you share effective strategies that can be employed to identify the key factors that contribute to [my/their] [team/group/department]'s [contextual challenge/opportunity]? Furthermore, could you suggest specific methods or actions that [I/Name/Role] can take to [desired outcome] among all members of [my/their] [team/group/department]?

PROMPT No 378

Cohesion - Purpose - Reflection

To acquire a comprehensive, actionable guide on methods for reflecting with a team on the deeper understanding they have gained about their collective purpose, with the aim of enhancing team cohesion, individual motivation, and overall organizational alignment.

As a **Purpose-Driven Leadership Coach** in the **non-profit industry**, could you provide an exhaustive guide outlining the methods **my team and I** can employ to reflect on the deeper understanding we have all gained about our **purpose**? Please include **both individual reflection exercises and group activities**. Break down your advice into specific sections, reinforcing each with **quantifiable metrics**. Explore unconventional approaches and diverse viewpoints. Let's dissect this carefully. Write using an **analytical** tone and a **structured** writing style.

As a [profession] in the [industry], could you provide an exhaustive guide outlining the methods [my team and I/Name/Role and their team] can employ to reflect on the deeper understanding we have all gained about our [purpose/specific goal]? Please include both [individual reflection exercises/group activities]. Break down your advice into specific sections, reinforcing each with [quantifiable metrics/scholarly literature]. Explore unconventional approaches and diverse viewpoints. Let's dissect this carefully. Write using a [type] tone and [style] writing style.

RELATIONSHIPS

PROMPT No 379

Impact - Morale - Emotional

To provide team leaders, managers, and executives with the tools and frameworks they need to assess the unforeseen impact of their successes and failures on their team members.

Act as a **Leadership Coach** specializing in **emotional intelligence and team dynamics** for the **manufacturing industry**. Could you help me understand how to **better assess the unforeseen**

impacts—both positive and negative—of my leadership decisions on my team? I want to understand how to **gauge these impacts in terms of team morale, productivity, and alignment with organizational goals**. Please provide **frameworks** for evaluating these impacts. Additionally, suggest strategies to rectify negative impacts and reinforce positive outcomes. Respond separately to each item of my request. Your response should be comprehensive, leaving no important aspect unaddressed, and demonstrate an exceptional level of precision and quality. Let's take this one step at a time. Write using a **probing** tone and a **systematic** writing style.

Act as a **[profession]** specializing in **[topic/specialization]** for the **[industry]**. Could you help me understand how to **[contextual challenge/opportunity]**? I want to understand how to **[desired objective]**. Please provide **[assessment tools/KPIs/frameworks]** for evaluating these impacts. Additionally, suggest strategies to rectify negative impacts and reinforce positive outcomes. Respond separately to each item of my request. Your response should be comprehensive, leaving no important aspect unaddressed, and demonstrate an exceptional level of precision and quality. Let's take this one step at a time. Write using a **[type]** tone and **[style]** writing style.

PROMPT No 380

Resilience - Problem-Solving - Support

To gain specific actions, techniques, or tools to improve the capacity to effectively support and lead a team in difficult situations, fostering resilience and effective problem-solving within the team.

As a **Leadership Development Consultant**, adopting a **solution-oriented and supportive tone**, could you provide specific actions, techniques, or tools that **I** can utilize to improve **my** capacity to effectively support and lead **my team** in **difficult situations**? This is particularly relevant given the goal of fostering resilience and effective problem-solving within the team.

As a **[profession]**, adopting a **[tone of voice]**, could you provide specific actions, techniques, or tools that **[I/Name/Role]** can utilize to improve **[my/their]** capacity to effectively support and lead **[my/their]** **[team/group/department]** in **[contextual challenge/opportunity]**? This is particularly relevant given the goal of **[desired outcome]**.

PROMPT No 381

Roles - Construction - Allocation

To acquire a comprehensive, actionable framework for determining the responsibilities of team members for a specific project, with the aim of optimizing resource allocation, enhancing team collaboration, and ensuring project success.

As a **Project Management Consultant** in the **construction industry**, could you provide a **detailed blueprint** outlining the **strategies I** can employ to determine the responsibilities of **my team members** for an **upcoming project**? Please include **both role-mapping exercises and**

communication protocols. Divide your insights into separate modules, each **authenticated by corroborative evidence from credible sources**. Explore unconventional approaches and diverse viewpoints. Let's examine each dimension meticulously. Write using a consultative tone and a narrative writing style.

As a **[profession]** in the **[industry],** could you provide a **[detailed blueprint/thorough toolkit/in-depth manual]** outlining the **[methods/tactics/strategies]** **[I/Name/Role]** can employ to determine the responsibilities of **[my/our/their]** **[team/group/department]** for **[a/an/the]** **[upcoming/current/specific]** project? Please include both **[role-mapping exercises/communication protocols/task delegation frameworks]**. Divide your insights into separate modules, each **[authenticated by/endorsed with]** **[corroborative evidence from/ data from/references from]** **[credible/reputable/authoritative]** sources. Explore unconventional approaches and diverse viewpoints. Let's examine each dimension meticulously. Write using a **[consultative/empathetic/balanced]** tone and a **[narrative/nuanced/concise]** writing style.

PROMPT No 382

Fulfillment - Implementation - Clients

To obtain a comprehensive, actionable framework that outlines the steps a leader can take to instill a sense of fulfillment in their team when working with clients. The aim is to enhance team morale, improve client relationships, and ultimately drive business success.

As a **Team Morale Specialist** in the **retail industry**, could you provide a **comprehensive strategy** detailing the **steps** I can take to bring **fulfillment** to my **team** when working with **clients**? Additionally, offer **actionable steps** for **immediate** implementation. Divide your recommendations into distinct areas, each supported by evidence from **reputable studies**. Investigate unexpected avenues and creative pathways. Let's **examine each dimension meticulously**. Write using a **motivational** tone and an **engaging** writing style.

As a **[profession]** in the **[industry]**, could you provide a **[comprehensive strategy/thorough toolkit/detailed blueprint]** detailing the **[steps/methods/tactics]** I can take to bring **[fulfillment/satisfaction/contentment]** to my **[team/group/department]** when working with **[clients/colleagues/stakeholders]?** Additionally, offer **[actionable steps/initial measures/immediate tactics]** for **[immediate/short-term/long-term]** implementation. Divide your recommendations into distinct areas, each supported by **[evidence from/references from/data from]** **[reputable studies/credible research/authoritative publications]**. Investigate unexpected avenues and creative pathways. Let's **[examine each dimension meticulously/dissect this carefully]**. Write using a **[motivational/inspirational/energetic]** tone and an **[engaging/innovative/nuanced]** writing style.

PROMPT No 383

Trust - Assessment - Collaboration

To understand, foster, and implement strategies that enhance trust and open communication between your team and other departments within the organization, thereby leading to improved collaboration and increased productivity.

Act as an **organizational psychologist** with a specialization in **interpersonal dynamics** for the **healthcare sector**. Could you guide me through the **intricacies of fostering a culture that promotes open and trusting relationships between my team and other departments**? Please include **methodologies for assessing trust levels and actionable steps to improve them.** Make sure to cover how **the role of communication in trust-building, and the impact of trust on inter-departmental collaboration could be further developed**. Delve into uncharted territories and groundbreaking concepts to sustain this practice. Let's dissect this in a structured manner. Write using an **empathetic** tone and a **narrative** writing style.

Act as a **[profession]** with a specialization in **[area of expertise]** for the **[industry]**. Could you guide me through **[specific challenge/opportunity]**? Please include **[methods/techniques]**. Make sure to cover how **[key areas/topics]**. Delve into uncharted territories and groundbreaking concepts to sustain this practice. Let's dissect this in a structured manner. Write using a **[type]** tone and **[style]** writing style.

PROMPT No 384

Satisfaction - Implementation - Interaction

To obtain a comprehensive, actionable framework that outlines methods for identifying what works well in the interactions between a team and its clients. The aim is to enhance client satisfaction, improve team performance, and contribute to business success.

As a **Client Interaction Analyst** in the **technology industry**, could you provide a **comprehensive strategy** detailing **methods** to identify what works well in **my team's** interactions with **clients**? Additionally, offer **actionable steps** for **immediate** implementation. Segment your insights into distinct modules, each supported by **evidence from reputable industry reports**. Investigate unexpected avenues and creative pathways. Let's **dissect this carefully**. Write using a **solution-oriented** tone and a **persuasive** writing style.

As a **[profession]** in the **[industry]**, could you provide a **[comprehensive strategy/thorough toolkit/detailed blueprint]** detailing the **[methods/techniques/approaches]** to identify what works well in **[my/our/their]** **[team/group/department]**'s interactions with **[clients/colleagues/stakeholders]**? Additionally, offer **[actionable steps/initial measures/immediate tactics]** for **[immediate/short-term/long-term]** implementation. Segment your insights into distinct modules, each supported by **[evidence from/references from/data from]** **[reputable journals/credible research/authoritative publications/industry reports]**. Investigate unexpected avenues and creative pathways. Let's **[examine each dimension meticulously/dissect this carefully]**. Write using a **[solution-oriented/pragmatic/analytical]** tone and a **[persuasive/engaging/innovative]** writing style.

PROMPT No 385

Tags

Perception - Alignment - Duties

Goal

To guide team leaders and managers in assisting their team members to comprehend the way they perceive and frame their duties. This understanding will enhance self-awareness, enable better communication and collaboration within the team, and align individual responsibilities with team goals and organizational values.

Prompt

Act as a **Team Dynamics Specialist** specializing in the **automotive industry**. Could you elucidate **the strategies and techniques that I can employ to help my team realize how they frame their duties in relation to their work and interactions with the rest of their team**? This understanding is vital for **fostering collaboration, aligning individual tasks with team objectives, and promoting a harmonious working environment**. Please provide a thorough and actionable guide that covers various approaches, psychological insights, communication methods, and **team-building activities**. Let's dissect this carefully. Write using an **instructive** tone and **engaging** writing style.

Formula

Act as a **[profession]** specializing in the **[industry]**. Could you elucidate **[contextual challenge/opportunity]**? This understanding is vital for **[desired outcome]**. Please provide a thorough and actionable guide that covers various approaches, psychological insights, communication methods, and **[specific factors or elements]**. Let's dissect this carefully. Write using a **[type]** tone and **[style]** writing style.

PROMPT No 386

Tags

Relationships - Communication - Collaboration

Goal

To establish principles, techniques, and best practices for building supportive and trusting relationships with colleagues. This includes understanding the foundations of trust, effective communication, empathy, collaboration, and ongoing support within professional relationships.

Prompt

Act as a **Corporate Relationship Building and Leadership Coaching expert** specializing in the **food & beverage manufacturing industry**. Trust and support among colleagues are vital for a harmonious and productive working environment. How can a **professional** at any level **cultivate supportive and trusting** relationships with **colleagues**? What are some **principles** and **behaviors** that can be **adopted**? Provide a **comprehensive** guide that includes **understanding** the **nuances** of trust, **developing empathy**, **active listening**, **conflict resolution**, **collaboration**, and **ongoing support**. Include **scenarios** that **exemplify** how these principles can be **applied** in the **food & beverage manufacturing industry**.

Formula

Act as a **[profession]** specializing in the **[industry]**. Trust and support among colleagues are vital for a harmonious and productive working environment. How can a **[professional/individual/team member]** **[cultivate/build/develop]** **[supportive/trusting/positive]** relationships with **[colleagues/peers/team members]**?

What are some **[principles/techniques/best practices]**, and **[behaviors/attitudes/strategies]** that can be **[adopted/implemented/fostered]**? Provide a **[comprehensive/thorough/complete]** guide that includes **[understanding/recognizing/identifying]** the **[nuances/elements/aspects]** of trust, **[developing/fostering/building]** **[empathy/compassion]**, **[active listening/effective communication]**, **[conflict resolution/problem-solving]**, **[collaboration/teamwork]**, and **[ongoing support/recognition/reinforcement]**. Include **[scenarios/case studies/examples]** that **[exemplify/illustrate/demonstrate]** how these principles can be **[applied/utilized/enacted]** in the **[industry]**.

<u>PROMPT No 387</u>

Self-awareness - Relationships - Dynamics

To equip leaders with a comprehensive framework that enables their teams to reflect on self-insights gained through interpersonal relationships. The aim is to foster self-awareness, improve team dynamics, and enhance individual contributions to collective goals.

Act as a **Relationship Dynamics Expert** specializing in the **tech industry**. What are the **most appropriate** strategies for my team to **reflect** on the **insights** they have **gained** about **themselves** through their **relationships** with **others**? Include **actionable steps, psychological theories, and real-world examples**. Let's systematically explore each facet. Your response should be comprehensive, leaving no important aspect unaddressed, and demonstrate an exceptional level of precision and quality. Write using an **introspective** tone and a **reflective** writing style.

Act as a **[profession]** specializing in the **[industry]**. What are the **[most appropriate/best/effective]** strategies for my team to **[reflect/ponder/consider]** on the [insights/lessons/understandings] they have **[gained/derived/obtained]** about **[themselves/their character/their personality]** through their **[relationships/interactions/engagements]** with **[others/teammates/colleagues]**? Include **[actionable steps/practical measures/tangible actions]**, **[psychological theories/conceptual frameworks/academic models]**, and **[real-world examples/case studies/practical illustrations]**. Let's systematically explore each facet. Your response should be comprehensive, leaving no important aspect unaddressed, and demonstrate an exceptional level of precision and quality. Write using a **[type]** tone and **[style]** writing style.

<u>PROMPT No 388</u>

Selection - Software - Team-building

To assist business leaders in effectively selecting the right team members for a project by considering technical knowledge, experience, and personality. The aim is to provide leaders with a comprehensive method to assess and match team members to project needs, thus enhancing the chances of project success.

Act as an **Executive Coach** with a specialization in **talent management and team formation** for the **software industry**. Could you guide me through **the process of selecting the right people to work on a project based on their technical knowledge, experience, and personality**? Please include **assessment tools, interview questions, and team-building exercises**. Make sure to cover how **to evaluate the suitability of a team member based on these three factors**. Delve into uncharted territories and groundbreaking concepts to optimize team selection. Let's dissect this in a structured manner. Write using a **practical** tone and a **how-to** writing style.

Act as a **[profession]** with a specialization in **[area of expertise]** for the **[industry]**. Could you guide me through **[specific challenge/opportunity]**? Please include **[methods/techniques]**. Make sure to cover how **[key areas/topics]**. Delve into uncharted territories and groundbreaking concepts to optimize team selection. Let's dissect this in a structured manner. Write using a **[type]** tone and **[style]** writing style.

PROMPT No 389

Authenticity - Presence - Interactions

To identify actionable strategies and techniques that enable team members to be fully present and authentic in their interactions with others. The aim is to enhance interpersonal relationships, foster a culture of trust, and ultimately improve team performance and well-being.

As a **Behavioral Scientist** in the **pharmaceutical industry**, could you delineate a **multi-layered approach** to help **my team** be fully **present and authentic** in their interactions with **senior management**? Include **actionable strategies** that can be **immediately implemented**. Organize your insights into **distinct themes**, each supported by **references from reputable academic sources**. Delve into **unconventional solutions and alternative perspectives**. Let's examine each dimension meticulously. Write using an **inspiring** tone and an **engaging** writing style.

As a **[profession]** in the **[industry]**, could you delineate a **[multi-layered approach/comprehensive plan/structured methodology]** to help **[me/us/them]** be fully **[present/authentic/engaged]** in their interactions with **[others/clients/colleagues]**? Include **[actionable strategies/practical solutions/immediate steps]** for **[immediate/short-term/long-term]** implementation. Organize your insights into **[distinct themes/separate focal points/clear categories]**, each supported by **[references from/evidence from/data from]** **[reputable academic sources/credible research/authoritative publications]**. Delve into **[unconventional solutions/alternative perspectives/innovative methods]**. Let's **[examine each dimension meticulously/deconstruct this subject stepwise]**. Write using an **[inspiring/empowering/motivating]** tone and an **[engaging/invigorating/energetic]** writing style.

PROMPT No 390

Goal

To enable individuals, especially leaders and managers, to identify areas in their work and relationships where they may unconsciously relinquish control or influence. This insight is crucial for self-awareness, empowerment, and effective leadership, ensuring that they maintain the appropriate level of authority and confidence in their interactions and decisions.

Prompt

Act as an **Executive Coach** specializing in the **finance industry**. Could you guide me through **a reflective analysis to discover the areas of my work and responsibilities where I tend to give away my power in work relationships**? Recognizing these areas is essential for **strengthening my leadership, enhancing collaboration, and maintaining the integrity of my role**. Please provide a detailed roadmap that includes **self-assessment tools, strategies for observation, guidance on seeking feedback, and methods to reclaim and assert my influence**. Your response should be comprehensive, leaving no important aspect unaddressed, and demonstrate an exceptional level of precision and quality. Let's dissect this carefully. Write using an **insightful** tone and **engaging** writing style.

Formula

Act as a **[profession]** specializing in the **[industry]**. Could you guide me through **[contextual challenge/opportunity]**? Recognizing these areas is essential for **[desired outcome]**. Please provide a detailed roadmap that includes **[specific components or methods]**. Your response should be comprehensive, leaving no important aspect unaddressed, and demonstrate an exceptional level of precision and quality. Let's dissect this carefully. Write using a **[type]** tone and **[style]** writing style.

PROMPT No 391

Tags

Presence - Engagement - Communication

Goal

To identify actionable strategies and techniques that can help an individual enhance the nature or quality of their presence in order to be fully engaged and present in various settings. This includes both professional and personal interactions, aiming to improve communication, leadership skills, and overall well-being.

Prompt

As a **Mindfulness Expert** in the **healthcare industry**, could you provide a **detailed roadmap** for enhancing the **quality** of my presence to be **fully engaged and present** in my interactions? Include **actionable steps** for **long-term application**. Organize your insights into **thematic clusters**, each substantiated by **evidence from reputable journals**. Probe into **alternative perspectives and groundbreaking concepts**. Let's **deconstruct this subject stepwise**. Write using a **visionary** tone and an **invigorating** writing style.

Formula

As a **[profession]** in the **[industry]**, could you provide a **[detailed roadmap/comprehensive guide/structured plan]** for enhancing the **[quality/nature]** of **[my/our/their]** presence to be **[fully engaged/fully present/both]** in **[my/our/their]** interactions? Include **[actionable steps/practical solutions/immediate measures]** for **[immediate/short-term/long-term]** application. Organize your insights into **[thematic clusters/distinct categories/individual segments]**, each substantiated by **[evidence from/references from/data from]** **[reputable** journals/credible research/authoritative publications]. Probe into [alternative perspectives/groundbreaking concepts/innovative methods]. Let's [deconstruct this subject stepwise/examine each dimension meticulously]. Write using a [visionary/inspiring/empowering] tone and an [invigorating/energetic/engaging] writing style.

PROMPT No 392

Self-awareness - Engagement - Motivating

To acquire a robust, actionable framework that outlines methods for assisting team members in describing the nature or quality of their presence when they are fully engaged and present. The objective is to enhance self-awareness, improve team dynamics, and foster a more engaged work environment.

As a **Mindfulness Consultant** in the **healthcare industry**, could you offer a **multi-layered strategy** for assisting **my team** in describing the nature or quality of their presence when they **are fully engaged and present**? Include **actionable steps** for **immediate application**. Divide your insights into **manageable sections**, each supported by **evidence from verified academic publications**. Explore unconventional solutions and alternative perspectives. Let's **deconstruct this subject stepwise**. Write using a **motivating** tone and an **innovative** writing style.

As a [profession] in the [industry], could you offer a [comprehensive strategy/multi-layered approach/detailed plan] for assisting [my/our/their] team in describing the nature or quality of their presence when they are [fully engaged and present/actively participating/focused]? Include [actionable steps/initial measures/immediate tactics] for [immediate/short-term/long-term] application. Divide your insights into [manageable sections/discrete units/clear categories], each supported by [evidence from/references from/data from] [reputable journals/credible research/authoritative publications/industry reports]. Explore unconventional solutions and alternative perspectives. Let's [deconstruct this subject stepwise/examine each dimension meticulously]. Write using a [motivating/inspiring/captivating] tone and an [innovative/engaging/relatable] writing style.

PROMPT No 393

Presence - Mindfulness - Contemplative

To develop a comprehensive and actionable strategy for identifying the factors that hinder one's ability to be fully present. The aim is to provide a roadmap for self-awareness and improvement, supported by evidence-based methods and practices.

As a **Mindfulness Consultant** in the **education sector**, could you delineate a **structured approach** to help **me** identify the factors that hinder **my** ability to be **fully present**? Include **actionable tactics** for **short-term** implementation. Organize your insights into **distinct themes**, each substantiated by **references from trustworthy studies**. Investigate unexpected avenues and creative pathways. Let's **examine each dimension meticulously**. Write using a **contemplative** tone and a **reflective** writing style.

As a **[profession]** in the **[industry]**, could you delineate a **[structured approach/comprehensive strategy/detailed plan]** to help **[me/us/them]** identify the factors that hinder **[my/our/their]** ability to be **[fully present/engaged/focused]?** Include **[actionable tactics/immediate steps/practical measures] for [immediate/short-term/long-term]** implementation. Organize your insights into **[distinct themes/clear categories/discrete units]**, each substantiated by **[references from/data from/evidence from] [trustworthy studies/credible research/authoritative publications]**. Investigate unexpected avenues and creative pathways. Let's **[examine each dimension meticulously/deconstruct this subject stepwise]**. Write using a **[contemplative/reflective/thoughtful]** tone and a **[reflective/insightful/nuanced]** writing style.

PROMPT No 394

Triggers - Interactions - Compassionate

To identify and understand the triggers that typically cause team members to withdraw or shrink back during interactions, and to develop actionable strategies for mitigating these triggers. The focus is on creating a psychologically safe and inclusive environment that enhances team performance and well-being.

As an **Organizational Psychologist** in the **supply chain industry**, could you outline a **multi-faceted approach** to help **me** identify the triggers that typically cause **my** team to **withdraw or shrink back** in interactions? Include **actionable strategies** for **long-term** implementation. Organize your insights into **separate focal points**, each supported by **evidence from reputable journals**. Probe into **overlooked factors and innovative solutions**. Let's **scrutinize this topic incrementally**. Write using a **compassionate** tone and an **empathetic** writing style.

As a **[profession]** in the **[industry]**, could you outline a **[multi-faceted approach/comprehensive plan/structured methodology]** to help **[me/us/them]** identify the triggers that typically cause **[my/our/their]** team to **[withdraw/shrink back/disengage]** in interactions? Include **[actionable strategies/practical solutions/immediate steps]** for **[immediate/short-term/long-term]** implementation. Organize your insights into **[separate focal points/distinct themes/clear categories]**, each supported by **[evidence from/references from/data from] [reputable journals/credible research/authoritative publications]**. Probe into **[overlooked factors/innovative solutions/alternative perspectives]**. Let's **[scrutinize this topic incrementally/deconstruct this subject stepwise]**. Write using a **[compassionate/empathetic/supportive]** tone and an **[empathetic/understanding/considerate]** writing style.

PROMPT No 395

Assessment - Leadership - Analytical

To provide leaders with a robust framework for self-assessment that identifies their unique contributions to team dynamics and performance. The objective is to enhance self-awareness, optimize individual strengths, and ultimately improve team outcomes.

Act as a **Leadership Assessment Specialist** specializing in the **tech industry**. How can I **rigorously** assess the **unique** ways in which I **contribute** to my **team's success**? Include **methodologies, key performance indicators, and real-world examples**. Let's sequentially unravel this issue. Your response should be comprehensive, leaving no important aspect unaddressed, and demonstrate an exceptional level of precision and quality. Write using an **analytical** tone and a **data-driven** writing style.

Act as a **[profession]** specializing in the **[industry]**. How can I **[rigorously/thoroughly/comprehensively]** assess the **[unique/specific/individual]** ways in which I **[contribute/add value/participate]** to my **[team's/group's/organization's]** **[success/performance/effectiveness]**? Include **[methodologies/techniques/tools]**, **[key performance indicators/metrics/measures]**, and **[real-world examples/case studies/practical illustrations]**. Let's sequentially unravel this issue. Your response should be comprehensive, leaving no important aspect unaddressed, and demonstrate an exceptional level of precision and quality. Write using a **[type]** tone and **[style]** writing style.

PROMPT No 396

Engagement - Persuasive - Organization

To obtain a comprehensive, actionable framework that outlines methods for creating a growth-mindset environment within a company and strategies for effectively communicating the benefits of such an environment to employees. The aim is to enhance employee engagement, improve performance, and contribute to overall organizational success.

As an **Organizational Psychologist** in the **technology sector**, could you provide a **detailed action plan** outlining **methods** to create a growth-mindset environment within **my** company and strategies to effectively communicate its benefits to employees? Additionally, offer **actionable steps** for **mid-term** implementation. Divide your insights into distinct modules, each supported by **evidence from reputable industry reports**. Investigate unexpected avenues and creative pathways. Let's **examine each dimension meticulously**. Write using a **persuasive** tone and a **visionary** writing style.

As a **[profession]** in the **[industry]**, could you provide a **[comprehensive strategy/thorough toolkit/detailed action plan]** outlining **[methods/techniques/approaches]** to create a growth-mindset environment within **[my/our/their]** company and strategies to effectively communicate its benefits to employees? Additionally, offer **[actionable steps/initial measures/immediate tactics]** for **[short-term/mid-term/long-term]** implementation. Divide your insights into distinct modules, each supported by **[evidence from/references from/data from]** **[reputable journals/credible research/authoritative** publications/industry reports]. Investigate unexpected avenues and creative pathways. Let's **[examine each dimension meticulously/dissect this carefully].** Write using a **[persuasive/inspiring/motivating]** tone and a **[visionary/engaging/innovative]** writing style.

PROMPT No 397

Creativity - Innovation - Framework

To obtain a comprehensive, actionable framework that outlines methods for sparking novel ideas and generating creative discussions within a team. The aim is to enhance team creativity, improve problem-solving capabilities, and contribute to overall organizational innovation.

As an **Innovation Facilitator** in the **publishing industry**, could you provide a **thorough action plan** detailing approaches to spark novel ideas and generate creative discussions with **my** team? Additionally, offer **actionable steps** for **immediate** implementation. Segment your insights into distinct modules, each supported by evidence from **reputable industry reports**. Investigate unexpected avenues and creative pathways. Let's **dissect this carefully**. Write using an **inspiring** tone and a **visionary** writing style.

As a **[profession]** in the **[industry]**, could you provide a **[comprehensive strategy/thorough action plan/detailed blueprint]** detailing **[methods/techniques/approaches]** to spark novel ideas and generate creative discussions with **[my/our/their]** team? Additionally, offer **[actionable steps/initial measures/immediate tactics]** for **[immediate/short-term/long-term]** implementation. Segment your insights into distinct modules, each supported by **[evidence from/references from/data from] [reputable journals/credible research/authoritative publications/industry reports]**. Investigate unexpected avenues and creative pathways. Let's [examine each dimension meticulously/dissect this carefully]. Write using a **[inspiring/energizing/motivating]** tone and a **[visionary/engaging/innovative]** writing style.

PROMPT No 398

Resourcefulness - Strategy - Human Resources

To equip business leaders with robust tools and strategies for accurately determining the additional human resources needed to complete a project successfully. This will cover various aspects such as skill sets, time commitment, and budget considerations.

Act as a **Business Strategist** with a specialization in **project management and human resources** for the **technology sector**. Could you guide me through **the methodology of assessing the extra human resources needed to successfully execute a project**? Please include **metrics, evaluation criteria, and time management strategies**. Make sure to cover how **to balance the allocation of existing and new resources**. Delve into uncharted territories and groundbreaking concepts. Let's dissect this in a structured manner. Write using a **comprehensive** tone and a **how-to** writing style.

Act as a **[profession]** with a specialization in **[area of expertise]** for the **[industry]**. Could you guide me through **[specific challenge/opportunity]?** Please include **[methods/techniques]**. Make sure to cover how **[key areas/topics]**. Delve into uncharted territories and groundbreaking concepts. Let's dissect this in a structured manner. Write using a **[type]** tone and **[style]** writing style.

PROMPT No 399

Engagement - Strategy - Implementation

To obtain a comprehensive, actionable framework that outlines methods for specifying the ways in which others need to be involved in a project and strategies for inviting them to join. The aim is to enhance stakeholder engagement, improve project outcomes, and contribute to overall organizational success.

As a **Project Management Expert** in the **retail industry**, could you provide a **comprehensive strategy** detailing **methods** to specify the ways in which others need to be involved in **my** project and how to invite them to join? Additionally, offer **actionable steps** for **immediate** implementation. Segment your insights into distinct modules, each supported by **evidence from reputable industry reports**. Investigate unexpected avenues and creative pathways. Let's **examine each dimension meticulously**. Write using a **diplomatic** tone and a **persuasive** writing style.

As a **[profession]** in the **[industry]**, could you provide a **[comprehensive strategy/thorough toolkit/detailed blueprint]** detailing the **[methods/techniques/approaches]** to specify the ways in which others need to be involved in **[my/our/their]** project and how to invite them to join? Additionally, offer **[actionable steps/initial measures/immediate tactics]** for **[immediate/short-term/long-term]** implementation. Segment your insights into distinct modules, each supported by **[evidence from/references from/data from]** **[reputable journals/credible research/authoritative publications/industry reports]**. Investigate unexpected avenues and creative pathways. Let's **[examine each dimension meticulously/dissect this carefully]**. Write using a **[diplomatic/strategic/inviting]** tone and a **[persuasive/engaging/innovative]** writing style.

PROMPT No 400

Collaboration - Accountability - Consultative

To equip leaders with a comprehensive framework for effectively involving external stakeholders in various project contexts, thereby enhancing collaboration, accountability, and project success.

Act as a **Leadership Consultant** specializing in the **technology sector**. Could you outline a **structured approach** for involving **external stakeholders** in a **software development project**? What are the **key considerations, best practices, and potential pitfalls**? Provide **actionable steps and innovative solutions**, each supported by **evidence or case studies**. Let's **methodically dissect each component**. Write using a **consultative** tone and an **advisory** writing style.

Formula

Act as a **[profession]** specializing in the **[industry]**. Could you outline a **[structured approach/methodology]** for involving **[external stakeholders/partners/clients]** in a **[specific project/context]**? What are the **[key considerations/critical factors/essential elements]**, **[best practices/recommended approaches]**, and **[potential pitfalls/common mistakes]**? Provide **[actionable steps/concrete measures]** and **[innovative solutions/creative ideas]**, each supported by **[evidence/case studies/references]**. Let's **[methodically dissect each component/examine each dimension meticulously]**. Write using a **[type]** tone and **[style]** writing style.

PROMPT No 401

Tags

Communication - Conflict-Resolution - Construction

Goal

To provide managers and team leads with a comprehensive framework for managing and navigating sensitive discussions with colleagues who have expressed concerns about them. This framework will include communication techniques, psychological insights, and best practices to ensure an outcome beneficial to both parties involved.

Prompt

Act as a **Human Resources Expert** with a specialization in **conflict resolution and communication** for the **construction industry**. Could you guide me through **a constructive approach for discussing concerns that a colleague has raised about me**? Please include **conversational frameworks, active listening techniques, and the role of nonverbal communication**. Make sure to cover how **to maintain professionalism and address the issue without escalating it further**. Delve into uncharted territories and groundbreaking concepts to ensure effective communication and problem-solving. Let's dissect this in a structured manner. Write using a **diplomatic** tone and a **how-to** writing style.

Formula

Act as a **[profession]** with a specialization in **[area of expertise]** for the **[industry]**. Could you guide me through **[specific challenge/opportunity]**? Please include **[methods/techniques]**. Make sure to cover how **[key areas/topics]**. Delve into uncharted territories and groundbreaking concepts to ensure effective communication and problem-solving. Let's dissect this in a structured manner. Write using a **[type]** tone and **[style]** writing style.

PROMPT No 402

Tags

Relationship - Diagnostics - Constructive

Goal

To equip team leaders, managers, and individual contributors with a well-rounded method to identify which work relationships may be in need of improvement. This includes assessments to gauge interpersonal dynamics, communication flows, and practical steps to act upon the findings.

Act as a **Business Psychologist** with a specialization in **organizational behavior** for the **banking sector**. Could you guide me through **the methods to identify a work relationship that may require focused improvement**? Please include **diagnostic tools, observation metrics, and emotional intelligence guidelines**. Make sure to cover how **to recognize signs of tension or ineffectiveness and how to address them constructively**. Investigate unexpected avenues and creative pathways. Let's dissect this in a structured manner. Write using an **analytical** tone and a **step-by-step** writing style.

Act as a [profession] with a specialization in [area of expertise] for the [industry]. Could you guide me through [specific challenge/opportunity]? Please include [methods/techniques]. Make sure to cover how [key areas/topics]. Investigate unexpected avenues and creative pathways. Let's dissect this in a structured manner. Write using a [type] tone and [style] writing style.

PROMPT No 403

Relationships - Communication - Barriers

To provide entrepreneurs and business leaders a structured approach for initiating relationship enhancement with clients or colleagues, fostering improved communication and collaboration.

Act as a **Relationship Development Specialist** specializing in **Communication Skills** within the **corporate business sector**. Could you guide me through a **systematic and actionable approach to take the initial step in enhancing relationships with clients or colleagues**? Please include **identification of potential barriers, communication strategies, and key metrics to evaluate the effectiveness of the relationship enhancement initiatives**. Make sure to cover how **to maintain a constructive and professional demeanor during this process**. Explore **innovative and possibly unconventional solutions** to **foster a culture of open dialogue and continuous relationship improvement**. Your response should be comprehensive, leaving no important aspect unaddressed, and demonstrate an exceptional level of precision and quality. Let's think about this step by step. Write using a **professional** tone and a **methodical** writing style.

Act as a [profession] specializing in [area of expertise] within the [industry]. Could you guide me through [specific challenge/opportunity]? Please include [methods/techniques]. Make sure to cover how [key areas/topics]. Explore [exploratory direction] to [desired outcome]. Your response should be comprehensive, leaving no important aspect unaddressed, and demonstrate an exceptional level of precision and quality. Let's think about this step by step. Write using a [type] tone and a [style] writing style.

PROMPT No 404

To furnish business leaders with a structured approach to initiate relationship enhancement with clients or colleagues, setting a foundation for improved communication and collaboration.

Act as a **Relationship Development Specialist** specializing in **Communication Skills** within the **corporate business sector**. Could you guide me through **a meticulous process to identify and execute the initial step in enhancing relationships with clients or colleagues**? Please include **analytical tools to assess the current state of relationships, communication strategies tailored for initiating relationship enhancement, and metrics to monitor the progress and effectiveness of the initiatives**. Ensure to cover how **to maintain a professional and constructive demeanor throughout this process**. Delve into innovative or unconventional solutions that could foster a culture of open dialogue and continuous relationship improvement. Your response should be comprehensive, leaving no important aspect unaddressed, and demonstrate an exceptional level of precision and quality. Let's think about this step by step. Write using a professional tone and a methodical writing style.

Act as a **[profession]** specializing in **[area of expertise]** within the **[industry]**. Could you guide me through **[specific challenge/opportunity]**? Please include **[methods/techniques]**. Ensure to cover how **[key areas/topics]**. Delve into innovative or unconventional solutions that could foster a culture of open dialogue and continuous relationship improvement. Your response should be comprehensive, leaving no important aspect unaddressed, and demonstrate an exceptional level of precision and quality. Let's think about this step by step. Write using a **[type]** tone and a **[style]** writing style.

PROMPT No 405

Recognition - Interpersonal - Reflective

To enable managers, team leaders, and even team members themselves to systematically evaluate the unique strengths and qualities each individual contributes to their interactions with clients or colleagues. By doing so, we aim to foster a culture of recognition, promote skills development, and improve team cohesion.

Act as an **Organizational Psychologist** with a specialization in **interpersonal relationships** for the **non-profit sector**. Could you guide me through **methods to reflect on the unique strengths and qualities my team members bring to their relationships with clients and colleagues**? Please include **assessment frameworks, reflective questions, and qualitative data gathering techniques**. Make sure to cover how **to encourage team members to recognize and leverage their own and others' strengths in these relationships**. Explore unconventional solutions and alternative perspectives to nurture these skills. Let's dissect this in a structured manner. Write using an **insightful** tone and a **how-to** guide style.

Act as a **[profession]** with a specialization in **[area of expertise]** for the **[industry]**. Could you guide me through **[specific challenge/opportunity]**? Please include **[methods/techniques]**. Make sure to cover how **[key areas/topics]**. Explore unconventional solutions and alternative perspectives to nurture these skills. Let's dissect this in a structured manner. Write using a **[type]** tone and **[style]** writing style.

PROMPT No 406

Tags

Alignment - Frameworks - Values

Goal

To equip teams with a robust framework for selecting actions that reflect active contribution and alignment with company values, thereby enhancing collective performance and organizational integration.

Prompt

Act as an **Organizational Behavior Specialist** specializing in **Performance Management** within the **technology industry**. Could you guide me through a **comprehensive process for my team to identify and select actions that best align with being active and contributing members of the company?** Please include **frameworks for evaluating potential actions, strategies for fostering alignment with company values, and metrics for assessing the impact of these actions on team and organizational performance**. Ensure to cover how **to maintain an environment of continuous improvement and feedback**. Explore **innovative or unconventional methods** to **cultivate a culture of active contribution and alignment with organizational objectives**. Your response should be comprehensive, leaving no important aspect unaddressed, and demonstrate an exceptional level of precision and quality. Let's think about this step by step. Write using an **analytical** tone and a **structured, instructional** writing style.

Formula

Act as a **[profession]** specializing in **[area of expertise]** within the **[industry]**. Could you guide me through **[specific challenge/opportunity]**? Please include **[methods/techniques]**. Enure to cover how **[key areas/topics]**. Explore **[exploratory direction]** to **[desired outcome]**. Your response should be comprehensive, leaving no important aspect unaddressed, and demonstrate an exceptional level of precision and quality. Let's think about this step by step. Write using a **[type]** tone and a **[style]** writing style.

PROMPT No 407

Tags

Presence - Engagement - Meetings

Goal

To facilitate a thorough exploration with the team on factors that enable full presence during meetings, fostering engagement, active participation, and collective focus, leading to productive and meaningful interactions.

Prompt

Act as a **Meeting Efficiency Expert** specializing in **Team Building and Collaboration** within the **manufacturing industry**. Could you guide me through **a comprehensive approach to explore with my team the elements that support us in being fully present during team meetings?** Please include **methodologies for assessing current levels of engagement,**

strategies for cultivating a conducive meeting environment, and tools for ongoing monitoring and improvement of presence and participation. Ensure to cover how **to address potential challenges and resistance.** Delve into innovative or unconventional approaches that could further enhance meeting effectiveness and team presence. Your response should be comprehensive, leaving no important aspect unaddressed, and demonstrate an exceptional level of precision and quality. Let's think about this step by step. Write using an **engaging** tone and a **structured, instructional** writing style.

Act as a **[profession]** specializing in **[area of expertise]** within the **[industry]**. Could you guide me through **[specific challenge/opportunity]**? Please include **[methods/techniques]**. Ensure to cover how **[key areas/topics].** Delve into innovative or unconventional approaches that could further enhance meeting effectiveness and team presence. Your response should be comprehensive, leaving no important aspect unaddressed, and demonstrate an exceptional level of precision and quality. Let's think about this step by step. Write using a **[type]** tone and a **[style]** writing style.

PROMPT No 408

Motivation - Implementation - Satisfaction

To obtain a comprehensive, actionable framework that outlines methods for reflecting on the factors that fuel passion for work among team members. The aim is to enhance job satisfaction, improve team cohesion, and contribute to overall organizational success.

As a **Motivational Strategist** in the **non-profit sector**, could you provide a **comprehensive strategy** detailing **methods** to help **me** and **my team** reflect on the factors that fuel **our** passion for work? Additionally, offer **actionable steps** for **immediate** implementation. Segment your insights into distinct modules, each supported by **evidence from reputable industry reports**. Investigate unexpected avenues and creative pathways. Let's **dissect this carefully**. Write using an **inspiring** tone and a **persuasive** writing style.

As a **[profession]** in the **[industry]**, could you provide a **[comprehensive strategy/thorough toolkit/detailed blueprint]** detailing the **[methods/techniques/approaches]** to help **[me/us/them]** reflect on the factors that fuel **[our/their/my]** passion for work? Additionally, offer **[actionable steps/initial measures/immediate tactics]** for **[immediate/short-term/long-term]** implementation. Segment your insights into distinct modules, each supported by **[evidence from/references from/data from]** **[reputable journals/credible research/authoritative publications/industry reports].** Investigate unexpected avenues and creative pathways. Let's **[examine each dimension meticulously/dissect this carefully].** Write using a **[inspiring/energizing/motivating]** tone and a **[persuasive/engaging/innovative]** writing style.

PROMPT No 409

Resilience - Fulfillment - Problem-Solving

To obtain a comprehensive, actionable framework that outlines methods for identifying resources that can be accessed to face obstacles at work in a more fulfilled manner. The aim is to enhance personal resilience, improve problem-solving capabilities, and contribute to overall job satisfaction.

As a **Professional Development Advisor** in the **education sector**, could you provide a **comprehensive action plan** detailing **methods** to identify resources **I** could access to face obstacles at work in a **more fulfilled manner**? Additionally, offer **actionable steps** for **immediate** implementation. Segment your insights into distinct modules, each supported by evidence from **reputable industry reports**. Investigate unexpected avenues and creative pathways. Let's **examine each dimension meticulously**. Write using a **solution-oriented** tone and a **persuasive** writing style.

As a **[profession]** in the **[industry]**, could you provide a **[comprehensive strategy/thorough action plan/detailed blueprint]** detailing the **[methods/techniques/approaches]** to identify resources **[I/we/they]** could access to face obstacles at work in a **[more fulfilled/more effective/more resilient]** manner? Additionally, offer **[actionable steps/initial measures/immediate tactics]** for **[immediate/short-term/long-term]** implementation. Segment your insights into distinct modules, each supported by **[evidence from/references from/data from]** **[reputable journals/credible research/authoritative publications/industry reports]**. Investigate unexpected avenues and creative pathways. Let's **[examine each dimension meticulously/dissect this carefully]**. Write using a **[solution-oriented/pragmatic/analytical]** tone and a **[persuasive/engaging/innovative]** writing style.

PROMPT No 410

Leadership - Effectiveness - Performance

To acquire a comprehensive, actionable guide on methods for determining the support or resources that the leaders of a company need to enhance their work performance, with the aim of improving leadership effectiveness, team productivity, and overall organizational success.

As an **Executive Coach** in the **telecommunications industry**, could you provide an exhaustive guide outlining the methods **I** can employ to determine the support or resources the leaders of **my company** need to enhance their **work performance**? Please include diagnostic **tools like 360-degree feedback and resource allocation strategies**. Segment the guide into **distinct categories**, and substantiate each with empirical data. Explore unconventional approaches and diverse viewpoints. Let's dissect this carefully. Write using an **analytical** tone and a **structured** writing style.

As a **[profession]** in the **[industry]**, could you provide an exhaustive guide outlining the methods **[I/Name/Role]** can employ to determine the support or resources the leaders of **[my/our/their]** **[company/organization]** need to enhance their **[work performance/specific area of performance]**? Please include **[diagnostic tools like X/resource allocation strategies like Y]**. Segment the guide into **[distinct categories]**, and substantiate each with **[empirical data/scholarly references]**. Explore unconventional approaches and diverse viewpoints. Let's dissect this carefully. Write using a **[type]** tone and **[style]** writing style.

PROMPT No 411

Resourcefulness - Mindset - Adaptability

To acquire a comprehensive, actionable guide on methods for exploring with a team the ways they can develop their own long-term resourcefulness, with the aim of enhancing individual adaptability, team resilience, and overall organizational sustainability.

As a **Resilience Coach** in the **renewable energy industry**, could you provide an exhaustive guide outlining the methods **I** can employ to explore with **my team** the ways they can develop their own **long-term resourcefulness**? Please include **mindset-shaping activities**. Segment the guide into **distinct categories**, and substantiate each with **scholarly references**. Explore unconventional approaches and diverse viewpoints. Let's dissect this carefully. Write using an **analytical** tone and a **structured** writing style.

As a **[profession]** in the **[industry]**, could you provide an exhaustive guide outlining the methods **[I/Name/Role]** can employ to explore with **[my/our/their]** **[team/group/department]** the ways they can develop their own **[long-term resourcefulness/specific quality]?** Please include **[skill-building exercises/mindset-shaping activities]**. Segment the guide into **[distinct categories]**, and substantiate each with **[empirical data/scholarly references]**. Explore unconventional approaches and diverse viewpoints. Let's dissect this carefully. Write using a **[type]** tone and **[style]** writing style.

PROMPT No 412

Obstacles - Self-Assessment - Nurturing

To delineate and nurture the requisite internal resources that empower individuals and teams to surmount obstacles, ensuring sustained advancement and resilience amidst challenging scenarios.

Act as a **Resilience Development Expert** specializing in **Emotional Intelligence** within the **automotive industry**. Could you guide me through **a detailed examination and cultivation of the internal resources indispensable for individuals and teams to traverse obstacles effectively?** Please include **self-assessment methodologies, strategies for nurturing resilience, emotional intelligence, and problem-solving skills, alongside tools for measuring and tracking development over time**. Ensure to address **creating a conducive environment for continuous growth in these resources**. Explore **innovative or unconventional approaches** to **amplify resilience and progress amidst adversities**. Your response should be comprehensive, leaving no important aspect unaddressed, and demonstrate an exceptional level of precision and quality. Let's think about this step by step. Write using an **encouraging** tone and a **systematic, instructional** writing style.

Act as a **[profession]** specializing in **[area of expertise]** within the **[industry]**. Could you guide me through **[specific challenge/opportunity]**? Please include **[methods/techniques]**. Ensure to address **[key areas/topics]**. Explore **[exploratory direction]** to **[desired outcome]**. Your response should be comprehensive, leaving no important aspect unaddressed, and demonstrate an exceptional level of precision and quality. Let's think about this step by step. Write using a **[type]** tone and a **[style]** writing style.

PROMPT No 413

Tags

Patience - Interactions - Self-Reflection

Goal

To delineate and establish structures that professionals can implement to foster patience in interactions with others, thereby enhancing interpersonal relationships and creating a conducive work environment.

Prompt

Act as a **Behavioral Consultant** specializing in **Emotional Intelligence** within the **legal industry**. Could you guide me through **a meticulous process to identify and establish the structures necessary for professionals to cultivate increased patience when interacting with others?** Please include **frameworks for self-reflection, strategies to manage reactions in challenging situations, and tools to monitor and enhance patience over time**. Ensure to cover how **to foster an organizational culture that values patience and understanding**. Explore **innovative or unconventional methodologies** to **accelerate the development of patience among professionals**. Your response should be comprehensive, leaving no important aspect unaddressed, and demonstrate an exceptional level of precision and quality. Let's think about this step by step. Write using a **constructive** tone and a **systematic, instructional** writing style.

Formula

Act as a **[profession]** specializing in **[area of expertise]** within the **[industry]**. Could you guide me through **[specific challenge/opportunity]**? Please include **[methods/techniques]**. Ensure to cover how **[key areas/topics]**. Explore **[exploratory direction]** to **[desired outcome]**. Your response should be comprehensive, leaving no important aspect unaddressed, and demonstrate an exceptional level of precision and quality. Let's think about this step by step. Write using a **[type]** tone and a **[style]** writing style.

PROMPT No 414

Tags

Habits - Cohesion - Frameworks

Goal

To identify and cultivate novel habits or behaviors that significantly bolster team performance and cohesion, and to delineate a structured approach for their development and integration within team dynamics.

Prompt

Act as a **Team Development Specialist** specializing in **Habit Formation** within the **advertising industry**. Could you guide me through **a thorough exploration of new habits or behaviors that would notably enhance my team's performance and cohesion, and**

outline the methods for developing and integrating them? Please include **frameworks for habit identification and assessment, strategies for habit cultivation, and tools for monitoring and reinforcing these new behaviors over time.** Ensure to cover how **to foster a supportive environment that encourages the adoption and sustained practice of these beneficial habits.** Delve into **innovative or unconventional approaches** to **habit formation that could further propel team effectiveness.** Your response should be comprehensive, leaving no important aspect unaddressed, and demonstrate an exceptional level of precision and quality. Let's think about this step by step. Write using a **motivational** tone and a **systematic, instructional** writing style.

Formula

Act as a **[profession]** specializing in **[area of expertise]** within the **[industry]**. Could you guide me through **[specific challenge/opportunity]**? Please include **[methods/techniques]**. Ensure to cover how **[key areas/topics]**. Delve into **[exploratory direction]** to **[desired outcome]**. Your response should be comprehensive, leaving no important aspect unaddressed, and demonstrate an exceptional level of precision and quality. Let's think about this step by step. Write using a **[type]** tone and a **[style]** writing style.

PROMPT No 415

Tags

Self-assessment - Motivation - Development

Goal

To meticulously identify and develop or modify personal attributes in a manner that significantly augments one's ability to achieve desired outcomes, fostering personal and professional growth.

Prompt

Act as a **Personal Development Consultant** specializing in **Self-awareness and Change Management** within the **technology sector**. Could you guide me through **a systematic approach to discerning the aspects about myself that can be developed or altered to better serve my ambitions**? Please include **frameworks for self-assessment, strategies for personal development or change, and tools for monitoring and evaluating progress over time.** Ensure to cover how **to maintain motivation and consistency during the transformation process.** Explore **cutting-edge or unconventional methodologies** to **expedite the identification and development of these aspects.** Your response should be comprehensive, leaving no important aspect unaddressed, and demonstrate an exceptional level of precision and quality. Let's think about this step by step. Write using an **insightful** tone and a **structured, instructional** writing style.

Formula

Act as a **[profession]** specializing in **[area of expertise]** within the **[industry]**. Could you guide me through **[specific challenge/opportunity]**? Please include **[methods/techniques]**. Ensure to cover how **[key areas/topics]**. Explore **[exploratory direction]** to **[desired outcome]**. Your response should be comprehensive, leaving no important aspect unaddressed, and demonstrate an exceptional level of precision and quality. Let's think about this step by step. Write using a **[type]** tone and a **[style]** writing style.

PROMPT No 416

Tags

Emotional-Intelligence - Cohesive - Resilience

To foster awareness and understanding within a team regarding how emotions and feelings can influence decision-making, particularly during challenging or high-pressure situations. This self-awareness aims to enhance emotional intelligence, encourage thoughtful response rather than reactive decisions, and contribute to a more cohesive and effective team dynamic.

Prompt

Act as an **Emotional Intelligence Coach** specializing in the **renewable energy industry**. Could you help **my team and me to recognize and understand our feelings or emotions that may be affecting our decision-making process when dealing with a challenging situation at work?** Insight into this area is crucial for **enhancing our collective emotional intelligence, improving our problem-solving abilities, and creating a more empathetic and resilient team environment**. Please provide an in-depth response that includes **techniques for self-awareness, team-building activities, emotional intelligence assessments, and strategies for mindful decision-making**. Let's explore this step by step. Write using an **empathetic** tone and **instructive** writing style.

Formula

Act as an **[profession]** specializing in the **[industry]**. Could you help **[contextual challenge/opportunity]?** Insight into this area is crucial for **[desired outcome]**. Please provide an in-depth response that includes **[specific components or methods]**. Let's explore this step by step. Write using a **[type]** tone and **[style]** writing style.

PROMPT No 417

Tags

Confidence - Empowerment - Leadership

Goal

To explore various tools, techniques, strategies, or mindset shifts that can be developed by a team to enhance their confidence and competence in handling their respective responsibilities, whether in daily tasks, projects, or long-term goals.

Prompt

Act as a **Leadership Confidence Coach** specializing in the **retail industry**. Could you delineate **the essential tools, techniques, strategies, or mindset shifts that my team needs to develop to empower themselves with the confidence to better deal with their responsibilities?** This includes **understanding individual capabilities, collective strengths, industry-specific challenges, and underlying psychological factors**. Provide unique insights and overlooked opportunities, considering various team dynamics and **levels of responsibility**. Let's analyze this piece by piece. Write using an **inspirational** tone and **engaging** writing style.

Formula

Act as a **[profession]** specializing in the [industry]. Could you delineate **[contextual challenge/opportunity]?** This includes **[desired outcome]**. Provide unique insights and overlooked opportunities, considering various team dynamics and **[other relevant factors]**. Let's analyze this piece by piece. Write using a **[type]** tone and **[style]** writing style.

PROMPT No 418

Tags

Empowerment   - Self-efficacy - Motivation

To proficiently facilitate team members in recognizing and harnessing their intrinsic capabilities towards crafting the career trajectory they aspire to, thereby promoting self-efficacy, motivation, and career satisfaction.

Act as a **Career Development Specialist** specializing in **Empowerment Strategies** within the **digital media industry**. Could you guide me through **an adept approach to assist my team in contemplating and accessing their own power to sculpt the career they desire**? Please include **frameworks for self-reflection, strategies for personal empowerment, and methodologies for aligning individual aspirations with actionable steps**. Ensure to cover how **to cultivate a supportive environment that encourages self-directed career development**. Probe into **innovative or unorthodox techniques** to **accentuate self-efficacy and proactive career management among team members**. Your response should be comprehensive, leaving no important aspect unaddressed, and demonstrate an exceptional level of precision and quality. Let's think about this step by step. Write using an **inspiring** tone and a **structured, instructional** writing style.

Act as a **[profession]** specializing in **[area of expertise]** within the **[industry]**. Could you guide me through **[specific challenge/opportunity]**? Please include **[methods/techniques]**. Ensure to cover how **[key areas/topics]**. Probe into **[exploratory direction]** to **[desired outcome]**. Your response should be comprehensive, leaving no important aspect unaddressed, and demonstrate an exceptional level of precision and quality. Let's think about this step by step. Write using a **[type]** tone and a **[style]** writing style.

PROMPT No 419

Resilience - Introspection - Decision-making

To meticulously explore and understand the requisites for cultivating self-trust, and to establish a personalized plan that fosters a strong foundation of self-trust, thereby enhancing decision-making, resilience, and personal satisfaction.

Act as a **Self-Trust Facilitator** specializing in **Personal Resilience** within the **mental health industry**. Could you guide me through **a comprehensive exploration to discern what it entails for me to access self-trust optimally**? Please include **frameworks for self-reflection, strategies for building self-trust, and tools for monitoring and nurturing self-trust over time**. Ensure to cover how **to address and overcome barriers that may impede the development of self-trust**. Investigate pioneering or unconventional approaches that could fast-track the cultivation of self-trust. Your response should be comprehensive, leaving no important aspect unaddressed, and demonstrate an exceptional level of precision and quality. Let's think about this step by step. Write using an **introspective** tone and a **structured, instructional** writing style.

Act as a **[profession]** specializing in **[area of expertise]** within the **[industry]**. Could you guide me through **[specific challenge/opportunity]**? Please include **[methods/techniques]**. Ensure to cover how **[key areas/topics]**. Investigate pioneering or unconventional approaches that could fast-track the cultivation of self-trust. Your response should be comprehensive, leaving no important aspect unaddressed, and demonstrate an exceptional level of precision and quality. Let's think about this step by step. Write using a **[type]** tone and a **[style]** writing style.

PROMPT No 420

Engagement - Tools - Creativity

To proficiently identify and utilize a range of tools or resources that can effectively inspire and motivate the team, fostering a culture of innovation, engagement, and high performance.

Act as a **Motivational Strategist** specializing in **Team Inspiration** within the **advertising industry**. Could you guide me through **the various tools or resources I could employ to significantly inspire my team**? Please include **both conventional and digital tools, methodologies for gauging their effectiveness, and strategies for integrating them into our daily operations**. Ensure to cover how **to tailor these tools or resources** to the **diverse needs and preferences of my team members**. Venture into novel or avant-garde insights that could provide a fresh perspective or ignite creativity among the team. Your response should be comprehensive, leaving no important aspect unaddressed, and demonstrate an exceptional level of precision and quality. Let's think about this step by step. Write using an **engaging** tone and a **well-organized, instructional** writing style.

Act as a **[profession]** specializing in **[area of expertise]** within the **[industry]**. Could you guide me through **[specific challenge/opportunity]**? Please include **[methods/techniques]**. Make sure to cover how **[key areas/topics]**. Ensure to cover how **[exploratory direction]** to **[desired outcome]**. Venture into novel or avant-garde insights that could provide a fresh perspective or ignite creativity among the team. Your response should be comprehensive, leaving no important aspect unaddressed, and demonstrate an exceptional level of precision and quality. Let's think about this step by step. Write using a **[type]** tone and a **[style]** writing style.

PROMPT No 421

Engagement - Productivity - Mindfulness

To adeptly devise and implement strategies that rejuvenate team engagement and presence, ensuring a conducive atmosphere for enhanced productivity, communication, and collective achievement.

Act as an **Engagement Revitalization Expert** specializing in **Mindful Leadership** within the **software development industry**. Could you guide me through **robust strategies to steer my team back to full presence whenever I discern a lapse in their engagement**? Please include **diagnostic tools to ascertain the level of engagement, mindfulness practices, and re-engagement techniques**. Ensure to cover how **to foster a culture of sustained presence and attentivenes**s. Delve into avant-garde or pioneering strategies that could provide a fresh impetus to team engagement. Your response should be comprehensive, leaving no important aspect unaddressed, and demonstrate an exceptional level of precision and quality. Let's think about this step by step. Write using a **focused** tone and a **step-by-step instructional** writing style.

Act as a **[profession]** specializing in **[area of expertise]** within the **[industry]**. Could you guide me through **[specific challenge/opportunity]**? Please include **[methods/techniques]**. Ensure to cover how **[key areas/topics]**. Delve into avant-garde or pioneering strategies that could provide a fresh impetus to team engagement. Your response should be comprehensive, leaving no important aspect unaddressed, and demonstrate an exceptional level of precision and quality. Let's think about this step by step. Write using a **[type]** tone and a **[style]** writing style.

PROMPT No 422

Role-Optimization - Responsibilities - Personal-Growth

To engage in a thoughtful reflection on the various elements that contribute to assigning meaningful responsibilities or roles within your team, facilitating both personal growth and team success.

Act as an **executive coach** with a specialization in **role optimization** for the **manufacturing industry**. Could you guide me through **dissecting the key factors that contribute to establishing meaningful roles and responsibilities for myself and my team**? Please include **models for role analysis and strategies for aligning these roles with organizational objectives**. Make sure to cover how **team members' individual strengths and aspirations fit into this scheme**. Navigate through unexplored realms and revolutionary paradigms to cultivate this practice. Let's dissect this in a structured manner. Write using an **introspective** tone and an **analytical** writing style.

Act as a **[profession]** with a specialization in **[area of expertise]** for the **[industry]**. Could you guide me through **[specific challenge/opportunity]?** Please include **[methods/techniques].** Make sure to cover how **[key areas/topics]**. Navigate through unexplored realms and revolutionary paradigms to cultivate this practice. Let's dissect this in a structured manner. Write using a **[type]** tone and **[style]** writing style.

PROMPT No 423

Resources - Implementation - Performance

To identify and evaluate the essential resources that could enhance the performance and satisfaction of your team. These resources may range from software tools to training programs, and from flexible work arrangements to mental health support systems.

Act as a **leadership coach** with a specialization in **resource optimization** for the **healthcare industry**. Could you guide me through **the identification and implementation of valuable resources that can assist my team in delivering top-tier performance**? Please include a **discussion on technological, educational, and emotional resources**. Make sure to cover how **the selected resources will fit within the work ecosystem and any potential constraints**. Explore unconventional solutions and alternative perspectives to continually refine our approach to resource allocation. Let's dissect this in a structured manner. Write using a **strategic** tone and a **problem-solving** writing style.

Act as a **[profession]** with a specialization in **[area of expertise]** for the **[industry]**. Could you guide me through **[specific challenge/opportunity]?** Please include **[methods/techniques].** Make sure to cover how **[key areas/topics].** Explore unconventional solutions and alternative perspectives to continually refine our approach to resource allocation. Let's dissect this in a structured manner. Write using a **[type]** tone and **[style]** writing style.

PROMPT No 424

Optimization - Assessment - Efficiency

To acquire a comprehensive, actionable guide on methods for optimally assessing the resources a company needs to better support the whole organization, with the aim of enhancing operational efficiency, employee satisfaction, and overall business performance.

As a **Resource Management Expert** in the **logistics industry**, could you provide an exhaustive guide outlining the methods **I** can employ to optimally assess the resources **my company** needs to better support the whole organization? Please include **both human capital and technological assets**. Organize your recommendations into thematic clusters, each supported by **data-driven**

evidence. Explore unconventional approaches and diverse viewpoints. Let's dissect this carefully. Write using an **analytical** tone and a **structured** writing style.

Formula

As a **[profession]** in the **[industry]**, could you provide an exhaustive guide outlining the methods **[I/Name/Role]** can employ to optimally assess the resources **[my/our/their]** **[company/organization]** needs to better support the whole organization? Please include both **[human capital/technological assets]**. Organize your recommendations into thematic clusters, each supported by **[data-driven evidence/academic citations]**. Explore unconventional approaches and diverse viewpoints. Let's dissect this carefully. Write using a **[type]** tone and **[style]** writing style.

PROMPT No 425

Tags

Reflective - Resourcefulness - Collaboration

Goal

To adeptly facilitate a reflective process for the team to identify, appreciate, and optimize their most valuable resources, thereby enhancing resourcefulness, collaboration, and overall productivity.

Prompt

Act as a **Resource Recognition Advisor** specializing in **Team Reflection** within the **renewable energy industry**. Could you guide me through **a thorough process to assist my team in reflecting upon and recognizing their most precious resources**? Please include **reflective exercises, identification methodologies, and strategies to leverage these resources effectively**. Ensure to cover how **to cultivate an ongoing awareness and appreciation of individual and collective resources**. Venture into innovative or unorthodox approaches that could unveil overlooked resources. Your response should be comprehensive, leaving no important aspect unaddressed, and demonstrate an exceptional level of precision and quality. Let's think about this step by step. Write using an **insightful** tone and a **structured, instructional** writing style.

Formula

Act as a **[profession]** specializing in **[area of expertise]** within the **[industry]**. Could you guide me through **[specific challenge/opportunity]**? Please include **[methods/techniques]**. Ensure to cover how **[key areas/topics]**. Venture into innovative or unorthodox approaches that could unveil overlooked resources. Your response should be comprehensive, leaving no important aspect unaddressed, and demonstrate an exceptional level of precision and quality. Let's think about this step by step. Write using a **[type]** tone and a **[style]** writing style.

PROMPT No 426

Tags

Resource Management - Utilization - Analytical Guide

Goal

To acquire a comprehensive, actionable guide on methods for identifying how a team can best utilize their existing resources to navigate current challenges, with the aim of enhancing problem-solving capabilities and operational efficiency.

Prompt

As a **Resource Management Expert** in the **logistics industry**, could you provide an exhaustive guide outlining the strategies **my team** and **I** can employ to identify how to utilize our current resources to navigate **our existing challenges**? Please include both **quantitative assessments and qualitative observations**. Segment the guide into **distinct categories**, and substantiate each with **empirical data and scholarly references**. Explore unconventional approaches and diverse viewpoints. Let's dissect this carefully. Write using an **analytical** tone and a **structured** writing style.

Formula

As a **[profession]** in the **[industry]**, could you provide an exhaustive guide outlining the strategies **[I/Name/Role]** and **[my/our/their]** **[team/group/department]** can employ to identify how to utilize our current resources to navigate **[current challenges/specific issues]**? Please include both **[quantitative assessments/qualitative observations]**. Segment the guide into **[distinct categories]**, and substantiate each with **[empirical data/scholarly references]**. Explore unconventional approaches and diverse viewpoints. Let's dissect this carefully. Write using a **[type]** tone and **[style]** writing style.

PROMPT No 427

Tags

Support - Emotional - Performance

Goal

To meticulously identify and establish structures or systems that provide robust emotional support to the team, promoting a nurturing work environment conducive to well-being, resilience, and optimal performance.

Prompt

Act as a **Well-being Systems Architect** specializing in **Emotional Support Infrastructure** within the **social work industry**. Could you guide me through **a methodical process to determine the structures or systems my team could have in place to offer substantial emotional support**? Please include **assessment tools, design principles for supportive structures, and strategies for fostering a supportive culture**. Ensure to cover how **to tailor these systems to the unique emotional needs and preferences of my team members**. Explore **groundbreaking or unconventional systems** to **provide a novel layer of support**. Your response should be comprehensive, leaving no important aspect unaddressed, and demonstrate an exceptional level of precision and quality. Let's think about this step by step. Write using a **compassionate** tone and a **detailed, instructional** writing style.

Formula

Act as a **[profession]** specializing in **[area of expertise]** within the **[industry]**. Could you guide me through **[specific challenge/opportunity]**? Please include **[methods/techniques]**. Ensure to cover how **[key areas/topics]**. Explore **[exploratory direction]** to **[desired outcome]**. Your response should be comprehensive, leaving no important aspect unaddressed, and demonstrate an exceptional level of precision and quality. Let's think about this step by step. Write using a **[type]** tone and a **[style]** writing style.

PROMPT No 428

Tags

To obtain a comprehensive, actionable guide on methods for facilitating a thought experiment within a team to explore what could be achieved if they had unlimited time and resources, with the aim of unlocking latent potential and inspiring innovative thinking.

As a **Futurist Consultant** in the **technology sector**, could you provide an exhaustive guide outlining the methods **my team** and **I** can employ to imagine what we could achieve in **our** work if we had **unlimited time and resources**? Please include both **brainstorming techniques** and **analytical frameworks**. Segment the guide into **distinct categories**, and substantiate each with **empirical data and scholarly references**. Explore unconventional approaches and diverse viewpoints. Let's dissect this carefully. Write using an **analytical** tone and a **structured** writing style.

As a **[profession]** in the **[industry],** could you provide an exhaustive guide outlining the methods **[I/Name/Role]** and **[my/our/their]** **[team/group/department]** can employ to imagine what we could achieve in **[our/their]** work if we had **[unlimited time and resources/other hypothetical scenarios]**? Please include both **[brainstorming techniques/analytical frameworks]**. Segment the guide into **[distinct categories]**, and substantiate each with **[empirical data/scholarly references]**. Explore unconventional approaches and diverse viewpoints. Let's dissect this carefully. Write using a **[type]** tone and **[style]** writing style.

SELF-ASSESSMENT

PROMPT No 429

Conflict - Communication - Legal

To acquire a comprehensive, actionable guide on best practices for speaking to a colleague about the factors that led him to have a fight with another colleague, with the aim of resolving the conflict, fostering a positive work environment, and maintaining team cohesion.

As a **Conflict Resolution Specialist** in the **legal industry**, could you provide an exhaustive guide outlining the best practices **I** should consider when speaking to a colleague about the factors that led **him** to have a fight with another colleague? Please include **both verbal communication strategies and non-verbal cues**. Structure your guidance into individual components, each backed by **statistical analysis and peer-reviewed studies**. Explore unconventional approaches and diverse viewpoints. Let's dissect this carefully. Write using an **analytical** tone and a **structured** writing style.

As a **[profession]** in the **[industry],** could you provide an exhaustive guide outlining the best practices **[I/Name/Role]** should consider when speaking to a colleague about the factors that led **[him/her/them]** to have a fight with another colleague? Please include both **[verbal communication strategies/non-verbal cues]**. Structure your guidance into individual components, each backed by **[statistical analysis/peer-reviewed studies]**. Explore unconventional approaches and diverse viewpoints. Let's dissect this carefully. Write using a **[type]** tone and **[style]** writing style.

PROMPT No 430

Tags

Leadership - Persuasion - Executive

Goal

To acquire actionable strategies, techniques, and frameworks for enhancing persuasion skills, with the objective of effectively influencing and leading a team in a business environment.

Prompt

As an **Executive Leadership Coach** in the **technology sector**, could you provide a comprehensive guide on the steps **I** need to take to improve my **persuasion skills** for **influencing and leading my team**? Please include both **theoretical foundations and practical applications**. Break down the guide into **key components**, and substantiate each with **empirical evidence and case studies**. Explore unconventional solutions and alternative perspectives. Let's dissect this carefully. Write using an **authoritative** tone and a **structured** writing style.

Formula

As a **[profession]** in the **[industry]**, could you provide a comprehensive guide on the steps **[I/Name/Role]** need to take to improve my **[skillset]** for **[contextual challenge/opportunity]** in **[my/their]** **[team/group/department]**? Please include both **[theoretical foundations/practical applications]**. Break down the guide into **[key components]**, and substantiate each with **[empirical evidence/case studies]**. Explore unconventional solutions and alternative perspectives. Let's dissect this carefully. Write using a **[type]** tone and **[style]** writing style.

PROMPT No 431

Tags

Presentation - Development - Consulting

Goal

To acquire a comprehensive, actionable guide on creating the optimal conditions that will enable a team to plan and take the first step toward enhancing their presentation skills, with the aim of improving communication effectiveness and professional development.

Prompt

As a **Professional Development Expert** in the **consulting industry**, could you provide an exhaustive guide outlining the conditions **I** need to create for **my team** to plan to take the first step in enhancing their **presentation skills**? Please include both **environmental factors and motivational strategies**. Segment the guide into **distinct categories**, and substantiate each with **empirical data and scholarly references**. Explore unconventional approaches and diverse viewpoints. Let's dissect this carefully. Write using an **analytical** tone and a **structured** writing style.

Formula

229

As a **[profession]** in the **[industry]**, could you provide an exhaustive guide outlining the conditions **[I/Name/Role]** need to create for **[my/our/their]** **[team/group/department]** to plan to take the first step in enhancing their [skillset]? Please include both **[environmental factors/motivational strategies]**. Segment the guide into **[distinct categories]**, and substantiate each with **[empirical data/scholarly references]**. Explore unconventional approaches and diverse viewpoints. Let's dissect this carefully. Write using a **[type]** tone and **[style]** writing style.

PROMPT No 432

Growth - Fulfillment - Optimization

To proficiently evaluate the current professional standing of a team member in relation to their desired career state, thereby crafting a structured pathway for aligned growth, fulfillment, and performance optimization.

Act as a **Career Alignment Specialist** specializing in **Professional Position Assessment** within the **aerospace industry**. Could you guide me through **a rigorous process to assess the current position of a team member relative to his/her desired professional state?** Please include **assessment tools, comparative analysis techniques, and discussions conducive to understanding their career aspirations**. Ensure to cover how **to create a supportive environment for team members to openly discuss their professional goals and current standing**. Examine novel or pioneering methodologies that could offer a deeper insight into this alignment. Your response should be comprehensive, leaving no important aspect unaddressed, and demonstrate an exceptional level of precision and quality. Let's think about this step by step. Write using an **analytical** tone and a **thorough, instructional** writing style.

Act as a **[profession]** specializing in **[area of expertise]** within the **[industry]**. Could you guide me through **[specific challenge/opportunity]**? Please include **[methods/techniques]**. Ensure to cover how **[key areas/topics]**. Examine novel or pioneering methodologies that could offer a deeper insight into this alignment. Your response should be comprehensive, leaving no important aspect unaddressed, and demonstrate an exceptional level of precision and quality. Let's think about this step by step. Write using a **[type]** tone and a **[style]** writing style.

PROMPT No 433

Introspection - Decision-making - Behavior

To provide leaders with a nuanced and actionable framework that enables their teams to engage in deep self-reflection, focusing on understanding their core identity and essence, which in turn informs their professional behavior and decision-making.

Act as a **Personal Development Coach** specializing in the **technology sector**. Could you outline a **structured approach** for **guiding** my team in **reflecting** on their **core identity** and **understanding who they are at their essence**? Include **exercises, questionnaires, and** other tools that **facilitate** this **introspective** process. Let's methodically dissect each component. Your response should be comprehensive, leaving no important aspect unaddressed, and demonstrate an exceptional level of precision and quality. Write using an **introspective** tone and an **analytical** writing style.

Act as a **[profession]** specializing in the **[industry]**. Could you outline a **[structured/comprehensive]** approach for **[guiding/leading]** my team in **[reflecting on/understanding]** their **[core identity/true essence]**? Include **[exercises/questionnaires/tools]** that **[facilitate/enable]** this **[introspective/deep]** process. Let's methodically dissect each component. Your response should be comprehensive, leaving no important aspect unaddressed, and demonstrate an exceptional level of precision and quality. Write using a **[type]** tone and **[style]** writing style.

PROMPT No 434

Talent - Assessment - Cohesion

To acquire a comprehensive, actionable guide on methods for identifying the unique qualities or attributes that make each team member stand out, particularly in alignment with the overall goals of the company. The aim is to foster individual growth, team cohesion, and organizational success.

As a **Talent Management Specialist** in the **financial sector**, could you provide an exhaustive guide outlining the methods **my team** and **I** can employ to identify the unique qualities or attributes that make each team member stand out, considering **our company's overall goals**? Please include both **assessment tools and interpersonal evaluation techniques**. Segment the guide into **distinct categories**, and substantiate each with **empirical data and scholarly references**. Explore unconventional approaches and diverse viewpoints. Let's dissect this carefully. Write using an **analytical** tone and a **structured** writing style.

As a **[profession]** in the **[industry]**, could you provide an exhaustive guide outlining the methods **[I/Name/Role]** and **[my/our/their]** **[team/group/department]** can employ to identify the unique qualities or attributes that make each team member stand out, considering **[our/their]** company's overall goals? Please include both **[assessment tools/interpersonal evaluation techniques]**. Segment the guide into **[distinct categories]**, and substantiate each with **[empirical data/scholarly references]**. Explore unconventional approaches and diverse viewpoints. Let's dissect this carefully. Write using a **[type]** tone and **[style]** writing style.

PROMPT No 435

Engagement - Passions - Cohesion

To equip leaders with a multi-faceted approach that fosters a culture of open sharing and engagement among team members, specifically focusing on the communication of individual passions within their professional lives, thereby enhancing team cohesion and motivation.

Act as a **Communication Coach** specializing in the **banking industry**. Could you outline a **structured** strategy for **facilitating** an environment where my **colleagues** can **openly share** what they are **passionate about** in their **professional lives**? Include **actionable steps, communication exercises, and best practices** that **facilitate** this **open sharing**. Let's methodically dissect each component. Your response should be comprehensive, leaving no important aspect unaddressed, and demonstrate an exceptional level of precision and quality. Write using an **encouraging** tone and a **persuasive** writing style.

Formula

Act as a **[profession]** specializing in the **[industry]**. Could you outline a **[structured/comprehensive]** strategy for **[facilitating/creating]** an environment where my **[colleagues/team members]** can **[openly share/discuss]** what they are **[passionate about/interested in]** in their **[professional lives/careers]?** Include **[actionable steps/communication exercises/best practices]** that **[facilitate/enable]** this **[open sharing/engagement]**. Let's methodically dissect each component. Your response should be **[comprehensive/thorough]**, leaving no important aspect unaddressed, and demonstrate an **[exceptional/high]** level of **[precision/quality]**. Write using a **[type]** tone and **[style]** writing style.

PROMPT No 436

Accountability - Success - Analysis

To provide leaders and professionals with a nuanced framework for effectively analyzing and articulating recent professional successes or failures, thereby fostering a culture of accountability, learning, and continuous improvement.

Act as a **Career Development Coach** specializing in the **finance sector**. Could you elucidate the **key** elements that **professionals** should consider when **describing** their **recent successes** in the **workplace**? Include **both qualitative and quantitative metrics, psychological factors, and organizational context** that **should** be **considered**. Let's methodically dissect each component. Your response should be comprehensive, leaving no important aspect unaddressed, and demonstrate an exceptional level of precision and quality. Write using an **analytical** tone and a **structured** writing style.

Act as a **[profession]** specializing in the **[industry]**. Could you elucidate the **[key/critical/essential]** elements that **[professionals/individuals/team members]** should consider when **[describing/analyzing/evaluating]** their **[recent/past/current]** **[successes/failures]** in the **[workplace/professional setting]?** Include **[both qualitative and quantitative metrics/psychological factors/organizational context]** that **[should/must/could]** be **[considered/taken into account]**. Let's methodically dissect each component. Your response should be comprehensive, leaving no important aspect unaddressed, and demonstrate an exceptional level of precision and quality. Write using a **[type]** tone and **[style]** writing style.

Organizational   - Reflection - Improvement

To obtain a well-rounded, actionable guide on the most effective methods for reflecting on and learning from both the successes and failures experienced by a team, with the aim of fostering continuous improvement and resilience in a business setting.

As an **Organizational Development Specialist** in the **financial sector**, could you provide an exhaustive guide outlining the most optimal ways for **me** to reflect on the lessons **my team** has learned from recent failures? Please include both **analytical frameworks and practical exercises**. Segment the guide into **distinct phases**, and substantiate each with **empirical data and scholarly references**. Explore unconventional approaches and diverse viewpoints. Let's scrutinize this topic incrementally. Write using an **analytical** tone and a **structured** writing style.

As a **[profession]** in the **[industry]**, could you provide an exhaustive guide outlining the most optimal ways for **[I/Name/Role]** to reflect on the lessons **[my/their]** **[team/group/department]** has learned from recent **[successes/failures]**? Please include both **[analytical frameworks/practical exercises]**. Segment the guide into **[distinct phases]**, and substantiate each with **[empirical data/scholarly references]**. Explore unconventional approaches and diverse viewpoints. Let's scrutinize this topic incrementally. Write using a **[type]** tone and **[style]** writing style.

Evolution - Mentoring - Perspectives

To equip leaders with a robust methodology for tracking and understanding the evolution of their team's perspectives on responsibilities and potential, thereby enabling more effective coaching, mentoring, and talent development strategies.

Act as an **Organizational Development Specialist** specializing in the **retail industry**. Could you provide a **comprehensive** framework for **examining** how my team's perspective on their **responsibilities evolves** over **time**? Include **qualitative assessment methods**, as well as **strategies** for capturing temporal changes for **assessment**. Let's methodically dissect each component. Your response should be comprehensive, leaving no important aspect unaddressed, and demonstrate an exceptional level of precision and quality. Write using an **analytical** tone and a **structured** writing style.

Act as a **[profession]** specializing in the **[industry]**. Could you provide a **[comprehensive/robust/detailed]** framework for **[examining/assessing/evaluating]** how my team's perspective on their **[responsibilities/potential/roles]** **[evolves/changes/shifts]** over **[time/periods/phases]**? Include **[qualitative/quantitative assessment methods/strategies]** for capturing **[temporal changes/psychological metrics]** for **[assessment/evaluation]**. Let's methodically dissect each component. Your response should be comprehensive, leaving no important aspect unaddressed, and demonstrate an exceptional level of precision and quality. Write using a **[type]** tone and **[style]** writing style.

<u>PROMPT No 439</u>

Self-awareness - Mindfulness - Growth

Goal

To meticulously develop and hone self-observance and self-awareness skills, fostering a deeper understanding of personal tendencies, behaviors, and responses, which in turn cultivates personal growth, enhanced interpersonal relations, and effective decision-making.

Prompt

Act as a **Self-Reflective Practices Expert** specializing in **Awareness Enhancement** within the **defense industry**. Could you guide me through **various strategies to significantly enhance my self-observance and self-awareness**? Please include **practical exercises, mindfulness techniques, and feedback mechanisms**. Ensure to cover how **to maintain a consistent practice of self-reflection and effectively utilize the insights gained for personal and professional development**. Explore **contemporary or avant-garde approaches** to **offer a fresh perspective on self-observance**. Your response should be comprehensive, leaving no important aspect unaddressed, and demonstrate an exceptional level of precision and quality. Let's think about this step by step. Write using an **introspective** tone and a **detailed, instructional** writing style.

Formula

Act as a **[profession]** specializing in **[area of expertise]** within the **[industry].** Could you guide me through **[specific challenge/opportunity]**? Please include **[methods/techniques]**. Ensure to cover how **[key areas/topics]**. Explore **[exploratory direction]** to **[desired outcome]**. Your response should be comprehensive, leaving no important aspect unaddressed, and demonstrate an exceptional level of precision and quality. Let's think about this step by step. Write using a **[type]** tone and a **[style]** writing style.

<u>PROMPT No 440</u>

Communication - Observational - Strategies

Goal

To acquire a multifaceted, actionable guide on indirect methods for gaining a deeper understanding of a boss's desires and vision for the future, with the aim of aligning team efforts and individual contributions more effectively in a business setting.

Prompt

As a **Corporate Communication Expert** in the **technology sector**, could you provide a comprehensive guide on indirect strategies **I** can employ to gain a deeper insight into **my** boss's desires for the future without directly asking **her**? Please include both **observational techniques and analytical tools**. Segment the guide into **specific categories**, and substantiate each with **empirical data and scholarly references**. Explore unconventional approaches and diverse viewpoints. Let's dissect this carefully. Write using an **analytical** tone and a **structured** writing style.

Formula

As a **[profession]** in the **[industry],** could you provide a comprehensive guide on indirect strategies **[I/Name/Role]** can employ to gain a deeper insight into **[my/their]** boss's desires for the future without directly asking [him/her/them]? Please include both **[observational techniques/analytical tools].** Segment the guide into **[specific categories],** and substantiate each with **[empirical data/scholarly references].** Explore unconventional approaches and diverse viewpoints. Let's dissect this carefully. Write using a **[type]** tone and **[style]** writing style.

PROMPT No 441

Data - Collaboration - Continuous-improvement

To empower teams with a clear, systematic, and insightful methodology for identifying relevant metrics and assessment techniques that accurately measure progress towards their defined goals, fostering a culture of continuous improvement and goal attainment.

Act as a **Performance Measurement Specialist** specializing in **Goal Progression Metrics** within the **technology sector**. Could you guide me through **comprehensive approaches for my team to elucidate on their own how to measure progress towards their goals**? Please include **metric identification, key performance indicators (KPIs) development, and data analysis techniques**. Make sure to cover how **to foster a collaborative environment that encourages continuous feedback and refinement of measurement strategies. Explore innovative or under-utilized methods** to **offer a fresh perspective on progress measurement**. Your response should be comprehensive, leaving no important aspect unaddressed, and demonstrate an exceptional level of precision and quality. Let's think about this step by step. Write using a **precise** tone and a **systematic, instructional** writing style.

Act as a **[profession]** specializing in **[area of expertise]** within the **[industry].** Could you guide me through **[specific challenge/opportunity]**? Please include **[methods/techniques].** Make sure to cover how **[key areas/topics].** Explore **[exploratory direction]** to **[desired outcome].** Your response should be comprehensive, leaving no important aspect unaddressed, and demonstrate an exceptional level of precision and quality. Let's think about this step by step. Write using a **[type]** tone and a **[style]** writing style.

PROMPT No 442

Executive - Priority - Organizational

To meticulously identify and comprehend the core values, priorities, and aspirations of a boss within the corporate landscape, facilitating a more aligned and harmonious work environment, and enabling a deeper understanding of organizational objectives and expectations.

As a **Priority Identification Specialist** specializing in **Executive Alignment** within the **pharmaceutical industry,** how can I rigorously identify and understand **what truly matters to my boss** in their work or within the company? Please elucidate a thorough process entailing **strategic conversations, observation methodologies, and feedback mechanisms, aimed**

at discerning their core values, priorities, and aspirations. The discourse should delve into creating a conducive environment for **open communication**, ensuring **accurate interpretation of these insights**, and strategies **for aligning team objectives with the identified priorities**. Your discourse should be exhaustive, addressing all crucial aspects, and reflecting a high degree of precision and quality.

Formula

As a **[Profession]** specializing in **[Specialization]** within the **[Industry]**, how can I rigorously identify and understand **[Specific Inquiry]** in their work or within the company? Please elucidate a thorough process entailing [Methodologies], aimed at discerning their **[Key Aspects]**. The discourse should delve into creating a conducive environment for **[Communication/Interaction]**, ensuring **[Relevant Assurance]**, and strategies for **[Alignment/Application]**. Your discourse should be exhaustive, addressing all crucial aspects, and reflecting a high degree of precision and quality.

PROMPT No 443

Tags

Feedback - Communication - Motivations

Goal

To adeptly discern the core values, aspirations, and motivations that significantly matter to the team in their work or within the company, fostering a conducive environment for engagement, satisfaction, and meaningful contributions.

Prompt

Act as an **Organizational Values Analyst** specializing in **Employee Engagement** within the **automotive sector**. Could you guide me through **an intricate approach to identifying what truly matters to my team in their work or within the company**? Please include **methods for value discovery, effective communication channels, and feedback gathering techniques**. Make sure to cover how **to create a safe and open environment that encourages honest expression**. Explore **novel and empathetic ways** to **delve into the team's core motivations and aspirations**. Your response should be comprehensive, leaving no important aspect unaddressed, and demonstrate an exceptional level of precision and quality. Let's think about this step by step. Write using an **insightful** tone and a **guided, explorative** writing style.

Formula

Act as a **[profession]** specializing in **[area of expertise]** within the **[industry]**. Could you guide me through **[specific challenge/opportunity]**? Please include **[methods/techniques]**. Make sure to cover how **[key areas/topics]**. Explore **[exploratory direction]** to **[desired outcome]**. Your response should be comprehensive, leaving no important aspect unaddressed, and demonstrate an exceptional level of precision and quality. Let's think about this step by step. Write using a **[type]** tone and a **[style]** writing style.

SKILLS

PROMPT No 444

Tags

Skills - Gap - Analysis

To meticulously evaluate the discrepancy between the existing skills of the team and the requisite skills for attaining the organizational objectives, employing systematic methodologies which yield precise insights, enabling targeted development initiatives and optimal resource allocation in the technology consultancy sector.

As a **Skills Gap Analyst** specializing in **Corporate Performance Optimization** within the **technology consultancy sector**, how can I meticulously evaluate the discrepancy between my team's existing skills and the requisite skills for attaining our organizational objectives? Please provide a thorough elucidation of systematic methodologies encompassing **quantitative assessments, qualitative analyses, and feedback mechanisms**, aimed at yielding precise insights. The discourse should further delve into leveraging these insights for **targeted development initiatives, optimal resource allocation**, and **strategic planning to bridge the skills gap effectively**. Your discourse should be exhaustive, addressing all crucial aspects, and reflecting a high degree of precision and quality.

As a **[Profession]** specializing in **[Specialization]** within the **[Industry]**, how can I meticulously evaluate the discrepancy between my team's existing skills and the requisite skills for attaining our organizational objectives? Please provide a thorough elucidation of systematic methodologies encompassing **[Assessment Techniques]**, aimed at yielding precise insights. The discourse should further delve into leveraging these insights for **[Development/Allocation Strategies]**, and **[Strategic Planning]** to bridge the skills gap effectively. Your discourse should be exhaustive, addressing all crucial aspects, and reflecting a high degree of precision and quality.

PROMPT No 445

Benchmarking - Development - Prioritization

To meticulously delineate and acquire the requisite new skills aligned with achieving specified key performance indicators or professional aspirations, thereby enhancing competency, performance, and career progression.

Act as a **Professional Development Strategist** specializing in **Skill Gap Analysis** within the **telecommunications industry**. Could you guide me through **a thorough methodology to identify the specific new skills I need to acquire to meet my key performance indicators or professional goals**? Please include **skill assessment tools, industry benchmarking, and personalized development plans**. Ensure to cover how **to prioritize these skills based on immediate and long-term objectives**. Explore **innovative approaches** to **skill acquisition that may expedite the attainment of my goals**. Your response should be comprehensive, leaving no important aspect unaddressed, and demonstrate an exceptional level of precision and quality. Let's think about this step by step. Write using a **structured** tone and a **strategic, actionable** writing style.

Act as a **[profession]** specializing in **[area of expertise]** within the **[industry]**. Could you guide me through **[specific challenge/opportunity]**? Please include **[methods/techniques]**. Ensure to cover how **[key areas/topics]**. Explore **[exploratory direction]** to **[desired outcome]**. Your response should be comprehensive, leaving no important aspect unaddressed, and demonstrate an exceptional level of precision and quality. Let's think about this step by step. Write using a **[type]** tone and a **[style]** writing style.

PROMPT No 446

Motivation - Skills - Optimization

To gain a nuanced understanding of the skills that motivate and uplift your team, aiming to further optimize these elements for enhanced team performance and morale.

As an **HR manager** specializing in **talent development** within the **healthcare industry**, provide an exhaustive and meticulous examination, incorporating innovative insights and inventive strategies for **reflecting** on the skills that **energize** and **inspire** your team as they **utilize** them. Explore strategies to **make the most of** these skills in **day-to-day operations and project management**.

As a **[profession]** specializing in **[area of expertise/focus]** within the **[industry]**, provide an exhaustive and meticulous examination, incorporating innovative insights and inventive strategies for **[reflecting/contemplating/considering]** on the skills that **[energize/motivate/invigorate]** and **[inspire/uplift/empower]** your team as they **[utilize/employ/use]** them. Explore strategies to **[optimize/maximize/leverage]** these skills in **[day-to-day operations/project management/team initiatives]**.

PROMPT No 447

Introspection - Evolution - Self-Assessment

To equip professionals with a nuanced framework for introspectively examining and articulating the evolution of skills that have energized and inspired them over the years, thereby fostering self-awareness, career adaptability, and personal growth.

Act as a **Career Development Specialist** specializing in the **technology industry**. Could you **guide** me through a **structured process** for **introspectively examining** and **articulating** how the **skills** that have **energized and inspired** me have **evolved** over the years? Include **reflective exercises, theoretical frameworks, and metrics for self-assessment**. Let's think about this step by step. Write using a **reflective** tone and an **introspective** writing style.

Act as a **[profession]** specializing in the **[industry]**. Could you **[guide/lead/direct]** me through a **[structured/nuanced/comprehensive]** **[process/methodology/approach]** for **[introspectively/experientially/self-reflectively]** **[examining/analyzing/evaluating]** and **[articulating/describing/expressing]** how the **[skills/competencies/abilities]** that have **[energized/inspired/motivated]** me have **[evolved/transformed/changed]** over the **[years/decades/time]?** Include **[reflective exercises/self-assessment tools/question** prompts], **[theoretical frameworks/conceptual models]**, and **[metrics/KPIs/evaluation criteria]** for **[self-assessment/self-evaluation/self-monitoring].** Let's think about this step by step. Write using a **[type]** tone and **[style]** writing style.

PROMPT No 448

Acquisition - Performance - Alignment

To meticulously devise an efficient, well-structured approach for acquiring new skills necessary for your team, ensuring this acquisition enhances overall team performance, and aligns with strategic objectives.

As a **Skill Development Strategist** specializing in **Effective Learning Pathways** within the **Management Consulting industry**, how can I meticulously devise and execute a well-structured, efficient approach for identifying and acquiring new skills crucial for my team, ensuring that this acquisition significantly amplifies overall team performance and aligns seamlessly with our strategic objectives? I am seeking an in-depth discussion outlining robust methodologies, actionable strategies, and measurable metrics, as well as the potential implications of such skill acquisition on **team dynamics, organizational alignment, and competitive advantage**. The discourse should encapsulate every critical facet of this endeavor with an exceptional degree of precision and quality.

As a **[Profession]** specializing in **[Specialization]** within the **[Industry]**, how can I meticulously devise and execute a well-structured, efficient approach for identifying and acquiring new skills crucial for my team, ensuring that this acquisition significantly amplifies overall team performance and aligns seamlessly with our strategic objectives? I am seeking an in-depth discussion outlining robust methodologies, actionable strategies, and measurable metrics, as well as the potential implications of such skill acquisition on **[team dynamics/organizational alignment/competitive advantage or other relevant impact areas].** The discourse should encapsulate every critical facet of this endeavor with an exceptional degree of precision and quality.

PROMPT No 449

Skill - Leverage - Metrics

To acquire a comprehensive, actionable guide on methods for identifying the areas where a team has the highest leverage in terms of skill development, with the aim of maximizing team potential and aligning with organizational goals.

As a **Skill Development Analyst** in the **software industry**, could you provide an exhaustive guide outlining the methods **my team** and **I** can employ to identify the areas where we have the highest leverage in terms of **skill development**? Please include both **quantitative metrics and qualitative assessments**. Segment the guide into **distinct categories**, and substantiate each with **empirical data and scholarly references**. Explore unconventional approaches and diverse viewpoints. Let's dissect this carefully. Write using an **analytical** tone and a **structured** writing style.

Formula

As a **[profession]** in the **[industry]**, could you provide an exhaustive guide outlining the methods **[I/Name/Role]** and **[my/our/their]** **[team/group/department]** can employ to identify the areas where we have the highest leverage in terms of **[skill development/specific skills]?** Please include both **[quantitative metrics/qualitative assessments]**. Segment the guide into **[distinct categories]**, and substantiate each with **[empirical data/scholarly references]**. Explore unconventional approaches and diverse viewpoints. Let's dissect this carefully. Write using a **[type]** tone and **[style]** writing style.

PROMPT No 450

Tags

Prioritization - Effectiveness - Diagnostics

Goal

To provide a robust framework that enables professionals to identify and prioritize new skills for improvement, thereby enhancing their effectiveness and adaptability in their respective roles.

Prompt

Act as a **Talent Development Specialist** specializing in the **manufacturing industry**. Could you **outline** a **methodical approach** for **identifying** and **prioritizing new** skills I need to **improve** on to become **more effective** in my **role**? Include d**iagnostic tools, actionable strategies, and key performance indicators** for **tracking progress**. Let's think about this **step by step**. Write using a **strategic** tone and a **forward-thinking** writing style.

Formula

Act as a **[profession]** specializing in the **[industry]**. Could you **[outline/delineate/provide]** a **[methodical/systematic/structured]** **[approach/methodology/plan]** for **[identifying/ascertaining/determining]** and **[prioritizing/ranking/organizing]** **[new/emerging/essential]** skills I need to **[improve/enhance/develop]** to become **[more effective/more efficient/more competent]** in my **[role/position/job]**? Include **[diagnostic tools/assessment methods/questionnaires]**, **[actionable strategies/practical steps/improvement plans]**, and **[key performance indicators/metrics/evaluation criteria]** for **[tracking/monitoring/assessing]** **[progress/development/improvement]**. Let's **[think about this step by step/systematically explore each facet]**. Write using a **[type]** tone and **[style]** writing style.

PROMPT No 451

Tags

Leadership - Feedback - Development

Goal

To proficiently assist a supervisor in identifying and honing new skills requisite for heightened effectiveness, fostering a mutually beneficial relationship, and contributing to organizational excellence.

Prompt

Act as a **Leadership Enhancement Specialist** specializing in **Executive Skill Development** within the **hospitality industry**. Could you guide me through **a tactful and systematic approach to help my boss identify the new skills they need to improve and become more effective in**? Please include **tools for skill identification, techniques for constructive feedback, and methods for supporting skill development**. Make sure to cover how **to maintain a respectful and supportive demeanor while addressing areas for improvement**. Explore **subtle and motivational methods** to **encourage the willingness for self-improvement**. Your response should be comprehensive, leaving no important aspect unaddressed, and demonstrate an exceptional level of precision and quality. Let's think about this step by step. Write using a **respectful** tone and a **tactful, encouraging** writing style.

Formula

Act as a **[profession]** specializing in **[area of expertise]** within the **[industry]**. Could you guide me through **[specific challenge/opportunity]**? Please include **[methods/techniques]**. Make sure to cover how **[key areas/topics]**. Explore **[exploratory direction]** to **[desired outcome]**. Your response should be comprehensive, leaving no important aspect unaddressed, and demonstrate an exceptional level of precision and quality. Let's think about this step by step. Write using a **[type]** tone and a **[style]** writing style.

PROMPT No 452

Tags

Collaboration - Analytical - Innovation

Goal

To acquire a comprehensive, actionable guide on identifying the skills or qualities required to foster collaborative creation within a specific industry, with the aim of enhancing innovation, team cohesion, and overall business performance.

Prompt

As a **Collaboration Expert** in the **automotive industry**, could you provide an exhaustive guide outlining the skills or qualities required to foster collaborative creation in **this sector**? Please include **both soft skills like** communication and **hard skills** like project management. Segment the guide into **distinct categories**, and substantiate each with **empirical data and scholarly references**. Explore unconventional approaches and diverse viewpoints. Let's dissect this carefully. Write using an **analytical** tone and a **structured** writing style.

Formula

As a **[profession]** in the **[industry]**, could you provide an exhaustive guide outlining the skills or qualities required to foster collaborative creation in [this/that] sector? Please include both **[soft skills like X/hard skills like Y]**. Segment the guide into **[distinct categories]**, and substantiate each with **[empirical data/scholarly references]**. Explore unconventional approaches and diverse viewpoints. Let's dissect this carefully. Write using a **[type]** tone and **[style]** writing style.

STRATEGIES

PROMPT No 453

Tags

Recognition - Resilience - Acknowledgment

To acquire a comprehensive, actionable guide on methods for genuinely acknowledging a team's courage or commitment, even when their strategy doesn't yield the desired outcome, with the aim of fostering resilience, team cohesion, and a culture of continuous improvement.

As an Organizational Psychologist in the e-commerce industry, could you provide an exhaustive guide outlining the methods I can employ to genuinely acknowledge my team for their courage or commitment, even if their strategy doesn't yield the desired outcome? Please include both verbal and non-verbal recognition techniques. Segment the guide into distinct categories, and substantiate each with empirical data and scholarly references. Explore unconventional approaches and diverse viewpoints. Let's dissect this carefully. Write using an analytical tone and a structured writing style.

As a **[profession]** in the **[industry]**, could you provide an exhaustive guide outlining the methods **[I/Name/Role]** can employ to genuinely acknowledge **[my/our/their]** **[team/group/department]** for their **[courage or commitment/specific quality]**, even if their strategy doesn't yield the **[desired outcome/specific goal]**? Please include both **[verbal/non-verbal recognition techniques]**. Segment the guide into **[distinct categories]**, and substantiate each with **[empirical data/scholarly references]**. Explore unconventional approaches and diverse viewpoints. Let's dissect this carefully. Write using a **[type]** tone and **[style]** writing style.

PROMPT No 454

Strategies - KPIs - Alignment

To proficiently formulate an array of effective strategies aimed at actualizing the key performance indicators (KPIs) of the team, ensuring a meticulous evaluation of each strategy for its potential impact and feasibility, within the context of strategic planning and execution.

As a **Strategic Performance Expert** specializing in **Outcome Optimization** within the **retail industry**, how can I proficiently devise a multitude of effective strategies targeted at actualizing my team's key performance indicators? I am seeking a thorough exposition on the methodological framework encompassing the generation, evaluation, and **iterative refinement** of strategies, infused with insights on **leveraging data analytics for informed decision-making**. The discourse should also articulate the importance of aligning these strategies with **organizational objectives**, while fostering a culture of **continuous improvement and adaptability** amidst **changing market dynamics**. Your elucidation should be comprehensive, addressing all critical aspects with a high degree of precision and quality.

As a **[Profession]** specializing in **[Specialization]** within the **[Industry]**, how can I proficiently devise a multitude of effective strategies targeted at actualizing my team's key performance indicators? I am seeking a thorough exposition on the methodological framework encompassing the generation, evaluation, and **[Iterative Aspect]** of strategies, infused with insights on **[Analytical/Technological Aspect for Informed Decision-making]**. The discourse should also articulate the importance of aligning these strategies with **[Organizational/Team Objective]**, while fostering a culture of **[Desired Cultural Aspect]** amidst **[Changing External**

Factor]. Your elucidation should be comprehensive, addressing all critical aspects with a high degree of precision and quality.

PROMPT No 455

Impediments - Proactive - Mitigation

To adeptly discern potential impediments that could thwart the progression and timely completion of tasks, through an exhaustive analysis employing proactive identification techniques, thereby fostering anticipatory measures to mitigate such hindrances, within the realm of Project Management in the construction industry.

As a **Risk Analysis Expert** specializing in **Proactive Obstacle Identification** within the **construction industry**, how can I adeptly discern potential impediments that could thwart the progression and timely completion of tasks? Please provide an in-depth elucidation on exhaustive analysis methodologies, proactive identification techniques, and **strategic foresight practices**. The discourse should extend to recommending anticipatory measures and **mitigation strategies** to address the identified hindrances, ensuring **uninterrupted task progression and adherence to timelines**. Your elaboration should be comprehensive, encapsulating all pertinent facets, and manifest a high degree of precision and quality.

As a **[Profession]** specializing in **[Specialization]** within the **[Industry],** how can I adeptly discern potential impediments that could thwart the progression and timely completion of tasks? Please provide an in-depth elucidation on exhaustive analysis methodologies, proactive identification techniques, and **[Additional Aspect]**. The discourse should extend to recommending anticipatory measures and **[Mitigation Strategies]** to address the identified hindrances, ensuring **[Desired Outcome]**. Your elaboration should be comprehensive, encapsulating all pertinent facets, and manifest a high degree of precision and quality.

PROMPT No 456

Innovation - Experimentation - Creativity

To identify innovative methodologies and frameworks that empower you and your team to explore new behaviors, thoughts, or approaches for enhanced problem-solving and creativity.

As a **project manager** specializing in **software development** within the **technology industry**, provide an exhaustive and meticulous examination, incorporating innovative insights and inventive strategies for **identifying** various avenues to **experiment** with new **behaviors, thoughts, or approaches**. Discuss how these could **benefit problem-solving** and **creativity** in the team.

As a **[profession]** specializing in **[area of expertise/focus]** within the **[industry],** provide an exhaustive and meticulous examination, incorporating innovative insights and inventive strategies for **[identifying/listing/uncovering]** various avenues to **[experiment/test/engage]** with new

[behaviors/thoughts/approaches]. Discuss how these could **[benefit/enhance/improve]** **[problem-solving/creativity/team performance]** in the team.

PROMPT No 457

Tags

Strategy - Efficiency - Planning

Goal

To empower business leaders, managers, and team leads to identify and implement strategies that will enable their team to achieve objectives in a manner that is both efficient and effective. This entails a deep dive into various planning methodologies, decision-making models, and performance metrics.

Prompt

Act as a **Strategic Management Consultant** with a specialization in **organizational efficiency** for the mining sector. Could you guide me through **the methods and frameworks for determining the most efficient and effective strategy for my team to achieve its goals**? Please include **strategic planning models, decision-making frameworks, and KPIs to monitor**. Make sure to cover how **to involve team members in the strategy formulation process**. Offer extraordinary advice and non-mainstream insights. Let's dissect this in a structured manner. Write using an **analytical** tone and a **step-by-step** guide style.

Formula

Act as a **[profession]** with a specialization in **[area of expertise]** for the **[industry]**. Could you guide me through **[specific challenge/opportunity]**? Please include **[methods/techniques]**. Make sure to cover how **[key areas/topics]**. Offer extraordinary advice and non-mainstream insights. Let's dissect this in a structured manner. Let's dissect this in a structured manner. Write using a **[type]** tone and **[style]** writing style.

PROMPT No 458

Tags

Effectiveness - ROI - Decision-making

Goal

To provide business leaders with a rigorous methodology for evaluating the effectiveness and efficiency of various strategies or plans, aimed at ensuring alignment with company objectives and maximizing ROI.

Prompt

Act as a **Strategic Planning Advisor** specializing in the **automotive industry**. Could you **elucidate** the most **optimal methods** for **assessing** which **strategy** will be most **effective and efficient** in **achieving** my company's **objectives**? Include **decision-making frameworks, key performance indicators, and risk assessment tools**. Let's systematically explore each facet. Your response should be comprehensive, leaving no important aspect unaddressed, and demonstrate an exceptional level of precision and quality. Write using a **data-driven** tone and a **structured** writing style.

Formula

Act as a **[profession]** specializing in the **[industry]**. Could you **[elucidate/explain/outline]** the most **[optimal/effective/efficient]** **[methods/techniques/approaches]** for

[assessing/evaluating/measuring] which **[strategy/plan/approach]** will be most **[effective/efficient/successful]** in **[achieving/meeting/fulfilling]** my company's **[objectives/goals/targets]**? Include **[decision-making frameworks/key performance indicators/risk assessment tools]** for **[evaluation/assessment/analysis]**. Let's systematically explore each facet. Your response should be comprehensive, leaving no important aspect unaddressed, and demonstrate an exceptional level of precision and quality. Write using a **[type]** tone and **[style]** writing style.

PROMPT No 459

Tags

Innovation - Realities - Resource

Goal

To equip business leaders with a robust framework for devising new strategies or plans that are not only innovative but also deeply aligned with the current situational realities, thereby ensuring practicality and effectiveness.

Prompt

Act as a **Strategic Innovation Coach** specializing in the **healthcare industry**. Could you **guide** me through the **process** of **formulating** a **new strategy** that is **congruent** with the **current realities** of my **business environment**? Include **steps** for **situational analysis, stakeholder engagement, and resource allocation**. Let's methodically dissect each component. Your response should be comprehensive, leaving no important aspect unaddressed, and demonstrate an exceptional level of precision and quality. Write using a strategic tone and a prescriptive writing style.

Formula

Act as a **[profession]** specializing in the **[industry]**. Could you **[guide/lead/direct]** me through the **[process/framework/methodology]** of **[formulating/creating/developing]** a **[new/fresh/innovative]** **[strategy/plan/approach]** that is **[congruent/aligned/synchronized]** with the **[current/present/existing]** **[realities/situations/conditions]** of my **[business/organization/team]**? Include **[steps/guidelines/measures]** for **[situational analysis/stakeholder engagement/resource allocation]**. Let's methodically dissect each component. Your response should be comprehensive, leaving no important aspect unaddressed, and demonstrate an exceptional level of precision and quality. Write using a **[type]** tone and **[style]** writing style.

STRENGTH

PROMPT No 460

Tags

Exhilaration - Strengths - Challenges

Goal

To provide leaders with a structured approach for facilitating team reflection on the specific strengths that are activated during exhilarating challenges, thereby enhancing self-awareness and optimizing performance.

Prompt

Act as a **Team Development Specialist** specializing in the **financial services industry**. Could you **outline** a **structured methodology** for helping my team **reflect** on the **strengths** they **leverage** when facing **exhilarating challenges**? Include **actionable exercises and assessment tools**. Let's methodically dissect each component. Your response should be comprehensive, leaving no important aspect unaddressed, and demonstrate an exceptional level of precision and quality. Write using an **analytical** tone and a **prescriptive** writing style.

Act as a **[profession]** specializing in the **[industry]**. Could you **[outline/guide/develop]** a **[structured/step-by-step/comprehensive]** **[methodology/framework/approach]** for helping my team **[reflect/analyze/consider]** on the **[strengths/abilities/skills]** they **[leverage/utilize/employ]** when facing **[exhilarating/challenging/demanding]** **[challenges/opportunities]**? Include **[actionable/practical/engaging]** **[exercises/activities/assessment tools]**. Let's methodically dissect each component. Your response should be comprehensive, leaving no important aspect unaddressed, and demonstrate an exceptional level of precision and quality. Write using a **[type]** tone and **[style]** writing style.

PROMPT No 461

Top-strengths - Progress - Motivation

To equip leaders with a robust framework that enables their teams to engage in reflective practices, focusing on identifying and leveraging their top three to five career strengths for further professional growth and development.

Act as a **Career Development Specialist** specializing in the **manufacturing industry**. Could you **provide** a **structured methodology** for **facilitating** team **reflection** on the **top three to five strengths** they **most frequently utilize** in their **careers**, and how these could be **leveraged for further progress**? Include **actionable exercises and validated assessment tools**. Let's systematically explore each facet. Your response should be comprehensive, leaving no important aspect unaddressed, and demonstrate an exceptional level of precision and quality. Write using a **motivational** tone and a **solution-oriented** writing style.

Act as a **[profession]** specializing in the **[industry]**. Could you **[provide/outline/design]** a **[structured/comprehensive/step-by-step]** **[methodology/framework/approach]** for **[facilitating/guiding/enabling]** team **[reflection/analysis/evaluation]** on the **[top/most critical/most impactful]** **[three to five/number]** **[strengths/skills/abilities]** they **[most frequently/often/regularly]** **[utilize/employ/leverage]** in their **[careers/professional lives/job roles]**, and how these could be **[leveraged/utilized/employed]** for **[further/additional/ongoing]** **[progress/growth/development]**? Include **[actionable/practical/effective]** **[exercises/activities/assessment tools]**. Let's systematically explore each facet. Your response should be comprehensive, leaving no important aspect unaddressed, and demonstrate an exceptional level of precision and quality. Write using a **[type]** tone and **[style]** writing style.

Innate - Strengths-based - Introspection

To provide leaders with a nuanced framework that enables their teams to engage in introspective analysis, focusing on identifying strengths that come naturally to them, and how these innate abilities can be strategically leveraged for organizational success and individual growth.

Act as a **Strengths-Based Leadership Consultant** specializing in the **renewable energy industry**. Could you **elucidate** a **structured methodology** for **my** team to **identify** and **consider** the **strengths** that **come naturally** to them? Include **actionable exercises and evidence-based assessment tools**. Let's methodically dissect each component. Your response should be comprehensive, leaving no important aspect unaddressed, and demonstrate an exceptional level of precision and quality. Write using an **insightful** tone and a **research-backed** writing style.

Act as a **[profession]** specializing in the **[industry]**. Could you **[elucidate/explain/provide]** a **[structured/comprehensive/step-by-step]** **[methodology/framework/approach]** for **[my/our/the]** team to **[identify/recognize/understand]** and **[consider/evaluate/reflect on]** the **[strengths/skills/abilities]** that **[come naturally/easily/effortlessly]** to them? Include **[actionable/practical/effective]** **[exercises/activities/assessment tools]**. Let's methodically dissect each component. Your response should be comprehensive, leaving no important aspect unaddressed, and demonstrate an exceptional level of precision and quality. Write using a **[type]** tone and **[style]** writing style.

Attraction - Roles - Inherent

One

To equip leaders with a robust analytical framework that allows them to interpret their team's consistent attraction to specific roles or tasks as indicators of inherent strengths, thereby facilitating more effective team management and individual development.

Act as an **Organizational Behavior Analyst** specializing in the **construction industry**. Could you **elucidate** the **analytical methods** for **interpreting my** team's consistent attraction to **certain roles or tasks** as indicators of their **inherent** strengths? Include **both qualitative and quantitative assessment techniques**. Let's methodically dissect each component. Your response should be comprehensive, leaving no important aspect unaddressed, and demonstrate an exceptional level of precision and quality. Write using a **diagnostic** tone and an **evidence-based** writing style.

Act as a **[profession]** specializing in the **[industry]**. Could you **[elucidate/explain/provide]** **[analytical/interpretive/assessment]** **[methods/mechanisms/frameworks]** for **[interpreting/understanding/analyzing]** **[my/our/the]** team's consistent attraction to **[certain/specific/individual]** **[roles/tasks/positions]** as indicators of their **[inherent/natural/latent]** strengths? Include **[both/and/or]** **[qualitative/quantitative/mixed]** **[assessment/evaluation/measurement]**

[techniques/methods/tools]. Let's **[methodically dissect each component/systematically explore each facet].** Let's methodically dissect each component. Your response should be comprehensive, leaving no important aspect unaddressed, and demonstrate an exceptional level of precision and quality. Write using a **[type]** tone and **[style]** writing style.

PROMPT No 464

Tags

Evolution - Passion - Self-assessment

Goal

To provide leaders with a comprehensive framework that enables their teams to introspectively evaluate the evolution of their passion or joy for utilizing specific strengths over time, thereby offering insights for personal and professional development.

Prompt

Act as a **Career Development Consultant** specializing in the **financial services industry**. Could you **delineate methods** for **my** team to **introspectively assess** whether their **passion** or **joy** for using a **particular** strength has **increased or decreased** over the years? Include self-assessment tools, key performance indicators, and reflective exercises. Let's methodically dissect each component. Write using an introspective tone and a research-based writing style. Your response should be comprehensive, leaving no important aspect unaddressed, and demonstrate an exceptional level of precision and quality. Write using an **empathetic** tone and a **community-focused** writing style.

Formula

Act as a **[profession]** specializing in the **[industry]**. Could you **[delineate/explain/outline]** **[methods/mechanisms/frameworks]** for **[my/our/the]** team to **[introspectively/analytically/self-reflectively]** **[assess/evaluate/examine]** whether their **[passion/joy/enthusiasm]** for using a **[particular/specific/defined]** strength has **[increased/decreased/remained stable]** over the **[years/months/period]**? Include self-assessment tools, key performance indicators, and reflective exercises. Let's methodically dissect each component. Your response should be comprehensive, leaving no important aspect unaddressed, and demonstrate an exceptional level of precision and quality. Write using a **[type]** tone and **[style]** writing style.

PROMPT No 465

Tags

Strengths - Engagement - Team-Dynamics

Goal

To guide leaders in assessing the specific strengths or sets of strengths that align well with their team's objectives and culture, thereby optimizing performance and engagement.

Prompt

Act as a **business leadership coach** with a specialization in **team dynamics** for the **health care industry**. Could you guide me through **assessing if there are any specific strengths or sets of strengths that feel particularly right for my team**? Please include **assessment methods and key performance indicators (KPIs)**. Make sure to cover how **these strengths relate to current projects and team morale**. Unearth hidden gems and non-traditional methods. Let's dissect this in a structured manner. Write using a consultative tone and a detailed writing style.

Act as a **[profession]** with a specialization in **[area of expertise]** for the **[industry]**. Could you guide me through **[specific challenge/opportunity]**? Please include [methods/techniques]. Make sure to cover how **[key areas/topics]**. Unearth hidden gems and non-traditional methods to boost team morale and efficiency. Let's dissect this in a structured manner. Write using a **[type]** tone and **[style]** writing style.

PROMPT No 466

Scrutinizing - Strengths - Patterns

To equip leaders with a robust methodology for scrutinizing the list of strengths within their team, thereby identifying recurring patterns that can be leveraged for strategic decision-making, team development, and performance optimization.

Act as an **Organizational Development Consultant** specializing in the **e-commerce industry**. Could you **elucidate** the **best practices** for **examining** the **list** of **strengths** within **my** team and **identifying** any **recurring patterns**? Include **data analytics techniques, qualitative assessments, and team dynamics theories**. Let's systematically explore each facet. Your response should be comprehensive, leaving no important aspect unaddressed, and demonstrate an exceptional level of precision and quality. Write using an **analytical** tone and a **methodical** writing style.

Act as a **[profession]** specializing in the **[industry]**. Could you **[elucidate/explain/outline]** the **[best practices/optimal methods/effective strategies]** for **[examining/scrutinizing/analyzing]** the **[list/collection/array]** of **[strengths/skills/talents]** within **[my/our/the]** team and **[identifying/detecting/uncovering]** any **[recurring/repeated/common]** **[patterns/trends/themes]**? Include **[data analytics techniques/qualitative assessments/team dynamics theories/psychometric tests]**. Let's systematically explore each facet. Your response should be comprehensive, leaving no important aspect unaddressed, and demonstrate an exceptional level of precision and quality. Write using a **[type]** tone and **[style]** writing style.

PROMPT No 467

Innate - Gifts - Psychometric

To provide leaders with a comprehensive framework for identifying and exploring the innate gifts and talents within their teams, thereby enabling more effective talent management, team cohesion, and individual development.

Act as a **Talent Development Specialist** specializing in the **fintech industry**. Could you **guide** me through the **methodologies** for **identifying and exploring** the **inner gifts or talents** of **my** team? Include **psychometric tests, one-on-one interviews, and team-building exercises**

that can be employed. Let's sequentially address each element. Your response should be comprehensive, leaving no important aspect unaddressed, and demonstrate an exceptional level of precision and quality. Write using an **insightful** tone and a **solution-oriented** writing style.

Act as a **[profession]** specializing in the **[industry]**. Could you **[guide/direct/assist]** me through the **[methodologies/frameworks/approaches]** for **[identifying/recognizing/uncovering]** and **[exploring/delving into/understanding]** the **[inner gifts/innate talents/core competencies]** of **[my/our/the]** team? Include **[psychometric tests/one-on-one interviews/team-building exercises/peer reviews]**. Let's sequentially address each element. Your response should be comprehensive, leaving no important aspect unaddressed, and demonstrate an exceptional level of precision and quality. Write using a **[type]** tone and **[style]** writing style.

PROMPT No 468

Strengths - Productivity - Morale

To identify robust methodologies that facilitate the comprehensive listing and nuanced description of team strengths for enhanced productivity and morale.

As a **Professional Team Coach** specializing in **team dynamics** within the **healthcare industry**, provide an exhaustive and meticulous examination, incorporating innovative insights and inventive strategies for **utilizing** methodologies that allow my team to **list** and **describe** their strengths **comprehensively**. Discuss the implications of these methods on **team productivity and morale**.

As a **[profession]** specializing in **[area of expertise/focus]** within the **[industry]**, provide an exhaustive and meticulous examination, incorporating innovative insights and inventive strategies for **[utilizing/applying/implementing]** methodologies that allow my team to **[list/enumerate/catalog]** and **[describe/explain/characterize]** their strengths **[comprehensively/fully/thoroughly]**. Discuss the **[implications/consequences/effects]** of these methods on **[team productivity/morale/team dynamics]**.

PROMPT No 469

Engagement - Strengths - Metrics

To provide leaders with a robust framework for engaging their teams in conversations that focus on identifying and discussing evidence of how individual strengths have manifested in their careers, thereby fostering self-awareness, career development, and team synergy.

Act as a **Career Development Specialist** specializing in the **finance industry**. Could you elucidate a **comprehensive** set of **best practices** for **initiating and conducting** a **conversation** with my team about the **tangible** evidence they have of how their **strengths** have been **instrumental** in their **career trajectories**? Include **conversation starters, relevant theories, and metrics** for **gauging the effectiveness of the discussion**. Let's think about this step by step. Write using a **consultative** tone and an **advisory** writing style.

Act as a **[profession]** specializing in the **[industry]**. Could you elucidate a **[comprehensive/robust/detailed]** set of **[best practices/guidelines/methodologies]** for **[initiating/conducting/facilitating]** a **[conversation/discussion/dialogue]** with my team about the **[tangible/concrete/observable]** evidence they have of how their **[strengths/skills/abilities]** have been **[instrumental/effective/critical]** in their **[career trajectories/career paths/professional journeys]**? Include **[conversation starters/question prompts/engagement techniques]**, **[relevant theories/academic frameworks]**, and **[metrics/KPIs/evaluation criteria]** for **[gauging/measuring/assessing]** the **[effectiveness/impact/success]** of the **[discussion/conversation/dialogue]**. Let's think about this step by step. Write using a **[type]** tone and **[style]** writing style.

PROMPT No 470

Ownership - Self-awareness - Strengths

To meticulously evaluate the degree of ownership and acknowledgement team members harbor towards their strengths, enabling a culture of self-awareness, self-efficacy, and continual professional growth.

Act as an **Organizational Psychologist** specializing in **Strengths-Based Leadership** within the **retail industry**. Could you guide me through **a comprehensive methodology to assess the level of ownership my team feels for their strengths**? Please include **assessment tools, feedback mechanisms, and reflective exercises**. Ensure to cover how **to foster an environment where team members can openly recognize and leverage their strengths for personal and organizational betterment**. Explore **innovative approaches** to **reinforce self-awareness and promote a strengths-based culture**. Your response should be comprehensive, leaving no important aspect unaddressed, and demonstrate an exceptional level of precision and quality. Let's think about this step by step. Write using an **insightful** tone and a **methodical, actionable** writing style.

Act as a **[profession]** specializing in **[area of expertise]** within the **[industry]**. Could you guide me through **[specific challenge/opportunity]**? Please include **[methods/techniques]**. Ensure to cover how **[key areas/topics]**. Explore **[exploratory direction]** to **[desired outcome]**. Your response should be comprehensive, leaving no important aspect unaddressed, and demonstrate an exceptional level of precision and quality. Let's think about this step by step. Write using a **[type]** tone and a **[style]** writing style.

PROMPT No 471

Growth   - Strengths - Development

To equip individuals with a reflective and analytical approach to keenly observe, understand, and leverage their inherent strengths, thereby fostering self-awareness, continuous learning, and personal and professional development.

Act as a **Personal Development Consultant** specializing in **Strengths-Based Self-Assessment** within the **healthcare industry**. Could you guide me through **the key considerations and methodologies to meticulously observe and reflect on any notable observations about my own strengths**? Please include **self-assessment tools, reflective exercises, and frameworks for analyzing and leveraging observed strengths**. Make sure to cover how **to maintain a growth mindset and how to actionably apply these insights for continuous personal and professional development**. Venture into innovative and perhaps unconventional strategies to deepen self-awareness and enhance strengths utilization. Your response should be comprehensive, leaving no important aspect unaddressed, and demonstrate an exceptional level of precision and quality. Let's think about this step by step. Write using an **insightful** tone and a **structured, actionable** writing style.

Act as a **[profession]** specializing in **[area of expertise]** within the **[industry]**. Could you guide me through **[specific challenge/opportunity]**? Please include **[methods/techniques]**. Make sure to cover how **[key areas/topics]**. Venture into innovative and perhaps unconventional strategies to deepen self-awareness and enhance strengths utilization. Your response should be comprehensive, leaving no important aspect unaddressed, and demonstrate an exceptional level of precision and quality. Let's think about this step by step. Write using a **[type]** tone and a **[style]** writing style.

PROMPT No 472

Self-awareness - Cohesion - Strengths-Utilization

To provide team leaders with actionable guidance for helping their team members recognize when they are using their strengths effectively, thereby increasing self-awareness and optimizing team performance.

Act as a **business leadership coach** with a specialization in **team dynamics** for the **automotive industry**. Could you guide me through **the process of enabling my team to determine when they are effectively employing their strengths**? Please include **self-assessment techniques and behavioral indicators**. Make sure to cover how **the recognition of using strengths impacts work quality and team cohesion**. Discover rare insights and pioneering ideas to enrich team self-awareness and performance. Let's dissect this in a structured manner. Write using a **consultative** tone and a **detailed** writing style.

Act as a **[profession]** with a specialization in **[area of expertise]** for the **[industry]**. Could you guide me through **[specific challenge/opportunity]**? Please include **[methods/techniques]**. Make sure to cover how **[key areas/topics]**. Discover rare insights and pioneering ideas to enrich team self-awareness and performance. Let's dissect this in a structured manner. Write using a **[type]** tone and **[style]** writing style.

PROMPT No 473

Development - Strengths - Metrics

To create a comprehensive development plan that identifies, leverages, and continuously refines the individual and collective strengths of your team, thereby driving performance, engagement, and overall business results.

As a **project manager** specializing in **data analytics** within the **automotive industry,** provide an exhaustive and meticulous examination, incorporating innovative insights and inventive strategies for **establishing a comprehensive development plan that identifies and leverages your team's key strengths in data interpretation, client interaction, and problem-solving**. Further, explore how to integrate this strengths-based approach into your **team's quarterly objectives and performance metrics**.

As a **[profession]** specializing in **[area of expertise/focus]** within the **[industry]**, provide an exhaustive and meticulous examination, incorporating innovative insights and inventive strategies for **[establishing a comprehensive development plan that identifies and leverages your team's key strengths in various competencies]**. Further, explore how to integrate this strengths-based approach into your **[quarterly objectives/performance metrics/ongoing projects]**.

PROMPT No 474

Evaluation - Strengths - Allocation

To conduct a detailed evaluation of your team's unique strengths in order to identify tasks or activities that will not only come naturally to them but also optimize performance, job satisfaction, and overall team efficiency.

As a **project manager** specializing in **digital transformation** within the **logistics industry,** provide an exhaustive and meticulous examination, incorporating innovative insights and inventive strategies for **pinpointing tasks or activities that will effortlessly align with your team's known strengths in analytical reasoning, adaptability, and collaboration**. Also, explore how to allocate these tasks for **maximized productivity**.

As a **[profession]** specializing in **[area of expertise/focus]** within the **[industry]**, provide an exhaustive and meticulous examination, incorporating innovative insights and inventive strategies for **[pinpointing tasks or activities that will effortlessly align with your team's known strengths in specific skill sets]**. Also, explore how to allocate these tasks for **[maximized productivity/well-being/efficiency]**.

PROMPT No 475

Tags

Exploration - Assets - Forward-thinking

Goal

To facilitate a deep-dive exploration with team members on leveraging their past assets and experiences as a substantial foundation for future endeavors, thereby promoting a culture of continuous learning, self-efficacy, and forward-thinking.

Prompt

Act as a **Leadership Development Consultant** specializing in **Experiential Learning and Future Preparedness** within the **manufacturing sector**. Could you guide me through **a comprehensive process to explore with my team how they can leverage the assets from their past to support their future endeavors?** Please include **methodologies for identifying and articulating past assets, frameworks for aligning these assets with future goals, and strategies for fostering a culture of continuous learning and forward-thinking.** Ensure to cover how **to engage the team in a constructive dialogue and how to create a supportive environment for such reflective exercises.** Your response should encourage innovative thinking and possibly venture into novel approaches to leveraging past experiences for future growth. Let's think about this step by step. Write using an **inspiring** tone and a **solution-oriented** writing style.

Formula

Act as a **[profession]** specializing in **[area of expertise]** within the **[industry]**. Could you guide me through **[specific challenge/opportunity]**? Please include **[methods/techniques]**. Ensure to cover how **[key areas/topics]**. Your response should encourage innovative thinking and possibly venture into novel approaches to leveraging past experiences for future growth. Let's think about this step by step. Write using a **[type]** tone and a **[style]** writing style.

PROMPT No 476

Tags

Evaluation - Strengths - Allocation

Goal

To equip leaders with a nuanced and actionable guide for facilitating team reflections focused on the active utilization of individual strengths, aiming to enhance self-awareness, team cohesion, and overall performance.

Prompt

Act as a **Team Dynamics Expert** specializing in the **manufacturing industry**. Could you delineate a **structured** methodology for facilitating a **reflection session** with my team on the **outcomes and experiences** they **encounter** when **actively employing** one of their **strengths?** Include **specific questions to ask, psychological theories that support this type of reflection**, and **potential metrics for evaluating its effectiveness.** Let's think about this step by step. Write using a **consultative** tone and an **advisory** writing style.

Formula

Act as a **[profession]** specializing in the **[industry]**. Could you delineate a **[structured/comprehensive/methodical]** methodology for facilitating a **[reflection session/group discussion/team meeting]** with my team on the **[outcomes/experiences/impacts]** they **[encounter/observe/realize]** when **[actively employing/utilizing/leveraging]** one of their **[strengths/skills/talents]?** Include **[specific questions/targeted queries/guiding prompts]**, **[supporting psychological theories/relevant frameworks]**, and **[potential metrics/KPIs/evaluation criteria]** for **[measuring/assessing/evaluating]** its **[effectiveness/impact/success]**. Let's think about this step by step. Write using a **[type]** tone and **[style]** writing style.

PROMPT No 477

Tags

Alignment - Strengths - KPIs

Goal

To meticulously analyze how the individual and collective strengths of your team align with their current goals or objectives, with the ultimate aim of maximizing performance, satisfaction, and achievement of key performance indicators (KPIs).

Prompt

As a **team leader** specializing in **sales** within the **healthcare industry**, provide an exhaustive and meticulous examination, incorporating innovative insights and inventive strategies for **assessing how your team's inherent strengths in communication, strategic thinking, and customer relationship management serve them in achieving their current quarterly sales targets and customer retention goals**. Further, delineate how to continuously align these strengths with **future objectives**.

Formula

As a **[profession]** specializing in **[area of expertise/focus]** within the **[industry]**, provide an exhaustive and meticulous examination, incorporating innovative insights and inventive strategies for **[assessing how your team's inherent strengths in various skill sets serve them in achieving their current/future goals or objectives]**. Further, delineate how to continuously align these strengths with **[future objectives/key performance indicators/long-term goals]**.

PROMPT No 478

Tags

Strengths - Performance - Methodology

Goal

To provide leaders with a robust methodology for leveraging their team's inherent strengths in a targeted manner to accelerate progress towards organizational goals or objectives, thereby enhancing team performance and job satisfaction.

Prompt

Act as an **Organizational Development Consultant** specializing in the **fintech industry**. Could you **delineate** a **comprehensive approach** for **exploring** ways to **utilize** my team's **strengths** to **propel** them towards **achieving** their **goals or objectives?** Include **evidence-based strategies, key performance indicators, and potential pitfalls to avoid**. Let's **think about this step by step**. Write using a **growth-oriented** tone and **expansion-minded** writing style.

Formula

Act as a [profession] specializing in the [industry]. Could you [delineate/outline/detail] a [comprehensive/robust/structured] [approach/methodology/plan] for [exploring/investigating/identifying] ways to [utilize/leverage/employ] my team's [strengths/capabilities/talents] to [propel/accelerate/drive] them towards [achieving/meeting/reaching] their [goals/objectives/targets]? Include [evidence-based strategies/research-backed methods], [key performance indicators/metrics/benchmarks], and [potential pitfalls/challenges] to [avoid/mitigate]. Let's [think about this step by step/methodically dissect each component]. Write using a [type] tone and [style] writing style.

PROMPT No 479

Understanding   - Strengths - Engagement

To develop a deep, actionable understanding of how each team member's strengths manifest in their work and responsibilities, thereby enabling the leader to foster a workplace that amplifies these strengths for enhanced productivity and employee engagement.

As a **team leader** specializing in **Human Resources** within the **finance industry**, provide an exhaustive and meticulous examination, incorporating innovative insights and inventive strategies, for consciously identifying observable indicators or patterns that signify how each team member's strengths manifest in **tasks such as data analysis, customer interactions, and project management**. Further, share detailed guidance on how to disseminate these insights to secure buy-in from stakeholders.

As a [profession] specializing in [area of expertise/focus] within the [industry], provide an exhaustive and meticulous examination, incorporating innovative insights and inventive strategies, for consciously identifying observable indicators or patterns that signify how each team member's strengths manifest in [specific tasks or responsibilities]. Further, share detailed guidance on how to disseminate these insights to secure buy-in from stakeholders.

PROMPT No 480

Overextension - Self-awareness - Diagnostics

To equip leaders with a robust framework for identifying scenarios where team members might overextend their strengths, potentially leading to counterproductivity or strain, and to cultivate an environment that fosters balanced utilization of strengths.

Act as an **Organizational Behavior Specialist** specializing in **Strengths Optimization** within the **pharmaceutical industry**. Could you guide me through **a meticulous process to identify situations or circumstances when my team tends to push their strengths to their extreme, and how to mitigate any negative repercussions**? Please include **diagnostic tools, observational techniques, and behavioral indicators**. Make sure to cover **strategies for fostering self-awareness among team members and creating a culture that**

encourages balanced utilization of strengths. Delve into innovative methods for maintaining a harmonious balance between leveraging strengths and avoiding overextension. Your response should be comprehensive, leaving no important aspect unaddressed, and demonstrate an exceptional level of precision and quality. Let's think about this step by step. Write using a **reflective** tone and a **solutions-focused** writing style.

Formula

Act as a **[profession]** specializing in **[area of expertise]** within the **[industry].** Could you guide me through **[specific challenge/opportunity]**? Please include **[methods/techniques].** Make sure to cover **[key areas/topics]**. Delve into innovative methods for maintaining a harmonious balance between leveraging strengths and avoiding overextension. Your response should be comprehensive, leaving no important aspect unaddressed, and demonstrate an exceptional level of precision and quality. Let's think about this step by step. Write using a **[type]** tone and a **[style]** writing style.

PROMPT No 481

Tags

Overleveraging - Performance - Adaptation

Goal

To facilitate reflective exploration among my team on the implications of overleveraging strengths, aiming to balance optimal strength utilization with avoiding over-extension to enhance individual and collective performance.

Prompt

As a **Performance Management Specialist** within the **Business Consulting industry**, how can I meticulously facilitate a reflective exploration among my team regarding the impact of extending their strengths to the extreme on their **performance and the resultant outcomes**? I am seeking a robust discussion that unravels **actionable strategies, potential repercussions, and adaptive measures** to ensure an **optimal utilization** of strengths that contributes to **enhanced performance**, without veering into over-extension. This discussion should also delve into the broader ramifications this understanding might have on **team dynamics, organizational culture, and client satisfaction**, ensuring a thorough analysis with an exceptional level of precision and quality.

Formula

As a **[Profession]** within the **[Industry]**, how can I meticulously facilitate a reflective exploration among my team regarding the impact of extending their strengths to the extreme on their **[performance/outcomes/other relevant areas]**? I am seeking a robust discussion that unravels **[actionable strategies/potential repercussions/adaptive measures]** to ensure an [optimal utilization/balanced approach] of strengths that contributes to **[enhanced performance/sustainable success/other relevant outcomes]**, without veering into over-extension. This discussion should also delve into the broader ramifications this understanding might have on **[team dynamics/organizational culture/client satisfaction or other relevant impact areas]**, ensuring a thorough analysis with an exceptional level of precision and quality.

PROMPT No 482

Tags

Indicators - Overutilization - Burnout

To identify reliable indicators that reveal when team members are overutilizing their strengths, thereby mitigating the risk of burnout and optimizing performance.

As a **Human Resources Manager** specializing in **employee well-being** within the **finance industry**, provide an exhaustive and meticulous examination, incorporating innovative insights and inventive strategies for **identifying signs or indicators** that suggest your team may be **overstretching** their **strengths**. Discuss how to **appropriately calibrate** their **efforts** to avoid **potential** drawbacks such as **burnout or diminished effectiveness**.

As a **[profession]** specializing in **[area of expertise/focus]** within the **[industry]**, provide an exhaustive and meticulous examination, incorporating innovative insights and inventive strategies for **[identifying/spotting/detecting]** **[signs/indicators/cues]** that suggest your team may be **[overstretching/**o**verextending/pushing]** their **[strengths/skills/talents]** **[too far/beyond limits]**. Discuss how to **[appropriately/wisely/optimally]** **[calibrate/adjust/tweak]** their **[efforts/activities/actions]** to avoid **[potential/possible]** drawbacks such as **[burnout/diminished effectiveness/reduced productivity]**.

PROMPT No 483

Consequences - Strengths - Mitigation

To equip leaders with a nuanced framework for reflecting on and mitigating any unintended consequences that may arise from leveraging their team's strengths, thereby ensuring a balanced and sustainable approach to team development and performance optimization.

Act as a Risk Management Consultant specializing in the software development industry. Could you provide a detailed reflection on any unintended consequences that may arise from the use of my team's strengths? Include risk assessment methodologies, potential impact on team dynamics, and actionable mitigation strategies. Let's think about this step by step. Write using a cautionary tone and risk-averse writing style.

Act as a **[profession]** specializing in the **[industry]**. Could you provide a **[detailed/comprehensive/thorough]** **[reflection/analysis/evaluation]** on any **[unintended consequences/unforeseen risks/unexpected outcomes]** that may **[arise/emerge/occur]** from the **[use/application/employment]** of my team's **[strengths/skills/talents]**? Include **[risk assessment methodologies/evaluation techniques]**, **[potential impact/effects]** on **[team dynamics/organizational culture]**, and **[actionable mitigation strategies/contingency plans]**. Let's **[think about this step by step/methodically dissect each component]**. Write using a **[type]** tone and **[style]** writing style.

PROMPT No 484

Impacts - Strengths - Cohesion

To provide leaders with a comprehensive framework for evaluating the impacts of their individual strengths on interpersonal dynamics and team relationships, thereby enabling them to optimize their leadership style for enhanced team cohesion and performance.

As a **Leadership Development Consultant** specializing in the **finance industry**, could you **elucidate** the **impacts** that my **strengths** have on **others** and the **dynamics** of our **relationships**? Include **psychological theories, empirical evidence, and actionable strategies** for **improvement**. Let's think about this step by step. Write using an **analytical** tone and a **data-driven** writing style.

As a **[profession]** specializing in the [industry], could you [elucidate/explain/clarify] the **[impacts/effects/consequences]** that my **[strengths/skills/abilities]** have on **[others/team members/colleagues]** and the **[dynamics/interactions/relations]** of our **[relationships/teamwork/collaboration]**? Include **[psychological theories/behavioral models]**, **[empirical evidence/research findings]**, and **[actionable strategies/practical steps]** for **[improvement/optimization/enhancement]**. Let's think about this step by step. Write using a **[type]** tone and **[style]** writing style.

PROMPT No 485

Transparency - Authenticity - Investigation

To develop a nuanced understanding and strategy for identifying circumstances where team members might feel compelled to conceal or underplay their strengths, thereby enabling a culture that encourages transparency, self-expression, and the optimal utilization of individual and collective strengths.

Act as an **Organizational Development Specialist** specializing in **Strengths Transparency** within the **technology sector**. Could you guide me through **an exhaustive exploration of situations or contexts in which my team feels tempted to hide or downplay their strengths**? Please include **investigative methodologies, psychological insights, and communication frameworks**. Ensure to cover **strategies for creating a supportive environment that encourages the open recognition and utilization of strengths**. Delve into **both conventional and unconventional approaches to fostering an organizational culture that values authenticity and the diverse capabilities of each team member**. Your response should be comprehensive, leaving no important aspect unaddressed, and demonstrate an exceptional level of precision and quality. Let's think about this step by step. Write using an **engaging** tone and an **exploratory** writing style.

Act as a **[profession]** specializing in **[area of expertise]** within the **[industry]**. Could you guide me through **[specific challenge/opportunity]**? Please include **[methods/techniques]**. Ensure to cover **[key areas/topics]**. Delve into **[additional exploration]**. Your response should be comprehensive, leaving no important aspect unaddressed, and demonstrate an exceptional level of precision and quality. Let's think about this step by step. Write using a **[type]** tone and a **[style]** writing style.

PROMPT No 486

Rejuvenation - Alignment - Assessment

Goal

To devise a meticulous process for reflecting on and addressing instances where team members possess strengths that they no longer enjoy utilizing, thereby fostering a rejuvenated engagement and alignment between personal satisfaction and organizational effectiveness.

Prompt

Act as a **Work Fulfillment Analyst** specializing in **Employee Engagement and Satisfaction** within the **manufacturing industry**. Could you guide me through **the most optimal process to reflect on any strengths my team possesses that they no longer enjoy using**? Please include **assessment tools, reflective exercises, and dialogic strategies**. Ensure to cover how **to realign these strengths with job roles in a manner that rejuvenates enjoyment and enhances productivity**. Investigate **both conventional wisdom and novel approaches to rediscovering job satisfaction through strengths alignment**. Your response should be comprehensive, leaving no important aspect unaddressed, and demonstrate an exceptional level of precision and quality. Let's think about this step by step. Write using a **motivational** tone and a **strategic** writing style.

Formula

Act as a **[profession]** specializing in **[area of expertise]** within the **[industry]**. Could you guide me through **[specific challenge/opportunity]**? Please include **[methods/techniques]**. Ensure to cover how **[key areas/topics]**. Investigate **[additional exploration]**. Your response should be comprehensive, leaving no important aspect unaddressed, and demonstrate an exceptional level of precision and quality. Let's think about this step by step. Write using a **[type]** tone and a **[style]** writing style.

PROMPT No 487

Misrepresentation - Integrity - Realignment

Goal

To equip leaders and team members with a robust methodology for identifying and rectifying misrepresented strengths, thereby enhancing team integrity, cohesion, and performance.

Prompt

Act as an **Organizational Behavior Analyst** with a specialization in **team dynamics** for the **manufacturing industry**. Could you guide me through **a meticulous approach to identify areas where my team may be feigning strengths they do not possess**? Please include **psychometric tests, observational metrics, and qualitative interview techniques**. Make sure to cover how **to confront these issues without damaging team morale and how to realign team roles for authentic performance**. Explore unconventional solutions and alternative perspectives to **ensure a holistic understanding and resolution**. Your response should be comprehensive, leaving no important aspect unaddressed, and demonstrate an exceptional level of precision and quality. Let's think about this step by step. Write using a **critical** tone and an **investigative** writing style.

Formula

Act as a **[profession]** with a specialization in **[area of expertise]** for the **[industry]**. Could you guide me through **[specific challenge/opportunity]**? Please include **[methods/techniques]**. Make sure to cover how **[key areas/topics]**. Explore unconventional solutions and alternative perspectives to **[desired outcome]**. Your response should be comprehensive, leaving no important aspect unaddressed, and demonstrate an exceptional level of precision and quality. Let's think about this step by step. Write using a **[type]** tone and **[style]** writing style.

PROMPT No 488

Optimization - Strengths - Stakeholders

To systematically identify and deploy high-impact strategies that optimize the unique strengths of each team member, thereby amplifying overall team performance, engagement, and effectiveness in achieving organizational goals.

As a **team leader** specializing in **organizational development** within the **healthcare industry**, provide an exhaustive and meticulous examination, incorporating innovative insights and inventive strategies, for discovering methodologies to leverage individual and collective strengths of your team in **patient care, resource management, and organizational leadership**. Also, delve into how to communicate these plans through different team layers to secure buy-in from stakeholders.

As a **[profession]** specializing in **[area of expertise/focus]** within the **[industry]**, provide an exhaustive and meticulous examination, incorporating innovative insights and inventive strategies, for discovering methodologies to leverage individual and collective strengths of your team in **[specific operational areas]**. Also, delve into how to communicate these plans through different team layers to secure buy-in from stakeholders.

PROMPT No 489

Alignment - Competency - Realignment

To equip leaders, professionals, and team members with a comprehensive methodology for assessing the alignment between the requirements of a team's role or position and their actual strengths, thereby enabling targeted development and optimized performance.

Act as an **Organizational Psychologist** with a specialization in **talent alignment** in the **logistics industry**. Could you guide me through **a rigorous approach to assess the alignment between the requirements of my team's role and their actual strengths**? Please include **competency mapping, performance metrics, and psychological assessments**. Make sure to cover how **to interpret discrepancies and formulate action plans for realignment**. Investigate unconventional **talent management strategies** and cutting-edge **assessment tools** to **ensure accurate evaluations**. Your response should be comprehensive, leaving no important aspect unaddressed, and demonstrate an exceptional level of precision and quality. Let's think about this step by step. Write using an **analytical** tone and a **diagnostic** writing style.

Act as a **[profession]** with a specialization in **[area of expertise]** in the **[industry]**. Could you guide me through **[specific challenge/opportunity]**? Please include **[methods/techniques]**. Make sure to cover how **[key areas/topics]**. Investigate unconventional **[area for innovation]** and cutting-edge **[technologies/methods]** to **[desired outcome]**. Your response should be comprehensive, leaving no important aspect unaddressed, and demonstrate an exceptional level of precision and quality. Let's think about this step by step. Write using a **[type]** tone and **[style]** writing style.

PROMPT No 490

Misalignment - Assessment - Realignment

To methodically assess and reflect on the ramifications of any misalignment between team members' roles and their strengths, aiming to generate actionable insights that will guide realignment strategies, enhance job satisfaction, and boost team performance.

Act as an **Organizational Alignment Specialist** with a focus on **Strengths-Based Development** within the **hospitality industry**. Could you guide me through **a detailed analysis to reflect on the impact of any misalignment between my team's roles and their strengths**? Please include **assessment methodologies, reflective discussions, and impact analysis techniques**. Ensure to cover how **to derive actionable insights from these reflections to realign roles with strengths, along with strategies to measure the improvements post realignment**. Examine **both the immediate and long-term impacts of such misalignments and the benefits of addressing them**. Your response should be comprehensive, leaving no important aspect unaddressed, and demonstrate an exceptional level of precision and quality. Let's think about this step by step. Write using an **analytical** tone and a **structured** writing style.

Act as a **[profession]** with a focus on **[area of expertise]** within the **[industry]**. Could you guide me through **[specific challenge/opportunity]**? Please include **[methods/techniques]**. Ensure to cover how **[key areas/topics]**. Examine **[additional exploration]**. Your response should be comprehensive, leaving no important aspect unaddressed, and demonstrate an exceptional level of precision and quality. Let's think about this step by step. Write using a **[type]** tone and a **[style]** writing style.

PROMPT No 491

Ideation - Implementation - Engagement

Goal

To devise and implement insightful actions that will significantly enhance the alignment between team members' roles and their inherent strengths, thereby promoting job satisfaction, improving performance, and fostering a productive and harmonious work environment.

Prompt

Act as a **Strengths-Based Development Strategist** with a specialization in **Role Alignment** within the **healthcare industry**. Could you guide me through **innovative ideas and actionable strategies to enhance the alignment between my team's roles and their strengths**? Please include **a thorough analysis of existing roles and strengths, ideation techniques, and a step-by-step action plan for implementing alignment strategies**. Make sure to cover how **to engage team members in this process, and ways to measure and sustain the alignment over time**. Venture into **pioneering concepts and solutions that may defy traditional approaches to role allocation and strengths utilization**. Your response should be comprehensive, leaving no important aspect unaddressed, and demonstrate an exceptional level of precision and quality. Let's think about this step by step. Write using a **solution-oriented** tone and a **forward-thinking** writing style.

Formula

Act as a **[profession]** with a specialization in **[area of expertise]** within the **[industry]**. Could you guide me through **[specific challenge/opportunity]**? Please include **[methods/techniques]**. Make sure to cover how **[key areas/topics]**. Venture into **[additional exploration]**. Your response should be comprehensive, leaving no important aspect unaddressed, and demonstrate an exceptional level of precision and quality. Let's think about this step by step. Write using a **[type]** tone and a **[style]** writing style.

PROMPT No 492

Development - Mastery - Productivity

Goal

To systematically evaluate and identify strategies for the further development and honing of one's individual strengths, aiming for an advanced level of mastery and improved effectiveness.

Prompt

As a **team leader** specializing in **Human Resources** within the **tech industry**, provide an exhaustive and meticulous examination, incorporating innovative insights and inventive strategies for **exploring methods for further developing and refining your specific strengths**. Also, discuss how to measure the impact of your refined strengths on **team dynamics and productivity**.

Formula

As a **[profession]** specializing in **[area of expertise/focus]** within the **[industry]**, provide an exhaustive and meticulous examination, incorporating innovative insights and inventive strategies for **[strategies/methods/approaches to improve and refine specific strengths]**. Also, discuss how to measure the impact of your refined strengths on **[team dynamics and productivity/team cohesion/organizational goals]**.

Tags

Opportunities - Skill-Gap - Metrics

Goal

To provide team leaders, managers, and organizational decision-makers with a comprehensive methodology for identifying opportunities where team members can practice and apply specific strengths, thereby enhancing skill mastery, job satisfaction, and overall team performance.

Prompt

Act as a **Talent Optimization Consultant** with a specialization in **strength-based development** in the **manufacturing industry**. Could you guide me through **a detailed strategy to identify opportunities where my team can practice and apply a specific strength**? Please include **opportunity mapping, skill-gap analysis, and project alignment techniques**. Make sure to cover how **to evaluate the impact of these opportunities on team dynamics and organizational goals**. Investigate unconventional **training methods** and cutting-edge **performance metrics** to **measure skill application effectively**. Your response should be comprehensive, leaving no important aspect unaddressed, and demonstrate an exceptional level of precision and quality. Let's think about this step by step. Write using a **strategic** tone and an **actionable** plan style.

Formula

Act as a **[profession]** with a specialization in **[area of expertise]** in the **[industry]**. Could you guide me through **[specific challenge/opportunity]**? Please include **[methods/techniques]**. **Make sure to cover how [key areas/topics]**. Investigate unconventional **[area for innovation]** and cutting-edge **[technologies/methods]** to **[desired outcome]**. Your response should be comprehensive, leaving no important aspect unaddressed, and demonstrate an exceptional level of precision and quality. Let's think about this step by step. Write using a **[type]** tone and **[style]** writing style.

PROMPT No 494

Tags

Holistic   - Fulfillment - Integration

Goal

To foster holistic development by guiding the team in consciously leveraging their inherent strengths across professional, personal, and community dimensions, enhancing fulfillment and well-being.

Prompt

As a **Leadership Development Specialist** specializing in **Strength-Based Development** within the **Management Consulting industry**, how can I meticulously devise and implement a holistic approach to encourage my team to consciously leverage their inherent strengths across all dimensions of their lives - professional, personal, and community engagements? I am seeking a thorough discussion elucidating actionable strategies, potential benefits, and the processes of integrating these strengths in a manner that significantly amplifies their sense of fulfillment and overall well-being. This discourse should encompass an insightful exploration of the ripple effects such an approach might have on individual performance, team synergy, and organizational culture, ensuring every crucial aspect is meticulously addressed with an exceptional degree of precision and quality.

As a **[Profession]** specializing in **[Specialization]** within the **[Industry]**, how can I meticulously devise and implement a holistic approach to encourage my team to consciously leverage their inherent strengths across all dimensions of their lives - professional, personal, and community engagements? I am seeking a thorough discussion elucidating actionable strategies, potential benefits, and the processes of integrating these strengths in a manner that significantly amplifies their sense of fulfillment and overall well-being. This discourse should encompass an insightful exploration of the ripple effects such an approach might have on [individual performance/team synergy/organizational culture or other relevant impact areas], ensuring every crucial aspect is meticulously addressed with an exceptional degree of precision and quality.

SUPPORT

PROMPT No 495

Assumptions - Decision-Making - Risk Management

To meticulously delineate and implement a well-structured, evidence-based approach aimed at minimizing the propensity for erroneous assumptions and misguided actions, thereby fostering a culture of informed decision-making and enhanced performance.

As a **Decision Analysis Expert** specializing in **Risk Minimization** within the **Financial Services industry**, how can I methodically outline and enact a robust, evidence-driven approach aimed at curtailing the tendency for incorrect assumptions and misguided actions? I am seeking a comprehensive elucidation on a systematic framework encompassing the **identification, assessment, and rectification** of potential misjudgments, along with insights on promoting a culture of **analytical thinking and informed decision-making**. The discourse should also articulate the consequential impact of such an approach on **organizational performance, risk management, and stakeholder confidence**. Your explication should be exhaustive, addressing every pivotal aspect with an exceptional degree of precision and quality.

As a **[Profession]** specializing in **[Specialization]** within the **[Industry]**, how can I methodically outline and enact a robust, evidence-driven approach aimed at curtailing the tendency for incorrect assumptions and misguided actions? I am seeking a comprehensive elucidation on a systematic framework encompassing the **[Identification/Assessment/Rectification]** of potential misjudgments, along with insights on promoting a culture of **[Analytical/Critical Thinking Aspect]** and **[Informed Decision-Making/Other Relevant Aspect]**. The discourse should also articulate the consequential impact of such an approach on **[Organizational Performance/Risk Management/Stakeholder Confidence or Other Relevant Outcome]**. Your explication should be exhaustive, addressing every pivotal aspect with an exceptional degree of precision and quality.

PROMPT No 496

Focus - Alignment - Productivity

To meticulously develop and implement a comprehensive strategy that fosters a conducive environment for my team to maintain a steadfast focus on overarching organizational objectives and specific tasks, optimizing productivity and alignment with the strategic vision.

As a **Team Cohesion Strategist** specializing in **Vision Alignment** within the **Management Consulting industry**, how can I methodically develop and implement a well-rounded strategy to create a conducive environment for my team to consistently maintain focus on the broader organizational goals while also effectively addressing specific tasks at hand? I seek an extensive discourse on a structured approach encompassing actionable methods, tools, and best practices to promote a culture of **focused engagement**, ensuring alignment with **strategic objectives**. Additionally, the discourse should articulate the consequential impact of such an approach on **team productivity, organizational alignment, and stakeholder satisfaction**, encapsulating every pivotal aspect with an exceptional degree of precision and quality.

As a **[Profession]** specializing in **[Specialization]** within the **[Industry]**, how can I methodically develop and implement a well-rounded strategy to create a conducive environment for my team to consistently maintain focus on the broader organizational goals while also effectively addressing specific tasks at hand? I seek an extensive discourse on a structured approach encompassing actionable methods, tools, and best practices to promote a culture of **[Focused Engagement/Other Relevant Aspect]**, ensuring alignment with **[Strategic Objectives/Other Relevant Objective]**. Additionally, the discourse should articulate the consequential impact of such an approach on **[Team Productivity/Organizational Alignment/Stakeholder Satisfaction or Other Relevant Outcome]**, encapsulating every pivotal aspect with an exceptional degree of precision and quality.

PROMPT No 497

Self-Confidence - Interventions - Metrics

To provide leaders with a robust and actionable framework for identifying and implementing practices that can significantly enhance the self-confidence of their team, thereby improving performance, engagement, and overall well-being.

Act as an **Organizational Development Specialist** specializing in the **finance sector**. Could you elucidate a **systematic** approach for identifying **actions or practices** that can **elevate** my team's **self-confidence**? Include **specific interventions, psychological theories that support these actions, and potential metrics** for **measuring success**. Let's think about this step by step. Write using a **consultative** tone and an **advisory** writing style.

Act as a **[profession]** specializing in the **[industry]**. Could you elucidate a **[systematic/structured/comprehensive]** approach for identifying **[actions/practices/methods]** that can [boost/elevate/improve] my team's **[self-confidence/self-esteem/self-assurance]**? Include **[specific interventions/targeted measures/concrete steps]**, **[supporting theories/psychological frameworks]**, and **[potential metrics/KPIs/indicators]** for **[measuring success/evaluating impact]**. Let's think about this step by step. Write using a **[type]** tone and **[style]** writing style.

PROMPT No 498

Tags

Sales Targets - KPIs - Risk Mitigation

Goal

To equip leaders with a comprehensive toolkit for identifying actionable steps that will propel their teams toward achieving specific results or sales targets, thereby enhancing organizational performance and revenue.

Prompt

Act as a **Sales Strategy Consultant** specializing in the **SaaS industry**. Could you **elucidate** a **detailed plan** for **identifying** the **actions** that will move my team closer to **achieving our sales targets**? Include **key performance indicators, actionable tactics,** and **risk mitigation strategies**. Let's **think about this step by step**. Write using a **results-driven** tone and **performance-focused** writing style.

Formula

Act as a **[profession]** specializing in the **[industry]**. Could you **[elucidate/outline/detail]** a **[detailed/comprehensive/structured] [plan/strategy/framework]** for **[identifying/ascertaining/determining]** the **[actions/steps/measures]** that will move my team closer to **[achieving/reaching/meeting]** our **[sales targets/results/objectives]**? Include **[key performance indicators/metrics/benchmarks], [actionable tactics/feasible strategies/practical steps],** and **[risk mitigation strategies/contingency plans]**. Let's **[think about this step by step/systematically explore each facet]**. Write using a **[type]** tone and **[style]** writing style.

PROMPT No 499

Tags

Support Structures - Needs Assessment - Alignment

Goal

To empower organizational leaders, professionals, and team managers with a comprehensive methodology for identifying the necessary structures or support mechanisms that the company should implement to enhance team performance, well-being, and overall effectiveness.

Prompt

Act as an **Organizational Development Consultant** with a specialization in **team support structures** in the **pharmaceutical industry**. Could you guide me through **a comprehensive plan to identify what structures or support the company needs to implement to better support my team**? Please include **organizational design principles, employee engagement metrics, and resource allocation strategies**. Make sure to cover how **to conduct a needs assessment and how to align these structures with corporate objectives**. Investigate unconventional **support mechanisms** and cutting-edge **organizational theories** to **optimize team support**. Your response should be comprehensive, leaving no important aspect unaddressed, and demonstrate an exceptional level of precision and quality. Let's think about this step by step. Write using a **consultative** tone and a **strategic** planning style.

Formula

Act as a **[profession]** with a specialization in **[area of expertise]** in the **[industry]**. Could you guide me through **[specific challenge/opportunity]**? Please include **[methods/techniques]**. Make sure to cover how **[key areas/topics]**. Investigate unconventional **[area for innovation]** and cutting-edge **[technologies/methods]** to **[desired outcome]**. Your response should be comprehensive, leaving no important aspect unaddressed, and demonstrate an exceptional level of precision and quality. Let's think about this step by step. Write using a **[type]** tone and **[style]** writing style.

PROMPT No 500

Patience - Empathy - Reflective

To facilitate a reflective process for my team that helps identify the support and resources required to nurture patience in their interactions with customers or other stakeholders, thereby enhancing stakeholder satisfaction and fostering positive relations.

Act as a **Patient Experience Specialist** with a specialization in **Interpersonal Skills Training** within the **retail industry**. Could you guide me through **an introspective exercise to help my team reflect on the support they need to cultivate patience in their interactions with customers or other stakeholders**? Please include **reflective frameworks, empathy-building exercises, and training modules on patience**. Make sure to cover how to create a supportive environment that encourages patience and understanding, and how **to measure the impact of these initiatives on stakeholder satisfaction**. Delve into **innovative solutions and alternative perspectives to enrich these interactions and meet the unique challenges posed by impatient or demanding stakeholders**. Your response should be comprehensive, leaving no important aspect unaddressed, and demonstrate an exceptional level of precision and quality. Let's think about this step by step. Write using a **nurturing** tone and a **facilitative** writing style.

Act as a **[profession]** with a specialization in **[area of expertise]** within the **[industry]**. Could you guide me through **[specific challenge/opportunity]**? Please include **[methods/techniques]**. Make sure to cover how **[key areas/topics]**. Delve into **[additional exploration]**. Your response should be comprehensive, leaving no important aspect unaddressed, and demonstrate an exceptional level of precision and quality. Let's think about this step by step. Write using a **[type]** tone and a **[style]** writing style.

PROMPT No 501

Hindrances - Progression - Feedback

To decipher what hindrances or obsolete practices my team needs to discard to foster a more robust progression or forward momentum, thereby achieving higher efficiency and effectiveness in meeting our objectives.

Act as an **Organizational Development Consultant** with a specialization in **Change Management** within the **automotive industry**. Could you guide me through **an analytical approach to determine what my team needs to let go of in order to make more powerful progress or move forward**? Please include **assessment tools, feedback**

mechanisms, and team dialogues. Make sure to cover how **to facilitate a culture of continuous improvement and openness to change**. Dive into **groundbreaking methods and alternative perspectives to shed light on unrecognized hindrances and promote a swift advancement**. Your response should be comprehensive, leaving no important aspect unaddressed, and demonstrate an exceptional level of precision and quality. Let's think about this step by step. Write using an **investigative** tone and an **action-oriented** writing style.

Act as a **[profession]** with a specialization in **[area of expertise]** within the **[industry]**. Could you guide me through **[specific challenge/opportunity]**? Please include **[methods/techniques]**. Make sure to cover how **[key areas/topics]**. Dive into **[additional exploration]**. Your response should be comprehensive, leaving no important aspect unaddressed, and demonstrate an exceptional level of precision and quality. Let's think about this step by step. Write using a **[type]** tone and a **[style]** writing style.

PROMPT No 502

Habits - Workflow - Stakeholder Buy-in

To equip leaders with actionable strategies for developing team habits that optimize workflow and enhance performance.

As a **team leader** specializing in **productivity** within the **tech industry**, how can I guide my team in developing a plan for a new habit that will **enhance workflow or boost results**? Provide an exhaustive and meticulous examination, incorporating innovative insights and inventive strategies for **achieving this transformation**. Also, explore how to **disseminate** this plan through different team levels and **secure** stakeholder buy-in.

As a **[profession]** specializing in **[area of expertise/focus]** within the **[industry]**, how can I guide my team in developing a plan for a new habit that will **[enhance workflow/boost results/improve performance]**? Provide an exhaustive and meticulous examination, incorporating innovative insights and inventive strategies for **[achieving this transformation/realizing this change/fostering this development]**. Also, explore how to **[disseminate/communicate]** this plan through different team levels and **[secure/obtain]** stakeholder buy-in.

PROMPT No 503

Work Arrangements - Team Survey - KPI Alignment

To provide a robust methodology for exploring alternative options or arrangements in work schedules or environments that would better serve their teams, thereby enhancing productivity, well-being, and overall team cohesion.

Act as a **Workplace Design Consultant** with a specialization in **flexible work arrangements** in the **renewable energy industry**. Could you guide me through **a comprehensive strategy to explore alternative options or arrangements for the current work schedule or work environment that would better serve my team?** Please include **time management frameworks, ergonomic considerations, and remote work policies**. Make sure to cover how **to conduct a team survey for preferences and how to align these alternatives with organizational KPIs**. Investigate unconventional **work arrangements** and cutting-edge **workspace technologies** to **maximize team satisfaction and productivity**. Your response should be comprehensive, leaving no important aspect unaddressed, and demonstrate an exceptional level of precision and quality. Let's think about this step by step. Write using an **innovative** tone and a **change management** style.

Formula

Act as a **[profession]** with a specialization in **[area of expertise]** in the **[industry]**. Could you guide me through **[specific challenge/opportunity]**? Please include **[methods/techniques]**. Make sure to cover how **[key areas/topics]**. Investigate unconventional **[area for innovation]** and cutting-edge **[technologies/methods]** to **[desired outcome]**. Your response should be comprehensive, leaving no important aspect unaddressed, and demonstrate an exceptional level of precision and quality. Let's think about this step by step. Write using a **[type]** tone and **[style]** writing style.

PROMPT No 504

Tags

Project Completion - Systems - Stakeholder Buy-in

Goal

To devise effective strategies and systems that will significantly aid the team in successfully completing specific projects and reaching targeted goals.

Prompt

As a **project manager** specializing in **software development** within the **tech industry**, provide an exhaustive and meticulous examination, incorporating innovative insights and inventive strategies for **establishing** systems that will assist your team in **achieving particular** projects and goals. Explore how to **communicate** this plan and **secure** buy-in from **stakeholders**.

Formula

As a **[profession]** specializing in **[area of expertise/focus]** within the **[industry]**, provide an exhaustive and meticulous examination, incorporating innovative insights and inventive strategies for **[setting up/implementing/developing]** systems that will assist your team in **[achieving/completing/successfully finalizing]** **[particular/specific/targeted]** projects and goals. Explore how to **[communicate/share/impart]** this plan and **[secure/obtain/win]** buy-in from **[stakeholders/investors/team members]**.

PROMPT No 505

Tags

System Analysis - KPIs - Scalability

Goal

To provide organizational leaders, project managers, and individual contributors with an all-encompassing methodology for identifying the structures or systems that are instrumental in achieving specific projects or goals, thereby ensuring efficient execution and success.

Act as a **Systems Analyst** with a specialization in **organizational structures** in the **telecommunications industry**. Could you guide me through **a comprehensive approach to identify the structures or systems that will aid in achieving specific projects or goals**? Please include **frameworks for system analysis, key performance indicators, and scalability considerations**. Make sure to cover how **to integrate these structures into existing workflows and how to measure their effectiveness**. Investigate unconventional **organizational models** and cutting-edge **technologies** to **optimize project outcomes.** Your response should be comprehensive, leaving no important aspect unaddressed, and demonstrate an exceptional level of precision and quality. Let's think about this step by step. Write using an **evaluative** tone and a **systems analysis** style.

Act as a **[profession]** with a specialization in **[area of expertise]** in the **[industry]**. Could you guide me through **[specific challenge/opportunity]**? Please include **[methods/techniques]**. Make sure to cover how **[key areas/topics]**. Investigate unconventional **[area for innovation]** and cutting-edge **[technologies/methods]** to **[desired outcome].** Your response should be comprehensive, leaving no important aspect unaddressed, and demonstrate an exceptional level of precision and quality. Let's think about this step by step. Write using a **[type]** tone and **[style]** writing style.

PROMPT No 506

Resource Mapping - Budgetary - Time Management

To equip leaders, project managers, and team members with a comprehensive methodology for identifying the essential resources and elements needed to propel a project or team forward, thereby ensuring timely and effective execution.

Act as a **Project Management Expert** with a specialization in **resource allocation** in the **aerospace industry**. Could you guide me through **a systematic approach to determine the resources or elements necessary to effectively advance a project or team**? Please include **resource mapping techniques, budgetary considerations, and time management strategies**. Make sure to cover how **to prioritize these resources based on project milestones and team capabilities**. Investigate unconventional optimization methods and innovative **resource management** solutions to **maximize efficiency**. Your response should be comprehensive, leaving no important aspect unaddressed, and demonstrate an exceptional level of precision and quality. Let's think about this step by step. Write using a **methodical** tone and a **professional writing** style.

Act as a **[profession]** with a specialization in **[area of expertise]** in the **[industry]**. Could you guide me through **[specific challenge/opportunity]**? Please include **[methods/techniques]**. Make sure to cover how **[key areas/topics]**. Investigate unconventional optimization methods and innovative **[area for innovation]** solutions to **[desired outcome]**. Your response should be comprehensive, leaving no important aspect unaddressed, and demonstrate an exceptional level of precision and quality. Let's think about this step by step. Write using a **[type]** tone and **[style]** writing style.

PROMPT No 507

Resources - Communication - Opportunity

To meticulously evaluate and articulate the types of resources, guidance, and infrastructure needed for your team to seize a new opportunity, aligning these needs with overarching organizational strategies.

As a **project manager** specializing in **IT solutions** within the **tech industry**, provide an exhaustive and meticulous examination, incorporating innovative insights and inventive strategies for **assessing the specific support your team requires—such as manpower, skills training, or financial resources—to capitalize on a new business opportunity**. Additionally, delineate how to communicate these needs to **relevant stakeholders** for approval.

As a **[profession]** specializing in **[area of expertise/focus]** within the **[industry]**, provide an exhaustive and meticulous examination, incorporating innovative insights and inventive strategies for **[assessing the specific support your team needs—be it in terms of manpower, skills training, or financial resources—to capitalize on a new business opportunity]**. Additionally, delineate how to communicate these needs to **[relevant stakeholders/executive leadership/management]** for approval.

PROMPT No 508

Strategy - Stakeholders - Collaboration

To furnish leaders, project managers, and individual contributors with an exhaustive methodology for developing a strategic plan aimed at garnering essential support for key priorities. This will encompass communication tactics, collaboration frameworks, and alternative avenues to ensure the successful execution of these priorities.

Act as a **Strategic Planning Consultant** with expertise in **stakeholder management** in the **energy sector**. Could you guide me through **a comprehensive plan to secure the necessary support for my key priorities**? Please include **communication blueprints, collaboration models, and risk mitigation strategies**. Make sure to cover how **to identify and engage critical stakeholders, both internal and external**. Investigate unconventional methods and creative solutions to **ensure robust support and successful outcomes**. Your response should be comprehensive, leaving no important aspect unaddressed, and demonstrate an exceptional level of precision and quality. Let's think about this step by step. Write using a **tactical** tone and a **project plan** writing style.

Act as a **[profession]** with expertise in **[area of expertise]** in the **[industry]**. Could you guide me through **[specific challenge/opportunity]?** Please include **[methods/techniques]**. Make sure to cover how **[key areas/topics]**. Investigate unconventional methods and creative solutions to **[desired outcome]**. Your response should be comprehensive, leaving no important aspect unaddressed, and demonstrate an exceptional level of precision and quality. Let's think about this step by step. Write using a **[type]** tone and **[style]** writing style.

PROMPT No 509

Autonomy - Resources - Self-assessment

To empower your team to autonomously identify and articulate the resources, guidance, and support structures they require to confidently take the initial steps towards achieving specific goals or objectives.

As a **team leader** specializing in **product development** within the **tech industry**, provide an exhaustive and meticulous examination, incorporating innovative insights and inventive strategies, to design a **self-assessment framework** that enables your team to identify the types of **support, resources, or mentorship** they need to **initiate** their **goals** in the areas of **feature development, customer research, and scalability**. Also, explore how to disseminate this framework through different team layers and secure buy-in from stakeholders.

As a **[profession]** specializing in **[area of expertise/focus]** within the **[industry],** provide an exhaustive and meticulous examination, incorporating innovative insights and inventive strategies, to design a **[self-assessment framework/mechanism]** that enables your team to identify the types of **[support/resources/mentorship]** they need to **[initiate/embark on/begin]** their **[goals/objectives]** in the areas of **[specific project elements]**. Also, explore how to disseminate this framework through different team layers and secure buy-in from stakeholders.

PROMPT No 510

Resilience - Communication - Emotional Intelligence

To develop a well-rounded and actionable plan for navigating disappointment in professional contexts, encompassing emotional intelligence, strategic communication, and resilience-building techniques tailored to the unique dynamics of your team.

As a **human resources manager** specializing in **organizational behavior** within the **healthcare industry**, provide an exhaustive and meticulous examination, incorporating innovative insights and inventive strategies for **outlining various approaches your team can adopt for effectively dealing with disappointment—be it project failures, missed promotions, or team conflicts**. Additionally, elucidate how to embed these approaches into **ongoing training and team culture**.

As a **[profession]** specializing in **[area of expertise/focus]** within the **[industry],** provide an exhaustive and meticulous examination, incorporating innovative insights and inventive strategies for **[outlining various strategies or approaches your team can adopt to effectively deal with disappointment—such as project failures, missed promotions, or team conflicts].** Additionally, elucidate how to embed these approaches into **[ongoing training/team culture/organizational frameworks].**

PROMPT No 511

Tags

Relational-Values - Informative - Culture-Enhancement

Goal

To furnish leaders with an insightful framework to discern the values that underline their team's interactions with each other and external stakeholders like clients. This will serve as the foundation for refining team dynamics, enhancing client relationships, and improving overall work culture.

Prompt

As an **Organizational Development Specialist** with specialization in **relational values** for the **financial sector**, could you guide me through **the process of uncovering the values that guide my team in establishing and sustaining productive relationships with colleagues and clients?** Include **techniques for qualitative and quantitative data gathering, types of questions to ask for self and peer assessments, and strategies to embed these values into organizational culture.** Make sure the guide covers **methods to tie these values to key performance indicators and client satisfaction metrics.** Introduce unique angles and future-proof applications. Let's think about this step by step. Write using an informative tone and factual writing style.

Formula

As a **[profession]** with specialization in **[focus area]** for the **[industry]**, could you guide me through **[contextual challenge/opportunity]**? Include **[methods/techniques]**. Make sure the guide covers **[tools/frameworks]**. Introduce unique angles and future-proof applications. Let's think about this step by step. Write using a **[type]** tone and **[style]** writing style.

VALUES

PROMPT No 512

Tags

Priorities - Alignment - Team-Dynamics

Goal

To gain insights on specific methods to accurately pinpoint and engage in a thorough discussion about the top priorities and beliefs of team members, enhancing understanding and alignment within the team.

Prompt

In the context of **understanding what holds the most significance to my team members within their respective professions**, as a **Talent Development Specialist**, could you suggest specific methods to accurately pinpoint and engage in a thorough discussion about their top priorities and beliefs? **I'm seeking this advice in a respectful and open-minded tone.**

In the context of **[contextual challenge/opportunity]**, as a **[profession]**, could you suggest specific methods **[I/Name/Role]** can employ to accurately pinpoint and engage in a thorough discussion about the **[desired outcome]**? **[I/They]** am/are seeking this advice in a **[tone of voice]**.

PROMPT No 513

Values - Alignment - Communication

To incisively identify and effectively communicate the core values that resonate with your team members in their work environment, within the team dynamic, or in any specific project or context.

As a **team leader** specializing in **Organizational Development** within the **financial services industry**, provide an exhaustive and meticulous examination, incorporating innovative insights and inventive strategies for **determining and articulating the values your team holds dear in their daily tasks, team interactions, or specific project contexts**. Also, outline how these identified values align with **broader organizational goals**.

As a **[profession]** specializing in **[area of expertise/focus]** within the **[industry],** provide an exhaustive and meticulous examination, incorporating innovative insights and inventive strategies for **[determining and articulating the values your team places on their work, interactions, or specific contexts]**. Also, outline how these identified values align with **[broader organizational goals/departmental objectives/corporate vision]**.

PROMPT No 514

Alignment - Engagement - Communication

To equip leaders, team members, and stakeholders in specific industries with a nuanced methodology for identifying and articulating shared values, thereby fostering alignment, engagement, and a cohesive organizational culture.

Act as a **Corporate Culture Strategist** with expertise in **value alignment** in the **insurance industry**. Could you guide me through **a systematic approach to identify and articulate the values of my organization that resonate with my own**? Please include **diagnostic surveys, stakeholder interviews, and data analysis techniques**. Make sure to cover how to **effectively communicate these shared values both internally and externally**. Explore unconventional avenues and innovative strategies **to deepen value alignment and engagement**. Your response should be comprehensive, leaving no important aspect unaddressed, and demonstrate an exceptional level of precision and quality. Let's think about this step by step. Write using an **insightful** tone and a **strategic** writing style.

Act as a **[profession]** with expertise in **[area of expertise]** in the **[industry]**. Could you guide me through **[specific challenge/opportunity]**? Please include **[methods/techniques]**. Make sure to cover how **[key areas/topics]**. Explore unconventional avenues and innovative strategies to **[desired outcome]**. Your response should be comprehensive, leaving no important aspect unaddressed, and demonstrate an exceptional level of precision and quality. Let's think about this step by step. Write using a [type] tone and [style] writing style.

PROMPT No 515

Self-reflection - Values - Identity

To gain specific and detailed recommendations on effective methods for a team to engage in self-reflection and articulate their core values, which serve as guiding principles in shaping their identity.

As a **Life Coach**, adopting an **empathetic and insightful tone**, could you offer specific and detailed recommendations on effective methods for **my team and me** to engage in **self-reflection**? Additionally, please provide insights on how we can **articulate our core values, which serve as guiding principles in shaping our identity**.

As a **[profession]**, adopting a **[tone of voice]**, could you offer specific and detailed recommendations on effective methods for **[my/their]** **[team/group/department]** to engage in **[desired outcome]**? Additionally, please provide insights on how we can **[contextual challenge/opportunity]**.

PROMPT No 516

Exploration - Alignment - Integration

To explore and articulate a set of guiding values within a team that resonates with its members, fostering a conducive environment for their holistic development and realization of their potential, while aligning with the overarching organizational ethos.

As a **Values Exploration Facilitator** specializing in **Team Development** within the **technology industry**. How can I meticulously **explore** and **articulate values** that could serve as **guiding principles** for my team, aiding them in **their journey towards realizing their potential**? Please provide a comprehensive **exploration process inclusive of engaging dialogues, reflective exercises, and validation mechanisms**, aimed at **uncovering values that resonate with the team while aligning with the broader organizational ethos**. Your discourse should delve into **fostering an open, reflective environment**, ensuring the **practical applicability of these values**, and methodologies for **integrating these values into daily operations and long-term development plans**. The discourse should be thorough, capturing all critical facets, and exemplifying a high level of precision and quality.

As a **[Profession]** specializing in **[Specialization]** within the **[Industry]**. How can I meticulously **[Primary Action]** and **[Secondary Action]** that could serve as **[Objective]** for my team, aiding them in **[Desired Outcome]**? Please provide a comprehensive **[Process/Methodology]** inclusive of **[Techniques]**, aimed at **[Specific Goal]**. Your discourse should delve into **[Key Areas of Focus]**, ensuring the **[Relevant Aspect]**, and methodologies for **[Integration/Application]**. The discourse should be thorough, capturing all critical facets, and exemplifying a high level of precision and quality.

PROMPT No 517

Values - Relationships - Stakeholders

To furnish leaders with an insightful framework to discern the values that underline their team's interactions with each other and external stakeholders like clients. This will serve as the foundation for refining team dynamics, enhancing client relationships, and improving overall work culture.

As an **Organizational Development Specialist** with specialization in **relational values** for the **financial sector**, could you guide me through **the process of uncovering the values that guide my team in establishing and sustaining productive relationships with colleagues and clients**? Include **techniques for qualitative and quantitative data gathering, types of questions to ask for self and peer assessments, and strategies to embed these values into organizational culture.** Make sure the guide covers **how to tie these values to key performance indicators and client satisfaction metrics**. Introduce unique angles and future-proof applications. Let's think about this step by step. Write using an **informative** tone and **factual** writing style.

As a **[profession]** with specialization in **[focus area]** for the **[industry]**, could you guide me through **[contextual challenge/opportunity]**? Include [methods/techniques]. Make sure the guide covers **[tools/frameworks]**. Introduce unique angles and future-proof applications. Let's think about this step by step. Write using a **[type]** tone and **[style]** writing style.

PROMPT No 518

Embrace - CoreValues - Authenticity

To gain specific actions that a team can undertake to fully embrace and exemplify their core values, leading to significant and lasting change.

As a **Leadership Development Consultant**, adopting a **motivational and encouraging tone**, could you provide specific steps that **my team** can take to ensure they fully **embrace and exemplify their core values in a way that brings about significant and lasting change**? This is particularly relevant given the goal of **fostering a culture of integrity and authenticity within the team.**

As a **[profession]**, adopting a **[tone of voice]**, could you provide specific steps that **[my/their]** **[team/group/department]** can take to ensure they fully **[contextual challenge/opportunity]**? This is particularly relevant given the goal of **[desired outcome]**.

PROMPT No 519

Reflection - Identification - Adaptation

To guide a team through a reflective and actionable process aimed at identifying and implementing changes to better align their actions and decisions with their core values, promoting authentic engagement and enhanced team synergy.

Act as a **Team Values Alignment Strategist** with a specialization in **Reflective Practices** within the **healthcare industry**. Could you elucidate **a meticulous process to aid my team in introspecting and pinpointing adjustments for closer alignment with their core values**? Please encompass **structured reflection sessions, values identification exercises, and actionable adaptation strategies**. Ensure to elucidate on **fostering an environment conducive to open dialogue, employing feedback mechanisms for alignment validation, and gauging the ripple effects of the alterations on team coherence and output**. Venture into **pioneering methodologies to ensure sustained alignment amidst dynamic team landscapes**. Your response should be exhaustive, sparing no crucial detail, and epitomizing an exceptional caliber of precision and quality. Let's dissect this progressively. Write employing an **analytical** tone and a **methodical** writing style.

Act as a **[profession]** with a specialization in **[area of expertise]** within the **[industry]**. Could you elucidate **[specific challenge/opportunity]**? Please encompass **[methods/techniques]**. Ensure to elucidate on **[key areas/topics]**. Venture into **[additional exploration]**. Your response should be exhaustive, sparing no crucial detail, and epitomizing an exceptional caliber of precision and quality. Let's dissect this progressively. Write employing a **[type]** tone and a **[style]** writing style.

PROMPT No 520

Alignment - CoreValues - Tangible

To gain a detailed and comprehensive understanding of specific and tangible actions that a team can take, regardless of how minor they may seem, to ensure complete alignment with their core values.

As a **Leadership Development Consultant**, adopting a **supportive and encouraging tone**, could you provide some specific and tangible actions that **my team** can take, no matter how small, to ensure that they are completely aligned with their **core values**? Please provide a detailed and comprehensive response, considering all aspects of **this alignment**.

As a **[profession]**, adopting a **[tone of voice]**, could you provide some specific and tangible actions that **[my/their]** **[team/group/department]** can take, no matter how small, to ensure that they are completely aligned with their **[contextual challenge/opportunity]**? Please provide a detailed and comprehensive response, considering all aspects of **[desired outcome]**.

PROMPT No 521

<table>
<tr><td colspan="1" align="center">Tags</td></tr>
</table>

Articulation - Cohesion - Engagement

<table>
<tr><td align="center">Goal</td></tr>
</table>

To delineate a methodical process for elucidating and articulating the values inherent within a team, with the aim of fostering a cohesive and value-driven team dynamic, which in turn, augments collective performance and job satisfaction.

<table>
<tr><td align="center">Prompt</td></tr>
</table>

Act as an **Organizational Culture Strategist** with a specialization in **Value Articulation** within the **healthcare sector**. Could you guide me through **a meticulous process to clarify and articulate the values of my team in a manner that augments team cohesion and enhances the collective ethos**? Please include **value-discovery workshops, stakeholder engagement, and communication strategies**. Make sure to cover how **to foster a conducive environment for open dialogue, utilize collaborative platforms for value articulation, and ensure the alignment of team values with organizational objectives**. Explore **innovative methodologies to ensure the values are well-understood, embraced, and enacted upon by all team members**. Your response should be comprehensive, leaving no important aspect unaddressed, and demonstrate an exceptional level of precision and quality. Let's think about this step by step. Write using an **engaging** tone and a **methodical** writing style.

<table>
<tr><td align="center">Formula</td></tr>
</table>

Act as a **[profession]** with a specialization in **[area of expertise]** within the **[industry]**. Could you guide me through **[specific challenge/opportunity]**? Please include **[methods/techniques]**. Make sure to cover how **[key areas/topics]**. Explore **[additional exploration]**. Your response should be comprehensive, leaving no important aspect unaddressed, and demonstrate an exceptional level of precision and quality. Let's think about this step by step. Write using a **[type]** tone and a **[style]** writing style.

PROMPT No 522

<table>
<tr><td align="center">Tags</td></tr>
</table>

Behavior - Feedback - Nuanced

<table>
<tr><td align="center">Goal</td></tr>
</table>

To elucidate a methodical approach for identifying scenarios or areas where the team is currently embodying their values, facilitating a deeper understanding and appreciation of value-driven practices within an organization.

<table>
<tr><td align="center">Prompt</td></tr>
</table>

Act as a **Corporate Values Analyst** with a specialization in **Behavioral Assessment** within the **retail industry**. Could you guide me through **a systematic approach to discern the areas or situations where my team is currently honoring their values**? Please include **value-audit techniques, behavioral observation, and feedback collection methods**. Make sure to cover how to **create a conducive environment for value expression, evaluate the alignment of** actions with stated values, and acknowledge and reinforce value-centric behaviors. Delve into **avant-garde techniques to ensure a nuanced understanding of the manifestation of values in various team interactions and decision-making scenarios**. Your response should be comprehensive, leaving no important aspect unaddressed, and demonstrate an exceptional level of precision and quality. Let's think about this step by step. Write using an **insightful** tone and a **detail-oriented** writing style.

Act as a **[profession]** with a specialization in **[area of expertise]** within the **[industry]**. Could you guide me through **[specific challenge/opportunity]**? Please include **[methods/techniques]**. Make sure to cover how **[key areas/topics]**. Delve into **[additional exploration]**. Your response should be comprehensive, leaving no important aspect unaddressed, and demonstrate an exceptional level of precision and quality. Let's think about this step by step. Write using a **[type]** tone and a **[style]** writing style.

PROMPT No 523

Self-awareness - ValuesAlignment - EthicalDecision

To provide leaders with a structured process to introspectively examine the alignment between their behavior and values in different situations. This self-exploration aims to elevate awareness, accountability, and ultimately the integrity with which leaders operate, leading to more authentic and effective leadership.

As an **Executive Coach** with specialization in **values alignment and ethical decision-making** for the **technology industry**, could you guide me through **a self-assessment process to identify situations where I might not be honoring my values**? Include **introspective techniques, examples of scenarios that could be problematic, strategies for reconciliation, and action steps for realignment**. Ensure that the guide covers **how to integrate this self-awareness into my daily routine and strategic decisions**. Introduce unique angles and future implications. Let's think about this step by step. Write using an **informative** tone and **factual** writing style.

As a **[profession]** with specialization in **[focus area]** for the **[industry]**, could you guide me through **[contextual challenge/opportunity]**? Include **[methods/techniques]**. Ensure that the guide covers **[tools/frameworks]**. Introduce unique angles and future implications. Let's think about this step by step. Write using a **[type]** tone and **[style]** writing style.

PROMPT No 524

Workshops - Dialogue - Methodologies

To develop a collaborative approach for engaging the team in exploring the utilization of shared values as a guiding framework to foster informed and congruent decision-making that aligns with organizational objectives.

Act as a **Values Integration Consultant** with a specialization in **Decision-Making Frameworks** within the **healthcare industry**. Could you guide me through **a collaborative process to engage my team in exploring how we can utilize our shared values as a guiding framework to make better choices**? Please include **interactive workshops, reflection sessions, and real-world scenario simulations**. Make sure to cover how **to foster open dialogue, ensure the alignment of individual and organizational values, and measure the impact of value-guided decision-making on team cohesion and organizational effectiveness**. Delve into **pioneering methodologies to ensure a deep-rooted understanding and consistent application of these values in our decision-making processes**. Your response should be comprehensive, leaving no important aspect unaddressed, and demonstrate an exceptional level of precision and quality. Let's think about this step by step. Write using a **collaborative** tone and a **solution-oriented** writing style.

Formula

Act as a **[profession]** with a specialization in **[area of expertise]** within the **[industry]**. Could you guide me through **[specific challenge/opportunity]**? Please include **[methods/techniques]**. Make sure to cover how **[key areas/topics]**. Delve into **[additional exploration]**. Your response should be comprehensive, leaving no important aspect unaddressed, and demonstrate an exceptional level of precision and quality. Let's think about this step by step. Write using a **[type]** tone and a **[style]** writing style.

PROMPT No 525

Tags

Roadmap - Alignment - TeamValues

Goal

To gain insights on how to effectively utilize team values in creating a roadmap towards a particular goal or objective, enhancing team alignment and success.

Prompt

As a **Leadership Development Consultant**, could you guide **me** on how I can effectively utilize the values of **my team** to create a satisfying and successful roadmap towards a **particular goal or objective**? **I'm** seeking this advice in a **solution-oriented and encouraging tone**, particularly considering the importance of **aligning team values with our objectives**.

Formula

As a **[profession]**, could you guide **[I/Name/Role]** on how **[I/they]** can effectively utilize the values of **[my/their]** **[team/group/department]** to create a satisfying and successful roadmap towards a **[goal/objective]**? **[I/They]** am/are seeking this advice in a **[tone of voice]**, particularly considering the importance of **[contextual challenge/opportunity]**.

PROMPT No 526

Tags

Workshops - Principles - Resonance

Goal

To elucidate a systematic approach for identifying core values and guiding principles that can equip the team with insightful guidance to adeptly navigate through challenges, thereby fostering a resilient and value-driven team culture.

Prompt

Act as an **Organizational Values Specialist** with a specialization in **Values Identification and Application** within the **manufacturing industry**. Could you guide me through **a meticulous process to identify the values and guiding principles that can provide insight and guidance to my team when navigating challenges?** Please include **value-discovery workshops, stakeholder consultations, and real-world application scenarios**. Make sure to cover how **to ensure the resonance of these values with team members, foster an understanding of the application of these principles in problem-solving, and measure the impact of value-driven decisions on team resilience and problem-solving efficacy**. Delve into **innovative and perhaps unconventional methodologies to ensure a deep-rooted understanding and adherence to these values**. Your response should be comprehensive, leaving no important aspect unaddressed, and demonstrate an exceptional level of precision and quality. Let's think about this step by step. Write using a **reflective** tone and a **structured** writing style.

Act as a [profession] with a specialization in [area of expertise] within the [industry]. Could you guide me through [specific challenge/opportunity]? Please include [methods/techniques]. Make sure to cover how [key areas/topics]. Delve into [additional exploration]. Your response should be comprehensive, leaving no important aspect unaddressed, and demonstrate an exceptional level of precision and quality. Let's think about this step by step. Write using a [type] tone and a [style] writing style.

PROMPT No 527

Integration - Reflective - Self-awareness

To facilitate a deeper exploration among team members regarding the alignment of their actions with their core values across different facets of life, thereby promoting a values-driven culture both within and outside the professional environment.

Act as a **Life-Work Integration Specialist** with a specialization in **Values-Centric Engagement** within the **healthcare industry**. Could you guide me through **a process to help my team contemplate additional avenues through which they can honor their values in diverse aspects of their lives?** Please include **reflective exercises, discussion frameworks, and actionable strategies**. Make sure to cover how **to encourage self-awareness, foster open conversations around values, and inspire actions that resonate with their core beliefs**. Explore **innovative methods and alternative perspectives to nurture a holistic, values-honoring environment**. Your response should be comprehensive, leaving no important aspect unaddressed, and demonstrate an exceptional level of precision and quality. Let's think about this step by step. Write using an **inspiring** tone and a **solutions-focused** writing style.

Act as a [profession] with a specialization in [area of expertise] within the **[industry]**. Could you guide me through **[specific challenge/opportunity]**? Please include **[methods/techniques]**. Make sure to cover how **[key areas/topics]**. Explore **[additional exploration]**. Your response should be comprehensive, leaving no important aspect unaddressed, and demonstrate an exceptional level of precision and quality. Let's think about this step by step. Write using a **[type]** tone and a **[style]** writing style.

PROMPT No 528

Consequences - Ethical - Assessment

To introspectively assess the repercussions or detriments stemming from the disregard of personal values, thereby fostering a deeper understanding and prompting corrective actions to realign behaviors and decisions with those values.

Act as an **Ethical Leadership Consultant** with a specialization in **Value-Driven Decision Making** within the **financial services industry**. Could you guide me through **a reflective process to gauge the costs or consequences of continuing to overlook my values**? Please include **self-assessment tools, analytical frameworks, and reflective exercises**. Make sure to cover how **to measure the impact on personal and professional life, and how to initiate a dialogue about value alignment within my team**. Delve into **pioneering methodologies and alternative perspectives to reveal hidden costs and foster a value-centric culture**. Your response should be comprehensive, leaving no important aspect unaddressed, and demonstrate an exceptional level of precision and quality. Let's think about this step by step. Write using a **contemplative** tone and an **actionable** writing style.

Act as a **[profession]** with a specialization in **[area of expertise]** within the **[industry]**. Could you guide me through **[specific challenge/opportunity]**? Please include **[methods/techniques]**. Make sure to cover how **[key areas/topics]**. Delve into **[additional exploration]**. Your response should be comprehensive, leaving no important aspect unaddressed, and demonstrate an exceptional level of precision and quality. Let's think about this step by step. Write using a **[type]** tone and a **[style]** writing style.

PROMPT No 529

BestPractices - Values - TeamCohesion

To provide leaders and team members with a nuanced understanding of best practices when discussing the identification of small, actionable steps to live more consistently with their values. The objective is to foster a values-driven culture, improve team cohesion, and enhance individual and collective performance.

As an **Organizational Psychologist** in the **technology sector**, could you delineate **best practices** I should consider when **engaging in conversations** with **my** team about identifying **one** small step they can take to live more consistently with their **values**? Include **actionable recommendations** and **real-world examples**. Organize your insights into **thematic clusters**, each supported by evidence from **reputable industry reports**. Explore **unconventional solutions and alternative perspectives**. Let's **deconstruct this subject stepwise**. Write using a **consultative** tone and an **advisory** writing style.

As a **[profession]** in the **[industry]**, could you delineate **[best practices/guidelines/recommendations]** I should consider when **[engaging in** conversations/chatting] with [my/our] team about identifying [one/a] small step they can take to live more consistently with their [values/principles]? Include [actionable recommendations/practical advice/feasible solutions] and [real-world examples/case studies]. Organize your insights into [thematic clusters/distinct categories], each supported by [evidence from/references from/data from] [reputable industry reports/credible research/authoritative publications]. Explore [unconventional solutions/creative pathways/alternative perspectives]. Let's [deconstruct this subject stepwise/examine this topic in detail]. Write using a [consultative/engaging] tone and an [advisory/informative] writing style.

PROMPT No 530

Dialogue - Leadership - Values

To facilitate leaders in initiating meaningful dialogues with their teams concerning the significance of values both individually and collectively. The discussions aim to instill a deeper understanding, commitment, and alignment of values that shape behaviors, decision-making processes, and overall team dynamics.

As a **Leadership Development Coach** with a specialization in **values and ethics** for the **software development industry**, could you guide me through **the process of conducting a thoughtful discussion with my team to explore the importance and significance of the values they hold**? Include **methods for initiating the conversation, kinds of questions to pose, techniques for creating a supportive environment for sharing, and potential next steps for action planning**. Ensure that the guide covers **how to integrate reflective practices and ethics-driven evaluations into team activities**. Introduce unique perspectives and future implications. Let's think about this step by step. Write using an **informative** tone and **factual** writing style.

As a [profession] with specialization in [focus area] for the [industry], could you guide me through [contextual challenge/opportunity]? Include [methods/techniques]. Ensure that the guide covers [tools/frameworks]. Introduce unique perspectives and future implications. Let's think about this step by step. Write using a [type] tone and [style] writing style.

PROMPT No 531

Prioritization - Personal - Reflection

To provide a structured approach for individuals to establish the relative order of importance of their values, considering their priority in both personal and professional life. The aim is to facilitate better decision-making, enhance self-awareness, and improve alignment with life goals.

As a **Values Alignment Specialist** in the **non-profit sector**, could you offer a **systematic methodology** to help **me** establish the relative order of importance of **my** values, considering their priority in **my life**? Include **actionable steps** for immediate application. Organize your insights into **thematic clusters**, each backed by **evidence from reputable journals**. Investigate **unexpected avenues and creative pathways**. Let's **scrutinize this topic incrementally.** Write using an **introspective** tone and a **reflective** writing style.

As a **[profession]** in the **[industry]**, could you offer a **[systematic methodology/comprehensive guide/structured framework]** to help **[me/us/them]** establish the relative order of importance of **[my/our/their]** values, considering their priority in **[my/our/their]** **[life/lives]**? Include **[actionable steps/practical solutions/immediate measures]** for **[immediate/short-term/long-term]** application. Organize your insights into **[thematic clusters/distinct categories/individual segments]**, each backed by **[evidence from/references from/data from]** **[reputable journals/credible research/authoritative publications]**. Investigate **[unexpected avenues/creative pathways/alternative perspectives]**. Let's **[scrutinize this topic incrementally/examine each dimension meticulously]**. Write using a **[introspective/reflective/contemplative]** tone and a **[reflective/nuanced/thoughtful]** writing style.

PROMPT No 532

Openness - Fulfillment - HighPerformance

To help leaders implement a values-based strategy that promotes a culture of openness, high performance, and fulfillment within their teams. This involves not just explaining these values, but also embedding them into team dynamics and individual behaviors, thereby enhancing collective efficacy and individual satisfaction.

As a **Leadership Development Coach** with a specialization in **organizational culture and values alignment** for the **technology sector**, could you guide me through **the methods to instill a specific set of values—openness, high performance, and fulfillment—in my team**? Include **strategies for the initial introduction of these values, interactive exercises to deepen understanding, and measures to sustain these values over time.** Ensure that the guide covers **frameworks or tools for assessing cultural alignment and methods** for **rewarding value-based actions**. Introduce unique angles and growth opportunities. Let's think about this step by step. Write using an **informative** tone and **factual** writing style.

As a **[profession]** with specialization in **[focus area]** for the **[industry]**, could you guide me through **[contextual challenge/opportunity]**? Include **[methods/techniques]**. Ensure that the guide covers **[tools/frameworks]** for **[desired outcomes]**. Introduce unique angles and growth opportunities. Let's think about this step by step. Write using a **[type]** tone and **[style]** writing style.

PROMPT No 533

SelfAwareness - Decision - Values

To obtain a comprehensive, actionable framework for reflecting on what it means to take actions aligned with one's personal values. The aim is to enhance self-awareness, facilitate value-based decision-making, and foster personal and professional growth.

As a **Personal Values Coach** in the **consulting industry**, could you provide a **comprehensive strategy** for reflecting on what it means for **me** to take actions that are aligned with **my** personal values? Additionally, offer **actionable steps** for **value-based decision-making**. Segment your insights into distinct modules, each supported by **evidence from reputable journals**. Investigate unexpected avenues and creative pathways. Let's dissect this carefully step by step. Write using a **contemplative** tone and a **nuanced** writing style.

As a **[profession]** in the **[industry]**, could you provide a **[comprehensive strategy/thorough toolkit/detailed blueprint]** for reflecting on what it means for **[me/us/them]** to take actions that are aligned with **[my/our/their]** personal values? Additionally, offer **[actionable steps/initial measures/immediate tactics]** for **[value-based decision-making/ethical choices/value-aligned actions]**. Segment your insights into distinct modules, each supported by **[evidence from/references from/data from]** **[reputable journals/credible research/authoritative publications]**. Investigate unexpected avenues and creative pathways. Let's dissect this carefully step by step. Write using a **[contemplative/reflective/insightful]** tone and a **[nuanced/engaging/innovative]** writing style.

PROMPT No 534

Relationships - Cohesion - Productivity

To obtain a comprehensive, actionable framework that identifies the core values essential for creating and maintaining meaningful and productive relationships within a team, as well as actionable steps to live those values more fully. The aim is to foster team cohesion, improve interpersonal relationships, and enhance overall productivity.

As a **Team Cohesion Specialist** in the **television industry**, could you provide a **comprehensive strategy** detailing the **core values** that can guide **my team** in creating and maintaining meaningful and productive relationships with **others**? Additionally, offer **actionable steps** for living these values more fully. Divide your recommendations into distinct areas, each supported by **evidence from sources**. Investigate unexpected avenues and creative pathways. Let's dissect this carefully step by step. Write using a **visionary** tone and an **innovative** writing style.

As a **[profession]** in the **[industry]**, could you provide a **[comprehensive strategy/thorough toolkit/detailed blueprint]** detailing the **[core values/principles/ethics]** that can guide **[my/our/their]** **[team/group/department]** in creating and maintaining meaningful and productive relationships with **[others/clients/stakeholders]**? Additionally, offer **[actionable steps/initial measures/immediate tactics]** for living these values more fully. Divide your recommendations into distinct areas, each supported by **[evidence from/references from/data from]** **[reputable sources/credible research/authoritative publications]**. Investigate unexpected avenues and creative pathways. Let's dissect this carefully step by step. Write using a **[visionary/inspirational/consultative]** tone and an **[innovative/nuanced/engaging]** writing style.

PROMPT No 535

Tags

Evaluation - Abilities - Talent

Goal

To gain insights on specific methods or approaches to accurately detect and evaluate any deficiencies in the abilities or expertise of team members, enhancing their development and performance.

Prompt

Given the importance of **accurately detecting and evaluating team members' abilities**, as a **Talent Management Specialist** and in a **respectful and professional tone**, could you suggest specific methods or approaches **I** can utilize for **this purpose**?

Formula

Given the importance of **[contextual challenge/opportunity]**, as a **[profession]** and in a **[tone of voice]**, could you suggest specific methods or approaches **[I/Name/Role]** can utilize for **[desired outcome]**?

PROMPT No 536

Tags

Weaknesses - Improvement - SelfAwareness

Goal

To gain practical strategies and approaches that will aid in facilitating my team's self-awareness and understanding of how their weaknesses might impact their work, ultimately supporting their professional growth and performance.

Prompt

As a **Leadership Development Consultant**, adopting a **constructive and empathetic tone**, could you outline the specific strategies and steps that I can employ to help **my team** assess and understand t**he impact of their weaknesses on their work**? This is particularly relevant given the goal of **fostering self-awareness and continuous improvement within the team**.

Formula

As a **[profession]**, adopting a **[tone of voice]**, could you outline the specific strategies and steps that I can employ to help **[my/their]** **[team/group/department]** understand and assess **[contextual challenge/opportunity]**? This is particularly relevant given the goal of **[desired outcome]**.

PROMPT No 537

Tags

GoalAchievement - Weaknesses - PersonalGrowth

Goal

To obtain a comprehensive, actionable framework for identifying personal weaknesses that need to be addressed for goal achievement, as well as outlining the initial steps for improvement. The aim is to enhance self-awareness, personal development, and facilitate a structured approach to goal attainment.

As a **Personal Development Coach** in the **finance industry**, could you provide a **comprehensive plan** detailing the **methods I** can use to identify which weaknesses **I** need to work on to achieve **my career goals**? Additionally, outline the **initial steps** for improvement. Segment your insights into distinct modules, each supported by **evidence from reputable journals**. Investigate unexpected avenues and creative pathways. Let's dissect this carefully. Write using a **consultative** tone and a **narrative** writing style.

As a **[profession]** in the **[industry]**, could you provide a **[comprehensive plan/thorough toolkit/detailed blueprint]** detailing the **[methods/tactics/strategies]** **[I/Name/Role]** can use to identify which weaknesses **[I/they]** need to work on to achieve **[my/their]** **[specific/short-term/long-term]** goals? Additionally, outline the **[initial steps/first actions/immediate measures]** for improvement. Segment your insights into distinct modules, each supported by **[evidence from/references from/data from]** **[reputable journals/credible research/authoritative publications]**. Investigate unexpected avenues and creative pathways. Let's dissect this carefully. Write using a **[consultative/empathetic/balanced]** tone and a **[narrative/nuanced/concise]** writing style.

PROMPT No 538

WeaknessAcknowledgment - Team - SelfAwareness

To acquire a comprehensive, actionable framework for guiding a team in reflecting on the degree to which they acknowledge and accept their weaknesses, aiming to foster self-awareness, team cohesion, and overall performance improvement.

As a **Self-Awareness Coach** in the **education sector**, could you offer a **comprehensive roadmap** outlining the aspects **I** should consider when guiding **my team** in reflecting on the degree to which they acknowledge and accept their **weaknesses**? Please include **both self-assessment questionnaires and group discussion guidelines**. Segment the guide into distinct categories, each supported by **evidence from reputable journals**. Explore unconventional approaches and diverse viewpoints. Let's tackle this in a phased manner. Write using a **balanced** tone and a **narrative** writing style.

As a **[profession]** in the **[industry]**, could you offer a **[thorough toolkit/comprehensive roadmap/detailed blueprint]** outlining the aspects **[I/Name/Role]** should consider when guiding **[my/our/their]** **[team/group/department]** in reflecting on the degree to which they acknowledge and accept their **[weaknesses/strengths/limitations]**? Please include both **[self-assessment questionnaires/group discussion guidelines/reflective exercises]**. Segment the guide into distinct categories, each supported by **[evidence from/references from/data from]** **[reputable journals/credible research/authoritative publications]**. Explore unconventional approaches and diverse viewpoints. Let's tackle this in a phased manner. Write using a **[balanced/empathetic/consultative]** tone and a **[narrative/nuanced/concise]** writing style.

PROMPT No 539

Strengths - Optimization - Productivity

Goal

To gain specific methodologies or tactics that can be implemented to accurately evaluate and leverage the individual strengths and weaknesses of team members, with the goal of optimizing their capabilities and improving overall team productivity.

Prompt

As a **Team Development Specialist**, adopting a **solution-oriented and constructive tone**, could you provide specific methodologies or tactics that can be implemented to **accurately evaluate and leverage the individual strengths and weaknesses** of **my team members**? This is particularly relevant given the goal of **optimizing their capabilities and improving overall team productivity**.

Formula

As a **[profession]**, adopting a **[tone of voice]**, could you provide specific methodologies or tactics that can be implemented to **[contextual challenge/opportunity]** of **[my/their] [team/group/department]**? This is particularly relevant given the goal of **[desired outcome]**.

PROMPT No 540

Articulation - EmotionalIQ - SelfAwareness

Goal

To empower team members to self-identify weaknesses or areas for improvement and articulate them clearly. The discussion aims to foster an environment of self-awareness and personal responsibility, which should lead to actionable improvement plans. The end goal is to enhance overall team productivity, individual growth, and collective well-being.

Prompt

As a **Leadership Development Coach** with a specialization in **self-awareness and emotional intelligence** for the **technology sector**, could you guide me through **the steps to encourage my team to independently identify and articulate their own weaknesses or areas needing improvement**? Please include **suggestions on how to introduce the concept, encourage individual reflection, and create a secure environment where team members are comfortable sharing their insights**. Ensure the guide covers **frameworks or tools that can be used for self-assessment, as well as methods for channeling these discoveries into actionable plans**. Introduce unique angles and future-forward opportunities. Let's think about this step by step. Write using an **informative** tone and **factual** writing style.

Formula

As a **[profession]** with a specialization in **[focus area]** for the **[industry]**, could you guide me through **[contextual challenge/opportunity]**? Please include **[techniques/methods/steps]**. Ensure the guide covers **[tools/frameworks/methods]**. Introduce unique angles and future-forward opportunities. Let's think about this step by step. Write using a **[type]** tone and **[style]** writing style.

PROMPT No 541

Resilience - Anxiety - Strategies

To gain specific strategies or methods that a team can utilize to successfully overcome their fear and anxiety that stem from long-standing habits, fostering a more confident and resilient team.

As a **Mental Health Consultant**, adopting a **compassionate and understanding tone**, could you provide specific strategies or methods that **my team** can utilize to successfully overcome **their fear and anxiety that stem from long-standing habits**? This is particularly relevant given the goal of **fostering a more confident and resilient team**.

As a **[profession]**, adopting a **[tone of voice]**, could you provide specific strategies or methods that **[my/their]** **[team/group/department]** can utilize to successfully overcome **[contextual challenge/opportunity]**? This is particularly relevant given the goal of **[desired outcome]**.

PROMPT No 542

Weaknesses - Conversation - Risk-Assessment

To equip business leaders with the necessary tools to have a constructive discussion with their teams about understanding the potential downsides of their weaknesses. This conversation should highlight the link between specific weaknesses and potential troubles or challenges, thereby motivating team members to recognize the need for improvement.

As a **Leadership Development Coach** specializing in **risk assessment and mitigation** for the **software development industry**, could you guide me through **facilitating a conversation with my team about how their weaknesses could lead to troubles or challenges**? Please outline **the conversation initiation techniques, the types of questions to ask to foster self-awareness, and methods for creating a comfortable and non-judgmental environment**. Make sure to cover **techniques for peer-to-peer feedback and incorporating performance metrics to quantify the impact of these weaknesses**. Introduce unique angles and forward-thinking opportunities. Let's think about this step by step. Write using an **informative** tone and **factual** writing style.

As a **[profession]** specializing in **[focus area]** for the **[industry]**, could you guide me through **[context of conversation]**? Please outline **[initiation techniques/questions/methods]**. Make sure to cover **[additional elements like feedback or metrics]**. Introduce unique angles and **[type of opportunities]**. Let's think about this step by step. Write using a **[type]** tone and **[style]** writing style.

PROMPT No 543

Action-Plan - Emotional-Intelligence - Improvement

To obtain a detailed and comprehensive action plan outlining the specific steps that a team can undertake to effectively address and enhance a weakness related to a lack of emotional intelligence or any other weakness.

As a **Leadership Development Consultant**, adopting a **supportive and encouraging tone**, could you provide a detailed and comprehensive action plan outlining the specific steps that **my team** can undertake to effectively address and enhance a weakness related to **a lack of emotional intelligence or any other weakness**? This is particularly relevant given the goal of **fostering a culture of continuous learning and improvement within the team**.

As a **[profession]**, adopting a **[tone of voice]**, could you provide a detailed and comprehensive action plan outlining the specific steps that **[my/their] [team/group/department]** can undertake to effectively address and enhance a weakness related to **[contextual challenge/opportunity]**? This is particularly relevant given the goal of **[desired outcome]**.

PROMPT No 544

Team-Weaknesses - Negative-Outcomes - Strategies

To gain a comprehensive understanding of potential negative outcomes that may arise from team's weaknesses at work and to effectively address them using specific strategies, methods, or approaches.

As a **Team Development Specialist**, adopting a **solution-oriented and analytical tone**, could you suggest specific strategies, methods, or approaches that **I** can use to **effectively explore and uncover any potential negative outcomes** that may arise from **our team's** weaknesses at work? This is particularly relevant given the goal of **gaining a comprehensive understanding and effectively addressing these issues**.

As a **[profession]**, adopting a **[tone of voice]**, could you suggest specific strategies, methods, or approaches that **[I/Name/Role]** can use to **[contextual challenge/opportunity]** that may arise from **[my/their] [team/group/department]**'s weaknesses at work? This is particularly relevant given the goal of **[desired outcome]**.

PROMPT No 545

Overlooked - Management - Opportunities

To gain insights on potential overlooked aspects of a team's work that they may be unaware of or not fully considering, helping to prevent negative consequences or missed opportunities.

Prompt

Considering the potential for **overlooked aspects of work leading to negative consequences or missed opportunities**, as a **Management Consultant** and in a **clear and concise tone**, could you identify some areas of **my team's** work that they may be unaware of or not fully considering?

Formula

Considering the potential for **[contextual challenge/opportunity]**, as a **[profession]** and in a **[tone of voice]**, could you identify some areas of **[I/Name/Role]'s [team/group/department]'s** work that they may be unaware of or not fully considering?

PROMPT No 546

Tags

Weaknesses - Growth - Team-Dynamics

Goal

To create a comprehensive strategy that equips business leaders with the tools and techniques to identify the genuine weaknesses within their teams. The end objective is to enhance productivity, teamwork, and professional development for each team member.

Prompt

As a **Leadership Development Coach** specializing in **team dynamics** for the **tech startup sector**, could you guide me through the **process of uncovering the real weaknesses within my team**? Additionally, can you help me outline an action plan **to turn these weaknesses into opportunities for growth**? Please provide guidance on **initiating the conversation, the types of questions to ask that elicit truthful responses, techniques** for **creating an open and non-threatening environment, and how to proceed after identifying the weaknesses to formulate actionable plans for improvement**. Include elements that emphasize **the importance of self-assessment, peer-to-peer feedback, and measurable outcomes**. Introduce unique angles and prophetic opportunities. Let's think about this step by step. Write using an informative tone and factual writing style.

Formula

As a **[profession]** specializing in **[topic/specialization]** for the **[industry],** could you guide me through the process of **[contextual challenge/opportunity]**? Additionally, can you help me outline an action plan to **[specific goal]**? Please provide guidance on **[methods/techniques/steps]** for **[specific aspects].** Include elements that emphasize **[aspects/topics to be covered].** Introduce unique angles and prophetic opportunities. Let's think about this step by step. Write using an **[tone]** and **[writing style].**

PROMPT No 547

Tags

Assessment - Career - Recognition

Goal

To gain specific techniques or approaches that can be utilized to effectively identify and assess any signs or indications of weaknesses in the career or professional performance of a team, ensuring accurate recognition and evaluation of these weaknesses.

As a **Leadership Development Consultant**, adopting a **supportive and analytical tone**, could you provide specific techniques or approaches that can be utilized to **effectively identify and assess any signs or indications of weaknesses** in the career or professional performance of **my team**? Please provide detailed and comprehensive suggestions that will **ensure accurate recognition and evaluation of these weaknesses**.

As a **[profession]**, adopting a **[tone of voice]**, could you provide specific techniques or approaches that can be utilized to **[contextual challenge/opportunity]** in the career or professional performance of **[my/their]** **[team/group/department]**? Please provide detailed and comprehensive suggestions that will **[desired outcome]**.

PROMPT No 548

Opportunities - Discussion - Strengths

To design an effective strategy for business leaders to facilitate conversations with their teams on how perceived weaknesses could have positive payoffs if enhanced. This would lead to increased productivity, stronger team unity, and overall growth on both personal and professional fronts.

As a **Leadership Development Coach** with specialization in **team effectiveness** for the **technology industry**, could you guide me through the **strategy of holding a compelling conversation with my team to explore the concept that their perceived weaknesses may actually be opportunities for growth with the right focus and effort**? Please include **tips for initiating the dialogue, types of questions that can lead to insightful responses, methods to ensure an environment conducive** for **open discussion, and steps for post-discussion action plans that aim at capitalizing on these newfound opportunities**. Ensure that the guide covers **techniques to encourage self-assessment and peer-to-peer reviews**. Introduce unique angles and prophetic opportunities. Let's think about this step by step. Write using an **informative** tone and **factual** writing style.

As a **[profession]** with specialization in **[topic/specialization]** for the **[industry]**, could you guide me through the **[contextual challenge/opportunity]**? Please include **[methods/techniques/steps]** for **[specific aspects]**. Ensure that the guide covers **[aspects/topics to be covered]**. Introduce unique angles and prophetic opportunities. Let's think about this step by step. Write using a **[type]** tone and **[style]** writing style.

PROMPT No 549

Reflection - Artificial-Intelligence - Weaknesses

To create an effective strategy for business leaders to initiate and facilitate an impactful discussion with their teams on identifying weaknesses at work. The conversation aims to encourage self-awareness, constructive feedback, and actionable plans for improvement. This will ultimately lead to increased productivity, team cohesion, and personal and professional growth.

As a **Leadership Development Coach** with a specialization in **team effectiveness** for the **artificial intelligence and machine learning industry**. Could you guide me through the **process of holding a thoughtful discussion with my team to explore their weaknesses at work**? Please include **methods for initiating the conversation, the types of questions to ask, techniques for fostering an environment where team members feel safe sharing, and follow-up steps for creating actionable improvement plans**. Ensure that the guide covers **how to encourage self-assessment, peer-to-peer feedback, and how to turn weaknesses into areas for growth**. Introduce unique angles and prophetic opportunities. Let's think about this step by step. Write using an **informative** tone and **factual** writing style.

As a **[profession]** with specialization in **[topic/specialization]** for the **[industry]**. Could you guide me through the [contextual challenge/opportunity]? Please include **[methods//techniques/steps]**. Ensure that the guide covers **[aspects/topics]**. Introduce unique angles and prophetic opportunities. Let's think about this step by step. Write using a **[type]** tone and **[style]** writing style.

PROMPT No 550

Self-Improvement - Experience - Reflective

To gain insights on how to encourage a team to reflect on the missed opportunities or experiences due to not actively working on their areas of weakness, promoting self-improvement.

In the context of **encouraging self-improvement**, as an **Executive Coach** and in a **reflective and patient tone**, could you advise on how **I** could make **my team** reflect on the specific things they are giving up or failing to experience as a result of not actively working to improve their **areas of weakness**?

In the context of **[contextual challenge/opportunity]**, as a **[profession]** and in a **[tone of voice]**, could you advise on how **[I/Name/Role]** could make **[my/their]** **[team/group/department]** reflect on the specific things they are giving up or failing to experience as a result of not actively working to improve their **[areas of weakness/shortcomings]**?

PROMPT No 551

Authenticity - Strengths - Downplaying

To gain insights on how to effectively identify situations where team members might be intentionally downplaying their strengths as weaknesses, and to learn strategies for accurately recognizing and addressing such instances, fostering a more transparent and authentic work environment.

Prompt

As a **Team Development Specialist**, adopting an **analytical and empathetic tone**, could you guide me on how to effectively identify situations where **my team** might be deliberately **downplaying their strengths by presenting them as weaknesses**? Please provide comprehensive strategies and detailed insights to assist **me** in **accurately recognizing and addressing such instances**.

Formula

As a **[profession]**, adopting an **[tone of voice]**, could you guide **[me/Name/Role]** on how to effectively identify situations where **[my/their]** **[team/group/department]** might be deliberately **[contextual challenge/opportunity]**? Please provide comprehensive strategies and detailed insights to assist **[me/Name/Role]** in **[desired outcome]**.

PROMPT No 552

Tags

Transformation - Confidence - Communication

Goal

To guide you in recognizing the value of mastering a current weakness, and how to understand the potential benefits and transformation that can result from this self-improvement. The prompt is aimed at both self-reflection and action planning, inspiring you to not only identify weaknesses but also to see the potential in transforming those areas.

Prompt

Act as a **Personal Development Coach** specializing in the **public sector**. If I were to **identify** a **current weakness** in my **professional life** and become **truly masterful** in that **area**, what could the **implications** be? How might it **impact** my **confidence, career trajectory, relationships, or overall satisfaction**? What **strategies** can I employ to transform the weakness of **lack of communication skills** into a **strength**? How can I **track progress** and **maintain** motivation in this **journey**? Respond to each question separately. Let's consider each facet of this topic. Write using an **inspirational** tone and **engaging** writing style.

Formula

Act as a **[profession]** specializing in the **[sector]**, if I were to **[identify/recognize/determine]** a **[current/existing/present]** **[weakness/flaw/shortcoming]** in my **[professional/personal/individual]** life and become **[truly/completely/absolutely]** **[masterful/expert/skilled]** in that **[area/field/aspect]**, what could the **[implications/consequences/ramifications]** be? How might it **[impact/affect/influence]** my **[confidence/career/relationships/overall satisfaction]**? What **[strategies/tools/methodologies]** can I **[employ/use/apply]** to **[transform/convert/change]** the **[weakness/flaw/shortcoming]** of **[insert weakness/flaw/shortcoming]** into a **[strength/asset/virtue]**? How can I **[track/monitor/observe]** **[progress/advancement/development]** and **[maintain/keep/sustain]** **[motivation/enthusiasm/drive]** in this **[journey/process/endeavor]**? Respond to each question separately. Let's consider each facet of this topic. Write using a **[type]** tone and **[style]** writing style.

PROMPT No 553

Evaluation - Skills - Productivity

Goal

To gain specific tactics or methods that can be utilized to thoroughly evaluate a team's weaknesses and pinpoint areas where they can improve their skills or knowledge.

Prompt

As a **Leadership Development Consultant**, adopting a **solution-oriented tone**, could you provide specific tactics or methods that **I** can utilize to thoroughly evaluate **my team's weaknesses and pinpoint areas where they can improve their skills or knowledge**? This is particularly relevant given the goal of **enhancing team performance and productivity**.

Formula

As a **[profession]**, adopting a **[tone of voice]**, could you provide specific tactics or methods that **[I/Name/Role]** can utilize to thoroughly evaluate **[my/their] [team/group/department]'s [contextual challenge/opportunity]**? This is particularly relevant given the goal of **[desired outcome]**.

PROMPT No 554

Tags

Improvement - HR - Competencies

Goal

To gain specific strategies for accurately assessing areas of improvement or skill acquisition for a team, and to learn about an actionable plan for helping the team acquire or develop these skills, thereby enhancing their overall abilities.

Prompt

As a **Human Resources Consultant**, adopting a **solution-oriented tone**, could you provide specific strategies that **I** can use to accurately assess the areas in which **my team** needs to **improve or acquire skills and competencies**? Furthermore, could you suggest a specific steps or action plan that can be implemented to aid them in **acquiring or developing these identified skills or competencies**, thereby enhancing their overall abilities?

Formula

As a **[profession]**, adopting a **[tone of voice]**, could you provide specific strategies that **[I/Name/Role]** can use to accurately assess the areas in which **[my/their] [team/group/department]** needs to **[contextual challenge/opportunity]**? Furthermore, could you suggest a specific steps or action plan that can be implemented to aid them in **[desired outcome]**, thereby enhancing their overall abilities?

PROMPT No 555

Tags

Performance - Qualities - Empowerment

Goal

To gain insights on the specific internal qualities or attributes to focus on developing within a team to enhance their overall performance.

Prompt

Given the objective of **enhancing team performance**, as a **Performance Coach** and in an **empowering and constructive tone**, could you specify the **internal qualities or attributes I** should focus on developing within **my team**?

Formula

Given the objective of **[contextual challenge/opportunity]**, as a **[profession]** and in a **[tone of voice]**, could you specify the **[qualities/attributes/skills] [I/Name/Role]** should focus on developing within **[my/their] [team/group/department]**?

Final Words

In the domain of coaching, mentoring, and leadership, navigating the complexities requires a disciplined approach. This book aims to be an instrumental guide, leveraging artificial intelligence and prompt engineering to provide actionable insights for those in any profession. I have presented a curated list of prompts, each serving a specific objective: to clarify roles, define leadership strategies, and optimize coaching techniques, to name a few.

The scope of this book goes beyond a mere compilation of prompts. My goal is to impart a strategic mindset for interpreting challenges as opportunities, seeing barriers as milestones for growth, and viewing the future as a dynamic environment that can be strategically managed.

For the reader who began with skepticism, I hope you conclude this book with a newfound confidence, equipped with a toolkit that elevates your professional standing. For the experienced practitioner, may the methods and strategies here serve to refine your existing approaches.

This journey, while individual in nature, is set against the backdrop of collective human experience. Artificial intelligence serves as a bridge to this collective wisdom, streamlining the path toward your professional and personal development objectives.

In summary, this book aims to leave you not just prepared but empowered. As you close this chapter and move forward in your career, be reminded that each decision and action point offers an opportunity for growth and leadership. This is not just preparation; it is empowerment for transformative impact.

The challenges you face should be viewed as opportunities for demonstrating your leadership and expertise. I encourage you to approach these with a strategic focus, grounded in the knowledge and insights you have gained from this book.

I wish you all the best.

Mauricio

PS: Enjoyed your book? Scan the QR code to quickly leave a review where you purchased it. Your feedback is invaluable!

APPENDIXES

Appendix No 1

Sign-In to Chatbots

1,1. Chat GPT

Step 1: Visit ChatGPT on https://chat.openai.com/chat Click on "Sign Up" and then create your account.

Step 2: Verify your Account. You'd have to enter your details, verify your email and give an OTP you'll receive on your phone.

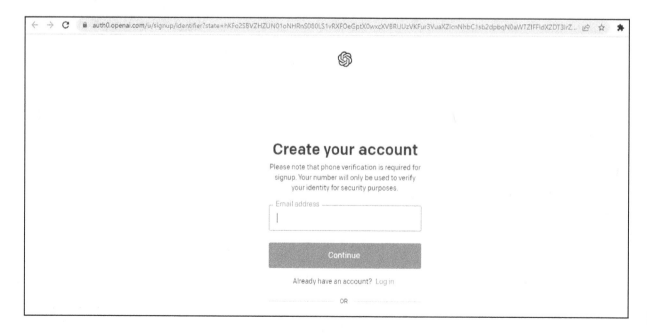

Once done, you'd have access to the free version of ChatGPT

As of April 2023, ChatGPT 3.5 is free to use and ChatGPT-4 costs $20 per month. As a beginner, you can easily test your skills on the free version.

This is how it looks:

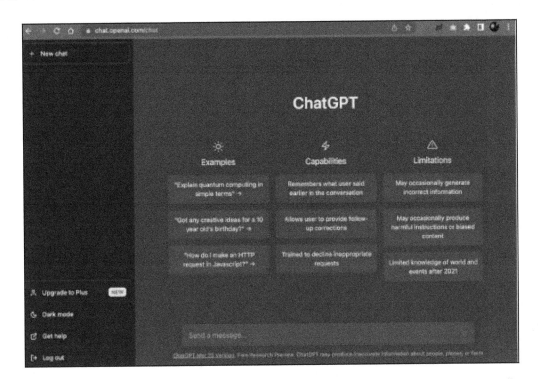

At the very bottom is where you'd chat:

You can now ask GPT anything you want, and it'll give you the desired result

Note: The procedure outlined was developed based on the instructions available at the time of writing. If you require further assistance with signing up for ChatGPT, please scan this QR code:

1.2. Bing Chat

Step 1: Go to the Microsoft website (www.microsoft.com).

Locate the download page for Edge or look for "Microsoft Edge" in the search bar. If you don't want to download Microsoft Edge, go directly to Step 6. For better results, we recommend using Microsoft Edge.

Step 2: Click the download button and choose the version that fits your system.

Step 3: Once downloaded, open the setup file.

Step 4: A User Account Control dialog box will appear – click "Yes" to grant permission.

The installation wizard will guide you through a series of prompts and options. Review them carefully.

Step 5: To open Microsfot Edge, press Win + R on the keyboard to open the Run window. In the Open field, type "microsoft-edge:" and press Enter on the keyboard or click or tap OK. Microsoft Edge is now open.

Step 6: Head to bing.com/chat

Step 7: From the pop-up that appears, click 'Start chatting'

Step 8: Enter the email address for the Microsoft account you'd like to use and click 'Next'.

If you don't have one, click 'Create one!' just under the text box and follow the instructions. Enter your password when prompted and click Next. From the following screen, choose whether you'd like to stay signed in or not. Click 'Chat Now'

Step 9: Choose your conversation style. If you've never used it before, it's best to stick with 'More Balanced'

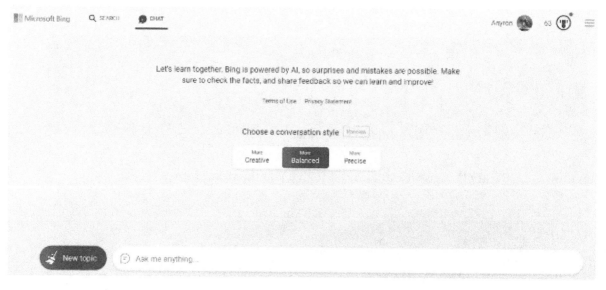

That's it! You can now start chatting.

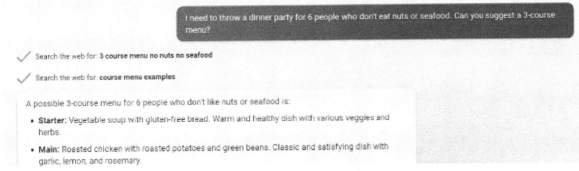

Chat mode is only available when you have access to the new Bing.

I need to throw a dinner party for 6 people who don't eat nuts or seafood. Can you suggest a 3-course menu?

✓ Search the web for: **3 course menu no nuts no seafood**

✓ Search the web for: **course menu examples**

A possible 3-course menu for 6 people who don't like nuts or seafood is:

- **Starter:** Vegetable soup with gluten-free bread. Warm and healthy dish with various veggies and herbs.
- **Main:** Roasted chicken with roasted potatoes and green beans. Classic and satisfying dish with garlic, lemon, and rosemary.

Welcome to the new Bing, your AI-powered co-pilot for the web.

✉ Start chatting   ⊞ Learn more

Note: The procedure outlined was developed based on the instructions available at the time of writing. If you require assistance with signing up for Bing Chat, please scan this QR code:

1.3. Google Bard

Step 1: Go to bard.google.com. Select Try Bard. Accept Google Bard Terms of Service

Bard ·····

⊙ Bard was last updated. See update

Bard can draft an email accepting the job offer and export it to Gmail

Meet Bard: your creative and helpful collaborator, here to supercharge your imagination, boost your productivity, and bring your ideas to life.

Bard is an experiment and may give inaccurate or inappropriate responses. You can help make Bard better by leaving feedback.

Try Bard

Step 2: Go to "Sign in"

Step 3: Enter a query or search term and then hit enter.

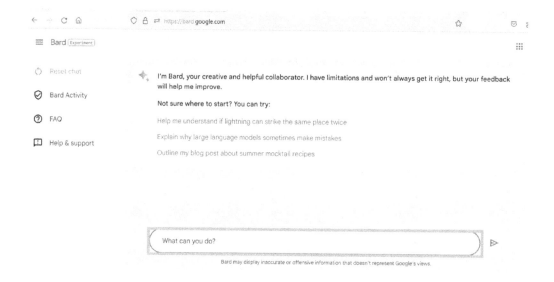

Wait for the AI to respond. You can then either continue the conversation or select Google It to use the traditional search engine.

Note: The procedure outlined was developed based on the instructions available at the time of writing. If you require assistance with signing up for Google Bard, please scan this QR code:

1.4. Meta LLaMA

Getting the Models

Step 1: Go to https://ai.meta.com/resources/models-and-libraries/llama-downloads/

Step 2: Fill the form with your information.

Step 3: Accept their license (if you agree with it)

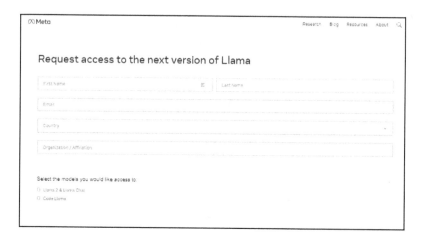

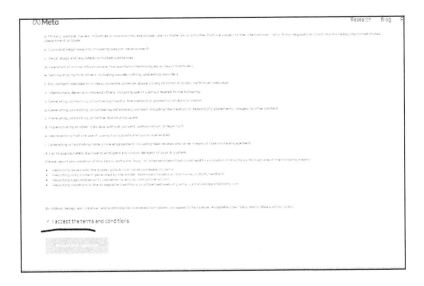

Step 4: Once your request is approved, you will receive a signed URL over email.

Step 5: Clone the Llama 2 repository (go to https://github.com/facebookresearch/llama).

Step 6: Run the download.sh script, passing the URL provided when prompted to start the download. Keep in mind that the links expire after 24 hours and a certain amount of downloads. If you start seeing errors such as 403: Forbidden, you can always re-request a link.

Appendix No 2

Follow-up Prompts

There are 1100 prompts that you can use as follow-ups in order to get more specific or revised information from ChatGPT and other Chatbots. Don't forget to tailor these prompts to your specific circumstances and to the response you previously received from the Chatbot.

Each of these prompt types serves a different purpose and can be used effectively in different scenarios. Depending on the context and the intended outcome, one type of prompt may be more suitable than another.

These prompts are divided into eleven distinct categories, each tailored to specific conversational needs: Generic, Enhancement, Clarification, Probing, Critical Thinking, Instructional, Exploration, Comparison, Summarization, Evaluation, and Hypothetical.

To have access to 1100 follow-up prompts, please scan this QR code:

Appendix No 3

A Beginner's Step-by-Step Guide to Using ChatGPT

If you're new to ChatGPT, don't fret. This guide is designed to walk you through its use, step by step. By the end, you'll have a solid grasp of how to harness the power of this incredible tool.

Step 1: Accessing the Platform

Visit OpenAI's Platform: Head to OpenAI's official website: ChatGPT [openai.com]

Sign Up/Log In: If you don't have an account, you'll need to sign up. If you already have one, simply log in.

Step 2: Navigating the Interface

Dashboard: This is your central hub, where you can access various tools and see your usage stats.

Start a New Session: To interact with ChatGPT, start a new session or use a predefined platform depending on the current interface.

Step 3: Interacting with ChatGPT

Input Field: This is where you'll type or paste the prompts from our book.

Submit: Once you've entered your prompt, press 'Enter' or click the 'Submit' button.

Review Output: ChatGPT will generate a response. Take a moment to read and understand it.

Step 4: Refining Your Interaction

Being Specific: If you need specific information or a particular type of response, make your prompts more detailed.

Iterate: If the first response isn't what you're looking for, tweak your prompt and try again.

Step 5: Utilizing the Prompts from This Book

Choose a Prompt: Browse the book's prompt section and select one that aligns with your current needs.

Input: Copy and paste or type the chosen prompt into ChatGPT's input field.

Customization: Feel free to adjust the prompts to be more specific to your situation.

Step 6: Safety and Best Practices

Sensitive Information: Never share sensitive personal information, such as Social Security numbers or bank details, with ChatGPT or any online platform.

Understanding Outputs: Remember, while ChatGPT can produce human-like responses, it doesn't understand context in the same way humans do. Always review its advice with a critical eye.

Step 7: Exploring Advanced Features

As you become more comfortable with ChatGPT:

Experiment: Play around with different types of prompts to see the diverse responses you can get.

Integrate with Other Tools: There are several third-party tools and platforms that have integrated ChatGPT. Explore these to maximize your work.

Step 8: Stay Updated

Technology, especially in the AI field, evolves rapidly. Periodically check OpenAI's official channels for updates, new features, or changes to the platform.

By following this guide, even the most tech-averse individuals will find themselves comfortably navigating and interacting with ChatGPT. As we delve deeper into the book and introduce specific prompts tailored for your work you'll be equipped with the knowledge to make the most of them.

Here is our "*Elevate Your Productivity Using ChatGPT*" Guide: To access this guide to boost your efficiency and productivity, please scan this QR code.

Appendix No 4

Mentoring, Coaching, and Leadership Professionals

This list encompasses professions pivotal in nurturing growth, leadership, and collaboration in work settings. They play crucial roles in guiding, training, and inspiring individuals towards achieving personal and organizational objectives.

1. Mentor: Provides guidance, support, and wisdom to less experienced individuals for personal and professional growth.
2. Coach: Assists in developing specific skills, improving performance, and achieving defined objectives through structured guidance.
3. Leader: Guides, inspires, and influences a group towards achieving common goals, fostering positive organizational culture.
4. Executive Coach: Assists executives in honing leadership skills, achieving goals, and navigating career transitions.
5. Life Coach: Guides individuals in personal development, goal-setting, and achieving life balance.
6. Career Counselor: Provides advice on career exploration, development strategies, and job search.
7. Organizational Consultant: Aids organizations in improving performance, culture, and change management.
8. Training and Development Manager: Plans, directs, and coordinates programs to enhance employee skills.
9. Human Resources Manager: Oversees recruitment, employee relations, and organizational development.
10. Management Consultant: Advises on business strategies, problem-solving, and organizational improvements.
11. Leadership Development Specialist: Creates programs to develop leadership capabilities within organizations.
12. Performance Coach: Helps individuals improve performance and achieve professional objectives.
13. Business Coach: Guides entrepreneurs in business growth, strategy, and problem-solving.
14. Conflict Resolution Specialist: Aids in resolving disputes and improving communication in workplaces.
15. Executive Search Consultant: Assists organizations in identifying and recruiting executive leadership talent.
16. Team Building Specialist: Designs and facilitates activities to enhance team cohesion.
17. Corporate Trainer: Provides training to improve employee skills and knowledge.
18. Sales Trainer: Develops and delivers training programs to improve sales team performance and effectiveness.
19. Communication Coach: Improves interpersonal communication skills within professional settings.
20. Industrial-Organizational Psychologist: Applies psychological principles to improve workplace dynamics.
21. Change Management Consultant: Guides organizations through change with strategies to ensure smooth transitions.
22. Culture Development Consultant: Aids in cultivating a positive, productive organizational culture.
23. Educational Consultant: Advises on educational strategies, curriculum development, and leadership.
24. Talent Development Specialist: Identifies and nurtures employee talents for organizational growth.
25. Learning and Development Specialist: Designs and implements training programs to promote employee growth and organizational success.

26. Supply Chain Manager: Oversees the end-to-end supply chain process to ensure efficiency and effectiveness.
27. Negotiation Consultant: Aids in enhancing negotiation skills and strategies.
28. Mediator: Facilitates resolution of disputes in a neutral manner.
29. Employee Engagement Consultant: Boosts employee satisfaction and productivity through engagement strategies.
30. Entrepreneurship Advisor: Guides individuals in launching and growing their own businesses.

Appendix No 5

Specializations for Mentors, Coaches and Leaders

1. This compilation presents specialized roles integral to fostering excellence, innovation, and resilience within professional landscapes, offering tailored guidance and support to propel individuals and businesses toward their aspirations.
2. Leadership: Enhancing skills for leading teams and organizations effectively.
3. Performance: Boosting individual or team productivity and output.
4. Career: Navigating career progression and transitions.
5. Sales: Increasing sales proficiency and results.
6. Marketing: Crafting and executing marketing strategies.
7. Strategy: Formulating and applying long-term business plans.
8. Innovation: Fostering creative thinking and new ideas.
9. Culture: Shaping positive organizational values and practices.
10. Conflict Resolution: Managing and resolving disputes effectively.
11. Communication Skills: Improving sharing and receiving of information.
12. Emotional Intelligence: Understanding and managing emotions for improved interactions.
13. Team Dynamics: Strengthening team cooperation and function.
14. Change Leadership: Guiding successful organizational change.
15. Diversity and Inclusion: Building respectful, diverse work environments.
16. Work-Life Balance: Balancing professional responsibilities with personal life.
17. Organizational Development: Enhancing organizational structures and efficiency.
18. Time Management: Prioritizing tasks and managing time wisely.
19. Customer Success: Ensuring clients achieve their desired outcomes.
20. Negotiation Skills: Reaching agreements effectively and advantageously.
21. Personal Branding: Crafting and communicating a personal image.
22. Corporate Governance: Directing company management and policies.
23. Business Ethics: Promoting ethical professional conduct.
24. Financial Coaching for Executives: Managing company finances and economic strategy.
25. Talent Development: Growing employee skills and career paths.
26. Digital Transformation: Integrating digital technology into all business areas.
27. Entrepreneurship: Starting and growing new business ventures.
28. Global Leadership: Leading across diverse cultures and markets.
29. Crisis Leadership: Leading effectively through emergencies.
30. Mindfulness and Well-being: Promoting mental health and mindfulness practices.

Appendix No 6

Tones

Tone reflects the emotional stance towards the subject or audience, impacting engagement and receptivity. In coaching or leadership, the right tone fosters trust, motivation, and effective communication, aligning with growth-oriented goals.

1. Motivational: Inspiring action and positivity towards achieving goals.
2. Empathetic: Demonstrating understanding and compassion towards others' experiences.
3. Authoritative: Exuding confidence and expertise in guiding others.
4. Inspirational: Provoking thought and encouraging higher aspirations.
5. Supportive: Offering encouragement and backing during challenges.
6. Reflective: Encouraging contemplation and self-assessment.
7. Directive: Providing clear, actionable guidance.
8. Analytical: Examining situations critically and logically.
9. Advisory: Offering suggestions based on expertise.
10. Challenging: Encouraging stretching beyond comfort zones.
11. Respectful: Honoring individuals' values, thoughts, and feelings.
12. Humorous: Adding levity to engage and ease tension.
13. Socratic: Encouraging critical thinking through questioning.
14. Constructive: Providing feedback for growth and improvement.
15. Patient: Showing understanding and tolerance during learning processes.
16. Optimistic: Highlighting the positive and potential success.
17. Realistic: Providing a practical and sensible perspective.
18. Encouraging: Boosting morale and self-efficacy.
19. Appreciative: Acknowledging efforts and achievements.
20. Reassuring: Alleviating concerns and instilling confidence.
21. Inquisitive: Encouraging exploration and curiosity.
22. Observational: Noting and reflecting on behaviors and outcomes.
23. Persuasive: Convincing others towards a certain viewpoint.
24. Resilient: Demonstrating toughness and adaptability in adversity.
25. Visionary: Focusing on long-term potential and broader horizons.
26. Collegial: Promoting a sense of partnership and teamwork.
27. Energizing: Infusing enthusiasm and vigor.
28. Compassionate: Showing care and understanding in dealing with others.
29. Professional: Maintaining a formal and respectful demeanor.
30. Mindful: Demonstrating awareness and consideration.

Appendix No 7

Writing Styles

Writing style denotes how ideas are expressed, encompassing word choice and narrative flow. In coaching, mentoring, and leadership, an apt style clarifies concepts, provides guidance, and facilitates meaningful exploration of ideas.

1. Expository: Explaining facts and information clearly and straightforwardly.
2. Descriptive: Painting a vivid picture to convey a particular scenario or idea.
3. Narrative: Telling a story or recounting events to convey lessons or insights.
4. Persuasive: Arguing a point or encouraging a particular action or mindset.
5. Concise: Delivering information in a brief, direct manner.
6. Analytical: Dissecting information to understand and convey underlying principles.
7. Reflective: Encouraging introspection and consideration of past experiences.
8. Dialogic: Engaging in a two-way conversation to explore ideas.
9. Illustrative: Using examples and anecdotes to clarify points.
10. Instructive: Providing detailed guidance or instructions.
11. Interpretive: Explaining and making sense of complex concepts.
12. Comparative: Analyzing similarities and differences between concepts.
13. Argumentative: Making a case for a particular stance or action.
14. Problem-Solution: Identifying issues and proposing solutions.
15. Evaluative: Assessing the value or effectiveness of certain practices.
16. Journalistic: Reporting facts in an objective, straightforward manner.
17. Exploratory: Delving into topics to discover new insights or perspectives.
18. Contemplative: Encouraging deep thought on certain topics.
19. Case Study: Delving into real-world examples to extract lessons.
20. Research-based: Grounding discourse in empirical evidence.
21. Informal: Adopting a casual, accessible approach.
22. Formal: Adhering to professional language and structure.
23. Technical: Utilizing specialized terminology relevant to the field.
24. Conceptual: Exploring ideas at a high level.
25. Practical: Focusing on actionable advice and real-world application.
26. Empirical: Relying on observation and experience.
27. Theoretical: Delving into theories and abstract concepts.
28. Storyboard: Unfolding ideas through a sequenced narrative.
29. Interactive: Encouraging active engagement from the reader.
30. Scenario-based: Outlining hypothetical situations to explore concepts.

Appendix No 8

Tags

	Chapter	Tag 1	Tag 2	Tag 3
Prompt 1	Accountability	Accountability	Leadership	Performance
Prompt 2	Accountability	RemoteWork	Self-Accountability	Commitment
Prompt 3	Accountability	Engagement	Virtual Environment	Team Presence
Prompt 4	Accountability	Accountability	Manager Review	Professionalism
Prompt 5	Accountability	Responsibility	Supportive Identification	Workplace Culture
Prompt 6	Accountability	Team Accountability	Solution-Oriented	Professional Setting
Prompt 7	Accountability	Strategic Plan	Team Motivation	Revenue Alignment
Prompt 8	Accountability	Courage Enhancement	Risk-Taking	Innovative Culture
Prompt 9	Accountability	Effort Acknowledgment	Team Commitment	Appreciative Strategy
Prompt 10	Accountability	Accountability	Relationships	Collaboration
Prompt 11	Accountability	Growth Cultivation	Fulfillment Fostering	Team Development
Prompt 12	Accountability	Client Acquisition	Business Development	Detailed Strategy
Prompt 13	Accountability	Strategic Planning	Competitive Advantage	Team Performance
Prompt 14	Accountability	Business Planning	Detailed Explanation	Organizational Structure
Prompt 15	Accountability	Team Resilience	Problem-Solving	Supportive Leadership
Prompt 16	Accountability	Management	Diversity	Strategies
Prompt 17	Accountability	Effective Communication	Team Cooperation	Initiative Implementation
Prompt 18	Accountability	Self-Discovery	Personal Development	Strengths
Prompt 19	Accountability	Team Dynamics	Goal Accomplishment	Behavioral Mitigation
Prompt 20	Accountability	Task Prioritization	Team Autonomy	Efficiency Enhancement
Prompt 21	Accountability	Sustainability	Expenses	Debt Mitigation
Prompt 22	Accountability	Relationship Maintenance	Collaborative Strategies	Professional Interaction
Prompt 23	Accountability	Decision-Making	Bold Choices	Informed Analysis
Prompt 24	Accountability	Motivational Strategies	Perspective Expansion	Opportunity Pursuit
Prompt 25	Accountability	Goal Achievement	Ambition Cultivation	Success Strategies
Prompt 26	Awareness	Self-Awareness	Work Ethic	High-Performance Culture
Prompt 27	Awareness	False Assumptions	Insightful Leadership	Self-Reflection
Prompt 28	Awareness	Emotional Intelligence	Fear Addressing	Team Morale
Prompt 29	Awareness	Professional Growth	Development Evaluation	HR Strategies
Prompt 30	Awareness	Resource Optimization	Allocation Efficiency	Task Management
Prompt 31	Awareness	Autonomous Assessment	Training Effectiveness	Work Enhancement
Prompt 32	Awareness	Goal-Setting	Prioritization Strategies	Task Management
Prompt 33	Awareness	Personal Growth	Achievement Strategies	Individual Development
Prompt 34	Awareness	Self-Awareness	Performance	Management
Prompt 35	Awareness	Positive Mindset	Motivation Maintenance	Supportive Leadership
Prompt 36	Awareness	Mission Influence	Organizational Culture	Team Mindset
Prompt 37	Awareness	Project Preparation	Team Equipping	Effective Tackling

Prompt 38	Awareness	Role Visualization	Value Articulation	Sense of Belonging
Prompt 39	Awareness	Identity Recognition	True Self	Personal Growth
Prompt 40	Awareness	Ideal Self	Self-Awareness	Professional Growth
Prompt 41	Awareness	Cohesive Culture	Organizational Success	Mission Cultivation
Prompt 42	Awareness	Effective Communication	Team Understanding	Self-Awareness Enhancement
Prompt 43	Awareness	Thought Awareness	Responsibility Management	Interaction Impact
Prompt 44	Awareness	Empowerment	Strategy	Contribution
Prompt 45	Awareness	Questioning	Insight	Understanding
Prompt 46	Awareness	Resilience	Virtue	Communication
Prompt 47	Awareness	Alignment	Beliefs	Performance
Prompt 48	Awareness	Recognition	Beliefs	Management
Prompt 49	Awareness	Learning	Access	Productivity
Prompt 50	Awareness	Mindset	Positive	Conversion
Prompt 51	Awareness	Reflection	Growth	Learning
Prompt 52	Awareness	Leadership	Action	Productivity
Prompt 53	Awareness	Empathy	Emotion	Interpretation
Prompt 54	Awareness	Assumptions	Strategies	Dynamics
Prompt 55	Awareness	Barriers	Detection	Progress
Prompt 56	Belief	Assessment	Workload	Balance
Prompt 57	Belief	Verification	Evidence	Strategy
Prompt 58	Belief	Counter-evidence	Critical-Thinking	Evaluation
Prompt 59	Belief	Empowerment	Beliefs	Goals
Prompt 60	Belief	Hindrance	Development	Mindset
Prompt 61	Belief	Alignment	Work-Ethic	Productivity
Prompt 62	Belief	Self-awareness	Improvement	Challenge
Prompt 63	Belief	Assumptions	Conflict	Resolution
Prompt 64	Belief	Mindset	Performance	Belief
Prompt 65	Belief	Assessment	Engagement	Strategies
Prompt 66	Belief	Improvement	Change	Mindset
Prompt 67	Belief	Identification	Covert	Motivations
Prompt 68	Belief	Contradiction	Values	Resolution
Prompt 69	Belief	Outcomes	Emotions	Evaluation
Prompt 70	Belief	Core-Values	Behavior	Professionalism
Prompt 71	Belief	Communication	Losses	Commitment
Prompt 72	Belief	Stakeholders	Interaction	Performance
Prompt 73	Belief	Satisfaction	Fulfillment	Communication
Prompt 74	Belief	Limitations	Independence	Progress
Prompt 75	Belief	Awareness	Outcomes	Decision-Making
Prompt 76	Belief	Beliefs	Progress	Work
Prompt 77	Belief	Viewpoints	Reevaluation	Diversity
Prompt 78	Belief	Transformation	Assumptions	Facilitation
Prompt 79	Belief	Qualities	Development	Professionalism
Prompt 80	Belief	Motivation	Analysis	Evidence
Prompt 81	Belief	Evolution	Beliefs	Identification
Prompt 82	Belief	Responsibilities	Clarity	Productivity

Prompt 83	Belief	Belief	Motivation	Action
Prompt 84	Challenge	Independence	Strategies	Motivation
Prompt 85	Challenge	Innovation	Encouragement	Challenges
Prompt 86	Challenge	Solutions	Proactivity	Challenges
Prompt 87	Challenge	Uncertainty	Capabilities	Support
Prompt 88	Challenge	Career	Assistance	Progression
Prompt 89	Challenge	Competencies	Emotional	Resolution
Prompt 90	Challenge	Self-awareness	Decision-Making	Beliefs
Prompt 91	Challenge	Exploration	Diversity	Analysis
Prompt 92	Challenge	Attitudes	Benefit	Mindset
Prompt 93	Challenge	Diversity	Problem-Solving	Strategies
Prompt 94	Challenge	Adaptability	Mindset	Leadership
Prompt 95	Challenge	Data	Relevance	Strategies
Prompt 96	Challenge	Development	Growth	Challenges
Prompt 97	Challenge	Motivation	Inspiration	Challenges
Prompt 98	Challenge	Resilience	Problem-Solving	Empowerment
Prompt 99	Challenge	Systematic	Organization	Guidance
Prompt 100	Challenge	Problem-Solving	Cultivation	Empowerment
Prompt 101	Challenge	Adaptation	Transition	Techniques
Prompt 102	Challenge	Thriving	Adaptation	Insights
Prompt 103	Challenge	Learning	Mistakes	Growth
Prompt 104	Challenge	Empowerment	Self-Discovery	Strategies
Prompt 105	Challenge	Team-Motivation	Leadership	Empowerment
Prompt 106	Challenge	Team-Leadership	Strategies	Professional-Development
Prompt 107	Challenge	Diverse-Thinking	Problem-Solving	Leadership
Prompt 108	Challenge	Communication	HR	Obstacle-Resolution
Prompt 109	Challenge	Risk-Taking	Team-Discussion	Positive-Outcome
Prompt 110	Challenge	Comfort-Zone	Performance	Team-Dynamics
Prompt 111	Challenge	Productive-Discussion	Impediment	Insight
Prompt 112	Change	Mindset-Change	Productivity	Organizational-Development
Prompt 113	Change	Relationship-Building	Collaboration	Work-Environment
Prompt 114	Change	Sales-Communication	Obstacle-Resolution	Client-Service
Prompt 115	Change	Change-Management	Innovation	Adaptability
Prompt 116	Change	Diplomacy	Communication	Team-Feedback
Prompt 117	Change	Celebration	Team-Morale	Appreciation
Prompt 118	Change	Future-Readiness	Leadership	Perspective-Shift
Prompt 119	Change	Self-Motivation	Performance	Change
Prompt 120	Change	Forward-Thinking	Impact	Strategy
Prompt 121	Change	Skills-Assessment	Implementation	Team-Development
Prompt 122	Change	Proposal-Development	Positive-Change	Work-Habits
Prompt 123	Change	Evaluation	Consequence	Work-Methods
Prompt 124	Change	Transformation	Mindset	Improvement
Prompt 125	Change	Prioritization	Decision-Making	Task-Management
Prompt 126	Change	Development	Skills	Adaptability
Prompt 127	Change	Assessment	Improvement	Team-Development
Prompt 128	Commitment	Motivation	Ownership	Vision

Prompt 129	Commitment	Distribution	Evaluation	Task-Management
Prompt 130	Commitment	Influence	Commitment	Goal-Orientation
Prompt 131	Commitment	Engagement	Productivity	Remote-Work
Prompt 132	Commitment	Communication	Promotion	Motivation
Prompt 133	Commitment	Dedication	Strategy	Goal-Progress
Prompt 134	Commitment	Accountability	Performance	Reliability
Prompt 135	Commitment	Composure	Support	Well-being
Prompt 136	Creativity	Collaboration	Innovation	Originality
Prompt 137	Creativity	Satisfaction	Engagement	Productivity
Prompt 138	Creativity	Self-Assessment	Evaluation	Improvement
Prompt 139	Creativity	Creativity	Empowerment	Individuality
Prompt 140	Creativity	Creativity	Problem-Solving	Innovation
Prompt 141	Creativity	Productivity	Behavior	Performance
Prompt 142	Creativity	Responsibility	Service	Contribution
Prompt 143	Creativity	Creativity	Innovation	Strategy
Prompt 144	Creativity	Trust	Satisfaction	Loyalty
Prompt 145	Creativity	Creativity	Enhancement	Responsibilities
Prompt 146	Creativity	Creativity	Connection	Inspiration
Prompt 147	Decisions	Timelines	Realism	Performance
Prompt 148	Decisions	Productivity	Time-Management	Prioritization
Prompt 149	Decisions	Evaluation	Strategy	Decision-Making
Prompt 150	Decisions	Meetings	Communication	Management
Prompt 151	Decisions	Data-Driven	Accuracy	Integration
Prompt 152	Decisions	Ethics	Decision-Making	Alignment
Prompt 153	Decisions	Quality	Motivation	Environment
Prompt 154	Decisions	Decision-Making	Balance	Open-Mindedness
Prompt 155	Decisions	Engagement	Discussion	Empowerment
Prompt 156	Decisions	Leadership	Empowerment	Positivity
Prompt 157	Excitement	Professional-Development	C-suite	Effectiveness
Prompt 158	Excitement	Motivation	Excitement	Strategy
Prompt 159	Excitement	Enthusiasm	Project-Management	Sustainment
Prompt 160	Excitement	Persuasion	Investors	Excitement
Prompt 161	Excitement	Virtual-Meetings	Creativity	Engagement
Prompt 162	Excitement	Rejuvenation	Support	Energy
Prompt 163	Excitement	CSR	Employee-Involvement	Brand-Reputation
Prompt 164	Excitement	Motivation	Energy	Analysis
Prompt 165	Excitement	Energy	Enhancement	Transition
Prompt 166	Excitement	Efficiency	Precision	Time-Management
Prompt 167	Excitement	Conflict-Resolution	Relationship	Positivity
Prompt 168	Excitement	Communication	Harmony	Openness
Prompt 169	Excitement	Motivation	Leadership	Environment
Prompt 170	Excitement	Feedback	Recognition	Empowerment
Prompt 171	Fear	Transparency	Empowerment	HR
Prompt 172	Fear	Empathy	Anxiety	Workplace
Prompt 173	Fear	Transparency	Communication	Support

Prompt 174	Fear	Goal-Setting	Fear	Strategy
Prompt 175	Fear	Empowerment	Ambition	Anxiety
Prompt 176	Fear	Motivation	Confidence	Leadership
Prompt 177	Fear	Resilience	Inspiration	Support
Prompt 178	Fear	Self-Criticism	Potential	Identification
Prompt 179	Feelings	Emotion-Management	Atmosphere	Leadership
Prompt 180	Feelings	Empathy	Relationships	Improvement
Prompt 181	Feelings	Well-being	Productivity	Workplace
Prompt 182	Feelings	Emotional-Intelligence	Leadership	Responsiveness
Prompt 183	Feelings	Information-Gathering	Emotions	Tactfulness
Prompt 184	Feelings	Commitment	Productivity	Assessment
Prompt 185	Feelings	Mental-Health	Support	Management
Prompt 186	Feelings	Self-Reflection	Emotions	Unconscious
Prompt 187	Feelings	Dissatisfaction	Morale	Promotion
Prompt 188	Feelings	Self-Awareness	Empowerment	Bias
Prompt 189	Feelings	Assessment	Growth	Satisfaction
Prompt 190	Feelings	Conversations	Understanding	Significance
Prompt 191	Feelings	Impact	Performance	Management
Prompt 192	Feelings	Roles	Emotional-Intelligence	Cohesion
Prompt 193	Flow	Focus	Evaluation	Effort
Prompt 194	Flow	Flow	Engagement	Environment
Prompt 195	Flow	Motivation	Productivity	Energy
Prompt 196	Flow	Obstacles	Flow	Strategies
Prompt 197	Flow	Metrics	Productivity	Influence
Prompt 198	Flow	Communication	Inner-Self	Professional-Growth
Prompt 199	Flow	Functioning	Optimization	Workplace
Prompt 200	Flow	Empowerment	Focus	Productivity
Prompt 201	Flow	Optimal-Self	Performance	Problem-Solving
Prompt 202	Flow	Diversity	Engagement	Fulfillment
Prompt 203	Fulfillment	Monotony	Enhancement	Boredom
Prompt 204	Fulfillment	Fulfillment	Challenges	Professional-Life
Prompt 205	Fulfillment	Guidance	Objectives	Potential
Prompt 206	Fulfillment	Cohesion	Development	Realization
Prompt 207	Fulfillment	Attributes	Leadership	Empathy
Prompt 208	Fulfillment	Exemplary	Boss	Effectiveness
Prompt 209	Fulfillment	Alignment	Passions	Fulfillment
Prompt 210	Goals	Purpose	Professional	Personal
Prompt 211	Goals	Values	Integration	Aspirations
Prompt 212	Goals	Evaluation	Growth	KPIs
Prompt 213	Goals	Synchronization	Learning	Objectives
Prompt 214	Goals	Empowerment	Recognition	Problem-Solving
Prompt 215	Goals	Synergy	Goal	Frameworks
Prompt 216	Goals	Empowerment	Leadership	Strategies
Prompt 217	Goals	Collaboration	Frameworks	Cohesiveness
Prompt 218	Goals	Prioritization	Goals	Alignment
Prompt 219	Goals	Feasibility	Evaluation	Decision-making

Prompt 220	Goals	Monitoring	Intervention	Accountability
Prompt 221	Goals	Resources	Development	Support
Prompt 222	Goals	Assessment	Performance	Accountability
Prompt 223	Goals	Learning	Engagement	Objectives
Prompt 224	Goals	Fulfillment	Conversations	Emotional
Prompt 225	Goals	Professionalism	Improvement	Objectives
Prompt 226	Goals	Self-Improvement	Career	Conflict
Prompt 227	Goals	Team-Reflection	Motivation	Goal-Setting
Prompt 228	Goals	Leadership	Conversations	Alignment
Prompt 229	Habits	Behavior	Analysis	Team-Dynamics
Prompt 230	Habits	Competency	Assessment	Talent-Assessment
Prompt 231	Habits	Quality	Efficiency	Error-Reduction
Prompt 232	Habits	Obstacles	Methodologies	Strategy
Prompt 233	Habits	Self-Sabotage	Transportation	Leadership
Prompt 234	Habits	Creativity	Perspective	Innovation
Prompt 235	Habits	Patterns	Management	Team-Development
Prompt 236	Habits	Productivity	SocialMedia	Distractions
Prompt 237	Habits	Communication	ActiveListening	Self-awareness
Prompt 238	Habits	Engagement	Meetings	Incentivize
Prompt 239	Habits	Networking	Efficacy	Optimism
Prompt 240	Learning	Learning	Techniques	Comprehension
Prompt 241	Learning	Reflection	Growth	Improvement
Prompt 242	Learning	Energy	Motivation	Leadership
Prompt 243	Learning	Assessment	Opportunities	Methodologies
Prompt 244	Learning	Self-Critique	EmotionalIntelligence	Plan
Prompt 245	Learning	Experiences	Beliefs	Self-Awareness
Prompt 246	Learning	Improvement	Recognition	Learning
Prompt 247	Learning	Opportunities	Vigilance	Identification
Prompt 248	Learning	Introspection	Conversations	Improvement
Prompt 249	Learning	Communication	Engagement	Curiosity
Prompt 250	Learning	Blindspots	Leadership	Biases
Prompt 251	Learning	Growth	Criteria	Evaluation
Prompt 252	Learning	Motivation	Reflection	Positivity
Prompt 253	Learning	Problem-solving	Communication	Safety
Prompt 254	Learning	Development	Environment	Learning
Prompt 255	Learning	Identification	Application	Performance
Prompt 256	Learning	Leadership	Wellbeing	Collaboration
Prompt 257	Learning	Reflection	ProjectManagement	Self-awareness
Prompt 258	Learning	LearningCulture	Innovation	Insurance
Prompt 259	Learning	Diplomacy	Self-Awareness	Improvement
Prompt 260	Learning	PositiveCulture	Productivity	KnowledgeTransfer
Prompt 261	Learning	CriticalReview	Solutions	ActionableInsights
Prompt 262	Learning	TalentDevelopment	Alignment	Interests
Prompt 263	Learning	Facilitation	Reflection	Assessment
Prompt 264	Learning	PersonalGrowth	Effectiveness	Construction
Prompt 265	Learning	ContinuousLearning	Self-awareness	LessonLearned

Prompt 266	Learning	Preparation	Conversation	Learning
Prompt 267	Learning	Investigation	Failure	Improvement
Prompt 268	Learning	Reflection	Sacrifices	Outcomes
Prompt 269	Learning	Challenge	Motivation	Goals
Prompt 270	Learning	Authenticity	Communication	Introspection
Prompt 271	Learning	Reflection	Improvement	Strategy
Prompt 272	Learning	Learning	Reflection	Actionability
Prompt 273	Learning	Understanding	Motivation	Alignment
Prompt 274	Learning	Learning	Engagement	Team-building
Prompt 275	Learning	Leadership	Risk-Management	Reflection
Prompt 276	Listening	Project-Management	Strategy	Progress
Prompt 277	Listenning	Performance-Enhancement	Conversation	Improvement
Prompt 278	Listenning	Resilience	Discussion	Failure
Prompt 279	Listenning	Communication	Obstacle-Identification	Team-Dynamics
Prompt 280	Listenning	Problem-Solving	Bottleneck-Identification	Innovation
Prompt 281	Listenning	Public-Speaking	Professional-Development	Confidence
Prompt 282	Listenning	Resilience	Mindfulness	Strategy
Prompt 283	Mindset	Self-Reflection	Growth	FinTech
Prompt 284	Mindset	Emotional-Intelligence	Relationship	Assessment
Prompt 285	Mindset	Work-Environment	Empowerment	Assessment
Prompt 286	Mindset	Operational	Efficiency	Barriers
Prompt 287	Mindset	Leadership	Transparency	Accountability
Prompt 288	Mindset	Mindset	Professionalism	Self-Reflection
Prompt 289	Mindset	Cognitive	Decision-Making	Fintech
Prompt 290	Mindset	Team-Dynamics	Awareness	Questioning
Prompt 291	Mindset	Comfort	Productivity	Workplace
Prompt 292	Mindset	Vulnerability	Well-being	Psychological-Safety
Prompt 293	Mindset	Growth-Mindset	Resilience	Learning
Prompt 294	Mindset	Curiosity	Innovation	Exploration
Prompt 295	Mindset	Possibilities	Reflection	Engagement
Prompt 296	Mindset	Communication	Leadership	Retention
Prompt 297	Mindset	Talent	Identification	Delegation
Prompt 298	Mindset	Self-Awareness	Performance	Optimization
Prompt 299	Mindset	Empowerment	Responsibility	Decision-Making
Prompt 300	Mindset	Empathy	Career	Feedback
Prompt 301	Mindset	Alignment	Goal-Setting	Entertainment
Prompt 302	Mindset	Transparency	Role-Clarity	Objectives
Prompt 303	Mindset	Purpose	Engagement	Mission
Prompt 304	Mindset	Leadership	Self-Management	Emotional-Intelligence
Prompt 305	Mindset	Readiness	Team-Dynamics	Project-Management
Prompt 306	Mindset	Resilience	Coping	Oil-and-Gas
Prompt 307	Options	Proactive	Collaboration	Bankruptcy
Prompt 308	Options	Decision-Making	Analysis	Strategy
Prompt 309	Options	Resilience	Challenge-Management	Personal-Growth

Prompt 310	Options	Opportunities	Development	Learning
Prompt 311	Options	Decision-Making	Development	Strategy
Prompt 312	Options	Resilience	Challenge-Management	Personal-Growth
Prompt 313	Options	Appreciation	Feedback	Listening
Prompt 314	Options	Innovation	Problem-Solving	Resilience
Prompt 315	Options	Stability	Individual-Preferences	Human-Resources
Prompt 316	Options	Risk-Mitigation	Opportunity-Leverage	Analysis
Prompt 317	Options	Decision-making	Frameworks	Participation
Prompt 318	Options	Organizational-Behavior	Empathy	Motivation
Prompt 319	Options	Reflecting	Effectiveness	Decision-making
Prompt 320	Options	Decision-Making	Transparency	Leadership
Prompt 321	Options	Leadership	Improvement	Finance
Prompt 322	Performance	Adaptability	Growth	Accounting
Prompt 323	Performance	Recognition	Team-Dynamics	Tech
Prompt 324	Performance	Underperformance	Methodologies	Advertising
Prompt 325	Performance	Self-Awareness	Performance	Coaching
Prompt 326	Performance	Outcomes	Alignment	Clarity
Prompt 327	Performance	Mindset	Transformation	Support
Prompt 328	Performance	Obstacles	Self-Improvement	Introspection
Prompt 329	Performance	Evaluation	Performance-Management	Productivity
Prompt 330	Performance	Communication	Trust-Building	Inclusivity
Prompt 331	Performance	Goals	Prioritization	Repercussions
Prompt 332	Performance	Goal-Attainment	Modification	Performance
Prompt 333	Performance	Benefits	Organizational-Psychology	Tech
Prompt 334	Performance	Leadership	Strategies	Step-by-Step
Prompt 335	Performance	Achievement	Self-Reflection	Marketing
Prompt 336	Performance	Leadership	Collaboration	OrganizationalCulture
Prompt 337	Preferences	Rapport	Creativity	Engagement
Prompt 338	Preferences	CognitivePsychology	Behavioral	DecisionMaking
Prompt 339	Preferences	Success	Resilience	Discussion
Prompt 340	Preferences	Trust-building	Mentorship	OpenDialogue
Prompt 341	Preferences	Prioritization	Facilitation	Reflection
Prompt 342	Priorities	Productivity	Diagnostics	Behavior Analysis
Prompt 343	Priorities	TimeManagement	Strategies	Priorities
Prompt 344	Priorities	Self-Management	Autonomy	Independence
Prompt 345	Priorities	Goal-setting	Finance	Strategic Planning
Prompt 346	Priorities	PositiveCulture	Communication	Team-building
Prompt 347	Priorities	Strategy	Decision-Making	Prioritization
Prompt 348	Priorities	Team-Management	Empathy	Satisfaction
Prompt 349	Progress	Communication	Success	Motivation
Prompt 350	Progress	Well-being	Mental-Health	Productivity
Prompt 351	Progress	Learning	Development	Professionalism
Prompt 352	Progress	Recognition	Morale	Engagement
Prompt 353	Progress	Inspiration	Alignment	Potential

Prompt 354	Progress	Self-Assessment	Transformation	Leadership
Prompt 355	Progress	Planning	Project-Management	Collaboration
Prompt 356	Progress	Performance	Measurement	Team
Prompt 357	Progress	Reflection	Self-awareness	Goals
Prompt 358	Progress	Satisfaction	Evaluation	Motivation
Prompt 359	Progress	Development	Strategies	Engagement
Prompt 360	Progress	Motivation	OrganizationalBehavior	Stagnation
Prompt 361	Purpose	Self-awareness	Career Trajectory	Introspection
Prompt 362	Purpose	Self-Perception	Dialogue	Performance
Prompt 363	Purpose	Consciousness	Alignment	Leadership
Prompt 364	Purpose	Purpose	Conversation	Hospitality
Prompt 365	Purpose	Emotional	Articulation	Morale
Prompt 366	Purpose	Framework	Articulation	Collaboration
Prompt 367	Purpose	Goal-setting	Articulation	Clarity
Prompt 368	Purpose	Metrics	Criteria	Quantitative
Prompt 369	Purpose	Communication	Resilience	Remediation
Prompt 370	Purpose	Commitment	Dialogue	Performance
Prompt 371	Purpose	Decision-Making	Communication	Articulation
Prompt 372	Purpose	Career Development	Software	Aspirations
Prompt 373	Purpose	Interpersonal	Inquiry	Non-Verbal
Prompt 374	Purpose	Contribution	Synergy	Alignment
Prompt 375	Purpose	Engagement	Purpose	Satisfaction
Prompt 376	Purpose	Self-Awareness	Media	Purpose
Prompt 377	Purpose	Leadership	Encouragement	Purpose
Prompt 378	Purpose	Cohesion	Purpose	Reflection
Prompt 379	Relationships	Impact	Morale	Emotional
Prompt 380	Relationships	Resilience	Problem-Solving	Support
Prompt 381	Relationships	Roles	Construction	Allocation
Prompt 382	Relationships	Fulfillment	Implementation	Clients
Prompt 383	Relationships	Trust	Assessment	Collaboration
Prompt 384	Relationships	Satisfaction	Implementation	Interaction
Prompt 385	Relationships	Perception	Alignment	Duties
Prompt 386	Relationships	Relationships	Communication	Collaboration
Prompt 387	Relationships	Self-awareness	Relationships	Dynamics
Prompt 388	Relationships	Selection	Software	Team-building
Prompt 389	Relationships	Authenticity	Presence	Interactions
Prompt 390	Relationships	Empowerment	Leadership	Self-awareness
Prompt 391	Relationships	Presence	Engagement	Communication
Prompt 392	Relationships	Self-awareness	Engagement	Motivating
Prompt 393	Relationships	Presence	Mindfulness	Contemplative
Prompt 394	Relationships	Triggers	Interactions	Compassionate
Prompt 395	Relationships	Assessment	Leadership	Analytical
Prompt 396	Relationships	Engagement	Persuasive	Organization
Prompt 397	Relationships	Creativity	Innovation	Framework
Prompt 398	Relationships	Resourcefulness	Strategy	Human Resources

Prompt 399	Relationships	Engagement	Strategy	Implementation
Prompt 400	Relationships	Collaboration	Accountability	Consultative
Prompt 401	Relationships	Communication	Conflict-Resolution	Construction
Prompt 402	Relationships	Relationship	Diagnostics	Constructive
Prompt 403	Relationships	Relationships	Communication	Barriers
Prompt 404	Relationships	Dialogue	Professional	Unconventional
Prompt 405	Relationships	Recognition	Interpersonal	Reflective
Prompt 406	Relationships	Alignment	Frameworks	Values
Prompt 407	Relationships	Presence	Engagement	Meetings
Prompt 408	Relationships	Motivation	Implementation	Satisfaction
Prompt 409	Relationships	Resilience	Fulfillment	Problem-Solving
Prompt 410	Relationships	Leadership	Effectiveness	Performance
Prompt 411	Relationships	Resourcefulness	Mindset	Adaptability
Prompt 412	Relationships	Obstacles	Self-Assessment	Nurturing
Prompt 413	Relationships	Patience	Interactions	Self-Reflection
Prompt 414	Relationships	Habits	Cohesion	Frameworks
Prompt 415	Relationships	Self-assessment	Motivation	Development
Prompt 416	Relationships	Emotional-Intelligence	Cohesive	Resilience
Prompt 417	Relationships	Confidence	Empowerment	Leadership
Prompt 418	Relationships	Empowerment	Self-efficacy	Motivation
Prompt 419	Relationships	Resilience	Introspection	Decision-making
Prompt 420	Relationships	Engagement	Tools	Creativity
Prompt 421	Relationships	Engagement	Productivity	Mindfulness
Prompt 422	Relationships	Role-Optimization	Responsibilities	Personal-Growth
Prompt 423	Relationships	Resources	Implementation	Performance
Prompt 424	Relationships	Optimization	Assessment	Efficiency
Prompt 425	Relationships	Reflective	Resourcefulness	Collaboration
Prompt 426	Relationships	Resource Management	Utilization	Analytical Guide
Prompt 427	Relationships	Support	Emotional	Performance
Prompt 428	Relationships	Futurist	Brainstorming	Innovation
Prompt 429	Self-assessment	Conflict	Communication	Legal
Prompt 430	Self-assessment	Leadership	Persuasion	Executive
Prompt 431	Self-assessment	Presentation	Development	Consulting
Prompt 432	Self-assessment	Growth	Fulfillment	Optimization
Prompt 433	Self-assessment	Introspection	Decision-making	Behavior
Prompt 434	Self-assessment	Talent	Assessment	Cohesion
Prompt 435	Self-assessment	Engagement	Passions	Cohesion
Prompt 436	Self-assessment	Accountability	Success	Analysis
Prompt 437	Self-assessment	Organizational	Reflection	Improvement
Prompt 438	Self-assessment	Evolution	Mentoring	Perspectives
Prompt 439	Self-assessment	Self-awareness	Mindfulness	Growth
Prompt 440	Self-assessment	Communication	Observational	Strategies
Prompt 441	Self-assessment	Data	Collaboration	Continuous-improvement
Prompt 442	Self-assessment	Executive	Priority	Organizational
Prompt 443	Self-assessment	Feedback	Communication	Motivations
Prompt 444	Skills	Skills	Gap	Analysis

Prompt 445	Skills	Benchmarking	Development	Prioritization
Prompt 446	Skills	Motivation	Skills	Optimization
Prompt 447	Skills	Introspection	Evolution	Self-Assessment
Prompt 448	Skills	Acquisition	Performance	Alignment
Prompt 449	Skills	Skill	Leverage	Metrics
Prompt 450	Skills	Prioritization	Effectiveness	Diagnostics
Prompt 451	Skills	Leadership	Feedback	Development
Prompt 452	Skills	Collaboration	Analytical	Innovation
Prompt 453	Strategies	Recognition	Resilience	Acknowledgment
Prompt 454	Strategies	Strategies	KPIs	Alignment
Prompt 455	Strategies	Impediments	Proactive	Mitigation
Prompt 456	Strategies	Innovation	Experimentation	Creativity
Prompt 457	Strategies	Strategy	Efficiency	Planning
Prompt 458	Strategies	Effectiveness	ROI	Decision-making
Prompt 459	Strategies	Innovation	Realities	Resource
Prompt 460	Strength	Exhilaration	Strengths	Challenges
Prompt 461	Strength	Top-strengths	Progress	Motivation
Prompt 462	Strength	Innate	Strengths-based	Introspection
Prompt 463	Strength	Attraction	Roles	Inherent
Prompt 464	Strength	Evolution	Passion	Self-assessment
Prompt 465	Strength	Strengths	Engagement	Team-Dynamics
Prompt 466	Strength	Scrutinizing	Strengths	Patterns
Prompt 467	Strength	Innate	Gifts	Psychometric
Prompt 468	Strength	Strengths	Productivity	Morale
Prompt 469	Strength	Engagement	Strengths	Metrics
Prompt 470	Strength	Ownership	Self-awareness	Strengths
Prompt 471	Strength	Growth	Strengths	Development
Prompt 472	Strength	Self-awareness	Cohesion	Strengths-Utilization
Prompt 473	Strength	Development	Strengths	Metrics
Prompt 474	Strength	Evaluation	Strengths	Allocation
Prompt 475	Strength	Exploration	Assets	Forward-thinking
Prompt 476	Strength	Evaluation	Strengths	Allocation
Prompt 477	Strength	Alignment	Strengths	KPIs
Prompt 478	Strength	Strengths	Performance	Methodology
Prompt 479	Strength	Understanding	Strengths	Engagement
Prompt 480	Strength	Overextension	Self-awareness	Diagnostics
Prompt 481	Strength	Overleveraging	Performance	Adaptation
Prompt 482	Strength	Indicators	Overutilization	Burnout
Prompt 483	Strength	Consequences	Strengths	Mitigation
Prompt 484	Strength	Impacts	Strengths	Cohesion
Prompt 485	Strength	Transparency	Authenticity	Investigation
Prompt 486	Strength	Rejuvenation	Alignment	Assessment
Prompt 487	Strength	Misrepresentation	Integrity	Realignment
Prompt 488	Strength	Optimization	Strengths	Stakeholders
Prompt 489	Strength	Alignment	Competency	Realignment
Prompt 490	Strength	Misalignment	Assessment	Realignment

Prompt 491	Strength	Ideation	Implementation	Engagement
Prompt 492	Strength	Development	Mastery	Productivity
Prompt 493	Strength	Opportunities	Skill-Gap	Metrics
Prompt 494	Strength	Holistic	Fulfillment	Integration
Prompt 495	Support	Assumptions	Decision-Making	Risk Management
Prompt 496	Support	Focus	Alignment	Productivity
Prompt 497	Support	Self-Confidence	Interventions	Metrics
Prompt 498	Support	Sales Targets	KPIs	Risk Mitigation
Prompt 499	Support	Support Structures	Needs Assessment	Alignment
Prompt 500	Support	Patience	Empathy	Reflective
Prompt 501	Support	Hindrances	Progression	Feedback
Prompt 502	Support	Habits	Workflow	Stakeholder Buy-in
Prompt 503	Support	Work Arrangements	Team Survey	KPI Alignment
Prompt 504	Support	Project Completion	Systems	Stakeholder Buy-in
Prompt 505	Support	System Analysis	KPIs	Scalability
Prompt 506	Support	Resource Mapping	Budgetary	Time Management
Prompt 507	Support	Resources	Communication	Opportunity
Prompt 508	Support	Strategy	Stakeholders	Collaboration
Prompt 509	Support	Autonomy	Resources	Self-assessment
Prompt 510	Support	Resilience	Communication	Emotional Intelligence
Prompt 511	Support	Relational-Values	Informative	Culture-Enhancement
Prompt 512	Values	Priorities	Alignment	Team-Dynamics
Prompt 513	Values	Values	Alignment	Communication
Prompt 514	Values	Alignment	Engagement	Communication
Prompt 515	Values	Self-reflection	Values	Identity
Prompt 516	Values	Exploration	Alignment	Integration
Prompt 517	Values	Values	Relationships	Stakeholders
Prompt 518	Values	Embrace	CoreValues	Authenticity
Prompt 519	Values	Reflection	Identification	Adaptation
Prompt 520	Values	Alignment	CoreValues	Tangible
Prompt 521	Values	Articulation	Cohesion	Engagement
Prompt 522	Values	Behavior	Feedback	Nuanced
Prompt 523	Values	Self-awareness	ValuesAlignment	EthicalDecision
Prompt 524	Values	Workshops	Dialogue	Methodologies
Prompt 525	Values	Roadmap	Alignment	TeamValues
Prompt 526	Values	Workshops	Principles	Resonance
Prompt 527	Values	Integration	Reflective	Self-awareness
Prompt 528	Values	Consequences	Ethical	Assessment
Prompt 529	Values	BestPractices	Values	TeamCohesion
Prompt 530	Values	Dialogue	Leadership	Values
Prompt 531	Values	Prioritization	Personal	Reflection
Prompt 532	Values	Openness	Fulfillment	HighPerformance
Prompt 533	Values	SelfAwareness	Decision	Values
Prompt 534	Values	Relationships	Cohesion	Productivity
Prompt 535	Weakness	Evaluation	Abilities	Talent
Prompt 536	Weakness	Weaknesses	Improvement	SelfAwareness

Prompt 537	Weakness	GoalAchievement	Weaknesses	PersonalGrowth
Prompt 538	Weakness	WeaknessAcknowledgment	Team	SelfAwareness
Prompt 539	Weakness	Strengths	Optimization	Productivity
Prompt 540	Weakness	Articulation	EmotionalIQ	SelfAwareness
Prompt 541	Weakness	Resilience	Anxiety	Strategies
Prompt 542	Weakness	Weaknesses	Conversation	Risk-Assessment
Prompt 543	Weakness	Action-Plan	Emotional-Intelligence	Improvement
Prompt 544	Weakness	Team-Weaknesses	Negative-Outcomes	Strategies
Prompt 545	Weakness	Overlooked	Management	Opportunities
Prompt 546	Weakness	Weaknesses	Growth	Team-Dynamics
Prompt 547	Weakness	Assessment	Career	Recognition
Prompt 548	Weakness	Opportunities	Discussion	Strengths
Prompt 549	Weakness	Reflection	Artificial-Intelligence	Weaknesses
Prompt 550	Weakness	Self-Improvement	Experience	Reflective
Prompt 551	Weakness	Authenticity	Strengths	Downplaying
Prompt 552	Weakness	Transformation	Confidence	Communication
Prompt 553	Weakness	Evaluation	Skills	Productivity
Prompt 554	Weakness	Improvement	HR	Competencies
Prompt 555	Weakness	Performance	Qualities	Empowerment

Appendix No 9

Unlock the Full Potential of This Book - Instantly

Dive into a world of convenience with our electronic copy! Feel free to seamlessly copy and paste any prompt that sparks your interest.

Customize them to fit your unique needs. Say goodbye to the hassle of retyping. Start crafting your perfect prompts with ease and efficiency!.

To access the electronic copy, please scan this QR code: